"I was humbled and inspired by Craig Detweiler's encyclopedic work. As a Christian screenwriter in postmodern Hollywood, I struggle every day to find the intersection between my faith and my craft. *Into the Dark* illuminates many such points of cohesion but in places one wouldn't think—or even dare—to look. Detweiler could have easily restricted his analysis to softer cinema: the anemic family dramas or self-important epics that try to pass as spiritual fare. Instead he chose to find wisdom in film's most profound shadows. As a result, *Into the Dark* does more than inform; it invites us to open our eyes and discover the divine in even the most brutal of movies."

—**Matt Greenberg**, screenwriter of *1408* and *Reign of Fire*

"Hallelujah! What a refreshing book. Rather than the usual fruitless wholesale condemnation of modern culture, Craig Detweiler has delivered a theologically truthful and joyous exploration of one of the most powerful forces in today's overwhelmingly visual society—the movies."

—**Valerie Mayhew**, former television writer; the Brehm Center for Worship, Theology, and Art, Fuller Theological Seminary

"Many books on the intersection of Christian theology and popular culture cut to the chase of cultural engagement without taking the time to develop the plotline of theological method. Thankfully, Craig Detweiler takes the time to explicate his method before engaging some of the most compelling films of our day. I've had the pleasure of sitting in a movie theater with Craig and of talking about the film over a cup of coffee afterward. Now you have that chance, too, with *Into the Dark*. I can think of no better companion than Craig to help us reflect on the most important storytelling medium of our time."

—**Tony Jones**, author of *The New Christians: Dispatches from the Emergent Frontier* and national coordinator of Emergent Village

culturalexegesis

William A. Dyrness
and Robert K. Johnston, series editors

The Cultural Exegesis series is designed to
complement the Engaging Culture series
by providing methodological and foundational studies that address the way to
engage culture theologically. Each volume
works within a specific cultural discipline,
illustrating and embodying the theory behind cultural engagement. By providing the
appropriate tools, these books equip the
reader to engage and interpret the surrounding culture responsibly.

Into the Dark

SEEING THE SACRED IN THE TOP FILMS
OF THE 21ST CENTURY

Craig Detweiler

B)

Baker Academic

a division of Baker Publishing Group
Grand Rapids, Michigan

 # 182737986

© 2008 by Craig Detweiler

Published by Baker Academic
a division of Baker Publishing Group
P.O. Box 6287, Grand Rapids, MI 49516-6287
www.bakeracademic.com

Printed in the United States of America

Library of Congress Cataloging-in-Publication Data

Detweiler, Craig, 1964–
    Into the dark : seeing the sacred in the top films of the 21st century / Craig Detweiler.
       p.   cm. — (Cultural exegesis)
    Includes bibliographical references (p.   ) and index.
    ISBN 978-0-8010-3592-0 (pbk.)
    1. Motion pictures—Religious aspects. 2. Motion pictures—Moral and ethical aspects.
I. Title.
  PN1995.5.D48 2008
    791.43′682—dc22
                                                      2008010374

Contents

Preface

A Hornet's Nest

I want to live where soul meets body.

Death Cab for Cutie[1]

An eight-year-old boy builds a house out of Lego blocks. He faces two obstacles: the orange shag carpeting that destabilizes everything that rests on it and the television. With the shag carpeting winning the war of (de)construction, the television becomes the primary distraction. The boy's mother is watching a war film starring Rock Hudson. It follows an American commando unit, dropped behind enemy lines in World War II Italy, assigned to blow up a bridge. When most of Rock Hudson's unit is killed, who become his allies? A gang of Italian street kids led by the defiant, cigarette-smoking Aldo. Rock becomes a surrogate father for the orphaned boys, training them to serve as a guerrilla army.

To a child raised on a steady diet of *Sesame Street*, the violence pouring from the television screen both attracts and repels. He can't bear to watch, and he can't imagine looking away. When Rock has the boys strip down to their underwear and frolic in the water in order to distract the enemy, it seems like a brilliant strategy. *Hornet's Nest* was made well before Rock Hudson's highly publicized death from AIDS in 1985. What may play as gay kitsch today worked as solid action-adventure for me as a young boy watching television in 1972. At the conclusion of the movie, with the mission endangered, Aldo, the gang leader, steps up. He climbs behind a submachine gun and blasts away at the Nazis who murdered his parents. Aldo makes a valiant effort, but he dies in a hail of bullets. As an eight-year-old, I was shaken to the core by Aldo's on-screen death. I shed real tears, as if I had lost a genuine friend or a close family member. I didn't understand how movies were made or how Ennio Morricone's score may have manipulated my emotions. Concepts like *honor*, *sacrifice*, and *community* would come much later. All I knew at that moment was that movies had a revelatory power to move me greater than any book, toy, or person I'd ever met.

Hornet's Nest is no cinematic classic. It hasn't even been deemed worthy of a DVD release. Rare, scattered copies remain on VHS for a decidedly limited fan base. Nevertheless, it propelled me on a lifelong obsession with film. From that moment on, I feigned Lego building on the floor as an excuse to watch movies on television. I pursued the chills, thrills, and pathos that washed over me in *Hornet's Nest*. Kids' movies like *That Darn Cat* would no longer suffice. I wanted truly moving pictures—the kind adults watched. I begged my parents to let me see a PG-rated movie in the theater. For my tenth birthday, I saw Irwin Allen's disaster film, *The Towering Inferno* (1974). It packed chills, thrills, and pathos into a burning high-rise. I was hooked on cinema—a fan for life.

I found a blank check register in my parents' closet. It had forty-three two-sided pages with room for thirty entries per page. This became my movie log: a place to record what I saw, when I saw it, and what I thought of it. I gave *Hornet's Nest* four stars. The special effects in *The Towering Inferno* seemed even more overwhelming on the big screen. It received four and a half stars. I was officially a movie critic, engaged in an active response to film. As the check register slowly filled up, my attention to detail grew. I started making lists of movie stars and noting the films in which I'd seen them. John Wayne, Clint Eastwood, and Sean Connery dominated the movie matinees on after-school TV. As I paid more attention to the credits, I discovered character actors like Ben Johnson, L. Q. Jones, and Richard Jaeckel getting plenty of supporting roles. When my hormones kicked in, I suddenly noticed Jill St. John, Connie Stevens, and Raquel Welch. Soon the lists included directors as well, with Alfred Hitchcock and John Ford dominating my register.

As the lists grew longer, my print grew smaller. It was tough to squeeze in all the movies Burt Reynolds was making. And I couldn't keep the actors in anything resembling alphabetical order. My record keeping had become an unwieldy chore. How to manage my scattered shards of movie memories? My trustiest companions were dog-eared copies of Leonard Maltin's *Movie Guide* and Ephraim Katz's comprehensive *Film Encyclopedia*.[2] They provided acres of alphabetized entries, perfect for perusing during late-night TV viewing. But they couldn't be updated immediately (although Maltin publishes new editions every year). They also couldn't be cross-referenced, like a dynamic database. If only I'd had the foresight (and ability) to create the Internet Movie Database!

The check register allowed me to track my viewing habits through my tumultuous teenage years. I grew up in Charlotte, the largest city in North Carolina.

Frustrated in his attempts to control the city during the Revolutionary War, British General Cornwallis described it as "a hornet's nest of rebellion." As a teenager, I too lived in a hornet's nest, learning how to sting and be stung by others.

As a high school student, my movie watching reached even higher frequencies. Between football practice, student government, and the occasional book report, I was seeing 180 films a year (on TV or in theaters). Amid a plethora of activities, the movies became my downtime, offering moments for quiet reflection, an opportunity to take stock.[3] While experimenting with adulthood, I turned to movies as my sounding board—a safe place in which to measure my manhood. Role models ranged from the rugged individualism of Humphrey Bogart to the ironic detachment of Sean Connery. As aspects of my home life grew uglier, movies also became a convenient escape. Like many teenagers, I felt trapped by my circumstances, hemmed in by family, friends, and expectations. Film became an effective coping mechanism—a way to keep hope alive in a dark period of my life. Movies offered a solace that bracketed my fears, managed my chaos, and calmed the hornet's nest raging inside me.

This personal preface chronicles how and why I came to consider film a source of divine revelation. It will track my transition from film fanatic to God follower, drawing parallels between moviegoing and religious devotion. As a student at Fuller Seminary, I discovered an underappreciated strand within the Christian tradition: general revelation. My journey offers theological categories to describe the habits of those who turn to film for entertainment *and* enlightenment. Blockbuster films such as *Star Wars* combined roller-coaster thrills with ultimate, philosophical questions. To a generation raised to follow "the Force," film became the gathering place for a community that believed in the transformative power of screen stories. Online communities like the Internet Movie Database are a natural extension of the critical film conversations forged in the 1970s.

Quentin Tarantino emerged as the ultimate fanboy—an adult fixated on entertainment who *borrows* moments from his favorite films to create his own postmodern pastiche. Tarantino's early films like *Pulp Fiction* (1994, IMDb #8) blended the sacred and profane in surprising and unprecedented ways. Like John the Baptist crying in the wilderness, Tarantino was a forerunner for the messy, transcendent movies that have followed. *Pulp Fiction* paved the way for the fractured, multilayered narratives discussed in subsequent chapters, such as *Memento, Eternal Sunshine of the Spotless Mind*, and *Crash*. To some, his success signaled the decline of Western civilization. But to dedicated fanboys (and girls), Tarantino's unlikely rise demonstrates the newer, democratic possibilities of filmmaking, film criticism, and even theology: general revelation in action.

In *The Gospel according to Hollywood*, Greg Garrett reflects, "What I took away from *Pulp Fiction* was not the violent action, dark humor, and crudity, but embedded themes of grace and redemption and the belief that God was real and powerful. For me, *Pulp Fiction* was a deeply spiritual film."[4] Tarantino opened up the religious possibilities of movies to the next generation. This book is written for those dedicated seekers of cinematic awe and wonder.

Unfortunately, Tarantino's increasing descent into bloody homage suggests postmodern posing at its worst. His recent films fetishize violence, demean women, and reduce movies to mere simulacra. Can we learn to separate the substantive from the superficial, embracing the best and leaving the rest? As a creative God brought forth light from darkness, so we wade into dark, chaotic films in search of the sacred. The Spirit of God that hovered over the waters in Genesis continues to stir up creativity.

Joining the Committed

I grew up during Hollywood's second golden age—the seventies.[5] The classic films from the thirties and forties (Hollywood's first golden era) defined and buoyed Americans during the challenges of the Depression and World War II.[6] Young directors just graduating from film school in the sixties were granted a prime opportunity to respond to the cultural turbulence that surrounded them. In the seventies, the possibilities of this populist medium finally caught up with the critical theory surrounding it. Art and commerce met in the films created by Hollywood's "holy trinity" of Coppola, Spielberg, and Lucas. Francis Ford Coppola served as the literal godfather to a new generation of filmmakers fresh out of film school. Coppola was slightly older than George Lucas and Steven Spielberg, and he was a step ahead of them as an award-winning director of *The Godfather* (1972, IMDb #1). He produced George Lucas's first features, *THX-1138* (1971) and *American Graffiti* (1973). Steven Spielberg's *Jaws* (1975, IMDb #83) awakened Hollywood to the potential profits lurking in the shores of the summer blockbuster. They each repackaged the most beloved movie matinees of their childhood into rousing adventures. In surpassing their unparalleled success with *The Godfather: Part II* (1974, IMDb #3), *Star Wars* (1977, IMDb #11), and *Raiders of the Lost Ark* (1981, IMDb #16), Coppola, Lucas, and Spielberg enshrined themselves atop the cinematic pantheon before they turned thirty-five.[7] Coppola played (God)Father, Spielberg emerged as Hollywood's Messiah, and Lucas became the mysterious Spirit, descending with new technologies from the Sky(walker ranch). I joined a generation of fanboys and girls whose imaginations were baptized by this cinematic trinity at the local cineplex.[8] We sat in awe, transfixed by the power of cinema. We walked out of theaters transformed by a *close encounter of the fourth kind*, where transcendent art broke box-office records. We were a community, united around a shared experience, a common text. We committed our lives to spreading the gospel of Obi-Wan. (The tragic McDonald's movie tie-ins and toys came later.)

For film critics, the seventies also constituted their first flush of fame and power. Andre Bazin and his coterie of *Cahiers du Cinema* critics/filmmakers (Godard, Truffaut, and Chabrol) had canonized the first wave of film auteurs, including John Ford, Howard Hawks, and Alfred Hitchcock.[9] Andrew Sarris popularized their auteur theory in the United States in his influential book, *The American Cinema: Directors and Directions, 1929–1968.*[10] Sarris defined a cinematic pantheon that remains relatively unchanged and unchallenged forty years later. Movies went from being a disposable entertainment to a legitimate art. Film studies gained academic credibility, and film critics became serious cultural commentators.[11] The first film-school graduates, like Coppola, Lucas, and Spielberg, redefined cinema by combining classic genres with a revolutionary 1960s sensibility.

Against this backdrop, I had a plethora of serious film critics and journals from which to choose. I scoured the stacks of my local library in search of heady reviews from Stanley Kauffman in *The New Republic* or Pauline Kael in *The New Yorker*. Kael's rapturous endorsements of *Last Tango in Paris* and *Nashville* intoxicated me.[12] At eleven years of age, I wasn't allowed to see such decidedly R-rated movies, but I knew about them thanks to Pauline and her circle of critics. Artsy film journals like *Sight and Sound* and *Film Comment* provided me with long lists of films that were never coming to a theater near me.[13] Only big-city critics got to see important films or relish retrospectives from legendary archives. I continue to depend on the finest film critics and scholars for recommendations and insights.

Then came video. In the prevideo era, obscure foreign film classics were only a distant dream. But as distribution expanded, so did the possibilities. Locally owned video stores were soon purchasing long-lost titles for eighty to one hundred dollars each. A rental fee of three or four dollars was a ticket to my own personal *Cinema Paradiso* (IMDb #102). Film studios began to mine their vaults in search of forgotten classics and hidden gems. Everything old suddenly became new again, resurrected on home video. The whole of cinematic history soon became available to the masses. Fanboys like Quentin Tarantino secured jobs as video-store clerks, paid to study movies all day. A visual literacy tied to a new cinematic canon resulted.

Film criticism also shifted from rarified journals or academic arenas to the mass medium of television. Dedicated cinephiles and youthful fanboys found solace in Chicago-based film critics Gene Siskel and Roger Ebert. I discovered these bickering film buffs while watching PBS in 1978. Their television program, *Sneak Previews*, allowed home viewers in the heartland to sit in on serious discussions of the latest releases from Samuel Fuller, Akira Kurosawa, and Ingmar Bergman. Even better, we saw sneak previews of actual scenes from significant new releases. Siskel and Ebert's real genius was boiling highbrow film debates into capsule, two-word reviews: "thumbs up" or "thumbs down." Their show proved so popular that it expanded into the much more profitable syndicated market as *At the Movies*. Siskel and Ebert were Pauline Kael's acolytes, popularizing her insightful reflections on all kinds of genres, from the art house to the grind house.[14] The lines between high art and broad cinematic appeal were vanishing. *The Godfather* won Oscars and conquered the box office at the same time. The unprecedented profits of films from Lucas and Spielberg recalibrated the studio's expectations of what they wanted in a movie. Populist entertainment and critical approval merged to form a highly democratic art—cinematic manna for the masses. The marriage did not last.

Not everyone was swept up by the fantasy world of *Star Wars*. A backlash against such unprecedented success and charges of "sellout" followed. As the sixties outsiders became Hollywood insiders, the cinematic revolution eventually stopped at the end of their own companies and compounds.[15] Coppola's American Zoetrope went bankrupt. Lucasfilm and Amblin Entertainment became cash cows and critical whipping boys. Film scholar Robin Wood wrote a famous essay on "the Lucas-Spielberg Syndrome," in which he (psycho)analyzed audience enthusiasm for their films.[16] Wood's critical theory suggested, "The success of the films is only comprehensible when one assumes a widespread *desire* for regression to infantilism, a populace who wants to be constructed as mock children."[17] For Wood, when audiences return to *Star Wars* and *Raiders of the Lost Ark* multiple times, they are demonstrating the childish behavior associated with fairy tales—"Tell me the story again, Daddy!" Wood was offended by how the films turned back the clock and echoed President Ronald Reagan's vision of morning in America. To Wood, "Patriotism, racism, and militarism are being indulged and celebrated." The token heroism of Princess Leia doesn't empower women but disguises the real agenda: "to put everyone back in his/her place, reconstruct us as dependent children, and reassure us that it will all come right in the end." Within Wood's political rereading of the films arose perhaps his most serious charge—that imagination and nostalgia are incompatible. He says, "Imagination is a force that strives to grasp and transform the world, not restore 'the good old values.'"[18] In reimagining their favorite films from childhood, Lucas and Spielberg brought hope to a depressed, post-Watergate America. But were they selling a new vision or repackaging an old one? Had my commitment to film arrested my development?

When the Hollywood studios saw how much gold could be mined from a blockbuster series, they stopped searching for stories and began investing in sequels. The idealism that defined an era and fueled a burgeoning art was consumed by greed, a victim of excess. J. Hoberman of *The Village Voice* lamented:

> If the sixties and seventies brought a film culture of unprecedented plurality, the last twenty years have been characterized by increasing self-absorption, a profound ignorance of world cinema, and a corresponding disinterest—among American critics, as much as American audiences—in other people's movies. More disturbing, perhaps, than diminished film enthusiasm is the failure of the sixties film culture . . . to establish itself as a lasting intellectual presence.[19]

Hollywood's second golden era ended as I graduated from high school. My faith in film waned.

Raging Bull (for Jesus)

Movies may have been my first love, but as I emerged from Martin Scorsese's *Raging Bull* (1980, IMDb #68), I was catapulted toward a different kind of obsession. Robert DeNiro's haunting portrait of boxing champ Jake LaMotta left me beaten and bruised. I watched the perils of self-immolation, as Jake destroyed his relationships with his brother, his wife, and his fans. Jake ends up alone, in jail, literally banging his head against the wall crying, "Why? Why? Why?" As a high school jock with an equally independent streak, I recognized far too much of myself in Jake. As the film ended, director Martin Scorsese offered a curious counterpoint. The credits read, "All I know is this, once I was blind, but now I can see." I recognized the blindness in Jake and me, but I wondered, "What does it mean to see?" A violent, profane, R-rated movie had provided the spark to a spiritual search—film forged theology.

I had no theological terms to describe this phenomenon. I did not recognize that "LaMotta is such a guilt-ridden individual that he 'atones for his sin by absorbing vicious punishment in the ring.'"[20] I was too young to understand how "the boxing ring has even been construed as 'a metaphorical re-creation of the

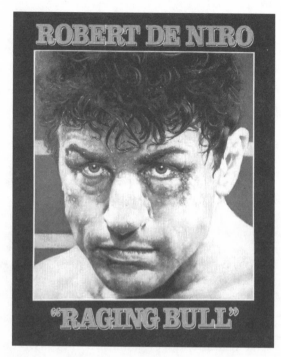

Raging Bull. © 1980 by United Artists.

crucifixion.'"[21] But like my transforming encounter with *Hornet's Nest*, a movie compelled me to action. I responded to a friend's invitation to attend a Young Life meeting. This wild and wacky youth ministry offered fresh and funny home theater. Students gathered in basements and living rooms for singing, games, and a moving discussion of Jesus. It was shockingly relevant, particularly as I saw the loving principles of Jesus embodied by Young Life's adult volunteers. I listened carefully and weighed the options for almost a year. As a freshman in college, at Young Life's Windy Gap Camp, I committed all I knew of myself to all I'd heard and read about Jesus. It was a wondrous meeting: the beginning of a propulsive wrestling match involving my heart and soul that continues unabated to this day. Jesus continues to address my blindness and offer sustaining sight.

As I was initiated into the Christian community, people challenged me to abandon my old ways. I was encouraged to give up R-rated movies and toss out my old Clash records. It was time to shift allegiance, change teams, exchange the profane for the sacred. Yet why would I discard the probing artists and angry revolutionaries who propelled me to Jesus in the first place? What I experienced as a unity was being bifurcated into a war between art and faith. To make peace with my Christian peers, I divided myself in half, adopting the anti-art rhetoric while keeping my passion for Scorsese, Kubrick, and Bertolucci a closeted secret. Such disintegration is difficult (and unhealthy) to sustain.[22]

Only years later, as a student at Fuller Theological Seminary, did I hear a theological term that approximated my experience of cinema and salvation: "general revelation." Something was revealed to me through *Raging Bull*—a sense of longing, need, and desperation. It was available to any viewer willing to endure two hours of pain for one final challenging dollop of grace. Paul Schrader wrote the screenplay, Martin Scorsese directed the movie, and Robert DeNiro gave the performance, but the Holy Spirit convicted me of sin. Later I found that John Wesley attributed my experience to "prevenient grace." Were my self-destructive tendencies restrained by the preceding grace of God? *Raging Bull* offered a sneak preview of where I was headed, but hadn't the Spirit been softening me up throughout high school? God chose to use a profane movie to reveal blinding truth to my parched and weary soul; the Spirit spoke through the big screen. At Fuller Seminary I discovered that God has always used unlikely means to communicate to mule-headed audiences.

From the beginning, since the Spirit of God was hovering over the waters, God has offered revelations. God spoke and there was light (Gen. 1:3). The heavens and the stars declare the glory of God (Ps. 19). God was also revealed within a burning bush. In Exodus 3, God engages in an extended conversation with Moses, answering his questions before revealing a holy and particular name, Yahweh—"I am who I am" (v. 14). This revelation crossed barriers of time and space, identifying God as both eternal and present, omniscient and personal.

God continued to appear in surprising places, from a pillar of fire (see Exod. 40:34–38) to Balaam's talking donkey (see Num. 22:21–41). Lowly prophets arose to offer object lessons on God's behalf. Ezekiel cooked dinner on a dung pile (Ezek. 4:12–15). Jeremiah strapped himself into a cattle yoke (Jer. 27–28). Hosea married a prostitute to send a message (Hosea 1:2–3). They proved the theological could also be theatrical.[23] God continually raised up outsiders to wake Israel from spiritual slumber. Both the righteous Melchizedek and the pillaging Babylonians served as representatives for the divine. The Proverbs of the Bible incorporated wisdom from ancient Egypt. The collected sayings of non-Israelites like Agur (Prov. 30) and King Lemuel (Prov. 31) were included in the canon of Scripture. Paul appeals to Greek art and poetry in his sermon on Mars Hill. Many have upheld Acts 17:16–34 as an example of how we can connect a culture's art to an explication of the gospel. But Paul goes even further. He actually incorporates the truth of Greek poetry (written to praise Zeus!)—"In him we live and move and have our being," and "We are his offspring"—into his argument (v. 28). Art created to honor false gods could contain timeless truth that not only agrees with our Christian faith but expands our understanding of

God. If the Spirit spoke through the best of Egyptian, Greek, or Roman art in biblical times, couldn't the same Spirit still be speaking through today's art?

Integration

I applied to film school on a whim. Somehow, a background in youth ministry and a Master of Divinity degree didn't strike me as keys to the University of Southern California's gated kingdom. To my surprise and delight, I joined forty entering students who all shared the same dream—to make movies. As we talked about our influences, one touchstone united most of us. My classmates spoke in rapturous terms: "When I saw *Star Wars*, I knew I wanted to be a filmmaker." They had experienced a sense of calling, an epiphany, within George Lucas's fantasy film. Could USC become the place to finally unite my two loves—film and faith?

But what about Robin Wood's scathing critique? He taught me that *Star Wars* sold people a false bill of goods, an ideology rather than a theology. What if Wood's own bias blinded him to how much more a movie could prompt? What scholars had reduced to politics, others had turned into religion. Movies can certainly become a distraction, a buffer from the world, a harmful escape. But as a teenager in Charlotte, North Carolina, films served as my lifeline and sustenance—more life raft than crutch. While my critical studies' professors stressed the unholy masking of ideology in film, I found my heart gravitating toward the blessed union of film and theology.

J. R. R. Tolkien described my initial, innocent experience of film in his essay, "On Fairy-Stories."[24] Tolkien affirmed the importance of escape, the "Consolation of a Happy Ending," which he termed a "eucatastrophe." He wrote:

> This joy, which is one of the things which fairy-stories can produce supremely well, is not essentially "escapist," nor "fugitive." In its fairy-tale—or otherworld—setting, it is a sudden and miraculous grace: never to be counted on to recur. It does not deny the existence of *dyscatastrophe*, of sorrow and failure: the possibility of these is necessary to the joy of deliverance; it denies (in the face of much evidence, if you will) universal final defeat and in so far is *evangelium*, giving a fleeting glimpse of Joy, Joy beyond the walls of the world, poignant as grief.[25]

Rather than deriding audiences for escaping their circumstances through stories, Tolkien affirmed it as a longing for joy, a hunger for miraculous grace. Hope and happy endings are so rare. We turn to movies for good news because we desperately need it.

Could my obsessive, youthful escape through movies have actually been a passionate, restless search for God? Maybe others shared my experience of finding God in the movies. Churches may condemn movies for serving as a substitute religion, "idol worship." Academic film scholars may dismiss movies as products of capitalist ideology, reinforcing "cultural hegemony." But I resolved to walk down the middle aisle, where most of us wander in the dark. In this book, I want to understand how an avowedly profane film like *Raging Bull* prompted my spiritual search. Hopefully, my questions will resonate with readers' experiences. Did God use my feelings generated in the dark, or did God inspire those feelings? Is my experience of faith an anomaly or an underreported (and underappreciated) grace of God?

This book begins as a personal effort to reintegrate my head and my heart, to unite my feelings about life, art, and God with the facts of faith. It is a study in film as an occasion for general revelation; a meditation on the Spirit of God, which blows where it wills, inspir(it)ing artists and audiences alike. It is also a work of theological aesthetics—an effort to reunite what the Enlightenment separated: beauty, goodness, and truth (in that order!). I want to practice what Jürgen Moltmann has preached: "It is possible to experience God *in, with and beneath* each everyday experience of the world, if God is in all things, and if all things are in God, so that God himself 'experiences' all things in his own way."[26]

The Numbers

Recent research demonstrates how the lines between church and Hollywood have blurred. Questions of lived religion have taken on tangible form in a comprehensive study of Brits' religious experience. Hay and Hunt conducted a "Soul of Britain Survey," comparing responses between 1987 and 2000. Respondents were asked about their awareness of the presence of God, receiving help in prayer, the presence of evil, a sacred presence in nature, or an experience that all things are "one." In 1987, 48 percent of the population surveyed affirmed one or more of these types of experiences. By 2000, 76 percent acknowledged at least one of these spiritual encounters. While traditional church attendance declined by 20 percent during the decade, spiritual experiences were breaking out across the British Isles. They concluded, "The figures might suggest that we are in the midst of an explosive spiritual upsurge not unlike the Methodist revival of the 18th century."[27] It just hasn't manifested itself in traditional church growth. While I leave the surveying to others, I am definitely suggesting that the anecdotal evidence from my own life, the preponderance of research on film and theology, and the ongoing passion of the film-going community gathered at the IMDb suggest that movies have become one surprising locus for the divine.

Recent research in America by pollster George Barna confirms this. In his book, *Revolution!* Barna finds that in the year 2000, 20 percent of Americans turned to "media, arts and culture" as their primary means of spiritual experience and expression. He expects that percentage to rise to 30 or 35 percent by 2025.[28] Barna's research suggests that the media's growing influence comes at the expense of the local church (which will decline from 70 percent to 35 percent as people's primary means of religious expression). He foresees American religious experience divided equally among the traditional church, alternative religious communities (like small groups), and the arts/media. Barna's numbers offer a potent wake-up call to the Christian community. They demonstrate why film and theology have emerged into a particularly prescient discipline.[29]

Unfortunately, the religious community has grown far too accustomed to controlling the conversation about God, keeping it safely within the doors of the local congregation. We have devoted plenty of pages to understanding theology within the special revelation of Scripture. It is important to deepen our Christology and soteriology, but religious expression has exploded beyond the walls of our churches or theological categories. If a third of all Americans will turn to media, arts, and culture as their primary means of spiritual experience, then we will desperately need a more robust theology of art, image, and culture, and those theologies must be rooted in an experience and explication of general revelation. My passion for the special revelation of the Holy Bible continues, but the rise of general revelation as God's growing means of communication demands our fervent attention.

Rather than bemoan the church's falling cultural impact, I have chosen to get in step with the Spirit and catch up with what's happening through the unlikely means of media. Perhaps our most populist art can inform our desperate need for a public theology. I begin by affirming the unique opportunity that accompanies our current context. The information age has resulted in the democratization of film, film criticism, academia, and theology. Our creative era, in which anybody can be a filmmaker, must be joined by a church that acknowledges that anyone can be (or already is) a theologian.[30]

I am grateful for my crucial companions along an arduous (but joyous) journey into the dark. Thanks go first and foremost to my wife, Caroline, who supported my first foray into Fuller Seminary while we were a newlywed couple. Caroline also experienced most of my film studies at the University of Southern California. She was a great actress during that season of our life. Caroline has also been my most faithful discussion partner, from child-free days of beaches and backpacking, through kid-centric excursions to Disneyland, Sea World, and Legoland. She has helped me process the ramblings punctuating these pages through two decades of testing her patience. We made it through a haunting experience of Hodgkin's lymphoma—a long, strange trip into the dark. Caroline has emerged on the far side of cancer (and my graduate studies!) with her faith and health intact. Thanks be to God!

I would not have undertaken the enormity of a PhD in Theology and Culture without the encouragement of Rob Johnston and Cathy Barsotti. They spelled out the costs and benefits of this course of action in a forthright manner. I trust they have enjoyed the sparks that have flown across our shared classrooms. The faculty in the Center for Advanced Theological Studies also shaped my words and deeds. The insights of William Dyrness and Terry Lindvall sharpened early drafts into a book. Robert Hosack and his team at Baker Academic polished it with the craft of Renaissance sculptors. Finally, I am so grateful for the support of Fred and Dottie Davison and the Brehm Center for Worship, Theology, and the Arts. It has been a privilege to serve as a canary in their academic coal mine. I made it through and hopefully can offer guidance for those who will follow me into the dark in years to come.

1

Methodology
Into the Darko

If there's no one beside you
When your soul embarks
Then I'll follow you into the dark.

Death Cab for Cutie[1]

One of the more haunting songs (and captivating videos) of recent years is Death Cab for Cutie's "I'll Follow You into the Dark." Lead singer Ben Gibbard looks at death, filtered through his painful Catholic parochial school experience. Even if heaven and hell are full, illuminated by "no vacancy" signs, he vows to accompany his love "into the dark." It is a poignant and haunting pledge, an agnostic's prayer. Gibbard believes there may be no blinding light or pearly gates awaiting us, but he and his love hold hands, "waiting for the hint of a spark." Death Cab for Cutie express *a hopeful doubt*. They are willing to watch and wait, satisfied to find a flicker of eternity, a glimpse of the divine.

I invite readers to follow me into the dark of the movie theater. It may not produce a blinding light or usher viewers into a vision of pearly gates.

But I hope it will provide a hint of a spark. A journey "into the dark" may seem like an odd invitation for a work in film and theology. Yet any light that theologians might lift up will arise at the end of the long and daunting tunnel through which we find ourselves crawling. Despite our unprecedented financial and scientific success in the modern era, the twenty-first century can be characterized as a return to the Dark Ages. We have discarded civil discourse in an effort to outshout each other. A new tribalism has resulted in civil wars and ethnic cleansings.[2] Ancient battles between Christianity and Islam, the West and the East, have reared their ugly heads, and they show no signs of abating. The critiques of religion offered by Richard Dawkins and Sam Harris have become best sellers because of their insight, not merely their folly. We have offered far too much judgment, anger, and vitriol in the name of God. We must ask for forgiveness for our "unChristian" attitudes and actions.[3] Any work of art, eager to offer hope, must be forged in the darkness of our current situation.

Teachers, ministers, and therapists who long to get involved in their postmodern constituents' spiritual growth will find vexing shadows cast by our otherwise prosperous lives. The paradoxical reports of today's adolescents as motivated but directionless, well-adjusted but wounded demonstrate the limits of unifying paradigms.[4] Our autonomy has not necessarily resulted in the freedom we expected. To get to the heart of our matters, we must be willing to explore the hidden spaces of our psyche, to peer below the surfaces we've constructed on MySpace. Yet the movies offer such promises every single day. We follow conflicted characters through confusing situations. They emerge either weary and wiser or dead and defeated. The challenges confronting fictional characters become a vicarious opportunity for viewers to forge *their character*. We may discover our blind spots, recognize the limits of individualism, and acknowledge our need for community. What a sweet deal! We invest two hours in the dark (and ten dollars—or more) in exchange for moments of levity and clarity, a shift in perspective, signs of life.

This chapter is divided into four parts. It begins with a discussion of the transcendent possibilities of film and the difficulties in determining which movies matter. How can God communicate through such unlikely means as movies? The second section delves into the theological concept behind this phenomenon: general revelation. Efforts to explain the mysterious ways in which God speaks have led to much confusion. This section will examine the variety of terms and biblical evidence surrounding general revelation. The third part of this introduction explores my methodology, the messy merging of film and theology. This chapter concludes with an example of film and theology in action: a discussion of the cult film *Donnie Darko* (2001).

Film: Forming a Canon

So what constitutes a must-see movie? How do we measure a film's impact across time? Filmmaker Paul Schrader wrestled with the concept of a cinematic canon in a lengthy 2006 article for *Film Comment*. In a brilliant essay incorporating the history of art, aesthetics, and criticism, Schrader describes the formation of a canon as a story: "To understand the canon is to understand its narrative. Art is a narrative. Life is a narrative. The universe is a narrative. To understand the universe is to understand its history. Each and every thing is part of a story—beginning, middle, and end."[5]

As a Calvin College graduate raised within a deep theological tradition, Schrader also reconnected canonization to its religious roots. The establishment of a rule, an order, allowed early Christians to move from competing claims to a more unified people. The canonization process gave a nascent movement base, language, and common ground on which to build. The Nicene Creed, established in AD 325, has served as a baseline for orthodox Christian faith across the centuries. It tells a potent story in a compact form.

Yet the 1945 discovery of the Gospels of Thomas and Philip at Nag Hammadi, Egypt, reopened questions of canonization. Why were the Gnostic Gospels excluded from the canon of Scripture? And why were the Gospels of Matthew, Mark, Luke, and John set apart as authoritative? Ancient debates about orthodoxy have turned into a surprisingly commercial industry, from the best-selling books of Elaine Pagels to the controversies surrounding Dan Brown's *The Da Vinci Code*.[6] Pagels connected the Gnostic Gospels to the historic suppression of female voices within church and society. Dan Brown highlighted the people and politics inherent in the process, turning ancient debates into page-turning drama. The process of elevating certain texts over others played into our contemporary fascination with conspiracy theories. Church authority has come into question. Issues that Christians thought were settled centuries ago have resurfaced, forcing everyone to examine the roots of orthodox Christian faith. Scholarly work regarding the canonization process and early church history has proven remarkably timely.[7]

The founders of "cinematic faith" have also been struggling to retain their authority. Paul Schrader has devoted his life to exploring the transcendent

possibilities of cinema. His legacy as critic, screenwriter, and director is secured.[8] Yet he approached the subject of a cinematic canon with a sense of
ennui, lamenting the decline of film criticism and the film industry. Schrader
recognized that "motion pictures were the dominant art for the 20th century."
But he saw his work as riding "the broken-down horse called movies into the
cinematic sunset." For Schrader, the formation of a cinematic canon suggests
that movies have run their course. His list of the sixty essential films reflected
his bias against recent movies, naming just four films created since 1990.[9] Are
movies bound for the museum destined to be embalmed? Boston University
film professor Ray Carney worries that a digitized, sensationalized cinema has
replaced the artful films of Ingmar Bergman, Michelangelo Antonioni, Federico
Fellini, and Jean-Luc Godard. Carney feels that "the 'spiritual' films have been
shoved aside, . . . those that offer 'a transformative experience,' those that 'expose
us to new ways of being and feeling and knowing.' "[10] Carney laments that even
recent critically acclaimed films of Abbas Kiarostami (*A Taste of Cherry*, 1997)
and Todd Haynes (*Far from Heaven*, 2002) have proven too difficult for contemporary audiences accustomed to easy gratification. Such critical doomsaying is
a time-honored tradition, echoing back to Rudolph Arnheim's 1939 complaints
about the death of silent cinema: "The talking film as a means of representation
precludes artistic creation."[11]

Yet the passion demonstrated on the bulletin boards of the Internet Movie
Database suggests that devoted film fandom has never been more vital. As a freshman at Pomona College, Kate Brokaw declared, "The more popular contemporary
movies in my circle of friends are the movies that are more challenging; the ones
that are doing something offbeat or different in a narrative or visual sense—like
anything by David Finch or Wes Anderson, or Richard Linklater's *Waking Life*."[12]
The emerging canon is just as *spiritual* as its forerunners but in different ways.
Bigger, louder, and faster films *can* be empty and illusory, but a rigorous cutting
pace has not ruined the transcendent possibilities of cinema. Shorter attention
spans need not squelch the Spirit. Rather, the increased availability of moving
images has resulted in an even greater hunger for enlightenment *within* entertainment. Given the nascent possibilities found in digital technology and Internet
distribution, I do not share the skepticism of Schrader and Carney. Movies as a
theatrical event may be waning. But moving images are just starting to animate us
in significant and spiritual ways. This volume will explore the emerging cinematic
canon, wading into the dark with enthusiasm rather than lament.

A few institutions have polled scholars, critics, and stars in an effort to construct a definitive list. The British Film Institute's *Sight & Sound* magazine has

taken the critical pulse of cinematic history each decade since 1952. *Citizen Kane* has topped the international film critics' list since the 1962 poll (with *The Godfather* and *Vertigo* slowly gaining on it).[13] Yet if you ask younger moviegoers about *Citizen Kane*, it will likely inspire modest enthusiasm. In 1996, to celebrate the centennial of cinema, the American Film Institute polled critics and filmmakers to create a list of "The 100 Greatest American Movies of All Time."[14] Once again, *Citizen Kane* topped the charts with *The Godfather* a close second. But how definitive or untainted is such a proposed canon, especially when the American Film Institute turned its lists into a series of television specials, raising money for its institution? Critic Jonathan Rosenbaum rightly took the AFI to task for its isolationism.[15] What of world cinema? Rosenbaum acknowledged the power and importance of a film canon as an educational tool. It *should* start arguments about the art of cinema, causing us to reflect on what matters and why. But Rosenbaum proposed his own alternate Top 100 (and eventually an essential, idiosyncratic Top 1000).[16]

Whose list should we pay attention to? Where are the most credible sources? Scholars attempt to measure a film's impact in a variety of ways. Honors and prizes like the Academy Awards or the Cannes Film Festival Golden Palm confer a certain status (although politics often influence the outcome). Weaker films can win in a year of lesser competition (like *The Greatest Show on Earth*'s Academy Award for Best Picture in 1952). Box office receipts can determine popularity but often indicate more about marketing rather than enduring influence. Movie reviews can also provide a snapshot of initial reactions to a film. What used to take hours of combing through libraries in search of critical reactions is gathered on Web sites like www.metacritic.com or www.rottentomatoes.com. Critical consensus is just a mouse click away.

Yet critics *and* audiences can often overlook a film that comments too closely on its current context. Frank Capra's *It's a Wonderful Life* was neglected on its initial 1946 release, failing to recoup a $500,000 budget.[17] Post–World War II audiences looking for escape found George Bailey's "what if" trip to Potterville too dark a vision. Despite five Academy Award nominations, it walked away without a prize. Only after the studio failed to renew the copyright for *It's a Wonderful Life* did it become the beloved Christmas classic through repeated television screenings. *The Shawshank Redemption* was also greeted with indifference in its 1994 theatrical release. With a domestic gross of only $28 million, it barely recouped its modest budget. Despite seven Oscar nominations, *Shawshank* never even reached one thousand theaters. Did assumptions about dark, prison dramas keep viewers away? *Shawshank*'s redemption took place everywhere but the big screen—in home video (it was the biggest rental of 1995), on DVD (through multiple releases), and on nonpremium cable television. Since its network television debut in June 1997, *The Shawshank Redemption* has run on TNT an average of six times per year—more than fifty times overall.[18] Obviously, home viewers join Andy and Red on their hard-earned trip out of Shawshank again and again. Readers of England's *Empire Magazine* recently ranked *Shawshank* as their favorite film of all time.[19]

Some cinematic treasures are often not discovered until after they've left theaters. It takes time to appreciate the depth of some filmmakers' vision. Today's bombs may become tomorrow's classics. Will appreciation for M. Night Shyamalan's *The Village* (2004) and *Lady in the Water* (2006) grow the further we get from September 11, 2001? Or were audiences and critics right to deride these postmodern fairy tales forged in our fearful times? The combustible mix of oil and religion in *There Will Be Blood* (2007) may have arrived too close to our war in Iraq to appreciate its prescience. The transcendent hope provided by *Into the Wild* (2007) may grow in appreciation the more we preserve our tenuous environment. As the sheer volume of entertainment grows, the process of separating cinematic gold from forgettable dross will prove increasingly important.

With so many variables to measure a movie's worth, how might a discerning filmgoer determine which films to watch? What about a poll of nonexperts comprised of average moviegoers who know what they like and who celebrate movies that moved them, even if they do not have the critical grids or categories to articulate why? Since film is among our most public arts—a truly mass medium—we need *an audience-driven, receptor-oriented methodology*. What films evoke ongoing passion and repeat viewings? Could we combine both the critical admiration for craft (in *Citizen Kane*) with the visceral thrill of entertainment (in *Star Wars*)? Where do art, commerce, and enduring impact coalesce?

The IMDb and the New Canon

To determine which movies inspired film fans across the world, I turn to the Internet Movie Database (www.imdb.com). As an online encyclopedia created and updated by moviegoers, the IMDb is a remarkable tool to determine the new cinematic canon. It is a receptor-oriented database, culling from the collective wisdom of the global film-watching community. It is driven by love and devotion and fueled by passionate opinions. Some may consider IMDb users a little obsessive. It may attract people who have too much time on their hands, who care more about movies than everyday life. How representative are people who invest too much time online? Yet I admire the unguarded responses that IMDb users offer up so freely and frequently. Nobody is paid for their reviews. Unlike the Oscars, the votes are not tainted by personal grudges or professional jealousy. While global in scope, all politics (and opinions) are local. As Amazon .com serves as the one-stop shop for book buying and reading capsule reviews, so the IMDb gathers information and posts reviews from both rabid and casual film fans. It is a dynamic, constantly evolving forum of opinions and insights. The IMDb offers both a long view of cinematic history and an immediate snapshot of a film's relative popularity and power.

The IMDb publishes an evolving list of the Top 250 films of all time (see appendixes A and C). It invites millions of users to rate films from one to ten stars and then compiles and sorts their responses to form a collective ranking. Like most of the Internet, the IMDb is a jumbled, postmodern morass of public opinion. It is tough to sort through all the inchoate feelings to determine what matters. While individual opinions can be mercurial, the aggregate effect is staggering. With forty million hits per month, the IMDb's fact-checking, correcting, and up-to-the-minute additions serve as a self-correcting, global community project. The IMDb ratings evolve over time. Loyal fans often praise a director's latest film upon its theatrical release, but as the movie rolls out on DVD or television, another wave of moviegoers weigh in, often counterbalancing the initial enthusiasm. Over two or three years, the best films find an audience, with ample time for word of mouth to build. Films overlooked on their theatrical release can take on new life and resonance within the collective wisdom of the Internet. (For example, *The Shawshank Redemption* is ranked at #2 on the all-time list, right after *The Godfather*). The IMDb offers an unparalleled, highly democratic portrait of films that have moved the human spirit.

For film scholars, what used to be guesswork rooted in hunches or slow, scientific surveys has been replaced by ongoing data gathering. But we must overcome our bias against these "average" moviegoers. The IMDb began as a community project of fanboys and girls (just like me). It was a Usenet bulletin board called rec.arts.movies.[20] It featured lists of actors, actresses, directors, and movies. In 1990 British film fan Col Needham created a program to allow the lists to be searched—a movie database was born. It hit the World Wide Web from a server at Cardiff University in Wales in 1993. Two years later, the name was changed from rec.arts.movies to the Internet Movie Database. The IMDb arrived earliest and captured the majority of the film-watching, review-writing, Internet-blogging market. As traffic and interest grew, the IMDb servers were stretched toward capacity. Jeff Bezos and Amazon.com arrived as a suitor with sufficient capital to establish the IMDb as the most effective and wide-ranging Internet gathering place for film facts. Film's fanboys and girls found a home that blends art and commerce, the special, artistic properties of film and the general popularity of the medium. Now every computer user can publish his or her thoughts on any film throughout cinematic history. My film students feel they've arrived when their films are posted and reviewed on the IMDb.

In the Internet era, film criticism evolved into a democratic art much to the chagrin of serious cineastes, who used to control the critical conversation. The IMDb allows anyone (with Internet access and a modest grasp of the English language) to become a critic. Thousands of ratings and reviews are posted on the site irrespective of merit. Yet the IMDb also offers an important corrective—reviews of the reviews. Each capsule review can also be voted on under the rubric, "Did you find the following comment useful?" The database collects the votes, sorts the data and compiles the list. The top-ranked films have each been seen (and affirmed) by thousands of voters. The IMDb serves as a clearinghouse to sort out the top films of the new century. Thus I choose to build this receptor-oriented study out of IMDb users' conclusions.

I recognize the pitfalls looming within such populist sentiments. Screenwriter William Goldman declared that in Hollywood, "Nobody knows anything."[21] Goldman did not question the intelligence of studio executives or the artistry of film directors (well, maybe a little bit). Rather, he acknowledged the mercurial nature of the moviegoing audience. The combined efforts of the finest storytellers, the most charismatic actors, and the best marketing minds still fail to connect with audiences *on a regular basis*. Yet small, independent films produced outside the studio apparatus often rise from obscurity to surprising box-office success and critical acclaim. Audiences' continuing ability to embrace new talent, fresh ideas, and artistic breakthroughs fuels the Hollywood dream.

Despite the entertainment industry's efforts to reduce filmmaking to formula, the restless longings of artists and audiences still gravitate toward creative ways to explore ultimate questions. The finest films chronicle our search for love, our longing for home, our hunger for community. Enduring classics wrestle with why we hide from one another, even sabotaging our best intentions. They document why we attack one another, undermining the community we seek. The most inspiring movies suggest that we can overcome our worst tendencies and engage in heroic efforts via courage, humility, beauty, and honor. But nobody knows why certain films capture the hearts and minds of audiences with such unpredictable (and often unrepeatable) power. It remains an elusive, ineffable mystery—an art rooted in faith and struggle.

Into the *Darko*

So what matters the most today? What films are addressing audiences' collective itch? What are movie lovers debating and raving about? Moreover, can the films that moved the human spirit also provide clues about the activity of the Holy Spirit? Can the voice of God emerge from among the passions of the people posting on the IMDb? This book seeks the sacred in the finest twenty-first-century films as identified by the users of the IMDb (see appendix B). I have watched and studied forty-five contemporary films that top the IMDb charts. The artists and their audiences set the cinematic agenda; I respond with theological observations and interpretations. The next generation of pastors, teachers, and therapists must not only learn the language of film but also develop the art of interpretation—seeing and hearing what's happening on big (and small) screens. This study is an opportunity to explain why we love certain movies. Thrilling scenes, memorable performances, touching stories all play a significant part, but have we overlooked the ultimate questions that fuel the most enduring art? I aspire to put words to moviegoers' inchoate feelings, to explore their enthusiastic but often ineffable ratings. This book complements my efforts to train people in the art of interpretive leadership.

The Proposition

The same God who spoke through dreams and visions in the Bible is still communicating through our celluloid dreams—the movies. As the Spirit of God raised up unexpected sources of wisdom during biblical times, so the same creative Spirit is inspiring actors, screenwriters, and directors today. The relative faith or righteousness of the artists has no bearing on their ability to become a conduit for revelatory insights. God is not only speaking through faith-fueled projects like *The Passion of the Christ* or *The Chronicles of Narnia*. The most important spiritual truths are often embedded within seemingly debased settings or sources. Entire sections of the biblical Proverbs were culled from sayings outside Israel. The wisdom of Agur in Proverbs 30 and King Lemuel in Proverbs 31 were lifted from Egyptian texts. The prophet Hosea was challenged to love a faithless wife, Gomer. How can a story rooted in whoring about serve divine purposes? Hosea's strained marriage was turned into a living illustration of God's faithfulness across time. To Habukkuk's cry for justice, God raised up the bitter and ruthless Chaldeans. How can God use such godless people to inaugurate divine judgment? The Oscar-winning movie *Amadeus* also questions the wisdom of God. It is easy to understand why Salieri raged against a God who distributes such talent and blessing to seemingly unworthy servants like Mozart. And yet the surprises continue. When horror-meister Stephen King serves as the source of inspiring films like *The Shawshank Redemption* and *The Green Mile*, we must question our assumptions about who God chooses and how the Spirit moves.

The theological term to describe this phenomenon is *general revelation*. It suggests that God can speak through anyone or anything at any time. Serious, thoughtful Christians have found themselves transformed by potent, R-rated films like *Magnolia* (IMDb #175), *Fight Club* (IMDb #32), and *American History X* (IMDb #44). The fervent discussions that swirl around *Memento* (IMDb #26), *Eternal Sunshine of the Spotless Mind* (IMDb #38), and *Million Dollar Baby* (IMDb #78) suggest that people with and without faith commitments find them to be occasions of searing insight, surprising comfort, and unexpected grace. Has a new wave of creativity, unleashed by the Spirit of God, descended on decadent Hollywood? My initial fascination in the power of cinema is reconfirmed by overwhelming evidence that the mysteries of life and faith are being communicated through filmmakers.

Too many film critics and scholars have underestimated (or even missed) the transcendent, revelatory possibilities of film.[22] Too many theologians have dismissed film as an academic trifle, unworthy of serious attention. Scholar Margaret Miles pushed past such biases, acknowledging how we "now gather about cinema and television screens rather than in churches to ponder the moral quandaries of American life."[23] The burgeoning field of film and theology seeks to unite what scholars have divided. It follows trails blazed by theologians like Friedrich Schleiermacher, Rudolph Otto, and Paul Tillich. Writing to an audience that had drained feeling from religion, Schleiermacher asked, "And how are religion and art related? They can hardly be quite alien, because, from of old, what is greatest in art has had a religious character."[24] Movies serve religious functions for filmgoers, offering them time for contemplation, a change in perspective, a glimpse of the divine. At Fuller Seminary's 2006 Reel Spirituality Conference, Sister Rose Pacatte, FSP, of the Pauline Center for Media Studies recounted a surprising story of a woman she met who came to the movies *because* she had heavy decisions to make and needed the time of contemplation in the dark. Film-going served as a form of retreat, a sacred space. Theology may be uniquely equipped to answer questions of why certain films endure. Skills used to determine the religious canon can deepen our understanding of the emerging film canon.

This book is an attempt to search for that wild, untamed God who reveals whatever to whomever whenever God chooses. It is about a theology not only from the top down but also from the bottom up. We search for God speaking from the margins to the margins, from the movie screen to the audience. I see mass entertainment as a form of Mass, a common grace. Christ remains our only saving grace, but movies can provide *moments* of grace as well. They dispense comfort and hope. Only God knows which debased art forms can still prove helpful to the mysterious ways of the Spirit. I have been trained theologically to move from facts to feelings, from propositional truths to personal applications. But what if we reverse the process, mirroring the way most people experience film? Can we start with beauty, art, and nature as a way into ethics and even theology? In a reverse hermeneutic, can our feelings lead us toward God? I join an emerging cloud of witnesses in undertaking this theological experiment, confident that the Spirit will guide us from art (beauty) to ethics (goodness) to theology (truth). God began with a beautiful creative act incarnated by Jesus. He is the most arresting image of God, the embodiment of kingdom ethics, and the ultimate lived Truth. Theology and doctrine *flowed out of* creation and incarnation.[25] We proceed with confidence because the Spirit behind the beauty of creation and the mystery of redemption is also the source of our discernment. We walk by faith, not by fear.

The Spirit of God that hovered over the waters at the genesis of the earth (Gen. 1:1–2) still hovers over the waters (deserts?) of Los Angeles. The same God who brought forth stars as proclamation (Ps. 19) continues to employ stars in Hollywood to tell his story. Just as the Israelites didn't expect to hear God through Cyrus, the king of Persia (Ezra 1:1–4), or Pharaoh Neco (2 Chron. 36), so the Christian community in America did not expect to hear about the power of God through Mel Gibson in *The Passion of the Christ*. Yet the surprising work of the Spirit knows no bounds. The mysteries of Christ cannot be contained within any walls or boxes. (Even when they tried to bury him, he literally emerged "outside the box"!) We must recover a more complete picture of God's communicative imagination. As the Holy Trinity engages in a three-way dialogue, so I challenge readers to move beyond binary categories of sacred/profane, good/evil, moral/immoral. The sacred life requires more mystery and nuance. Those who presume to know the limits of God have surely stopped seeking, listening, and seeing. General revelation is an underappreciated theological category, an underexplored catalyst for revitalizing our faith and practices.

Am I equating cinema with Holy Scripture? Heavens no! The Word of God is a special revelation unequaled in human history. I am not baptizing all art as sacred or all inspiration as divine. Yet God has revealed himself in ways beyond the written word. The Bible itself is a litany of unlikely communiqués. Christ promised if his people did not praise God, the rocks would cry out (Luke 19:40).

Perhaps those rocks have recently taken on pop cultural forms. It does not denigrate a sacred text to study other texts; I am merely affirming what the Spirit is already doing. God does not discriminate. The Spirit can communicate via inspiring films like *The Shawshank Redemption* (IMDb #2) or cautionary tales like *The Godfather* (IMDb #1). We need role models *and* warning signs. While the religious community questions prophets' credentials, divinely inspired artists keep on singing songs, telling stories, making movies.

Art-making emerges from divine action. As God created the heavens and earth, so artists create—in a reflection of the divine image. As the Spirit of God was hovering over the chaotic waters in Genesis 1, so the Spirit of God inspires filmmakers to craft art out of chaotic experience. Enduring art emerges from the depths of our human longing and reaches out in hunger for the divine. The revelation given to John suggests that the finest art, "the glory and the honor of the nations," will be brought into the new Jerusalem, securing a place in eternity (Rev. 21:26). I want to recover the biblical bookends of Genesis and Revelation. We've been so busy living within the pain of a broken world that we've missed the glory and wonder at each end of God's story. We recognize the shame and disintegration that fractured human identity in Genesis 3. We lament the tragic genocide that shattered community in Genesis 4. We celebrate the glorious redemption found in Jesus's death, resurrection, and ascension. The Spirit of God extends across biblical history, from the act of creation in Genesis 1 to the eternal invitation to all who are thirsty: "Come!" (Rev. 22:17). German theologian Jürgen Moltmann describes the hope embedded within the divine story: "In God's creative future, the end will become the beginning, and the true creation is still to come and is ahead of us."[26] The promise of eschatology still arises from our damaged anthropology and fragile ecclesiology. David Dark has suggested that the apocalyptic literature of the Bible "maximizes the reality of human suffering and folly before daring a word of hope. . . . The hope has nowhere else to happen but the valley of the shadow of death. Is it any surprise that we often won't know it when we see it?"[27] What theological partners can enhance our understanding of enduring cinema and divine revelation?

Theology: For General Audiences

> The theology of revelation is church theology, a theology for pastors and priests.
> The theology of experience is pre-eminently lay theology.
>
> Jürgen Moltmann[28]

General revelation is a term created by theologians to describe the experience of God available to all people. Such revelations may arrive as a word, a thought, a vision, a touch, or a feeling. These divine breakthroughs wake us up, surprise us, reassure us that we are not alone. They may also put us in our place, reminding us how small or self-imposed our problems may be amid hurting humanity. In a contentious world, the revelations of the Spirit move us toward peace, patience, and compassion. While it is tempting to define and delimit general revelation for the purpose of study, God resists our efforts to place boundaries around divine means and methods. General revelation remains an underexplored area of theological inquiry precisely because it often involves feelings, surprises, and exceptions. Of course, not all feelings are from God. The terror created by horror films does not necessarily stem from the fear of the Lord. Yet God may still speak through a horror film, scaring us straight or drawing us closer to divine comfort. The power of general revelation often resides in God's ability to sneak up on us, to speak through unlikely people or unexpected situations (even horror movies).

Revelation has echoes in the Greek word for *apocalypse*, which means to uncover, reveal, disclose, or make known. David Dark says, "Apocalyptic cracks the pavement of the status quo. It irritates and disrupts the feverishly defended norms of whatever culture it engages."[29] We associate the word with the book of Revelation and John's vision of an impending cosmic showdown. Mel Gibson's *Apocalypto* (2006) revealed what may have happened to a once-mighty Mayan culture. The film's graphic violence was intended as a prophetic warning for our own self-destructive times. But we are considering the term *revelation* much more broadly. It is more than mere doomsaying. I am also interested in what contemporary cinema may reveal about our selves, our communities, and our deepest longings. Apocalyptic moments offer blinding insight and clarity within decidedly fuzzy circumstances. I also hope to discover plenty about God, the Bible, and our eschatological hope. I expect contemporary cinema to serve as a vexing but rewarding source of divine inspiration.

Because sunsets and stars are available to all people, they are considered *general* sources of revelation. General revelation has also been linked to human reason, the nudge of our conscience. Christian scholars reserve the words *particular* or *special* for the revelation of God in Scripture. The Bible began as a highly specific word from God, about God. God self-identifies as "I AM THAT I AM" (Exod. 3:14 KJV). God the Father describes Jesus, "This is my beloved Son, in whom I am well pleased" (Matt. 3:17 KJV). Christ points to the Spirit, promising, "And I will pray the Father, and he shall give you another Comforter" (John 14:16 KJV). The names and manifestations of God are quite specific; the Holy Trinity engages in an interdependent relationship. While we may read these pronouncements as directed toward a general audience, the revelation itself was special—one-time events, recorded in biblical texts that bear repeated study across the centuries. The spirited debates about how inspired or infallible the Bible may be revolve around key questions of special revelation.

While I respect and value the importance of those scholarly undertakings, I focus on the underrepresented side of the academic canon. This study of general revelation highlights the hints and whispers of God available to us all. Is God still speaking? Can the Spirit still inspire and comfort? What might provide the means of general revelation today? Despite our neglect of the environment, we still have beaches, mountains, and butterflies to remind us of the Creator. God continues to speak through priests and prophets, dreams and distractions. But can God also communicate through the clatter of electronic information? Are the hours spent in front of computers, televisions, and movie screens solely a break from reality, an escape from providence? I want to sharpen our ability to see and hear the divine amid everyday life, even as we wander "into the dark." I adopt the observations of Jürgen Moltmann: "The theology of experience is pre-eminently lay theology."[30] A study of general revelation should be accessible to general audiences. As the liturgy was originally understood as the work of the people, so this study is a theology of the people. I am interested in how God speaks through people, places, and experiences *outside of Scripture*, specifically, within the feature-film-going experience.

Broadening the Conversation

Any study of general revelation must also wade into the fuzzy but related theological concepts of common grace, natural theology, and the Spirit in creation. This book is about catching glimpses of God among common people and everyday places (like the movies). But how do we describe it?

Some Reformed Protestant traditions have labeled this phenomenon "common grace."[31] The sun shines and the rain falls on all the earth, irrespective of people's beliefs or practices (Matt. 5:45). Gifts and talents are not distributed according to merit but by unmerited favor, the grace of God. The Oscar-winning film *Amadeus* (1984, IMDb #79) demonstrated that Mozart's music may be divine even while his personal life was a mess. Common grace creates theological problems for those of us who wish to have a corner on God's favor. How could a horror writer like Stephen King pen *The Shawshank Redemption* (1994, IMDb #2)? How can we explain the profoundly Christian truths emerging from the collaborative efforts of Tim Robbins, Susan Sarandon, and Sean Penn in *Dead Man Walking*? Common grace reminds us that the gifts of God and the ways of the Spirit are mysterious, beyond our understanding.

Those within the Roman Catholic tradition prefer the term *natural theology*, as in "the heavens declare the glory of God" (see Ps. 19:1–6). St. Thomas Aquinas looked for proof of God within nature. Creation arises from the Word of God and becomes a form of proclamation. The apostle Paul points to how the "invisible things" of God are seen via the wonders of the natural world. Nature reveals ample proof of God's eternal power; therefore, "men are without excuse," everyone is under divine judgment (see Rom. 1:18–20). Paul traces humanity's descent from not glorifying and thanking God to becoming "vain in their imaginations." Natural theology presents a compelling case for how humanity continues to ignore, deny, or dismiss the testimony found in creation. Yet what about the faith inspired by beauty? Natural theology provides a rationale for the environmental movement, for preservation of creation as a godly act of obedience. Theologian Sallie McFague suggests we need a total mind shift, "a conversion from a narrow, self-centered consumer mentality of abundance for the fortunate to an earth-centered, inclusive, long-term vision of the good life for all, including the planet."[32] In this study, I hope to awaken the underexplored *possibilities* of natural theology, the *opportunities* presented by general revelation.

A third strand of the Christian tradition prefers to talk about the Spirit in creation. Surely the natural world involves more than a blanket condemnation for humanity. Orthodox churches emphasize the trinitarian "glory of the Lord," encouraging believers to become "partakers of the divine nature" (2 Pet. 1:4 KJV). They stress the fullness of humanity found in Genesis 1 and 2 *prior to* the fall in Genesis 3. David Bentley Hart has pointed to the wondrous testimony contained in *The Beauty of the Infinite*. He suggests, "The things of the senses cannot of themselves distract from God. All the things of the earth, in being very good, declare God, and it is only by the mediation of their boundless display that the declaration of God may be heard and seen."[33] If God is present in the world, speaking through creation to creation, then we must listen closely. What are we missing? Can our humanity and imagination be recovered? How can we sharpen our hearing and perceiving to get in tune with the Spirit of God that was present at the creation? The same Spirit guides us in our current context and calls us toward a renewed creation in the future. All three Christian traditions—Protestant, Catholic, and Orthodox—point to revelation existing outside the church within creation and creativity.

To some degree, terms like *common grace* or *general revelation* are used interchangeably. Yet the differences arise in the faith traditions' view of humanity rather than God. How much can we perceive? Is God the sole initiator of the revelatory process, or do we respond to promptings around us, reaching God after searching for clues? Discussions of general revelation have tended to start with Augustine and Aquinas and trace their tensions back to Plato and Aristotle.[34] Augustine suggested we need illumination to appreciate and apprehend God. Faith trumps reason. Aquinas believed that the natural world was autonomous and God's dealings with creation were accessible via natural (human) reason. Thus Aquinas separated philosophy (reason) from religion. He put the intellect first, postulating five ways to demonstrate God. Augustine insisted that the effects of sin have crippled natural man's cognitive powers. Reasoning does not create truth but discovers it.

I lean toward a blended approach—not faith or reason, but faith *and* reason, God above us and God all around us. The old *either/or* dialectic seems exhausted. The simplistic division of our world into binary tensions has proven unhelpful.[35] In the postmodern era, we desperately need an integrative approach to general revelation (what Death Cab for Cutie describes as the place where "Soul meets Body"). Jürgen Moltmann considers natural theology "a *recollection* of creation and an eschatological *hope* for creation. . . . It brings us to what must be called a mystical perception of God's presence in all things and in our innermost being. By virtue of his Spirit, God is present in the heart of the world, and in our own hearts."[36] Moltmann moves beyond the limits that accompany common grace. General revelation is not merely what convicts us of sin but the Spirit that animates our art, our imagination, and our dreams. The Spirit of creation is the Spirit of redemption, and the same Spirit drives enduring creativity.

I prefer the term *general revelation* because it echoes the notion of general audiences. Movies are made for the masses, yet they touch us in such specific and individual ways. We are surprised by how an escapist entertainment suddenly moves us to tears or laughter, inspires us to express love to our family or an estranged friend. General revelation works in similar ways. We're pierced by an unexpected truth or comforted by a compassion we didn't request. There are no limits of time, place, people, or means. We may be moved by comedies, dramas, horror, or fantasy. Like the rain that falls indiscriminately, every genre is created under the sovereignty of God. Every film, every experience, every moment in our lives (including dreams) is potentially loaded with theological possibilities. Jesus constantly reminded his disciples that they simply needed "eyes to see and ears to hear" (Matt. 13:16). Such seeing takes time; listening takes patience. Both activities are dependent on the gift of discernment, meditated by the Spirit, sorted out in a truth-seeking community. This will be the ground of our conversation.

Key Partners

My personal experience of general revelation (within the movies) sparked my search for propositional truth to explain it. An appreciation of art or nature does not diminish the importance of biblical truth. In Psalm 19 we see how general revelation in the stars both precedes and confirms special revelation. Psalm 104 describes how God the great production designer is wrapped in light as with a garment. Plants are given to us that we may cultivate them, bringing forth food and wine. The Psalmist's inspired words of praise arise in response to the glory of God's creation. Consider the surprising attention N. T. Wright devotes to general revelation in his apologetic *Simply Christian: Why Christianity Makes Sense*.[37] While the title appeals to logic, the book begins with our experience of the divine. To a post–World War II audience, C. S. Lewis presented philosophical arguments in *Mere Christianity*. To our post-9/11 contexts, N. T. Wright offers four chapters on general revelation, including thoughts on our sense of injustice, our longing for relationships, and the beauty of nature. Wright calls these nagging notions "echoes of a voice." Only after appealing to our artistic and cultural instincts does Wright discuss God as revealed in history and Scripture, through the nation of Israel and the person of Jesus. This book will focus on the first half of Wright's apologetic—films that start the conversation rather than offer the answers. Where Wright hears "echoes of a voice," I invite readers "into the dark" to see and hear glimpses of the divine.

My hunger for reconciliation echoes H. D. McDonald's conclusions regarding general revelation. McDonald recalls, "There was set up an antithesis between 'Spirit' and 'Truth.' Is there not, however, a need for, and a possibility of, re-wedding these two views, and thus bringing into an acceptable unity the idea of revelation as 'Spirit' and the idea of revelation as 'Truth'? A less one-sided relationship between the Scriptures and the Spirit needs to be thought out, a relationship, indeed, more akin to the historic Evangelical position."[38] As Nancey Murphy has suggested, the old categories of liberal and conservative may not apply in this new, integrated paradigm.[39] In the meantime, those attempting to walk a fine line between the competing camps will receive shots from both sides. Evangelicals can help liberalism recover propositional truth. Liberalism can help evangelicals put hands and feet to their faith, turning beliefs into practices. I echo Paul's prayer for the Ephesians: "I keep asking that the God of our Lord Jesus Christ, the glorious Father, may give you the Spirit of wisdom and revelation, so that you may know him better" (see Eph. 1:17).

Thankfully, theologians Hans Urs von Balthasar and Jürgen Moltmann have provided viable, valuable frameworks that can bridge the theological divide. With a faith born amid the horrors of World War II, German theologian Jürgen Moltmann pushed beyond ideologically driven belief systems. He saw the destructive results of dualistic polarities. While embodying rigorous academic standards, Moltmann embarked on a public theology. He revived Martin Luther's notion that "all are theologians, that means every Christian. All are said to be theologians so that all may be Christians."[40] For Moltmann, that meant listening to alternative voices within theology, sitting under feminist theologians or leaders of liberation in Central or South America in an effort to gain a more complete picture of God. The vitality of Christian expression emerging from Africa, Asia, and Latin America suggests that the Western church still has plenty to learn.

Perhaps Moltmann's most daring (and yet obvious) notion is that atheists are also theologians with plenty to offer the Christian community. He asks, "Is not every unbeliever who has a reason for his atheism and his decision not to believe a theologian too?"[41] Moltmann learned plenty about God from Nietzsche, Feuerbach, Marx, and Freud. Can't the same principle extend to contemporary artists, musicians, and writers? Moltmann locates legitimate questions of God *within Scripture.* "There is a protest atheism that wrestles with God as Job did, and for the sake of the suffering of created beings which cries out to high heaven denies that there is a just God who rules the world in love."[42] This is the ancient conundrum known as *theodicy:* How can a good God be reconciled with so much evil and suffering? This is the starting point for probing films such as *21 Grams, In America,* and *Signs.*[43] Characters deal openly with grief, wondering why the innocent suffer, why beloved spouses and children die. They confront God with the same question Jesus asked from the cross: "My God, my God, why have you forsaken me?" (Matt. 27:46; Mark 15:34). Thank God for protest atheism that expresses our anger and gives voice to our unanswered cries. Anybody can be a theologian if they're willing to ask the hard questions, to address God directly with their deepest hurts and darkest doubts. This is where enduring films begin.

Balthasar also offered a potential way forward in his prescient theological aesthetics, *The Glory of the Lord.* This massive life's work attempts to reverse the fall of theology by reclaiming the glory of art. He considers the separation of beauty from truth and goodness as theology's original sin. Balthasar indicts both Catholics and Protestants in the great divorce, begging a new generation to restore the unity of art, ethics, and dogma. For Balthasar, there is no hierarchy within truth, goodness, and beauty. Like the Holy Trinity, they are equal partners, utterly independent. He begs for a recovery of revelation as a God-initiated action that emanates from the Spirit. Balthasar places Christ at the center of that revelation, as simultaneously fact and form, the ultimate beauty. Yet how many artists, spurned by the church, have ended up worshiping their creation rather than their Creator? Balthasar places blame on both sides of the cultural-religious divide.

> The word "aesthetic" automatically flows from the pens of both Protestant and Catholic writers when they want to describe an attitude which, in the last analysis, they find to be frivolous, merely curious and self-indulgent. And for the champions of an aesthetic world-view, the exact reverse is true: the ethical-religious in general and, in particular that which is positively Christian, is precisely what either clouds or simply destroys the "right" attitude to life.[44]

In other words, in the religious community, nothing is a bigger slight than the throwaway phrase, "It's (just) art." For the art community, "religious art" equals tacky, pedantic, and preachy. Balthasar challenges the artistically inclined not to dismiss morality or religion as an inherent assault on creativity. He challenges both communities to look closer, to think deeper.

As an artist *and* a person of faith, I was presented false choices resulting in a malnourished faith *and* a formless art. It is tough to be an artist, and it is difficult to be a Christian. Combining the two is exponentially challenging.[45] To heal the breach, Balthasar distinguishes between a theological aesthetic and an aesthetic theology.

> It seems both advisable and necessary to steer clear of the theological application of aesthetic concepts. A theology that makes use of such concepts will sooner or later cease to be a "theological aesthetics"—that is, the attempt to do aesthetics at the level and with the methods of theology—and deteriorate into an "aesthetic theology" by betraying and selling out theological substance to the current viewpoints of an inner-worldly theory of beauty.[46]

This distinction would have improved my first book, *A Matrix of Meanings: Finding God in Pop Culture*.[47] It was written to correct the anti-art, anticulture bias that characterizes too much of Christian theological reflection. In an effort to counteract the lack of aesthetics in most religious circles, my coauthor,

Barry Taylor, and I neglected to point out the limits of pop culture. We veered toward blanket enthusiasm for all things popular. Our critics wanted to hear more methodology, a tighter grid for sorting the good and the true from the popular.

Balthasar enabled me to see why we left ourselves open to such criticism. As artists, we started with the beautiful and then went toward the good and the true. We recognized such a reverse hermeneutic violated the dominant paradigm, but we did not have enough of the historical picture to understand just how revolutionary such a seemingly minor adjustment would seem. Consider this volume a more extended argument on behalf of general revelation/reverse hermeneutics/theology from the bottom up. Balthasar identifies his theological process (and God's revelation) as:

Theo-phany = Aesthetics
Theo-praxy = Dramatic Theory
Theo-logy = Logic[48]

God acts in creation (Genesis), in history (Exodus), in Christ (the Gospels). This divine drama unspools across the ages like a three-act (or maybe five-act) play. Our ethical notions flow out of God's beautiful and dramatic actions. The law arose *after* God freed Israel from slavery in Egypt. Paul's doctrines for the early church followed *in response to* the embodied faith and practices of Jesus. It took three hundred years for the nascent Christian community to sort out what had happened. Theology and doctrine are the logical results of trying to explain and organize glorious, artistic realities. Our religious rituals are designed to remind us of God's dramatic actions. The Jewish Passover and the Christian Eucharist are inherently dramatic, theatrical in their scope, reflecting the active and beautiful aspects of our faith.

We are so far from the dramatic act of creation that it is easy to lose sight of theology as story. Balthasar allowed me to recover what I inherently, aesthetically sensed: "This revelation, however, in its total shape, in large-scale and small-scale matters, is dramatic. It is the history of an initiative on God's part for his world, the history of a struggle between God and the creature over the latter's meaning and salvation."[49] Christian theology begins as divine drama: soul meets body in Jesus's incarnation. A creative age must be met by a creative theology. Emerging theologian Kevin J. Vanhoozer builds on Balthasar's beautiful work, uncovering "the drama of doctrine."[50] Vanhoozer suggests that understanding history as "theo-drama" frees us to serve as actors/performers/players in the ongoing work of God. Can we start to see ourselves as an essential part of God's play? Will we learn our lines and rehearse our roles with an unprecedented commitment to craft? Rather than rejecting our entertainment culture, we may rediscover how to present an eternal drama on a cosmic stage. We are just beginning to grasp the enormous and energizing implications of Balthasar's simple theological shift.

This study will broaden Balthasar's definition of beauty. Many of the films discussed herein could be considered ugly. They follow questionable characters into seedy surroundings. Women will be raped, addicts will get high, and children will be murdered. In no way will we consider such actions *beautiful*. But as we reflect on the dramatic choices and actions within the movies, we will consider whether they represent *truthful* actions. Theologian Richard Viladesau explains:

> God is not always revealed in art in what the Scholastics call the "splendor" of beauty or in the "glory" of which Balthasar speaks. Art may pose the question of the ultimate goal of human love, rather than give an answer; to this extent, it may evade beauty, or may be beautiful in a painful or anxious or anguished way. But even such a question, arising from a desiring in darkness rather than from the "clarity" of divine beauty, may be the communication of God's love.[51]

Movies are more effective at asking questions or depicting problems than proposing answers. Their truths are more *descriptive* than *prescriptive*.[52] If filmmakers describe the toughest aspects of life truthfully, then we will respond to their art with appropriate attention. Like many in the emerging generation, I prefer dark, R-rated truths to bright, G-rated lies.[53] We long to merge the messy text of life with the biblical testimony. An academic method must make room for the mysterious aspects of art and life, film and theology.

My Metier: Film and Theology

> My function is to make whoever sees my films aware of his need to love and to give his love, and aware that beauty is summoning him.
>
> Russian director, Andrey Tarkovsky[54]

While film critics from the print media were bemoaning their falling influence, the emerging discipline of theology and film witnessed explosive growth.[55] I am proud to follow terrain charted by Andre Bazin and Paul Schrader.[56] Their humane, theological criticism deepened my art and my humanity. The plethora of recent titles flooding the marketplace suggests a genuine movement. Theology and film pioneers like James Wall and John May should be encouraged by these developments. What began as a limited discussion of directors like Ingmar Bergman and Federico Fellini has crossed over into pews across America. The Barna media group found American adults watched an average of forty-five films in 2005. They also discovered virtually no difference in the movie-going habits of religious or nonreligious people.[57] As more churches incorporate film clips into their worship services, the need for theological reflection on moving images has expanded exponentially.

In my first book, *A Matrix of Meanings*, I adopted a reverse hermeneutic originally proposed by Oxford theologian Larry Kreitzer. He described his method: "The aim is to reverse the flow of influence within the hermeneutical process and examine select New Testament passages or themes in light of some of the enduring expressions of our own culture, namely great literary works and their film adaptations."[58] By examining how modern literature or film deals with the Bible, Kreitzer suggests, "We can often discover something fresh and new about the Scriptures themselves."[59] Kreitzer's approach has roots in the Yale school of narrative theology but applies biblical interpretations specifically through film. Rather than approaching film from a fixed theological grid, Kreitzer suggested we view films *on their own terms*, allowing them to inform and interact with our own theological assumptions. Principally a biblical scholar, Kreitzer searches for parallels in the creative process between filmmakers adapting a classic novel and the Gospel writers who expanded and adapted source material to create their literary genre. He is most interested in watching "the hermeneutical process in action."[60] Kreitzer points out the biblical sources of so much classic literature and film, hoping to awaken interest in an understanding of Scripture. He offers an interdisciplinary approach to the problem of interpretation—how we adapt texts. While this is a novel and important approach, I feel Kreitzer stops short of the full implications of his call to reverse the hermeneutical flow.

To me, films are not merely useful for appreciating overlooked biblical texts or comparing interpretive processes. The best movies are revelatory in nature, not just talking about God and ultimate questions but becoming an occasion for the hidden God to communicate through the big screen. Cinema is a *locus theologicus*, a place for divine revelation. Eyes sharpened by cinema may pick up a Bible and come to Scripture with more openness to the Spirit. But for plenty of filmgoers, the general revelation experienced inside a movie theater serves as a divine encounter unto itself. Consequently, my methodology in this book also starts with the texts themselves—the art of postmodern movies. That is where I am most comfortable, most at home. In fact, God continues to meet me via general revelation in the movies. I am not merely reversing a hermeneutical flow but affirming the way many people experience life and encounter the divine.

I am also attempting to push the discipline of theology and film beyond its literary roots.[61] Robert K. Johnston's *Reel Spirituality* and Paul Jewett's series on *Saint Paul at the Movies* served as essential foundations for the discipline. Jewett approached films "on the assumption that they disclose truth in their own right and thus qualify as valid conversation partners in dialogue with Pauline letters."[62] Jewett bridges the divide between biblical texts and contemporary films via "the idea of an interpretive arch, which operates by seeking analogies between ancient and modern texts and situations."[63] While offering profound insights into both Pauline letters and recent film, Jewett admits, "I am not much interested in evaluating films on the basis of aesthetic criteria as in discerning the message these interacting 'stories' disclose for our society."[64] I propose a both/ and approach to theology and film, upholding the best in aesthetic evaluation and a firm emphasis on the message, the story, the meaning of movies.

The two editions of Robert K. Johnston's *Reel Spirituality* display the growth of theology and film. The first edition (2000) offered a comprehensive look at how to respond to movies theologically.[65] Johnston transposed H. Richard Niebuhr's *Christ and Culture*[66] into a cinematic context. He also offered a helpful summation of the critical circle, from auteur and genre theory to cultural and thematic criticism. This book incorporates elements of all four approaches. Johnston expanded and updated *Reel Spirituality* (and the discipline) in his second edition (2006) by focusing on the cinematic elements seemingly outside the script or story. He notes how the meaning of a movie "is also embedded in the very techniques the filmmaker uses to bring the story to the screen."[67] How crucial to affirm the role of editing, the power of music, or the formal characteristics of *mise en scene* to the overall meaning of movies. I build on Kreitzer, Jewett, and Johnston's foundations but seek to counterbalance their biblical-literary backgrounds by coming at theology and film as a *filmmaker* (as well as a scholar). While I respect the power and authority of theology, I approach the discipline as "film and theology," allowing the films to drive the conversation, with theology arising *out of* the art, rather than imposing it *within* the text. This is the full implication of reversing the hermeneutic flow.

Among the key forerunners within film and theology who form the backbone of this discipline, Terry Lindvall and William D. Romanowski's efforts to uncover the hidden history of Protestants and Hollywood empower me. Scholars like Margaret R. Miles, Adele Reinhartz, Chris Deasy, Joseph G. Kickasola, and Bryan P. Stone apply expertise forged in religious studies to the art of film appreciation. Brent Plate, John Lyden, and Gaye Ortiz have challenged me to draw on seemingly irreligious film studies for theological understanding. Andrew Greeley, Richard Blake, Joe Cuneen, Peter Malone, and Rose Pacatte broadened my understanding of Catholic theology and the art of cinema. The ongoing journalistic efforts of articulate reviewers like Jeffrey Overstreet, Frederica Matthewes-Green, and Peter Chattaway and editors like Mark Moring, David Bruce, Rick Bonn, and Michael Kress make www.hollywoodjesus.com, www.beliefnet.com, and www.christianitytoday.com/movies dynamic places to discuss faith and film. These online communities make film and theology an appropriately democratic discipline.

Lived Religion

I ask therefore, that you turn from everything usually reckoned religion, and fix your regard on the inward emotions and dispositions, as all utterances and acts of inspired men direct.

Friedrich Schleiermacher[68]

Scholars in theology and film compare cinematic texts with remarkable ease. We are a discipline dedicated to moving images but steeped in words. Alongside the rigorous dedication to the text, I would like to emphasize *context*. I am empowered by British cultural studies forged by scholars like Richard Hoggart, Raymond Williams, and Stuart Hall, who focused on "how our everyday lives are constructed, how culture forms its subjects."[69] They offered an important corrective to the pioneering work of Theodor Adorno, Walter Benjamin, and the Frankfurt Institute for Social Research. While the Frankfurt school analyzed the messages embedded within pop cultural products and texts, the British cultural studies movement concentrated on audience reception, particularly among England's working class.[70] The British school, formerly housed at the Birmingham Centre for Cultural Studies, moved past the determinism of Frankfurt, giving audiences more credit and power in the interpretive process.

Working from the semiotic principles of linguist Ferdinand de Saussure, Stuart Hall distinguished between the meaning initiated by the creators of pop culture (coding) and the interpretative process of audiences (decoding).[71] Hall applied his coding/decoding theory to the television industry, suggesting at least three possible audience responses to producers' intentions. Audiences often receive the intended message, reinforcing a dominant-hegemonic position. In other cases, viewers adopt a negotiated position. Global concepts created by a producer are localized and internalized by the audience, resulting in give and take.[72] Hall also sees a third, oppositional, code operating between creators and receptors. In this case, the original artists' code is dismantled and replaced by the viewers' alternative code. Hall explains the gap between a filmmaker's intentions and an audience's response—why William Goldman proclaimed, "Nobody knows anything" in Hollywood. But where Hall may attribute the opposition code to power moves and politics, I see a realm of mystery and divine action—the possibility of general revelation. While I share Hall and company's concerns regarding media representation and resulting issues of race, gender, and class, I diverge from their Marxist politics. Jesus offered the ultimate oppositional code, reimagining Hebraic law, decoding the false signals sent by those who turned a blessing into a burden. He sided with the outcast, the downcast, those removed from the corridors of power. Consequently, I find cultural studies' populist, audience-based, reception studies an important resource for the discipline of theology and film.

While appreciating the narrative roots of the discipline, I seek to incorporate elements of ethnographic studies by examining the phenomenon of general revelation within the Internet Movie Database's massive online community. Clive Marsh's *Cinema and Sentiment* is among the first attempts to measure the religious responses of filmgoers.[73] Marsh compares the practice of regular film-going to attendance at worship and the practice of religious rites. Lynn Schofield Clark has contributed equally groundbreaking work in audience studies, particularly among adolescents watching supernatural films and television shows.[74] Like Marsh and Clark, I am interested in how film functions as a form of lived religion. I employ film viewers' responses, gathered at the Internet Movie Database, to broaden and deepen my understanding of film and theology. I incorporate the stories of IMDb users into my own experience of the movies. I also hope to offer a theological base for why people talk about movies in religious ways. As a filmmaker, my projects usually begin with themes, ideas, and hunches. This inductive approach to art coincides with Balthasar's "aesthetics first" methodology. I expect to come to strong theological conclusions, but I will allow film to steer the theological conversation.

Danish filmmaker Carl Theodor Dreyer made rigorous, haunting, and highly spiritual classics like *The Passion of Joan of Arc* (1928). I would like to appropriate a phrase from the title of a documentary chronicling Dreyer's life and art to define my methodology: my metier.[75] Today's academia was forged in a scientific era that valued objectivity over all. A methodology that kept the subject at a safe, objective distance was preferred. Yet the postmodern age of personal narratives caused many to question the myth of objectivity. Today we are much more comfortable discussing things "from my perspective," "from where I sit," or "the way I see it." It is a humbler posture, recognizing our limited perspective. Consequently, I will begin each chapter with personal reflections, rooted in my own biography. I consider my approach more *metier* than *method*. I will start with autobiography because this book is a work of passion, rooted in a sense of calling and vocation, *a métier*.

This emphasis on the practice of faith parallels adjustments in methodology *across disciplines*.[76] Interviews and personal narratives have supplemented (and even supplanted) objective surveys. The questions have shifted from what we did to what we do to *why we do it*. We have come to recognize that removing the personal or the present from scholarly activity can drain the life right out of histories, sociologies, and theologies. I write, study, and dissect in order to animate my sense of calling, not to negate it. So consider this volume an exercise in the emerging field of "lived religion."[77] Historian Robert Orsi defines lived religion as "religious practice and imagination in ongoing, dynamic relation with the realities and structures of everyday life in particular times and places."[78] This survey deals with our particular time and place—the twenty-first century, dominated by an American empire that disseminates movies to a global audience.

I consider the religious insights arising from the practice of film viewing. This is a receptor-oriented study of general revelation. While professional film critics may offer helpful standards to establish a cinematic canon, I choose to elevate the insights of the amateur critics gathered at the IMDb. Just as the early Christian community established the canon of Scripture, so the dedicated film fans of the IMDb sort out the essential from the incidental. Film studies professor Crystal Downing notes how "opinion, or dogma arises out of an interpretive community whose members believe with all their hearts, souls, and minds that their shared opinion is truth."[79] We turn to the chaotic world of the Internet Movie Database as our interpretive community.

God has always used the overlooked and the unlikely to communicate words of correction and inspiration. As the Old Testament prophets shook up a complacent people, perhaps the creative fury of independent filmmakers and their fans are waking up a sleeping church. We now recognize the words of the biblical prophets as revelatory, but they were viewed with substantial suspicion and confusion in their era. As Jesus spoke in parables rooted in his contemporary context, so filmmakers and IMDb users craft revelatory stories from their fragmented, postmodern positions. Jesus took his stories to the marketplace, engaging the common people in conversation. The IMDb users' love of movies

Into the *Darko*

motivates these everyday people to rank their favorites and post thousands of capsule reviews. Such "religious" devotion offers clues about the emerging film canon. It offers hints about what to watch (and study) and suggests where (or through whom) God may be speaking. What movies are moving people most profoundly? What films have challenged (or forged) our beliefs and altered (or affirmed) our practices?

As deep and detailed as disciplines have become, I find myself increasingly interested in blending studies, drawing from diverse sources. This book can be described as an intertextual study; each chapter looks at multiple films in multiple ways. I include elements of auteur theory, genre categories, and textual analysis. Film studies and critical theory inform my work, but I am trained in practical film production. (I am a graduate of the USC School of Cinematic Arts' production program rather than critical studies.) While I may analyze a director's shot selection and framing, I also recognize that the practical considerations of budget, unions, and the setting sun determine many artistic choices. Seeking to recover the democratic impulses inherent in the collaborative art of film, I draw on theologians, sociologists, and film scholars in an eclectic manner. I also incorporate elements of philosophy, history, and literature, but these are auxiliary. They serve a secondary role, more *ministerial* than *magisterial*. I follow the *via media* blazed by the growing field of lived religion. It seeks to bridge the gap between "lofty" academia and "lowly" subjects. Harvard professor of religion David D. Hall explains: "Where lived religion goes its own way is in breaking with the distinction between high and low that seems inevitably to recur in studies of popular religion. That is, these case studies are not built around a structure of opposition."[80] While it would be premature to declare the death of the dialectic, we can at least entertain other ways of accessing popular culture and spiritual experience.

A Freeze Frame

So what does a freeze frame of the IMDb's Top 250 films captured on January 1, 2007 (see appendix A), reveal about our tastes, preferences, and religious needs? The frequent users of the IMDb have affirmed forty-five films from 2000 to 2006 as all-time classics (see appendix B). This book will focus on this emerging canon.

While I would welcome the opportunity for in-depth reflection on each film, space precludes it. I go deeper with select films that represent particularly resonant themes. They may have inspired the most vigorous debate or the most rapturous reviews. Rarely have they been recognized for overtly religious content. But the devotional language attached to the most impactful films will hopefully confirm my suspicions and support my thesis that postmodern movies have become a source of general revelation—a medium from which God speaks. The IMDb identifies what viewers consider the most enduring recent films. My job is to explain *why* those films may have moved filmgoers so deeply.

I do not focus on recent cinema out of faddishness, in an effort to locate the next cultural hot spot or theological trend. C. S. Lewis offers a great warning against such folly through his devilish character, Screwtape. In counseling his nephew on how to distract a client, Screwtape advises him to cultivate a "horror of the Same Old Thing."[81] No community is more obsessed with the trendy, the new, and the faddish than Hollywood. So why do I focus exclusively on twenty-first-century cinema? I want to discern what God is revealing through the Holy Spirit *today*. General revelation happens in the present moment. It may illuminate the past or anticipate the future, but the moments of insight occur *now*. The best of recent cinema suggests we have forgotten significant portions of our roots. We desperately need to uncover ancient and timeless truths; we also have considerable anxiety regarding the future. Yet only when we hear the cry of our hearts and recognize the face of God in our contemporary context will we figure out how to proceed. This is the power of *genuine* revelation.

The list of recent films (appendix B) is not infallible or inerrant. It skews overwhelmingly male in its tastes. How sad to discover that not one woman directed any of the IMDb's Top 250 films. Phallocentrism and "the male gaze" still predominate a generation after the astute observations of critics like bell hooks and Laura Mulvey. It is equally shocking to discover there are no films from black directors on the IMDb list. How can Spike Lee's powerhouse *Do the Right Thing* (1989) be considered anything less than an instant classic? Continuing disparities along racial and economic lines are obviously relevant to continuing gaps in Internet access (around the globe). Asian cinema has four representatives on the list of twenty-first-century films. France (*Amelie*) and Germany (*Der Untergang*) each have a single film on the list, while Spain can boast of *Hable con ella* (*Talk to Her*). The burgeoning Mexican cinema provides *Amores perros* (*Love's a Bitch*) and *El Laberinto del fauno* (*Pan's Labyrinth*), with *Children of Men* still rising in the rankings. Christopher Nolan emerges as the most acclaimed new director with three films (*Memento*, *Batman Begins*, and *The Prestige*) on the list. Clint Eastwood concludes his distinguished career with poignant and timeless films like *Mystic River*, *Million Dollar Baby*, and *Letters from Iwo Jima*. Surprisingly, no horror films (and almost no science fiction) made the aggregate viewers' list.

The list continues to evolve. Since I began this study, *Lost in Translation, Almost Famous, 21 Grams*, and *No Man's Land* slipped off the list. Multiple films, including *Hot Fuzz, The Lives of Others*, and *The Departed*, were added. The IMDb provides a dynamic, moving target. By limiting the voting to unidentified and vaguely defined "regular voters," the webmasters have preserved an air of mystery (and the possibility of editorial adjustments). It is a democratic list with just a hint of elitism.[82] I have taken any ranking within the all-time classics as sufficient reason for close readings and concentrated studies. The canon is far from closed, but it is definitely coalescing.

The canon of Scripture was refined over time. It can take years for the most enduring art to emerge, but the sorting process starts immediately. Those who pay the most attention, who listen most attentively, may provide advance notices. Like spies scoping out the Promised Land, the film fans of the IMDb come back from excursions to the cineplex with enthusiastic reports. Despite all the distractions in the land, there are precious resources ready to be discovered. IMDb rankings allow us to reduce our risk, to avoid potential pitfalls, and to head straight to the gold. They also provide us with a locus classicus for theological dialogue. Here are movies that stretch our minds, stir our hearts, and trouble our souls. I didn't discover the new vein of postmodern movies that demand repeat viewings and postscreening conversations; I'm arriving after the fact, loaded with gear, ready to separate the fool's gold from the genuine article. Plenty of dross may still emerge, but careful and patient attention to detail will hopefully yield revelatory rewards.

A Sneak Preview: Emerging Themes in the New Canon

The IMDb community provides a list of forty-five essential films. Now it is time to make the theological connections. I follow Hans Urs von Balthasar's method of working from aesthetics toward ethics and, eventually, theology proper. The art of the films drives the discussion, with scriptural connections and theological applications arising *out of* the movies. In surveying the top-ranked movies of the new century, several themes emerge. I organize the films into six broad, thematic groups, concentrating on a representative film or filmmaker within each chapter.

Movies in the first part of the book (chaps. 2 and 3) challenge the myth of the ahistorical, autonomous individual. They demonstrate how bankrupt the

Enlightenment notion of a detached observer has become. These mind-bending films deal with the question of identity. They focus on anthropology, wrestling with God's initial question to Adam: "Where are you?" (Gen. 3:9). Why was Adam hiding from his Maker, already living in fear? In hiding our true selves, we can so easily forget who we are and where we've come from. Without a frame of reference, how do we get back to the garden? How do we recover our memory?

Chapter 2 examines the resurgence of film noir. *Memento* explores the dangers of memory loss. What happens when our autonomous selves lose our frame of reference? Self-deception becomes a deadly trap. Christopher Nolan explores humanity's dual (and dueling) nature in *Memento, Batman Begins*, and *The Prestige*. Addictions can lead to a harrowing *Requiem for a Dream*. The fractured mirror held up by *Amores perros, City of God*, and *Oldboy* demonstrate that evil is not just an American problem. Seasoned master directors like Martin Scorsese (*The Departed*) and David Lynch (*Mulholland Dr.*) show emerging filmmakers like Robert Rodriguez (*Sin City*) and Guy Ritchie (*Snatch*) how to wed style with substance. The finest film noirs suggest that crime never pays. Hard-boiled detectives locate a heart of darkness within each of us. As the Old Testament prophet Nathan used storytelling to unmask King David's sin, so film noir can cause us to recognize (and even confess) our sin.

Chapter 3 examines postmodern relationships via romantic comedies. *Amelie* offers a valentine to Paris and the possibilities of love. From our darkness and unchecked individualism arises a need for connection. Love can correct our self-deception. Yet the characters in *Eternal Sunshine of the Spotless Mind* sabotage their relationships, distancing themselves from the people who can rescue them from isolation. An air of wistful regret hangs over *Before Sunset* and *Walk the Line*. Is love worth the risk? Will we dare to care about someone outside ourselves? I find parallels within the songs of innocence and experience contained in the Song of Songs and Ecclesiastes.

The second part of this study (chaps. 4 and 5) echoes God's second question to humanity, "Where is your brother?" (Gen. 4:9). After Cain has murdered his brother Abel, God asks him to take responsibility. Yet Cain dodges the question by asking, "Am I my brother's keeper?" Such evasive actions do not change our innate interconnectivity. We are not alone. We will focus on the complications of community. What do we do when confronted by *the other*? How do we learn to live together despite our differences? How can we approximate the mutuality embodied in the Holy Trinity of Father, Son, and Holy Spirit? After we have dealt with identity, we must consider community, the possibilities contained within our ecclesiology.

Chapter 4 focuses on communities in crisis. In *Little Miss Sunshine*, the ultimate dysfunctional family learns to love each other despite their comedic differences. But in *Mystic River*, the horrible, hidden childhood secrets of three friends spiral into even thornier adult complications. Three of our messiest, real-life cultural hot spots inspired haunting movies: *Crash* deals with racism in Los Angeles, recalling the flames that arose from the Rodney King verdict. *Hotel Rwanda* depicts the Hutus' nightmarish genocide against the Tutsi tribe, finding hope in an individual's heroic choice to get involved despite others' indifference. *United 93* puts viewers inside the plane before it crashed on September 11, 2001. Can community survive such piercing challenges? Film serves as an opportunity for audiences to come together despite significant differences in race, class, gender, and beliefs. These echo Jesus's call to kingdom ethics that the early Christian community struggled to put into practice.

Chapter 5 analyzes everyday ethics in *Million Dollar Baby* and *Hable con ella* (*Talk to Her*). Both Oscar-winning films confront medical ethics and questions of euthanasia. What constitutes a human life? How do we alleviate pain and suffering while still allowing room for God's providence and the possibility of miracles? While *Million Dollar Baby* descends into despair, *Talk to Her* suggests that beauty can overcome our most debilitating circumstances. They are studies in everyday ethics found in ancient biblical proverbs.

The third section of this book confronts history. How do we move forward when so many painful memories still haunt us? Many are tempted to turn back the clock, clinging to nostalgia instead of facing present realities. Historical films and costume dramas appeal to our yearning for an earlier, seemingly simpler time. Yet the hard-won hope found in the biblical Revelation of John suggests we must embrace the future. Rather than trying to get back to the garden, we must anticipate and usher in a new heaven and a new earth. The rise of fantasy films reflects our longing for escape and our hunger for hope. We conclude with a cinematic eschatology. Perhaps fantasy films can help us abandon childishness but recover childlikeness.

Chapter 6 deals with nostalgia. War films, historical epics, and costume dramas all appeal to a longing for the past. *Gladiator* and *Cinderella Man* celebrated the virtues of sacrifice and honor portrayed by Russell Crowe. *The Pianist* and *Der Untergang* put a human face on the Holocaust, challenging us to "never forget." *Finding Neverland* appeals to our nostalgic impulse but ultimately affirms the need for imagination to transform our most painful memories. As the biblical prophets called Israel to abandon their fixation on a faded glory, so the finest filmmakers challenge viewers to push past nostalgia in order to forge a future.

Chapter 7 offers flights of fantasy. The harsh realities accompanying the war on terror have sparked an unprecedented wave of fantasy films. Pixar's digitally animated *Finding Nemo*, *The Incredibles*, and *Monsters, Inc.* transport audiences back to the wonders of childhood, preserving our sense of security for a few, satisfying minutes. *Shrek* and *Wallace & Gromit in The Curse of the Were-Rabbit* offer affectionate jibes at preestablished conventions of fairy tales and horror, demonstrating that old stories can be reimagined for postmodern audiences. *Pirates of the Caribbean: The Curse of the Black Pearl*, *Hero*, and *Crouching Tiger, Hidden Dragon* allow us to fight wars vicariously in faraway times and magical places. Digital effects have distanced the real wars raging in Iraq and Afghanistan, taking us to a more symbolic or eschatological plane. *V for Vendetta* mines the future to comment on the present. *Big Fish* affirms the importance of storytelling as a coping device. Hayao Miyazaki's *Spirited Away* challenges viewers to remember their roots, to reconnect with earth, to rediscover divinity within nature. Fantasy films take us back to the garden, offering a vision that corresponds to Genesis and Revelation, the beginning and end of the Christian story.

Identity, community, and history offer a strong starting place for theological reflection. I conclude with a study of the IMDb's highest-ranking recent films, *The Lord of the Rings* trilogy. Director Peter Jackson's towering achievement inspired a new generation of filmgoers and filmmakers. Rooted in J. R. R. Tolkien's timeless Christian vision, *The Lord of the Rings* trilogy combines the best of God's special and general revelation. It reimagines God's *special* shaping story in creative ways that captivate the broadest, *general* audience possible. *The Lord of the Rings* movies embody the revelatory possibilities of film. This imaginative story challenges us to remember our shaping story, to reconnect with our communities, and to forge a future for our fellowships. To the postmodern problem of memory, the *Rings* trilogy offers a strong corrective. The Jewish and Christian traditions are remembering religions, rooted in ritual, the ultimate mnemonic devices.

Donnie Darko: A Cinematic Paradox

I conclude this chapter with an example of my methodology in action. Of the forty-five films on the IMDb list, no picture started smaller or has grown in reputation more than *Donnie Darko* (IMDb #103).[83] Despite a cast that included Drew Barrymore, Patrick Swayze, and Jake Gyllenhaal, when it opened in October 2001, *Donnie Darko* played in just fifty-eight theaters and earned only $517,375.[84] Studios did not know how to market a genre blending teen

Jake Gyllenhaal and Drew Barrymore portray a disturbed student and a concerned teacher in the cult film *Donnie Darko*. © 2001 by Newmarket Films.

sex comedy, psychological drama, and superhero story. They failed to sell it as a horror movie. Arriving one month after the tragic events of September 11, 2001, *Donnie Darko* seemed a little too prescient—it opens with a devastating plane crash.

Yet three years later, *Donnie Darko* received the rarest of honors, being re-released theatrically in an extended director's cut.[85] How did an overlooked box-office bomb become *the cult film* for the emerging generation? Twenty-six-year-old director Richard Kelly's debut feature was messy, ambitious, and complex. It had to be discovered on DVD, where repeat viewing allowed movie lovers to unravel its complicated plot. A majority of its most rabid fans still cannot articulate why they love *Donnie Darko*. It serves as a talisman, offering revelations that promise to unlock the nature of the universe. The mystery both within and around the film will provide an appropriately enigmatic illustration of my methodology.

Donnie Darko portrays teenagers' schizophrenic bind with compassion and originality. It illustrates how crazy we can get when our head is isolated from our experience. But it also affirms the importance of listening to God even when those in authority may not understand our actions. Only alternative communities

---

may offer the freedom and support we need to follow God's call. *Donnie Darko* presents a dark, twisted, but redemptive version of the cost of discipleship.

Donnie Darko hides in his room because nobody understands him. He sees a therapist who has medicated his sleepwalking and mood swings. His mother worries about the twisted drawings on his bedroom walls. Donnie's teachers would like to get involved, but they are limited by their school district in how much they can say. Despite these adults' best efforts to connect, Donnie remains basically alone in his struggles. And they are considerable. For one, an airplane engine has crashed into his bedroom. For another, the world may end unless he takes action. And of course, there are always the class bullies.

We all struggle with Donnie's tension of how much to reveal versus how much to conceal. Everyday we consider how much of ourselves to disclose in the classroom, at work, on awkward first dates. We have aspects of our lives that we bracket, hold back, and protect. How much we reveal or conceal is often rooted in issues of trust. Are we willing to be exposed? Do we have faith that our trust will be honored, our secrets and selves appreciated rather than exploited? We may choose to reveal ourselves in our words, our actions, our art, our appearance. It is almost always a risk, but removing the veils on our past, our present, and our future dreams is an essential part of communication and community. Self-revelation is a gamble most of us are willing to take.

God shares our struggle: how much to say, how much to reveal, how much to conceal. No one wants to cast their pearls before swine. Director Richard Kelly keeps his story purposefully obscure. It is understandable why Kelly and God would want to preserve an air of mystery. Jesus describes the elusive ways of salvation: "The wind blows where it chooses, and you hear the sound of it, but you do not know where it comes from or where it goes. So it is with everyone who is born of the Spirit" (John 3:8 NRSV). Surely the Spirit behind our hints and rumors of God remains equally mysterious and intriguing. General revelation refers specifically to God's self-disclosure: when we catch glimpses of the divine in a shooting star, a reflection on a lake, the warm smile of a friend or companion, a work of art. Most people would probably consider finding God a *special* occasion. We hold such experiences close to our heart, drawing on them for sustenance and hope. Donnie Darko ponders his divine encounter privately, uncertain whom to trust.

Donnie Darko defies genre categories. It blends a coming-of-age story with time travel. Donnie has a comic book name and psycho-killer feelings. The many layers in the movie parallel Donnie's multilayered life. All the teens (and adults) in the film seem to harbor deep secrets. Chap Clark, an expert on adolescents describes the layers within which teens hide.[86] They are one person in class, another with parents, a third at church, and their most genuine selves with friends. They must remember who they are within each group or subculture. Donnie's schizophrenic tendencies are nearly normal for the average adolescent.

Donnie desperately wants to figure out life. He must solve a mystery, unlock clues, and rescue others. His companions on the journey are his new girlfriend, Gretchen, a crazy old lady (Grandma Death), and a giant talking rabbit named Frank. Donnie must sort out the voices in his head. What makes Donnie so dark? He seems highly teachable, but the educational system has been reduced to simplistic cheerleaders and Christian motivational speakers. Donnie and his friends feel they've been offered false choices, a dialectic between *fear* and *love*. His psychotherapist hasn't helped either. She wants him to stop listening to the voices and acknowledge there is no God, only an autonomous "Donnie."

Donnie fights back by dumping his meds and cranking up the noise in his head. He enters a strange zone, almost an alternative reality. At a Halloween double feature of *The Last Temptation of Christ* and *Evil Dead*, Donnie gets a message. He gathers an axe, floods Middlesex High School, and wages war on the town role model, Jim Cunningham. Donnie seems dangerously deluded—until the movie's secrets are revealed. The motivational speaker, Jim Cunningham, is exposed as a pedophile. Donnie's actions become heroic, reversing the events that threatened to hurt his family and kill his girlfriend. The creepy pronouncements of Frank, the giant rabbit, turn out to be a prophetic message from God. Donnie willingly sacrifices his life to save others. He dies, laughing for the first time, at the wonder of the divine plan unfolding. It is one of the most robust, poetic, and faith-affirming films of all time—a dark but divine comedy.

So why did *Donnie Darko* make such a small initial splash? The enormity of director Richard Kelly's vision was too much to take in. *Donnie Darko* demands thoughtful reflection and multiple screenings. Even then, viewers are still likely to exit confused, ambivalent about what they witnessed. What makes its revelations so veiled? *Donnie Darko* embraces paradox. It echoes the emotions of Tears for Fears's enigmatic song "Mad World." It describes a depressed society of "worn out places, worn out faces" who are "going nowhere, no expression, no tomorrow." Yet the chorus declares,

> The dreams in which I'm dying
> Are the best I've ever had.[87]

This is the wistful and weird resignation that crosses Donnie's face as he embraces death so that others might live. It may be a "mad world," but it echoes the song by enlarging your world. As Donnie accepts his sacrificial role, the other characters wake from their dreams, full of wonder and regret. Donnie has collapsed time, putting them into a position of eschatological appreciation. They catch a glimpse of all he has accomplished on their behalf and move forward with conviction and remorse.

Darko's Cult Status

Cultural influence can be measured in many ways. Box office is not always the best determinant. After its initial failure, *Donnie Darko* played for twenty-eight months as a midnight movie at the Pioneer Theater in Manhattan's East Village.[88] Two years after *Donnie Darko*'s release, the poignant acoustic version of "Mad World" from the sound track topped England's famed Christmas music charts. Domestic DVD sales eventually topped $10 million. *Donnie Darko* became the first cult film of a new generation.[89] What fueled the enthusiastic word of mouth that elevated Donnie from the dustbin of history to a hallowed classic?

Nuanced art may not always announce its intentions. On the director's commentary for the original *Donnie Darko*, Richard Kelly admits to obscuring his point. Buried within the extended scenes for the film, Kelly talks about *Donnie Darko* as a story of "divine intervention." But rather than reveal the religious implications of Frank the Bunny as a messenger from God, Kelly shortened the bunny's dark encounter with Donnie on a golf course. Kelly recounts, "Ultimately for me, it's more powerful to leave the mystery intact, to not spoil it by over-explaining everything, which tends to happen a lot."[90] Unfortunately, Kelly failed to follow his own advice, releasing a longer, less-nuanced "Director's Cut" of *Donnie Darko* in 2004. It drained too much of the mystique from the movie. Kelly admits, "Ultimately, I can't explain it. What's the voice. It's open to interpretation. That's the mystery of the entire film, really."[91] As director, Kelly seems to step into the role of Frank the Bunny, serving as an unlikely conduit for the divine.

Donnie Darko is nostalgic about the 1980s; its sound track cribs from the filmmaker's childhood. But it ultimately transcends time and space, tapping into cosmic history. Richard Kelly turned chaos theory into a postmodern version of *It's a Wonderful Life*. *Donnie Darko* deals with variables of space, time, and motion tracked by Edward Lorenz in his famous "Butterfly Effect."[92] The paradoxical universe of *Donnie Darko* is random and deterministic at the same time, but Richard Kelly and his postmodern audience have no problem holding such metaphysical paradoxes in tension. *Donnie Darko* is a sci-fi, fantasy film unfurled in what appears to be a normal, suburban setting. Kelly resacralized the most mundane of settings—high school.

Donnie Darko is also about the potential for self-deception. Like Leonard in *Memento*, Donnie has notes and numbers scribbled on his arm. He searches for clues, even though others may consider him crazy or deluded. Donnie would like to find a "normal" frame of reference, but the adults in his world lack imagination, so he must turn to the crazed and outcast for advice. It is a cinema of outsiders.

The teens in *Donnie Darko* are on a desperate search for connection. They recognize that they've been sold a simplistic view of life, but they will listen to people who give them genuine answers. Unfortunately, they are left to form their own alternative community, united around shared frustrations. In *Revolution!* George Barna's polls indicate that in the next twenty years alternative churches, gathered in small groups around mutual affinities, will replace large numbers of traditional churches.[93] In smaller circles, the "Donnies" and "Gretchens" of the world will find a safe place. Young people whom the authorities dismiss as dark or delusional ultimately will be vindicated. While skulking around in a hooded sweatshirt, Donnie Darko becomes a mythic superhero—the sacred emerges within the profane.

The rapturous reviews on the IMDb include self-proclaimed critics like evilmatt-3's description of *Donnie Darko* as "beautiful, terrifying." He praises the film because "it manages to inspire hope, love, dread, laughter, and tears at different points throughout the movie without making you feel the least bit like there is a contradiction between those states."[94] Another IMDb user, identified as Lwjoslin, gets at the paradoxes: "A lot goes on here. There's a meditation on the possible overlap between madness and the ability to perceive the divine. There's a demonstration of why, in the Bible, angelic messengers (if that's what 'Frank' can be taken to be) are often so terrifying that they have to start by saying 'Fear not.'"[95] As in the best fairy tales, viewers must learn to discern. What appears demonic may actually be godly (Frank the Bunny), and what appears godly may be masking horrible truths, like Jim Cunningham (or shamed evangelical minister Ted Haggard).

Donnie Darko confronts all the neuroses we will trace throughout this study. He is victimized by the myth of the autonomous individual; he must overcome mental problems; he needs to find his true identity; he learns to feel; he decides to enter into a risky romantic relationship; he acts on behalf of the community. Like the finest of fantasy films, *Donnie Darko*'s final actions occur in an alternative world. Donnie considers the cost of obedience and willingly adopts Jesus's sacrificial ways. Against an apocalyptic background, Donnie changes history, becoming a timeless, mythical cinematic hero. It is not an easy journey; *Donnie Darko* requires careful attention and extended reflection. Donnie wades into dark grottos full of scary surprises. But at the end of the arduous test, he laughs with an understanding of divine drama. Shall we follow him into the dark?

This book is a genuine experiment. I began with a bounded set of films. I had no preconceptions about what they might communicate. I only asked God to guide and surprise me. Consider this journey into the dark as a form of theological adventure. We will travel light, with limited preconceptions. We will walk by faith rather than fear. If God's word is a lamp unto our feet, then perhaps it will be illuminated even further by a journey into the dark. The light of Scripture may seem dim in comfortable, well-lit settings. But in the dark, a single spark can illuminate our every step.

Part I

Identity

And they heard the sound of the Lord God
walking in the garden in the cool of the evening
and the man and his wife hid themselves
from the presence of the Lord God
among the trees of the garden.

But the Lord God called to the man
and said to him,
"Where are you?"

And he said, "I heard the sound of you in the garden,
and I was afraid, because I was naked,
and I hid myself."

Genesis 3:8–10 ESV

2

Memento

Duped in Film Noir

Cidade de Deus (2002, IMDb #18)

Memento (2000, IMDb #26)

Requiem for a Dream (2000, IMDb #58)

Sin City (2005, IMDb #67)

The Departed (2006, IMDb #80)

Batman Begins (2005, IMDb #88)

Kill Bill: Vol. 1 (2003, IMDb #94)

Kill Bill: Vol. 2 (2004, IMDb #120)

Oldboy (2003, IMDb #122)

Amores perros (2000, IMDb #141)

Snatch (2000, IMDb #195)

The Prestige (2006, IMDb #216)

Mulholland Dr. (2001, IMDb #242)

What I like about experience is that it is such an honest thing. . . . You may have deceived yourself, but experience is not trying to deceive you. The universe rings true whenever you test it.

C. S. Lewis, *Surprised by Joy*[1]

I left the movie theater angry. How could I have been cheering for a murderer? I couldn't believe the director of *Memento* had played such a cheap trick on me. I wasn't bothered by the mind games within the movie. I loved trying to piece together the plot from the shards of Leonard Shelby's fractured memory. The mnemonic devices he employed to keep his life in order (Polaroids, tattoos) played like more extreme examples of the "notes to self" we all rely on to jog our memory, to remember to buy milk, or to return a phone call. I was genuinely involved in Leonard's search for his wife's murderer. The lowlifes like Teddy and Natalie who exploited his short-term memory loss were suitably slimy. The succession of bars, diners, and abandoned factories gave the picture a seedy charm. I joined Lenny in scanning hotel rooms for clues. But when the ending suggested that Leonard's quest for his wife's killer was a mere fiction, a way to justify his existence, I felt duped, cheated, abused. *Memento* seemed to undercut any efforts to assemble facts or organize our lives in a logical fashion. It eliminated all objectivity from our being, slipping into the worst kind of postmodern relativism. Our efforts to find meaning in life are doomed! Had I been victimized just like Leonard? *Memento* had betrayed my trust, mocked the audience, and played a game of "gotcha."

Standing on the sidewalk outside the theater, I huffed and I puffed until my fellow filmgoer blew my house of cards down. Robert, my best friend from film school, challenged me to look closer. Maybe what I mistook as the bleakest of nihilism was actually the smartest of commentaries on the human condition. Perhaps the director tricked me in an effort to wake me up. My trust in Leonard proved to be misplaced. Where else had I misplaced my confidence? Hmmm. Don't I filter out selective memories in creating my own personal history? Don't I choose which facts to inscribe on my heart and mind (if not my body)? Robert asked all the right questions, until I finally got it. Pointing out how limited our perspective can be does not eliminate objective truth. The film illustrated the arrogance of alleged objectivity. The road to hell has often been paved with good intentions. *Memento* dramatized the postmodern shift in epistemology, from surety to suspicion. It suggested we need a frame of reference bigger than our personal blinders. That sounded suspiciously close to an existential leap of faith, an acknowledgment that I need more than my autonomous self can offer. This is the unlikely means of general revelation in action. How odd or perhaps appropriate that it took my agnostic friend Robert to reveal the most basic truth: *Memento* reveals our endless capacity for self-deception. It is the ultimate cinematic portrait of original sin.

Theologian Cornelius Plantinga Jr. has pointed out how rarely the word *sin* appears in the public arena.[2] Corrupt politicians blame their indiscretions on alcoholism or childhood abuse. Corporate profits have been falsified to boost stock prices under the justification that "everybody's doing it." Few acknowledge their own culpability or dare to confess their own sin. Even ministers have grown sheepish about using the word *sin* in sermons, preferring to talk about "psychological self-abuse." Yet against this backdrop of hemming and hawing, filmmakers have been pouring out stories of widespread corruption, deceit, and self-deception. At a time when right and wrong seem to have blurred, film noir has emerged as an important corrective. When the wicked prosper, when the innocent suffer, when evil triumphs over good, life is "not the way it's supposed to be." Film noir echoes the cries of biblical prophets who rail against injustice and lament the human condition. Yet when film noir misses the mark, it stylizes violence and glorifies evil. This chapter considers the problems of memory and forgetting, the shifting ground of epistemology, and the important frames of reference being rediscovered in our postmodern context. To combat our blindness, we need revelatory moments. To sharpen our sight, we need a community that corrects our misperceptions. But to receive both gifts, we need that rarest of cinematic virtues, humility.

The most accomplished expressions of film noir simultaneously stretch our minds and insist on the limits of our knowledge. Enduring movies must do more than tease our brains or barrage our senses. The finest of contemporary film noir doesn't revel in evil but haunts our soul by acknowledging our failings and exposing our calculated cover-ups. Film noir demonstrates how far we fell from the *imago Dei* and how desperately we need to be rescued. But while the darkest films illustrate our fallen nature expressed in Romans 1, the most insightful filmmakers resist the temptation to place viewers above a character's worst behavior. At its best, film noir combines the truths of Romans 2 and 3: that because all have sinned and fallen, we are in no position to judge others. General revelation in film noir demonstrates our need but isn't satisfied by appealing to our basest instincts or sense of superiority. Audiences are convicted of their sinful complicity right alongside the corrupt characters.

Neo-Noir

Memento is a reimagination of film noir. French movie critics coined the term *dark film* or *black film* to describe the hard-boiled detective stories shot in high contrasting, black-and-white shadows. The genre exploded in the wake of World War II. Film noir began as low-budget filmmaking—"B movies" shot quickly, with minimal lighting. Rooted in the pulp fiction of James M. Cain, Raymond Chandler, and Dashiell Hammett, film noir offered audiences a trip to a netherworld of nefarious activities and questionable characters. The stories take place in cities, amid dark alleys laden with danger. Audiences follow the trail of a private eye investigating the murder of a client or a partner. Our haunted hero meets a femme fatale—a deadly woman who lures him into a scheme to commit extortion or murder. The plot is so convoluted that the mystery becomes almost incidental to the overall theme of paranoia, suspicion, and distrust.

Film scholars have debated whether film noir constitutes a distinct genre or primarily a style. Paul Schrader's influential essay, "Notes on Film Noir," identifies it by *tone*.[3] He traces the roots of film noir to German expressionistic filmmaking of the 1920s and 1930s. The harsh, consciously exaggerated lighting of movies such as *The Cabinet of Dr. Caligari* (1920, IMDb #165) eventually merged with a commitment to realism forged in war. The horrors uncovered at Dachau and Hiroshima revealed dark sides of humanity that mocked human progress. Film noir protagonists were often war veterans, dogged by psychological traumas. They are confronted by changes in economics, gender roles, and an increasingly urbanized life.[4] These private eyes have a world-weariness embodied in the gruff exterior of stars like Humphrey Bogart. In film noir the men alternately worship and fear women, making the genre ripe for psychosexual analysis.[5] Yet Paul Schrader cautions those who wish to psychoanalyze noir that it has always been characterized more by cinematography than social psychology. Groundbreaking early classics in the genre include *The Maltese Falcon* (1941, IMDb #57), *Double Indemnity* (1944, IMDb #62), and *The Big Sleep* (1946, IMDb #100).

Philosophically, film noir reflects existential angst—not even the bad guys win. It presents a hopeless universe, devoid of feelings other than lust, revenge, and will to power. The "kill or be killed" attitude of noir characters suggests a malevolent world without God or a moral core. Film noir reports from an urban jungle where survival of the wiliest often prevails.[6] This makes sense in a post–World War II context. Painful realities set in after the victory parties. Where was God during the Holocaust? Didn't the Divine abandon the Japanese amid nuclear bombs? Or did we abandon God when we dropped the bomb? The theological questions were potent given the shocking realities. While a popular phrase suggested there were "no atheists in foxholes," many who survived German concentration camps found their faith had vanished in the face of so much suffering.[7] "If there is a God, how could He let this happen?" Film noir arose from the potentially godless universe created by human carnage.

What accounts for the recent resurgence in film noir? Have notions of human progress been replaced by despair? The specter of September 11, 2001, looms heavy over our hearts. In the West, the problem of evil was awakened by the actions of Osama bin Laden and Al-Qaeda. But the stylistic homage to and updates of film noir began prior to 9/11. *The Usual Suspects* (1995, IMDb #17), *L.A. Confidential* (1997, IMDb #54), and *The Big Lebowski* (1998, IMDb #179) all begin with film noir conventions. They each feature delicious plot twists and double crosses that cause the audience to rewind the movie in their mind. But their fractured narratives take audiences to unexpected places, delicious "aha" moments. All three films play on the limits of our knowledge, how foolish we are when we think we have figured out life. Perhaps film noir has returned as the outgrowth of our postmodern context in which we are skeptical of absolute claims and have lost faith in our leaders and institutions. The resurgence of film noir also seems to coincide with a desensitized era. With so much violence occurring in the real world, film noir may simply be reflecting the cruelty that characterizes the postmodern condition. Once we have stooped to torture in the name of freedom, the moral high ground has eroded. There are many faces of terrorism and victims of barbarism in a time of war. The challenge is to portray the atrocious possibilities of human behavior without glorifying it. Fatalism and sensationalism lurk in the shadows of film noir. Can film noir present the human predicament as a painful problem rather than a license to thrill? Does the stain of sin cause us to grieve or merely reinforce a cycle of mindless violence? Recent film noir is a decidedly mixed bag of profundity and provocation. We need an interpretive community to sort out the difference.

The Apostle's Disciples

In *Pulp Fiction* (1994, IMDb #8), Quentin Tarantino married postmodern surfaces and brutal violence with the transcendent possibilities of film. Tarantino's disciples were inspired by the psychic power of cinema to simultaneously outrage and inspire. While some were attracted to Tarantino's "higher calling," others unleashed even flashier (and emptier) forms of film noir. These two resulting schools illustrate film noir's best and worst tendencies, both the rehumanization and dehumanization that accompanies potent portrayals of human sin.

Darren Aronofsky took Tarantino's aggressive filmmaking techniques to new levels of intensity. *Requiem for a Dream* (2000, IMDb #58) is an alarming anti-drug tract. Through bravura camera work and razor-sharp editing, Aronofsky pummels the audience with junkies' highs and lows. Based on Hubert Selby's harrowing novel, *Requiem* tracks the descent of four characters from casual users to hard-core addicts. Brooklyn's Coney Island offers a suitably decaying backdrop that parallels their unraveling lives. Aronofsky shows the visceral thrill provided by heroin and cocaine, but he also chronicles the horrendous chills that accompany withdrawal. *Requiem* also portrays the equally devastating effects of something as "innocent" as television or diet pills. The performances by Ellen Burstyn, Jared Leto, Jennifer Connolly, and Marlon Wayans are all heartbreakingly real. *Requiem* is a tragedy that evokes profound empathy. IMDb reviewer Eric226 said, "As I sat watching the credits roll, I began crying, but I'm still not sure why. Partly in reaction to the devastatingly tragic ending, partly the beauty (yes) of the film, partly my gratitude for good things in my life."[8] The final requiem blends horrid images and frightening music (from Clint Mansell and the Kronos Quartet) into one of the most memorable nightmares I've ever experienced. In a sad irony, Aronofsky's piercing meditation on the danger of drugs was deemed unsuitable for audiences under seventeen. Harry Knowles, creator of "Ain't It Cool News," ranted against the MPAA: "This film should be REQUIRED VIEWING by every friggin High School kid in the country. It should be unleashed upon them. Will it disturb them? Will it shake their fragile little minds? Will it possibly make a lifestyle change for them? Oh God YES. YES YES YES."[9] Evidently, Aronofsky's cautionary tale about the wages of sin (or certainly addictions) was too realistic. Are we afraid to confront our frailty or acknowledge our weakness?

Tarantino's influence also extended south of the United States border. Virtuoso director Alejandro Gonzalez Inarritu teamed up with screenwriter Guillermo Arriaga to suggest *Amores perros* (*Love's a Bitch*, 2000). They connect disparate characters in a gritty, back-alley Mexico City around a car crash. With clear debts to *Pulp Fiction*, *Amores perros* (IMDb #141) mixes high culture and low culture, rich and poor, with a strong emphasis on the hit man as the hand of God. It uses dogfighting as a metaphor for humanity's brutal foaming at the mouth. But Inarritu surpasses Tarantino with his larger social concerns. He shows a real rage against the system that produces assassins like El Chavo. The propulsive force of the film is driven by a sense of injustice, an understanding that both people and the system are broken. *Amores perros* shows that we are all connected despite the differences of time, place, and finances.

Cidade de Deus (*City of God*, 2002) plunges viewers into Rio de Janeiro's toughest favela. The title of the film (and the neighborhood) is loaded with irony, as circumstances pressure kids toward a life of crime (and anything but God).

It tells the history of a neighborhood through the divergent paths of three boys: Rocket, Bene, and L'il Dice. Viewers come to understand the lure of gangs as L'il Dice grows into a ruthless drug lord, L'il Ze. It plays with time, jumping from a bloody street fight in the eighties to more innocent beginnings in the sixties. We see a tender trio turn into a brutal gang of thugs. *City of God* (IMDb #18) has all the visual panache of a Tarantino film, but it adds a layer of social commentary often lacking in American films. The limited options available to Brazilian teens both shocks and repulses.

City of God is about a community in crisis with almost no way to change its circumstances. Only Rocket rises above the downward spiral through the gift of photography. Learning to see, to document the drama unfolding before him, Rocket serves as our narrator—the voice of reason amid a chaotic world. *City of God* offers art as a way out of the favela. Even runts born into the roughest scenarios can choose to rise above their circumstances. Character is not determined by even the toughest surroundings. Individual choice remains in even the poorest of communities.

Style over Substance

The downside of the Tarantino legacy comes from the triumph of film noir style over thematic substance. In England, Guy Ritchie reveled in the lowlifes of *Lock, Stock and Two Smoking Barrels* (1998, IMDb #211) and *Snatch* (2000, IMDb #195). Both films feature London gangs engaged in complex plans that played with time and expectations. They are almost escapist in their depictions of English lads as lovable scamps, providing a diverting romp, but not much more. Korean director Chan-wook Park pushes the boundaries of violence set by Tarantino in his vengeance trilogy, *Sympathy for Mr. Vengeance* (2002), *Oldboy* (2003, IMDb #122), and *Sympathy for Lady Vengeance* (2005). *Oldboy* won the Grand Prix at the 2004 Cannes Film Festival (where Tarantino served as the head of the jury). The film's fans rightly praise the cinematography, sound, and editing. They compare it to Greek tragedies in its blood-drenched, emotional extremes. Like Tarantino, Park tortures his characters and the audience. The plot of *Oldboy* borrows from *The Count of Monte Cristo* but substitutes a guilty protagonist, Dae-su, for a noble innocent.[10] Fueled by revenge, *Oldboy* portrays maiming, incest, self-mutilation, and even the eating of a live octopus as entertainment. While remarkably stylish and involving, IMDb user schnofel from Austria found *Oldboy* an "ultimately hollow and repugnant exercise in genre filmmaking."[11]

Dj bassett from Philadelphia says, "I guess you could argue that the movie shows revenge is futile from the bad guy's point of view. Then why are we watching Dae-su at all? Maybe the point is that everyone feels themselves righteous until they realize the true dimensions of their 'sin.' But I don't see a lot of people facing up to facts in the movie: I see a lot of denial, in fact."[12] After enduring the torturous scenes of *Oldboy*, Hakapes from Budapest, Hungary, declared, "I am hungry to see something beautiful, harmonious, with true feelings and a clear message."[13] Film noir that used to sneak up on audiences with plot twists and startling repartee was reduced to camera tricks, body counts, and bloody squibs. *Oldboy* is one long, bad joke—definitely not worth the ride.

Tarantino's equally bloody response to his disciples' work was the two-volume *Kill Bill* (2003, IMDb #94; 2004, IMDb #120). Tarantino poured everything he ever loved about movies into *Kill Bill*. It plays like a PhD thesis on celluloid, borrowing from samurai stories and cowboy myths to create an *eastern western*. The press kit contained *sixty-nine pages* of movie minutia, including arcane footnotes like, "The glass nightclub floor at the House of Blue Leaves comes from Seijun Suzuki's hallucinatory 1965 gangster-pic *Tokyo Drifter*."[14] Tarantino acknowledges his mania: "If you're a movie lover and have good knowledge, you can't help but smile at this thing, because it's just so movie-mad obsessed. It makes its own universe out of all these different genres."[15] His devoted fans consider the *Kill Bill* movies cinematic heaven. A Canadian IMDb user described it in religious terms:

> The film is so much more than a movie to me. As I was watching, I felt like I was a child dreaming and listening to my wise Grandfather tell me a story about a mythic woman on the quest for her own brand of justice. The images I saw on screen were the vivid dreams I thought I could only visualize in my mind. As I watched it I sweated, cried, laughed, and felt this movie inside and out. I didn't watch this movie with my eyes; I watched it with my soul. Movies like this make me want to pursue an occupation in the art form. God bless the anarchic mind of Quentin.[16]

Such high praise! Yet, one IMDb rater suggested, "No thinking human being who isn't lurid and disturbed at heart could find this repellent puddle of blood fetishism and wanton dismemberment a masterpiece of anything but gratuitous and unsettling rubbish."[17] Is it a priceless artifact or a painful endurance test?

As promised in its opening epigraph, "Revenge is a dish best served cold," the *Kill Bill* movies left me cold, wanting more. *Kill Bill* offers a cautionary condemnation of patriarchy.[18] Bill's efforts to control Beatrix's life (from her job

Identity

training to her pregnancy) ultimately blow up in his face. As Bill ripped a child from her womb, so Beatrix separates his barely beating heart from his chest. Bill's heartlessness is repaid with her five-point-palm-exploding-heart technique. As Bill falls and Beatrix and her daughter try to put the painful past behind them, we're left to consider the killer lurking within us. Is Beatrix a devoted mother or a natural-born killer? Can an assassin retire, or do our sins exact a price? Can we overcome our bloodlust? Not through movies that make murder look incredibly cool, like the ultimate high.

While I have witnessed the power of maternal love in my own household, I did not consider graphic scenes of torture, dismemberment, and abuse worth enduring for such a simple payoff. Where is the transcendence, the hard-earned hope? Beatrix and her daughter B. B. may be reunited, but they are anything but whole (the loss of Bill notwithstanding). Through obvious visual allusions, Tarantino connects Kill Bill to John Ford's cautionary revenge story, The Searchers. Neither John Wayne's Ethan Edwards nor Beatrix Kiddo can be tamed—there is no home on the range in their future. But unfortunately, Tarantino makes her revenge "cool" rather than chilling. He demonstrates the danger of cinematic portraits of sin. When killing is rendered with such high style, it becomes a thrill rather than a warning. Perhaps Quentin's movie love overwhelmed his openness to the Spirit. Access to bigger budgets may have expanded his technique, but it muddied his message. Kill Bill appeals to our base nature without lamenting it—edging closer to cinematic irresponsibility rather than artistry. The transcendent promise of Pulp Fiction has devolved into genre exercises like Deathtrap. How sad to see such vigor sink into one long, talkative, and pointless ride. Tarantino still has a loyal fan base, but the man has misplaced his spiritual mojo.

The apotheosis of film noir is Robert Rodriguez's collaboration with graphic novelist Frank Miller in Sin City (2005). (Tarantino served as a "special guest director" of one segment.) It returns the genre to its pulpy roots, reveling in its comic book look. Recapitulating Pulp Fiction's multiple story lines, Sin City's overlapping tales introduce audiences to a series of antiheroes, each put into compromising situations. The graphic violence and blatant sexuality of Sin City push film noir well past its 1940s roots. No one would expect any less from such a title. It satisfied Miller's hard-core fans, delivering the extreme gore and titillation they expected.

As an exercise in style, Sin City proved a remarkable trendsetter. The graphics that bookend each episode are the closest cinema has come to a seamless merger with comics. Rodriguez and Miller are to be commended for their groundbreaking use of digital effects. It contrasts the black-and-white style of film noir with shocking bursts of color. As an IMDb user raved, "A case could be made that this was the movie CGI was invented for."[19] Yet, as a dramatic whole, *Sin City* left this viewer wanting much more (despite a rapturous reception from IMDb's fanboys).

The misogyny and cruelty at the core of *Sin City* offers telling commentaries on our American empire. The men in *Sin City* deify their women (Marv calls Goldie a "goddess"), yet we are subject to repeated scenes of their kidnapping and torture. The "heroic" women in the story take up arms to repay their assailants. Yet no one feels any sense of remorse, regret, or even joy. It is violence as an end in itself with no overriding sense of justice guiding the characters. Our justification for war in Iraq was also undercut by reports of torture, abuse, and exploitation. The torture in *Sin City* or Abu Ghraib serves as "entertainment" to relieve our boredom. Like the antiheroes of *Sin City*, America seems to have forgotten what initiated our mission in Iraq. We have destroyed a nation in order to save it.

Despite its potential relevancy, *Sin City* makes me question whether the genre has lost its humanity. Film noir at its best reveals our cold, cold hearts. It understands the murderous impulses that lurk beneath our civil veneer. General revelation can cut through the depths of our depravity: *Raging Bull* showed me my blindness, but it never reduced people to mere animals. Our humanity may be flawed and fallen, but it is never beyond redemption. We may be blind, but seeing remains an arresting possibility. *Sin City* revels in our depravity rather than lamenting it. Can film noir raise awareness *and* regret in regard to sin? Leave it to a few wily veterans to offer a much-needed corrective.

Style and Substance

Nobody does creepy surfaces and nightmarish visions better than David Lynch. From *Blue Velvet* (1986) to *Lost Highway* (1997), Lynch has juxtaposed idealized visions of small-town America with twisted tales straight from the id. He appeals to our prurient interests in an effort to reveal their emptiness. To those with strong voyeuristic tendencies, Lynch will either be feeding an addiction or attempting to administer a bracing wake-up from our delusions. In *Mulholland Dr.* (2001), Lynch rips the façade off Hollywood itself. Like *Memento*, a character named Rita suffers from amnesia (caused by a car wreck). She just wants to remember who she is. Rita finds a friend and confidante in Betty, an innocent in search of acting stardom. Lynch preys on our voyeuristic instincts, sucking us into the mystery Rita and Betty try to unravel. *Mulholland Dr.* follows dream logic, starting viewers in a fantasy and gradually moving us to a painful truth. "Betty" is no innocent, and "Rita" is suffering from much more than an accident. Lynch offers his usual series of bizarre red herrings—a cowboy, a dwarf, and even a movie director—that could frustrate rationalist filmgoers. He manipulates sound, color, and the audience in revolutionary ways. The DVD offers no chapter stops. One must watch *all* of the film to get *any* of the film. But to those who are willing to surrender their preconceptions regarding narrative (and a strong moral grid), *Mulholland Dr.* offers a surreal and memorable commentary on Hollywood and human deceptions. It is a recurring nightmare that makes us question our confidence in logic, story, and personal identity. Lynch strips his actors and the audience down to their raw, manipulative souls. He uses style to get below our surface. *Mulholland Dr.* suggests our lives are often nightmares that no amount of Hollywood makeup can disguise. Left alone in a dark room, cut off from a larger shaping story, we may devolve into an autonomous hell.

Martin Scorsese's *The Departed* (2006) demonstrates the grim consequences of a world without God. It is a dark, masterful, highly cinematic story about hearts of darkness. *The Departed* (IMDb #80) opens with Frank Costello (Jack Nicholson) dispensing advice, "I don't want to be a product of my environment. I want my environment to be a product of me. Years ago we had the church. That was only a way of saying—we had each other." As the local crime boss, Frank has established his own kingdom and rules, "Church wants you in your place. Kneel, stand, kneel, stand. If you go for that sort of thing, I don't know what to do for you. A man makes his own way. No one gives it to you. You have to take it."[20] Frank suggests that a thin line separates cops and criminals. He believes in the modernist notion of the self-made man, mastering his own universe via a will to power. Based on the celebrated Hong Kong police drama, *Mou gaan dou* (*Internal Affairs*, 2002), *The Departed* follows the overlapping careers of Billy (Leonardo DiCaprio) and Colin (Matt Damon). Each goes undercover, playing a character for the sake of a larger mission. Yet *The Departed* sends all the characters to a bloody end. Scorsese shows how rats infest the corridors of power.

Given Scorsese's strong Catholic background and previous work, one expects hints of redemption within *The Departed*. Like *Raging Bull* (IMDb #68), it is a cautionary tale that offers a cold slap in the face. In *The Departed*, early decisions to remove an external frame of reference (like the church) sow horrific ends. An amoral universe ends in senseless bloodshed. This is a hard and ugly truth, a diagnosis without a prescription. I prefer the living hell that concludes *Mou gaan dou* rather than the nihilistic ending of *The Departed*. Scorsese's crooked cops cop out. *Mou gaan dou* leaves the evil in a simmering stew of their own making. *The Departed* anesthetizes audiences while *Mou gaan dou* wakes us up.

Joel and Ethan Coen's Oscar-winning adaptation of Cormac McCarthy's *No Country for Old Men* placed film noir along the Rio Grande. Sheriff Ed Tom Bell is approaching retirement, shocked by the dismal tide of violence he sees. He opines, "The crime you see now, it's hard to even take its measure." *No Country for Old Men* offers a chilling world where killers like Anton Chigurh take out innocent victims even while they plead, "You don't have to do this." The evil represented by Anton is an unstoppable force.

No Country for Old Men is an instant masterpiece, never wasting a shot or a gesture. It is a perfect merging of style and substance. Anton's air gun leaves a haunting mark on his victims (and the audience). The Coen brothers trust McCarthy's words. The actors offer brilliant, understated performances. Having wrestled with unmitigated evil, the sheriff is content to retire early. Ed Tom Bell admits to hoping "God would sorta come into my life somehow. And he didn't." Yet Ed doesn't blame God: "If I was him I would have the same opinion of me that he does." But a dim hope does arrive in a shrouded vision: in a quiet ending, Ed dreams of his deceased father going before him to prepare a fire. It is a distant flicker, a slight consolation compared to the mayhem that preceded the dream. In film noir, a comforting spark competes against a wave of depravity.

At its best, film noir reveals general truths about the human condition. We are brutal, heartless, and hopeless; the situation is bleak. Film noir begs for special revelation, longs for redemption. But that is a different story in a different genre. Film noir must resist the vexing temptation to glorify sin. When we embrace our worst instincts, then we have failed to learn the lesson inherent within the genre. Audiences must also resist the temptation to stand in judgment above the characters. "Why were they so easily seduced? Why did they take the money? How foolish to pull that trigger." While the hard truth of Romans 1:18–25 suggests that we have all rejected the images of God all around us, the lesson to be learned from Romans 2:1–4 is *empathy*. Because we are fallen, our judgment is clouded; therefore, do not judge. Because you are capable of just as much self-deception, do not consider yourself more highly than you ought. "All have sinned and fallen short of the glory of God" (Rom. 3:23). Surely even a hardcore Calvinist committed to total depravity and annihilation of the *imago Dei* can summon enthusiasm for film noir. Yes, it can devolve into a glorification of evil. But when handled with the most brutal honesty, it becomes a bracing self-assessment, a glimpse in the mirror at a double-minded man.

So how do we remove the plank that blinds our eyes? British filmmaker Christopher Nolan's smart narratives combat the myth of self-sufficiency. They are constructed like elaborate puzzles to suck in the most engaged, postmodern viewer. With three consecutive features ranked among the IMDb's Top 250 of all time, Nolan has demonstrated a mastery of movie magic and audience expectations. Thematically, Nolan takes on two holy tenets of Enlightenment thinking: (1) All knowledge is attainable through a careful assembly of the facts. (2) I do not need anyone or anything beyond my autonomous self. In Nolan's cinematic universe, misjudgments are not minor matters to be adjusted in the laboratory of life. Even our noblest obsessions can lead to murder.

The Unreliable Narrator

Fact One: "Just because there are things I don't remember, doesn't make my actions meaningless."

Leonard Shelby[21]

Memento (IMDb #26) begins with all the familiar film noir tropes. It starts with a flashback and the weary voice of Leonard Shelby. He functions as a self-employed private eye, hunting for his wife's murderer. The places he inhabits are shabby and unexceptional—trailer parks, cheap motels, parking lots. A femme fatale named Natalie drags Leonard into a multileveled conspiracy. Yet *Memento* never feels like homage to an earlier film from a bygone era. It doesn't fall into the trap of playing dress up, with style trumping substance. Director Christopher Nolan made some highly conscious decisions to avoid the feeling of a museum piece. "When you look at what film noir was, and what it is remembered as, you see that those are two very different things. And I get very annoyed when people refer to this as retro noir. It's not retro noir—it's a film noir. It's contemporary. We have the dark shadows but we don't have the guy in a trench coat in the alleyway."[22] *Memento* has film noir's urban feeling, but it takes place against the anonymous backdrop of Burbank, California. Nolan comments:

This fringe urban could be the edge of any mid-size town, the gas station and the motels. You're talking about a setting for a story where a character wakes up and doesn't know where the hell he is. There's a widespread American story about trying to place yourself in this very anonymous environment. That's kind of exciting. To me, that's like a guy out of film noir.[23]

Christopher Nolan, accomplished director of *Memento*, *Batman Begins*, *The Prestige*, and *The Dark Knight*. © Warner Brothers.

Like shattered veterans of World War II, Leonard represents an autonomous individual who has lost his frame of reference.

Nolan respected the film genre without becoming a slave to its conventions. He doesn't indulge in oblique camera angles or extreme lighting, but he does capitalize on the black-and-white film stock associated with classic noir. We associate black and white with the past, with films (and thoughts) gone by. Yet Nolan inverts our assumptions by putting the black-and-white scenes in the present, while organizing the color sequences backwards—in the past. This adds to viewer disorientation, until the central scene that starts the movie finally catches up with the narrative. As Leonard shakes the Polaroid of his latest victim, black, white, and color finally merge. Our clarity of vision develops alongside the picture. The past and the present blend, forming a seamless transition. Nolan has respected his sources, borrowed from the best, and managed to make something wholly original.

One of the secrets of *Memento*'s success is its undercutting of genre expectations. It reenergized film noir through its unreliable narrator. Audiences are used to hearing voice-over from people we've come to trust, people like Sam Spade and Philip Marlowe. So Leonard's mission seems to fall into the same historical trajectory—the wronged man, out for revenge/vindication/the truth. Leonard invokes even more sympathy than the traditional private eye. They take on cases for money; Leonard pursues justice out of love and grief. The genesis of the story actually belongs to Nolan's younger brother, Jonathan. Chris Nolan recalls:

Identity

While my brother and I were driving from Chicago to Los Angeles, he told me he was writing this story called "Memento Mori." It literally means "remember death" or "remember to die." It's like you're going to croak one day, so don't be too proud of all your worldly goods. So he told me the concept with the idea of this guy who has anterograde memory dysfunction and is tattooing things on his body and looking for revenge and all these cool concepts. And I was like, "Can I go and write a screenplay for this while you write the story?" And together we had decided that in it we were going to try and tell the story in the first person, me in film and him in a short story.[24]

Jonathan's short story eventually appeared in *Esquire Magazine* (March 2001) well after *Memento*'s movie premiere.

The Nolan brothers' most important artistic decision was to put the viewers into Leonard's situation so we feel just as lost as our lead. The film doesn't analyze Leonard; it puts you literally inside his head. The director explains it this way:

> Film, it seems to me, is this fantastic medium for drawing the audience into somebody else's point of view, more so than books, in a funny sort of way. What we tried to do in *Memento* is simply show the film from the character's point of view. So as he walks into a room, you're exploring the room as he does. There's a conscious attempt to keep the camera that way, but there's always this illusion of objectivity.[25]

Memento raises viewer identification with the "hero" to unprecedented heights. This makes Leonard's choice to deceive himself all the more devastating (and applicable).

I cheered for Leonard in the same way I cheer for myself. "Of course I am right. Everyone else is crazy; part of a larger conspiracy of evil, threatening to undo me. But I will be affirmed, avenged, justified—someday." My anger at the filmmaker when I walked out of the theater that day should have been directed at myself. How could I be so gullible—so eager to champion those who play victim, cry wolf, and protest their innocence? Yes, *Memento* made me angry, as my friend helped me discern, because it revealed more about me than I wanted to believe. If Leonard could justify his murderous mission, then what kinds of duplicitous intentions could I turn into a moral crusade? *Memento* put me in touch with my own inner hypocrite. Revelations arrived from two unexpected sources: a gritty film noir and the patient questions of my agnostic friend, Robert. This is the power of general revelation and support for my central thesis.

Remembering Death Wrongly

Fact Two: "But, even if you get your revenge, you won't remember it. You won't even know it's happened."

Natalie

The title, *Memento*, works on multiple levels. Initially we consider Leonard a role model. He is honoring his wife's death by pursuing her murderer. His reflective speeches about memory and healing challenge us to focus on the present, to take stock of our lives, to cherish precious moments of life before it's too late. As a *memento mori* it is also about remembering death in unhealthy ways. Leonard holds on too tightly to the past. He thinks he can't let go because of his condition, yet the movie reveals that he uses it as a crutch. Ultimately, Leonard refuses to move on. So in remembering his wife's death, he consigns himself to his own living hell. Like a rabbit on a treadmill, he repeats the cycle of revenge, his designated drug of choice for coping with grief and guilt.

Theologian Miroslav Volf has dealt with equally painful memories. In *The End of Memory* he recalls the psychological abuse he experienced during compulsory military service in the former Yugoslavia. Like Leonard, Volf has plenty of reasons to be angry, to want revenge against his enemies. Volf notes how crucial therapy and acknowledgment can be to the healing of memory. But clinging to memories is not sufficient. Failure to integrate traumatic events into the broader pattern of one's life story can lead to tragic results. Volf points out, "Victims will often *become* perpetrators precisely *on account of* their memories. It is *because they remember* past victimization that they feel justified in committing present violence."[26] Leonard has turned his wounding into a weapon. Memories that could have been a shield have become his sword. The general truth, "remember death," must be transformed by grace, forgiveness, and reconciliation—the power of special revelation.

Memento also raises troubling questions of a future-focused Western culture. It suggests the dangers of an ahistorical perspective. Leonard tries to piece together what happened but can't quite remember the key events or the key players. While proclaiming a rigorous commitment to the facts, Lenny has blacked out key pieces of evidence from his own police file. He has erased his wife's actual death date in an effort to make it conform to his fictionalized version of history. He justifies his actions through a selective interpretation of history.

Historical amnesia is a danger to both individuals and societies. Yet many nefarious books have attempted to rewrite history. Denial of the Holocaust

Identity

seems unconscionable and impossible, yet a steady stream of self-proclaimed Holocaust "revisionists" propagate detestable material like *The Protocols of Zion*.[27] Teachers worry about Germany or Japan editing their history books to lessen their atrocities committed during World War II. Filmmakers like Steven Spielberg embark on the Shoah project to record and preserve history before it is forgotten (or altered). Others lobby for covered up facts to finally be revealed. The slaughter of Lakota ghost dancers at Wounded Knee, South Dakota, became a rallying cry for a host of injustices directed against Native Americans. The Armenian community has yet to receive any formal recognition or apology from the nation of Turkey for the Armenian genocide of 1915. If the winners often draft the first version of what happened, those "losers" who suffer under persecution must become tireless crusaders committed to correcting the historical record. We must not only argue the facts but also be ever vigilant to make sure they are neither glossed over nor forgotten.

Consider our ahistorical view of Iraq. Had America paid attention to the origins of Iraq, we may have recognized that a nation established as a marriage of convenience for British petroleum interests in 1920 may not be a country worth freeing. The three provinces gathered together by the Treaty of Sevres have continued to see themselves as distinct religious and cultural entities (Kurdish, Sunni, and Shia) irrespective of Iraq's arbitrary boundaries. How many of us knew about Saddam Hussein's long and complex relationship with America, dating back to his days as a CIA-authorized Ba'athist freedom fighter who was trying to undercut a royal regime propped up by the West in 1959? We also have managed to overlook the previously cozy relationship of Saddam Hussein and Donald Rumsfeld. In the seventies and eighties, when we needed Hussein to serve our interests in the region, he was our strategic ally in keeping Iran in check. When he killed 182,000 Kurdish Iraqis in 1987, the United States offered no commentary or opposition. Yet these facts were blacked out in the ashes of the World Trade Center. How quickly the American people lost sight of Osama bin Laden and Al-Qaeda amid our post-9/11 grief. The war on terror began with clear enemies and targets, but the fog of war allowed us to be dragged into an unrelated conflict in Iraq.

In *Memento*, Leonard undoubtedly began his personal war with the best of intentions. But his amnesia got the best of him (or at least gave him a convenient excuse). *Memento* stands as an ongoing indictment of our collective amnesia, our need to place ourselves beside Leonard in the white suit (or hat). But what is the best way to remember death? Will retaliation satisfy even the most unjust murder? Leonard becomes addicted to revenge. To satisfy his habit, Lenny needs stronger doses of both blood and selective memory loss. Falsehood feeds on fresh fictions. We need hard truths to combat our love of lies. Who or what will reveal the sin and self-deception in our lives? Can a firm grasp of the facts undermine our convenient fictions?

Just the Facts, Ma'am

> Fact Three: "Facts, not memories. That's how you investigate. I know, it's what I used to do."
>
> Leonard Shelby

Our postmodern moment has magnified the problem of interpretation. How do we overcome the blindness attached to our limited perspective? Can we turn our situatedness into a strength rather than a weakness? *Memento* highlights the problem of identity while suggesting a potential corrective to our misperceptions.

One of the quickest ways to launch a rigorous debate is to ask the simple question, "What happened in *Memento*?" In my classes, the debate veers wildly as people reconstruct the facts. The online debate is just as vigorous.[28] Most people eventually agree that:

Leonard Shelby was an insurance investigator.

Leonard Shelby was married.

His wife was a diabetic who needed insulin shots.

His home was burglarized.

Burglars assaulted Leonard and his wife.

As a result, Leonard suffers from permanent short-term memory loss.

After that, the facts get fuzzy. Some think his wife was murdered; others suggest that Leonard murdered her.

Frustration rises as my classes attempt to discuss the film. Art is already a highly subjective experience. With differing aesthetics, it's tough to standardize what constitutes a good film. Some question whether the arts can even be known in any kind of objective manner. But *Memento* is an especially vexing movie. Students wonder how we can even have a conversation when people seem to have seen such different movies. If we can't agree on the facts of what we saw, how can we engage in a meaningful dialogue? My students' inability to agree on the basic facts of the case mirrors the Christian community's argument with the broader culture. We seem to prefer what Umberto Eco has called a "closed text"—one that leaves little room for interpretation.[29] Why would an "open text" like *Memento* make us nervous?

Those who wish to establish certain foundational assumptions about God, the Bible, and the life of Christ seem to grow increasingly frustrated with an industrialized world that doesn't share their assumptions. Philosopher Nancey Murphy has noted how modern theologians borrowed from science, constructing a justification of knowledge "that imagines a belief system to be like a building which cannot stand without a solid foundation—a 'bottom layer' of beliefs that cannot be called into question."[30] Theology was divided into two sides: "Conservative theologians have chosen to build upon Scripture; liberals are distinguished by their preference for experience."[31] Yet the empirical basis of science (and theology) has been crumbling since the 1930s. Writing in 1935, philosopher of science Karl Popper admitted, "Science does not rest upon solid bedrock. The bold structure of its theories rises, as it were, above a swamp."[32] Who will stand as the authority when we have fundamental disagreements about the swamp we're swimming in? The anger that emanates from televangelists is but one telling sign of the frustration borne by competing paradigms. But no amount of shouting will change *the fact* that people cannot agree on *the facts*. This doesn't mean that objective truths do not exist. It does mean that multiple perspectives and competing interpretations frustrate foundationalists. Pluralism demands a willingness to consider others' viewpoints, to look at the text of life from many vantage points. Surely we can be civil even if we don't all agree. And revelations can occur even as we meander in the dark.

Yet foundationalists (within all religions) have a right to be frustrated with the field of religious studies. Reducing belief to a science of comparisons from within an "areligious" framework can rob religions of their power and purpose. It is informative but not transformative. The vital dialogue that must take place is between adherents who have experience with the facts of faith and its lived practices. Jürgen Moltmann posits:

> It is only after we are at home in our religion that we shall be able to encounter the religion of someone else. The person who falls victim to the relativism of the multicultural society may be capable of dialogue, but that person does not merit dialogue; for after all, the representatives of other religions do not want to talk to modern religious relativists. They are interested in convinced Christians, Jews, Muslims, and others. Pluralism is not such a religion.[33]

Only when we agree that we have things worth discussing, convictions worth dying for, can we engage in meaningful dialogue. Of course we have all witnessed the downside of conviction versus conviction, when dialogue breaks down. But attempts to heal the breach by putting everyone on equally *relative* ground have brought only frustration. Facts still exist in an epoch marked by opinions. Nancey Murphy suggests that we must move beyond the old dichotomies of Scripture versus experience, facts versus feelings. She expresses, "My projection (and hope) is that theologians from both left and right will find resources in the new (postmodern) worldview for many fresh starts in theology—not fresh starts in content so much as fresh approaches to issues of method, to conceptions of the nature of the theological task."[34] How might *Memento*'s handling of Leonard's "facts" advance that process?

Check Your Mirror

Fact Four: "You don't know who you are anymore. . . . Maybe it's time you start investigating yourself."

Teddy

To overcome the limits of our perception, we need frames of reference beyond ourselves. In his concluding speech, Lenny says, "I have to believe in a world outside my own mind. I have to believe actions still have meaning, even if I can't remember them. . . . We all need mirrors to remind ourselves who we are. I'm no different." This is the all-important frame of reference we all need to remind ourselves of our place and purpose. So what kind of mirror are we looking at? Is it cracked? Distorted? If ours is broken, how do we get a new, more accurate mirror? *Memento* raises core questions of epistemology. It forces us to examine our receptors, our mirrors, lenses, and recording devices—basically our entire mental capacity. How do we know what we know? What kind of information do we trust? Are there objective facts or only subjective experiences?

The uncertainty raised by postmodern philosophy has left many of us feeling like Leonard. We don't know who to trust or where to place our faith. We may be tempted to consider the search for meaning a pointless exercise in existential frustration. The widely divergent responses to postmodern problems may be mirrored in viewers' responses to *Memento*. What some consider energizing, others may find unduly frustrating. The journey to piece together the clues will enthrall some and annoy others. And so it goes. Film critic Ella Taylor sums up the dilemma:

For the philosophically inclined, I doubt whether anyone—even in the glory of film noir—could have come up with a tale as vertiginously relativistic as this one. If nothing else, *Memento* is a savvy comment on the queasy uncertainties of the postmodern condition, in which history goes no further back than yesterday's news, and knowledge is supplanted by "information" from a tumult of spin-controlled, unreliable narrators.[35]

Memento so accurately reflects our unease that it may cause people to dismiss it as another unsolved mystery in a sea of uncertainty.

Director Christopher Nolan recognizes the different learning styles and epistemological grids that order our private worlds. He exploits our different ways of knowing (or remembering), recalling:

> By the time I finished writing *Memento*, it was apparent that the different devices I was using to make up for Leonard's memory were either visual or verbal, either written or photographic or tattoos. So you present those to people when the devices are at odds with each other and see what people choose to believe. What divides people along the question of whether Teddy is lying or not is whether they favor their visual memory or their verbal memory, if you like. . . . It's a question of which type of memory you favor, which you think has more weight. It seems to be an element in the way people sift through the information of the film.[36]

Do we trust what we hear or what we see? What happens when our experience doesn't line up with our beliefs and assumptions? Drawing on his own limitations, Lenny questions all our minds, telling Teddy, "Memory's not perfect. It's not even that good. Ask the police. Eyewitness testimony is unreliable. . . . Memory can change the shape of a room or the color of a car. It's an interpretation, not a record."[37]

I initially read the film's ending as anarchy, a cop-out of enormous proportions. If Leonard's search was mere self-deception, then *Memento* must be questioning all searches. It can be read as a mockery of our hunger for meaning. Lenny has settled for a purpose-driven lie. To some degree, this is true. The postmodern context demands that we recognize the limits of our perceptions. If the Enlightenment was about how much we know, then our postmodern context is about how little we know. This can lead to despair (my initial reaction) or to humility (the posture I aspire to). Maybe a little knowledge isn't as dangerous a thing as a lot of knowledge. But recognition of subjective limits does not rule out the possibility of objective truth elsewhere. We still need a moral frame of reference by which to measure our actions and the actions of others. One man's false purpose doesn't negate the possibility of a higher purpose or calling. Nolan explains: "It's very important for people to understand that I had to know, in my own mind, what the supposedly 'objective' facts were. . . . I wouldn't be able to create a subjective experience that contained multiple interpretations without hanging it on a consistent story."[38] Nolan balances the subjective experience of his protagonist with the objective facts of the case. Our tendency to conflate and thereby confuse the two creates the "movie magic" that fuels *Memento*'s classic status. Viewers who cannot learn to separate what Leonard says from what happened will be hopelessly frustrated.

I saw *Memento* at a prerelease screening. No reviews or expectations clouded my judgment. I was in the precarious position of not knowing what I was about to see. With no advance reviews to tell us what to think, we may come out cloudy in our vision. I wasn't prepared to work so hard to get at a movie and its meaning. *Memento* tricked me because I relied on pat notions of heroes and villains. Our assumptions about where truth resides can cloud our judgment. The church, the government, and Wall Street have all played on our confidence and later been convicted of lying. From ambitious reporters like Jayson Blair and Stephen Glass to investigative journalist shows like *60 Minutes*, those designated as watchdogs have proven suspect. When the Fourth Estate of journalism resorts to fabrication to boost its bottom line, we have run out of institutions to trust.

In a world of spin, *Memento* challenges viewers to dig deeper, to look closer, and to become more active listeners. So what if a manipulative cop like Teddy becomes the only person to tell Lenny (and the audience) the truth about Sammy Jenkus? Revelations can arrive in unexpected ways from unlikely sources. The biblical testimony from Isaiah, Ruth, or Habakkuk demonstrates how diverse God's spokespeople can be. God's story was communicated by a long tradition of eccentric outsiders—theology from the bottom up. Whether dealing with the arts or Scripture, Jesus's question remains, "Do you have ears to hear?" The truth is out there, but unless we develop eyes that see and ears that hear, we may end up as blind and self-deceived as poor Leonard Shelby.

One Theme/Many Films

Fact Five: "I always thought the joy of reading a book is not knowing what happens next."

Leonard Shelby

The issues explored in *Memento* turn out to be ongoing concerns of Christopher Nolan expressed throughout his artistic oeuvre. He has repeatedly returned to issues of self-deception, of transference, of trusting the wrong people—especially ourselves! Nolan's first film, *Following* (1998), was shot on the cheap as a weekend project in his native London. It begins with an ingenious premise: What if a voyeur becomes a victim of voyeurism? *Following* unfolds like a warm-up for *Memento*, turning on a film noir moll, "the Blonde," who proves unreliable. Nolan's fractured narrative also plays with time, and *Following* ends with a massive twist that forces audiences to rewind everything they've seen. Our "hero" has allowed others to pull out the worst voyeuristic tendencies within him, with frightening results. This final revelation forces us to replay all we have thought and believed about the universe contained within *Following*.

Like *Following* and *Memento*, *Insomnia* (2002) suggests that evil resides within all people. It deals with secrets, with guilt, with confronting our demons. It includes the adage, "A good cop can't sleep because part of the puzzle is missing. A bad cop can't sleep because his conscience can't let him."[39] *Insomnia* deals with painful memories. How do we process our regrets? Nolan says, "To me the film is about responses to guilt, and you've got two characters who deal with guilt in opposite ways, in fact that's what makes the relationship between them quite interesting. I think on a thematic level the film says something about the role of guilt in defining morality or suggesting morality. Both characters in some sense have transgressed to cause their reacting to guilt."[40] But rather than the shadowy world of film noir, *Insomnia* takes place in broad and unforgiving daylight. The dueling murderers in *Insomnia* will find no rest until their ugly secrets are revealed.

Batman Begins (2005, IMDb #88) is about doppelgängers, about facing our own inner demons. It delves into the origins of Batman, constructing a new mythology for the celebrated crime fighter. Christian Bale plays millionaire playboy Bruce Wayne as brooding and angry, haunted by guilt surrounding his parents' murder. How will he respond to such overwhelming grief? What can he do in the face of the corrupt politicians and criminalized courts? He goes on a worldwide search to understand the criminal mind. Bruce picks fights in foreign locales, running away from his past and his responsibilities. He becomes a study in self-imposed crime and punishment until a mysterious mentor, Henri Ducard, rescues Bruce from prison. Henri takes Bruce on a spiritual pilgrimage to Tibet, introducing him to Ra's Al Ghul and the League of Shadows. He teaches Bruce to turn his anger into a source of strength. But when the League insists he purge his compassion, Bruce strikes back, destroying their Himalayan outpost.

He returns to a Gotham City besieged by criminality. Like Leonard in *Memento*, Bruce becomes a vigilante, out to avenge a murder. But what will keep Bruce from sinking into the same self-deluded abyss? Bruce has gained the one thing Lenny lacked: sage wisdom. He learns to control his fears, to check his worst tendencies, and to keep his guilt from consuming him.

As the movie develops, Christopher Nolan offers a realistic and psychological cinematic portrait of the Dark Knight. Bruce's test comes in his confrontation with the mind-altering tricks of the Scarecrow. The Scarecrow springs from the psyche of a demented psychiatrist, Jonathan Crane. He serves as a willing pawn for Gotham City's organized crime syndicate, using his expert testimony to plead for criminals' psychological treatment rather than incarceration. Like Bruce Wayne, he hides behind a public mask for so long that his darker alter ego takes over. The Scarecrow gathers the worst offenders in a psychological Hall of Shame, prepping them for a sordid plot. Cillian Murphy portrays the Scarecrow with such unpredictable malevolence that it rises above the cartoonlike villains of previous Batman movies. His plan to poison Gotham's water supply with fear gas exploits Batman's weakest link.

All the skeletons (and bats) in Bruce's family closet come roaring out. His childhood fear of bats *did lead* to his parents' murder. The Scarecrow, an avowed agent of evil, becomes a source of necessary, revelatory truth. Bruce must acknowledge his own fears and his own evil impulses (confessing his sin). What separates Batman from the Scarecrow and the League of Shadows is his way of dealing with human depravity. Mastermind Ra's Al Ghul wants to purge Gotham of all evil in an act of judgment recalling Sodom and Gomorrah. But Batman refuses to acquiesce to a vision of a God of wrath. His strong sense of justice is balanced by compassion for everyday people. His city is worth saving. Nolan juxtaposes the absolutes of the League of Shadows with a superhero who is willing to consider individual cases. Batman clearly believes in right and wrong, but he has seen enough of his own conflicted history to recognize his own limitations. When we have all sinned, who are we to judge? Omniscience belongs to no one (but God).

The Prestige (2006, IMDb #216) uses the background of magicians in Victorian London to explore Nolan's theme of misdirection, deceit, and obsession. Robert Angier and Alfred Borden duel over magic tricks, the love of a woman, and prestige itself. They each have particular strengths—one as more showman, the other more a craftsman. The desire to reveal each others' secrets and possess each others' power leads them to murderous lengths. Like *Memento*, *The Prestige* plays with time; the narrative shifts seamlessly. As in *Insomnia*, neither character can be considered pure or heroic. The audience must question the reliability of

Leonard (Guy Pearce) is deceived by Natalie (Carrie-Anne Moss) and his own unreliable tattoos in *Memento*. © 2000 by Summit Entertainment.

Robert, Alfred, and their respective diaries. Whether as stand-ins for nations or our leaders, the obsessive one-upmanship of Robert and Alfred proves costly to all. Nolan (with a script cowritten by his brother, Jonathan) proves to be a master magician, keeping the audience off balance, guessing about the outcome right to the end. While some may have been put off by the heartless actions of the protagonists, *The Prestige* opens and closes with a basic truth: we must learn to "watch closely."

Christopher Nolan may be the smartest emerging director currently at work, yet he never condescends toward viewers. Like a master magician, he provides all the clues we need to solve the mysteries. General revelation is available to all, although "special revelations" found in online chat rooms may be necessary to unscramble the plot so all viewers may "get it." Isolated viewers will likely miss much of his movies. Nolan's tricky pictures require the help and insight of an interpretive community to solve their riddles. Nolan's films also resonate with audiences because they acknowledge our limitations in knowing and seeing. As a fan on the IMDb said of *Memento*, "You come out of the cinema questioning yourself, your memories, your truths."[41] Yet in a confusing world of shadows, Nolan refuses to demonize others. He makes us all complicit in our gaping social problems. Our ills are not rooted in them but in *us*. So how do we get beyond *our* failings?

Seeing and Hearing: The Hermeneutic Key

Fact Six: "You don't want the truth; you make up your own truth."

Teddy

Memento mirrors our postmodern problem in that it is ultimately about faith. Director Christopher Nolan talked about the different learning styles embedded within *Memento*'s puzzle. Some trust what they hear; others rely on sight. We overcome our blindness by learning to see and hear clearly (with one another's help). But throughout life, we are in a vulnerable position. Whom do we trust? Many of us rely on our own wits and wiles. What can we lean on as a firm foundation?

To cope with his condition, Lenny has constructed a closed, mnemonic system. So what's the problem? Leonard's tattoos are a self-imposed deception. He ends the film at a tattoo parlor, ready to put on another lie. Lenny has also had to remove a genuinely truthful tattoo: "I killed him." The putting on and taking off of truths to suit our intentions will continue to bedevil us. Every tattoo involves a leap of faith. What we desperately need is discernment—revelations to root out self-deception from our truth gathering. How do we acquire wisdom and develop the gift of discernment?

Humble subjectivity can lead to revelatory objectivity if and only if we put ourselves in a position to see and hear. We must get in step with the Spirit. Moses led an exodus out of Egypt, but not all the eyewitnesses recognized God's presence within it. Moses told Israel, "You have seen all that the LORD did before your eyes in the land of Egypt, to Pharaoh and to all his servants and to all his land, the great trials which your eyes saw, the signs, and those great wonders; but to this day the LORD has not given you a mind to understand, or eyes to see, or ears to hear" (Deut. 29:2–4 RSV). Seeing an event doesn't mean we've truly grasped it; revelation is a gift from God. It is available to all, but human sin clouds our lenses and muddies our ability to receive. Proximity to God doesn't guarantee insight.

Jesus spoke in parables, often frustrating his audience. He echoed Moses's challenge, concluding his teaching with the open-ended: "He who has ears, let him hear" (Matt. 13:9 RSV). His stories could seem like riddles rooted in a secret knowledge that he was withholding. Jesus recognized that hearing his words or even a close encounter with God is not sufficient to transform a person's life. So how do we learn to see? The apostle Paul tells the Corinthians, "So also no one comprehends the thoughts of God except the Spirit of God" (1 Cor. 2:11 RSV). There is a mysterious aspect to seeing and hearing. It is our openness to the truth, to the promptings of the Spirit through whatever unlikely means that will drive our transformation. Teddy gives Leonard a moment of blinding revelation. He tells him the whole truth. But Leonard rejects it. He rejects a genuine, communal source of truth and puts on a personal half-truth instead.

By questioning the reliability of memory, *Memento* raises the key issue of hermeneutics—the art of interpretation. Consider Christopher Nolan's intention:

> It was very important to never fully depart from the subjective terms of the storytelling that we set up at the beginning. What that means is, the film does not present objective truth. It presents subjective experience. And the audience is left very much in the same position as the protagonist: the audience is in possession of all the facts by the end of the film, but it's very much open to subjective interpretation. Just like real life.[42]

Nolan inadvertently hits on the distinction between historical biblical scholarship and hermeneutics. We must not mistake a New Testament survey class with a New Testament exegesis class. Each informs the other, but it is our hermeneutic, our interpretative lens that colors whatever the facts may be. Questioning people's objectivity is not the same thing as questioning objective truth. Nolan expounds:

> Film in general is so often used for the cathartic experience of seeing a universe . . . where the objective truth is presented in a way that we never have to access it in everyday life. In everyday life, all trust and objective truth is a complete leap of faith, as it has to be for Leonard. And that's what makes Leonard interesting: he is all of us, and he is a very useful character for highlighting this very human dilemma.[43]

The filmmaker plays God, arranging all the pieces. But the question of interpretation, of hermeneutics, remains for all of us an ongoing problem rooted in faith. Whether dealing with general or special revelation, we must invite the Spirit into the process and humbly be willing to receive.

Where you stand will determine what you see. To move beyond foundationalism is not to reject truth claims.[44] We must travel "beyond fragmentation" as well. Nancey Murphy emphasizes the importance of integrating Scripture and experience. She says, "It is impossible to do theology except in light of current experience if what one wants to do is to *apply* the text in one's own context."[45] Nolan reminds us that a subjective experience does not demand a fragmentation of all knowledge: "It's not a question of anything can happen—something did happen. And that's a crucial distinction. The degree to which you believe it's imperceptible to the protagonist affects the degree to which we wanted to present it to the audience. My view is in the film, but I as a filmmaker never attempted to put any authoritative stamp of approval on that one view."[46] This open-endedness is a conscious artistic choice. It invites viewers into an extended conversation around the film. It forces audiences back into the theater, to rewind the film in an effort to piece it together. Nolan summarizes his hopes: "I find it quite satisfying that people will come out of this film arguing about who the good guys and the bad guys are. Not because there isn't one, but because we are using an unreliable narrator, calling into question the judgments of who's the good guy and who's the bad guy, which I think is like real life."[47] Nolan plunges viewers into the dark (or at least the fog) of Leonard's life in an effort to bring enlightenment. The space between certainty and chaos constitutes *living in faith*. Leonard has relied on the wrong people, especially himself. A community of truth is a humbling, troubling, but necessary antidote to self-assurance.

Perhaps the enduring power of the Bible comes not from its simplicity but from its complexity. What we have reduced to a unified whole may be more attractive and engaging as sixty-six different takes on God's actions throughout human history. The Bible is multiple stories with shifting perspectives on the call and character of God. It is easy to get lost amid the many characters and story lines. But perhaps inviting people to discover the multifaceted story rather than offering a CliffsNotes version will yield a more-enduring transformation. At least that is what the early church recognized as it heard God speak through four Gospel writers—Matthew, Mark, Luke, and John. Their differing perspectives and emphases could have been collapsed or harmonized into one text, yet four takes on Jesus made our understanding of his life and work *that much more compelling*.

We are blessed by multiple perspectives, a communal wisdom that takes us beyond the tyranny of the autonomous self. Little revelations along the way will feed our hunger for greater knowledge. But telling readers (or viewers) what to think will surely stop the search even before it commences. Both the IMDb and the Christian church are communities of interpretation gathered around their most precious texts, engaging in dialogue in an effort to mine the depth, beauty, and wonder of their shaping stories. They will argue, fuss, and fight. Whether dealing with the general revelation of film or the special revelation of Scripture, the act of interpretation becomes a thrilling example of communal discernment when we engage in active listening.

Smart Bombs

Fact Seven: "I had to see through people's bullshit. It was useful experience, 'cause now it's my life."

Leonard Shelby

Identity

Memento sneaks up on viewers like a smart bomb, but distributors passed on the film, considering it "too smart." Steven Soderbergh, the éminence grise of independent film, found such a collective snubbing quite foreboding. Soderbergh lamented, "When a film like Chris Nolan's *Memento* cannot get picked up, to me independent film is over. It's dead."[48] Certainly, it says plenty about the contempt studios have for their audience. Yet that makes *Memento*'s box-office success that much sweeter. Peter Broderick, president of First Look Films, flips the script: "When a *Memento* comes along and gets the press attention that it has, and the business I think it will get [and it did], it's a hopeful sign. It says that formulaic studio movies are not the only game in town. It means that people can make the distinction between something tired and something fresh. It's reassuring."[49] For those who have reduced following God to a formula, *Memento*'s success serves as a wake-up call. Simplicity may allow a message to spread quickly, but complexity keeps us coming back for more. It stands up to repeated readings (or viewings). In fact, *Memento*'s special limited edition DVD makes even playing the disc into a puzzle to be solved.[50] Viewers must answer a series of questions *before* they can even access the movie. (This echoes ancient Christian catechism, where new believers were expected to demonstrate a certain level of knowledge before they were welcomed into such church rites as the Eucharist.) Nolan raises audience interest and devotion by making things harder, smarter, and more difficult to attain.[51]

Memento gained status as an instant classic not because of novelty but because of mystery. It leaves room for audiences to discover the truth for themselves. Kristina posted on the IMDb, "Memento is one of those pictures that will have you sitting in the theater after the lights come up so you can talk to everyone else about what they thought of the movie."[52] An IMDb rater identified as ltlrags celebrates the communal aspect of such mystery: "You will be talking about *Memento* at work, at the grocery store (to total strangers!), and you will find yourself joining conversations when you hear the word 'Memento.'"[53] Isn't that the type of participatory enthusiasm the gospel is supposed to engender? *Memento* invites us to enter into conversation with one another, gathering wisdom from multiple sources to solve a complex problem. It allows the Spirit to surprise us with unexpected insights.

How does revelation work in the Bible? What kind of smart bombs does God drop on an audience? My experience of *Memento* parallels the revelatory power of story demonstrated in Nathan's confrontation of King David in 2 Samuel 11 and 12. This biblical account of King David has just as much sex, violence, and duplicity as the darkest film noir. Gazing from the rooftop of his palace, David becomes sexually obsessed with a literal bathing beauty named Bathsheba. He acts impulsively and ends up impregnating Bathsheba while her soldier husband, Uriah, is off to war. David tries to cover up her pregnancy by rushing Uriah home. Yet Uriah's solidarity with his fellow soldiers prevents him from enjoying his royally appointed leave. David resorts to plan B: getting Uriah drunk in an effort to drive him home to Bathsheba's arms. But Uriah will not compromise. He will not enjoy the pleasure of his wife's company while his comrades are engaged in combat. With his best-laid plans thwarted, David exploits his power to have Uriah eliminated. David sends Bathsheba's husband to the front lines of battle, conveniently removing him from the picture. Bathsheba and David's illicit affair can now be legitimized, along with their child. They bury Uriah and end up seemingly happily married parents. This parallels the backstabbing world of film noir.

But David's nefarious plans come back to haunt him. God sends a prophet named Nathan to tell David a story about a rich man and a poor man and their possessions. The poor man has one little ewe lamb that he has raised and nurtured, until the rich man needs a quick meal to feed a visitor. The rich man steals the poor man's lamb. David responds to Nathan's story with considerable anger, demanding the death penalty for the rich man and suggesting reparations for the poor man of four times the value of the lamb. Then Nathan adds one final twist. He holds up his parable as a mirror and tells David, "You are the man!"—the rich guy who stole a poor man's wife. Nathan's story becomes a revelatory occasion where a man blinded by might finally recognizes his sin. As Teddy makes Lenny see his murderous ways in *Memento*, so Nathan unmasks a colleague's self-deceit.

This dark saga adds a poignant epilogue. David's illegitimate child dies. David and Bathsheba are blessed with the gift of another child, named Solomon. This demonstrates God's ability to redeem our past and heal our sin. Out of David's foolishness arises the famed wisdom of Solomon. Solomon's life is informed by the pain, regret, and wisdom David gained from his experience with Nathan. David and Bathsheba's lamentable choices demonstrate the revelatory power of story. As Nathan undercut David's self-deceit, so *Memento* (and *Raging Bull*) cut through my best defenses—divine revelation in action.

Conclusion

Memento challenges me to consider the ways in which I've made myself the ruler of my own private kingdom. Do I have people in my life who will question my actions? *Memento* flies in the face of the Western paradigm of the autonomous hero. It demonstrates the dangers of vigilante justice. Leonard the Lone Ranger is no better than those who use him. While Natalie and Teddy accomplish their purposes through Leonard, he also uses them to keep his self-deceiving mission intact. They give him another hit, a person to kill, a reason to live. What kind of pact have I made with my worst enablers? What will it take to knock the scales off my eyes? Or did I end my days the same way Leonard concluded his? "Do I lie to myself to make myself happy? Sure. Don't we all?"

We need the mirror of other people to keep us in focus. They don't necessarily have to be friends. Those outside our circle sometimes offer much-needed perspective. Jürgen Moltmann suggests, "Scholars belonging to other religions often perceive the particular character of Christianity more distinctly than Christian theologians. If we wish to know ourselves, it is important for us to see ourselves in the mirror of other eyes too."[54] We must be willing to see and hear God from unexpected sources—general revelations. Wisdom and discernment flow from an ability to sort out facts from fallacies, self-deceptions from the whisper of the Spirit.

We must walk in confidence that the same God who inspired Nathan to speak truth to power will raise up prophets today. While Nathan makes the moral of his story clear, Christopher Nolan is content to leave the questions dangling. This type of postmodern distance makes many nervous. We are used to having the points spelled out. But Jesus's parables remain enigmatic and intriguing. They are smart bombs that detonate when we least expect it. To a culture that has grown deaf to a reductionist "Four Spiritual Laws" come new puzzles that demand to be solved. Like Lenny, we wonder, "How did we get in this mess?" To the voyeur who observes others as sport comes a cautionary tale that *Following* can lead to trouble. To the self-interested who squander their riches comes *Batman Begins*—an avenging angel who rights wrongs out of his own sense of darkness. The Spirit speaks through cautionary tales of avarice and indifference. From the addicts in *Requiem for a Dream* to the crooked cops of *The Departed*, non–role models can inspire us to question our path and clean up our lives. God has stories to tell even amid the shady veneer of *Mulholland Dr.* But who is willing to hear them?

While epistemology remains Christopher Nolan's primary interest, audience enthusiasm for his films suggests that *we will listen* to hard truths when they are delivered in arresting and original parables. We must not allow style to overwhelm substance. Film noir can revel in our depravity, leaving us beguiled by *Sin City*. Form matches function when the characters' blindness parallels the viewers' surprise (and delight) in unexpected twists. In Nolan's films, nobody saw it coming. But thankfully, we have an opportunity to learn from Lenny's and Robert's and Alfred's and even Bruce Wayne's mistakes. Their blindness offers us the revelatory gift of sight, rooted in repentance. Rather than rejecting the notion that we are fallen and sinful, the dedicated film fans of the IMDb eagerly await Nolan's next variation on our historical (and hysterical) blindness. In Nolan's accomplished hands, film noir becomes a surprisingly potent cure. As we grow frustrated with Lenny's inability to see the speck in his mnemonic devices, Nolan challenges us to remove the log from our own eyes.

Remember my own journey with this movie: from frustrated anger to humble appreciation? The Spirit (and the community) showed me how much I don't know, how easy it is to stand in self-righteous judgment over everybody but myself. The truth of Romans 1 is revealed when we use it to judge others (and when, according to Romans 2, we inadvertently pour condemnation on ourselves). Romans 3:9 wonders, "What shall we conclude then? Are we any better? Not at all!" Nolan understands how cleverly disguised metaphors can clarify our vision. His self-deluded heroes are designed to root out the hardness from our hearts. I can't imagine more revelatory artistic intentions. May the Spirit of Truth continue to inspire Christopher Nolan, to keep him humble, and to work through his bracing art.

3

Eternal Sunshine
The Risky Rewards of Romance

Le Fabuleux destin d'Amélie Poulain (*Amelie*, 2001, IMDb #31)
Eternal Sunshine of the Spotless Mind (2004, IMDb #38)
Before Sunset (2004, IMDb #190)
Walk the Line (2005, IMDb #197)

> Love is the triumph of imagination over intelligence.
>
> H. L. Mencken

> To fall in love is to create a religion that has a fallible god.
>
> Juan Luis Borges

A Date Movie?

Once a couple has kids, date night becomes a precious and rare commodity. Babysitters and bedtimes constrict energy that used to be directed to simply having fun. The sheer work involved in walking out of the house can hamstring romantic intentions. It is also costly. Something as casual as dinner and a movie requires a hundred dollar minimum commitment. And what if the movie disappoints? Squandering both time and money has led to many a postdate debate. It is easy to see why home theaters grow ever more appealing. To rent or buy (or download) a movie makes sense when a night out costs twenty dollars for movie tickets, five dollars for gas, and fifty dollars for the babysitter. One can purchase a voluminous supply of microwaveable popcorn for the difference!

So my wife, Caroline, and I screen our movies carefully. If we're going to the movie theater, the film has *got* to be good. Since movies are my profession *and* pastime, the selection process usually begins with me. Yet my desire to be surprised within the movie theater makes me wary of reading too many reviews. I cover the broad strokes through compilation Web sites like metacritic.com and rottentomatoes.com. They offer an overview of the critical consensus and a percentage approval rating. But rapturous reviews are not always sufficient. Caroline wants to know small things like, "What's it about?" and "Will I like it?" Films like *There Will Be Blood* or *No Country for Old Men* are undoubtedly powerful, but they can also become painful endurance contests. We may admire their craft and acknowledge their power but still consider them less than ideal date movies (particularly for already exhausted parents).

I pitched *Eternal Sunshine of the Spotless Mind* (IMDb #38) as a romantic comedy. My sophisticated, PhD-earning wife is a big fan of *Ace Ventura 2: When Nature Calls*, so the presence of Jim Carrey suggested plenty of laughs. We both admire Kate Winslet's eclectic, artistic roles, but would the film be romantic? I had read enough to know *Eternal Sunshine* was about relationships, breaking up and getting back together. But I'd also seen enough of screenwriter Charlie Kaufman's work to expect the unexpected. His screenplays for *Being John Malkovich* (1999) and *Adaptation* (2002) were angst-ridden fever dreams, self-loathing puzzles. His first collaboration with director Michel Gondry, *Human Nature* (2001), came off as more creepy than comforting as innocent people became lab rats in a scientific experiment. We were willing to take a risk by stepping into Kaufman's cinematic lab. *Eternal Sunshine* and romantic comedy won out.

Then we saw the mind-bending, spellbinding movie. It was definitely a wild ride, with a premise rooted in science fiction. But Caroline didn't find it very romantic. A long, slow review of everything that went wrong with a relationship didn't make her laugh either. It failed as romance and comedy—at least, given her expectations. An IMDb user from the United Kingdom declared it "a feeble attempt to do the 'flashback' genre so wonderfully mastered by Tarantino and it fails in every respect.... It's being clever for being clever's sake."[1] So why did I find it so sublime, captivating, and transporting? When had I last left the theater so intoxicated by the sheer possibilities of cinema or so confronted by the complexities of life? *Eternal Sunshine* blew into my soul like the fresh wind of the Holy Spirit, clarifying, cleansing, renewing. On the IMDb, IllyriasAcolyte called it, "The only romantic movie that I can stand. It is a beautiful statement that no matter what, true love endures."[2] I joined the parade of critics praising *Eternal Sunshine* as the most original movie of the year and possibly the decade.[3] It was recorded in my big book of movies as a beguiling, "instant classic." How to reconcile these divergent reactions? Did my wife's disdain for the material reveal the distancing quality of Kaufman's earlier works like *Being John Malkovich* and *Adaptation*? Was he just playing clever mind games with an unsuspecting audience? Or had Kaufman and company achieved something else, something unprecedented—the first truly successful deconstruction of the romantic comedy?[4]

This chapter will focus on the risky rewards of romance. What does the relative paucity of recent cinematic love stories reveal about the human predicament? Are we drawn to the innocence and good deeds of *Le Fabuleux destin d'Amélie Poulain*, (*Amelie*, IMDb #31) or the regrets that drive the reunion in *Before Sunset* (IMDb #190)? They offer divergent visions of Paris, a city associated with romance. *Walk the Line* (IMDb #197) follows the tangled, real-life love of Johnny Cash and June Carter. It demonstrates how personal demons can block our best intentions and frustrate love. *Juno* (2007) inverts traditional notions of courtship, marriage, and reproduction. It starts with a pregnancy and slowly moves toward appreciative love. Most of all, we will turn to the twisted tales of Charlie Kaufman embodied by *Eternal Sunshine* (IMDb #38). What does a desire to erase the past suggest about postmodern romance? What might God be communicating through these messy portraits of lovers at odds? Our survey of romantic comedies will find surprising parallels in two overlooked books of the Bible. While traditional cinematic love stories mirror the passion found in the Song of Songs, recent romantic comedies resemble the more seasoned and complex love celebrated in Ecclesiastes. While movies may tell us how to fall in love, it is the rare film like *Eternal Sunshine* that reveals how to remain in love despite repeated disappointments. To an audience afraid of commitment, God has raised up films that demonstrate the wisdom and power of long-term love.

Auteur of Angst

Our whole being by its very nature is one vast need; incomplete, preparatory, empty yet cluttered, crying out for Him who can untie things that are now knotted together and tie up things that are still dangling loose.

C. S. Lewis, *The Four Loves*[5]

Charlie Kaufman's movies start with Gordian knots of vexing proportions. They wrestle with contemporary questions of nature versus nurture. Is biology destiny? Who are we? Can we transcend our existence? In *Being John Malkovich* (1999) Kaufman explored celebrity culture and our longing to inhabit others' lives (and skin). *Human Nature* (2001) satirizes our efforts to civilize our savage tendencies. Perhaps a state of nature is preferable to the pretense of sophistication. *Adaptation* (2002) questions the artistic process, challenging the conventional Hollywood wisdom found in story seminars taught by writing guru Robert McKee. Assigned to adapt Susan Orleans's novel about orchids, Kaufman the writer places himself (and his fictionalized twin brother) at the center of the movie, revealing the bald egotism that characterizes our inner lives. Such brazen navel-gazing is almost beyond criticism. His directorial debut, *Synecdoche, New York* (2008), blurs the lines between stage and screen as a celebrated theater director overindulges in doppelgängers. Kaufman revels in what others disguise. Yet the neurotic mind games that dominate his films have ended up more admired than loved. They are endlessly interesting but emotionally distancing. This was my wife's initial response to *Eternal Sunshine*.

Unlike Alexander the Great, viewers do not have the luxury of taking out a knife and cutting their Gordian knots in two, because Kaufman has already done all the dissecting, breaking down our mental and emotional processes to elemental levels. John Malkovich's greatest nightmare arrives when he's stuck in his own brain, where everybody looks and speaks only about "Malkovich." In *Adaptation*, Kaufman literally divides himself into two parts, creating a fictional twin brother (Donald) for his on-screen persona (Charlie). The strands of memory and meaning knotted together in *Eternal Sunshine* (2004) have already been separated out and analyzed in graphic detail by Kaufman himself. He brings years of introspection and psychoanalysis to bear on each one of his convoluted screenplays. Yet in *Eternal Sunshine*, Kaufman finally unites mind and body, discovering his heart and soul.

Eternal Sunshine flirts with the traditional Hollywood romance but ultimately forges a more complex and convoluted path. The movie twists and turns in an effort to refine and refind love in our divisive world. Kaufman scrambles our expectations not as a game but as a gift—a way to reveal the wonder before us. So how best to unscramble *Eternal Sunshine*? This chapter will deal with the basic facts of what happened before veering into the larger context of Kaufman's intentions. He cribs from the conventions of romantic comedy before subverting them in revelatory ways. Kaufman joins other significant filmmakers in reinventing romance for the twenty-first-century context. But he tries to unite

Identity

what others have divided—our greatest hopes and our devastating disappoint-ments. He acknowledges the pain of relationships while affirming their promise. To the risk-averse world of dating games, *Eternal Sunshine* beams a message of pressing on, through the hurt, with adjusted expectations and eyes to see the simple pleasures of everyday life.

We will also consider *Eternal Sunshine*'s visual style. *How* director Michel Gondry visualizes the story reveals just as much as the ramblings from our protagonist's brain. How do we portray and talk about memory? What are the possibilities and limits of science? The mundane details of the doctor's office ground this science fiction premise in our common, everyday world. What role does psychology play in our personhood? Gondry and his creative team play with shapes and sizes to approximate Joel Barish's childhood scars. This heady film offers an unforgettable glimpse into the dangers of losing our minds and erasing our pasts.

Finally, how does theology comment on and fill out the gaps created by *Eternal Sunshine*? The film's dueling quotations from Friedrich Nietzsche and Alexander Pope may offer some glimpses into Kaufman's intentions. They highlight the eternal tension between earthly and divine love. But *Eternal Sunshine* challenges the either/or choices that have haunted couples and doomed lovers. Perhaps the divergent visions of the biblical Song of Songs and Ecclesiastes can offer an integrated approach to life and romance. Like all of Charlie Kaufman's films, *Eternal Sunshine* asks the enduring questions, "Why am I here?" and "How do I get out of this mess?"[6] Will those fundamental questions result in revelations? Let's turn to the movie and find out.

Piecing Together the Puzzle

The cinematic inventiveness of *Eternal Sunshine* is one of its primary strengths but also what undoubtedly depressed the box office. Despite near universal critical acclaim, *Eternal Sunshine*'s ticket sales in America stopped at $34 mil-lion. An Oscar win for Best Original Screenplay arrived too late to revive viewer interest. Why did the broad, movie-going audience avoid *Eternal Sunshine*? It doesn't spell out what is happening or even when it is happening. The movie's rewinding plot rewards only an active mind. Therefore, one must piece together the puzzle of the plot before starting to discuss the issues, themes, and theology of *Eternal Sunshine*.

The first problem is that most of *Eternal Sunshine* takes place within Joel Barish's mind. Kaufman explained, "I think generally I'm kind of interested in subjective experience, what goes on inside someone's head, that being all they really know of the world."[7] The film follows the backward trajectory of Joel's memory as his tumultuous relationship with Clementine is systematically erased. Kaufman says he was attracted to "a story that takes place in two years that also takes place in one night."[8] *Eternal Sunshine* plays with time, telescoping years of experience into one arduous Valentine's Day massacre (of memories). It juxtaposes seemingly normal, everyday behavior with fractured recollections and hazy dreams. For audiences expecting to believe what they're shown, *Eternal Sunshine* provides an immediate contradiction.

After a seemingly straightforward introduction of Joel (Jim Carrey) and Clementine Kruczynski (Kate Winslet) and their romantic first day together, a strange character knocks on Joel's window. They have an awkward conversation, talking past each other. The youthful Patrick (Elijah Wood) asks Joel, "What are you doing here?" Joel responds, "I'm not really sure what you're asking." Patrick comes back with an equally obscure, "Oh, thanks. . . ." There is an air of familiarity and strangeness at the same time—like bad juju or depressing déjà vu. The film cuts to Joel crying in his car. The opening credits roll *eighteen minutes* into the movie. While Beck sings "Everybody's Gonna Lose Sometime," the audience is experiencing their first sense of loss—having lost the forward momentum of the plot.[9] From the moment Joel gets a knock on his window, we've been knocked off-kilter, playing catch-up.

Eternal Sunshine takes us down a rabbit hole that requires constant attention. Only at the end of the film do we understand the beginning. What viewers took as the first meeting was actually just a remeeting, after two years of dating and fighting and trying to forget each other. Only on second viewing do we begin to pick up on the multiple clues that suggested this story would unfold in reverse. But the filmmakers built multiple viewings into their original plans. Kaufman recalls, "I think we always wanted it to be a movie that you would watch more than once. And have differing reactions to it with the more information you have." Confused? Follow the clues provided by Clementine's hair.

Joel and Clementine meet at a beach party in Montauk, New York. She has green hair. As they slowly fall in love, they experience moments of genuine bliss, rolling under covers, playing on a frozen pond. She has orange hair. Over time, the spark in their relationship fades. As they share dinner together in a Chinese restaurant, Joel wonders how they've become "the dining dead." They have an intense fight at an outdoor market and end up eating Chinese takeout at

"Meet in Montauk": Joel and Clementine wake up on the beach in *Eternal Sunshine of the Spotless Mind*. © 2004 by Focus Features.

home, sulking. Ever a free spirit, Clementine goes out on her own, only to return home drunk, having wrecked Joel's car. She storms out. Joel tries to reconnect with her at the bookstore where she works, but he's rebuffed. Clementine hires Lacuna Inc. and Dr. Howard Mierzwiak to erase her memory of Joel. Patrick, a support technician at Lacuna, takes advantage of Clementine, using her mementos of Joel to woo her. Joel gets a card from Lacuna notifying him of her procedure. When he confronts Clementine at the bookstore, she is smooching with the new (but faceless to Joel) man in her life, Patrick. Joel decides to have the same procedure. He doesn't want to suffer through a Valentine's Day full of painful memories. The movie begins as Joel wakes up on Valentine's morning. Instead of going to work, Joel follows the suggestion planted by Clementine in his memory to "meet me in Montauk."[10] As they meet again, (as if for the first time), she has blue hair.

What might have appeared random on first viewing (wow, she sure changes her hair a lot) becomes a clear connection to the timeline. The filmmakers have gone to great lengths to make the story work both logically and emotionally.

Yet some critics couldn't get past the plot. They saw the twists as a distancing device, taking them out of the emotional heart of the movie. Stephanie Zackarek of Salon admired so much of *Eternal Sunshine* that she lamented Kaufman's use of tricks. She wonders:

In grappling with these perplexing riddles, we're supposedly exercising our intellect. But isn't it also possible that we're using them as a handy diversion, a way of distancing ourselves from emotions that might be too strong for us to deal with easily? Labyrinthine plots are supposed to stimulate us. But are they really just distracting us from the work at hand—the work of feeling?[11]

Kaufman acknowledges the tension: "If you have to complicate the structure, [you have to be careful] that it comes about in a way that's organic to the movie. That the complicated structure serves the movie and isn't a window dressing thing."[12]

Being John Malkovich and *Adaptation* are both so clever that you end up admiring their structure rather than engaging with the characters on screen. They serve as fascinating pawns in a big cinematic game. *Eternal Sunshine* appears complicated, but the narrative follows a classic, three-act structure: boy meets girl, boy loses girl, boy gets girl back. It springs from the same convoluted psyche as *Malkovich* and *Adaptation*, but *Eternal Sunshine* arrives with much more heart. Kaufman himself may not even be aware of the difference. He says, "Your emotions, as I understand it, are in your brain, so that seemed a natural place to put the story. The story's about emotions and it's about memory, and both of those things are in your brain. If I put it in the heart, it would just be about pumping blood."[13] Whether his feelings come from his head or his heart, Kaufman's romantic impulses betray him. Perhaps despite their best efforts to remain distant or disengaged, Joel and Clementine's hunger for connection trumps reason, experience, and emotions. Their humanity is both their weakness and their strength. Kaufman and Dr. Mierzwiak may be tempted to reduce emotions to a mental process, but their characters and their audience know better.

Forgotten Cinema

Eternal Sunshine of the Spotless Mind stands as a fine example in the growing corpus of memory-loss movies, such as *Mulholland Dr.* and *Memento*. It bears similarities to themes explored by sci-fi films based on the stories of Philip K. Dick, such as *Blade Runner* (1982) and *Total Recall* (1990). Director David Fincher also played mind games in suspense films like *The Game* (1997) and *Fight Club* (1999). As technology advances, humanity seems to move further from our roots. We've forgotten who we are or perhaps *whose* we are. *Eternal Sunshine*'s tone is closer to the romantic leanings of *Abre los Ojos* (1997) and the American remake, *Vanilla Sky* (2001). When we cut ourselves off from each other, we have reached genuine madness. We are made for relationship, built to love. Science that erases our past cannot be considered a friend. Recent cinema suggests that dehumanization is an evil that must be resisted.

One of the primary distinctions between *Eternal Sunshine* and its cinematic predecessors is the source of the memory loss. In most amnesia movies, the hero has been victimized—subjected to an accident or experiment by malevolent or chaotic cosmic forces. In *Eternal Sunshine*, Clementine and Joel choose amnesia. They want to forget, and they're willing to pay for it. The enemy is no longer technology but our longing to erase the past. Our capacity for enduring pain has been replaced by a procedure. In hiring Lacuna Inc., Joel and Clementine embrace the devil they don't know.

This extends the critique of humanity proposed by *Memento*. The pain inflicted by life makes forgetting attractive. Miroslav Volf notes the vulnerability that results from surrendering ourselves to *the other*. Volf writes of the risk of relationships in general: "Their problem is not so much exclusion of the other from their will to be oneself, but a paradoxical exclusion of their own self from the will to be oneself—what feminist theologians call, 'diffusion of the self.'"[14] Joel and Clementine have fused in unhealthy ways. They have lost their selves in relationship and are willing to do more damage to remedy it. The emotional truth of love and loss makes scientific options like erasing our memories remarkably attractive. We understand Joel and Clementine's reasons, just like we come to understand (but lament) Lenny's choices in *Memento*. Charlie Kaufman acknowledged the specter of *Memento* on his creative horizon. Upon seeing Christopher Nolan's whodunit, Kaufman called Gondry in despair, saying, "I'm canceling this."[15] Thankfully, Gondry talked him off the creative ledge and challenged him to press on. But how could he tell a story in reverse without subjecting *Eternal Sunshine* to too many comparisons? Tattoos were definitely out. Plans to have Joel write notes on the walls of his old haunts were also nixed. The conundrum resulted in a much more visual movie. Gondry and Kaufman had to figure out ways of showing rather than talking about the memory loss. In the process, *Eternal Sunshine* presses past the despair of *Memento* with a hint of promise.

Gondry and Kaufman resisted the temptation to resort to (too much) digital magic. Their science fiction story is rooted in real-world photography—tricks accomplished onstage and in camera. Cinematographer Ellen Kuras added smoke to flashbacks that took place in Joel's apartment. The hazy, gauzy feel of those scenes comes across as even more real than a strict documentary style. It looks the way we remember things: slightly golden, a little indistinct, close but not microscopic in detail. Gondry and Kuras also filmed most of Joel's "freak-out" scenes in real time—without special effects. On the *Eternal Sunshine* DVD, Gondry recounts how Jim Carrey went back and forth behind the camera, changing his sweater to appear both inside and outside Joel's nightmare. The crew applauded at the conclusion of the scene, sensing the genuine accomplishment of simply capturing the complex scene on film. The spotlight that dominates Joel's nightmarish recollections is so simple yet profound in its emotional resonance. As Joel's brain goes under the doctor's microscope, an impersonal and disorienting white light blasts his face. This is the opposite of a divine vision. It is without warmth, just a cold, interrogating vision. Even those scenes that do resort to digital effects incorporate as many human elements as possible. Gondry took the haunting image of the blank books from a personal nightmare and used composites of his own legs and knees to create the faceless Dr. Mierzwiak. It makes for a scary trip.

Brain Damage

In Joel's hunger for autonomy, individual human identity has been removed. The facelessness of the doctor and Patrick can be read as a telling indictment of the scientific method. Dr. Mierzwiak relates the facts of Clementine's case with clinical detachment. He says to Joel, "Suffice it to say, Miss Kruczynski was not happy and she wanted to move on. We provide that possibility." Lacuna offers the (false) promise of new life. The cheery secretary, Mary, explains their services to Joel. The aim is "to let people begin again. It's beautiful. You look at a baby and it's so fresh, so clean, so free. Adults . . . they're like this mess of anger and phobias and sadness . . . hopelessness. Howard just makes it go away." This echoes the biblical appeal of having our transgressions removed from us (Ps. 103:12). In Isaiah 43:25, God makes the attractive promise to remember our sins no more. Yet, unlike God, Dr. Mierzwiak requires no confession of sin in order to cleanse us (1 John 1:9). A spotless mind replaces any need for psychology or religion. Science provides a clean slate (for a price).

Eternal Sunshine holds the claims of the self-improvement industries up to the microscope. The casualness with which Dr. Howard Mierzwiak initiates the process is both comic and frightening. An anxious Joel expresses a legitimate fear, "Is there any risk of brain damage?" Howard reassures him, "Well, technically speaking, the operation is brain damage, but on a par of a night of heavy drinking. Nothing you'll miss." Lacuna's extreme makeover generates a literal nightmare. The scientific high priest turns out to be a charlatan.

Amid Lacuna's bold claims resides a frightening ethical indifference. With their client Joel sedated, Stan, Patrick, and Mary reveal their true selves, literally drinking, dancing, and smoking in the patient's bed. Kaufman says, "I was thinking of that as a customer-service kind of job. You have to deal with people, and you don't really like them. And you have to pretend you like them. And this is a situation where you don't have to pretend because the person is unconscious."[16] *Eternal Sunshine* raises relevant questions about responsibility. Patrick's exploitation of a wounded and unconscious Clementine borders on emotional rape. The filmmakers wanted viewers to feel a legitimate sense of outrage or loss toward the procedure. Kaufman comments, "There's just a little red light that goes off, and [the doctor] says, 'That's it.' That's so devastating to me. There's the contrivance of this story, but I think it's based on the reality that . . . these things that are important to us don't exist. They're gone."[17] Science intends to free us but instead annihilates our humanity. We're left as a living *lacuna*, haunted by blank spaces and missing parts. How will Joel fill the hole in his soul?

The subplot of Howard and his secretary, Mary, may provide the most cogent critique of Lacuna's methods. While their adulterous relationship has seemingly been cleaned up by a simple procedure, their tangled emotions reside just below the surface. The original script included the additional complication of Mary's pregnancy and abortion. All of the unresolved tensions boil to the surface in the middle of a Valentine's evening. Left alone, Howard and Mary revert to their flirtatious tendencies. And science cannot erase the complications of wives and boyfriends. As Howard and Mary rekindle their feelings with a kiss, Howard's wife arrives. Mary's new boyfriend, Stan, honks the horn. The tangled relationships spill out into an ugly street scene. The entire neighborhood becomes a witness to something Lacuna was supposed to have erased. Procedures cannot erase our painful pasts.

The filmmakers offer a glimpse of hope, though. At the conclusion of the film, Mary becomes the surprising catalyst of genuine change. She confiscates Lacuna's files and returns all the tapes to their sources. Joel and Clementine rediscover each other because of Mary's decision to blow the whistle. Mary's regrets become a life-giving occasion for others. Personal conscience trumps the myth of an objective, detached science. Unlike the title of the film (or the promises of Howard), Mary comes to believe that informed pain is preferable to the ignorant bliss of a spotless mind.

Hiding in Our Humiliation

While *Eternal Sunshine* questions the infallibility of science, it seems to affirm a particular kind of psychological awareness. Joel must confront his worst fears in order to save and protect Clementine. He digs deeper into his subconscious as a means of preserving her memory. The key piece of advice: Clementine's call (within Joel's brain) to "hide me in your humiliation." Notice the parallels to Adam's behavior in the Garden of Eden. When confronted and exposed, Adam and Joel attempt to cover themselves. Where can they hide?

Joel snaps back to a comforting scene from childhood—hiding from his mother under the kitchen table. Yet, Clementine has taken his mother's place, even wearing her clothes. Joel's primal Oedipal urges peek out. As Joel's mind wanders, Clementine points to her panties to keep him focused. Joel the man and Joel the boy both want versions of the same motherly love. Why does the love impulse drive us all so profoundly? *Eternal Sunshine* suggests that our endless longing for relationship is rooted in the parental hugs and approval we're still searching for. Yet shame and social stigma conspire against love. Joel's mental projection of Clementine challenges him, "Hide me somewhere deeper. Somewhere really buried." The memories that Joel covers up include the discovery of his masturbation and his capitulation to peer pressure. Ultimately, Clementine is hidden amid Joel's memory of smashing a dead pigeon with a hammer. Director Michel Gondry recalled how hesitant Jim Carrey was to act out the grisly scene. It evokes potent images and unresolved issues from adolescence in the actor, the filmmaker, and the audience.

Joel's journey is similar to the acting process itself, as artists get in touch with primal emotions in order to evoke tears and laughter. There's a reason method acting and Freudian psychoanalysis arose concurrently. Their processes bear remarkable similarities. Gondry discusses his commitment to getting a genuine tear from Jim Carrey as Joel's final memory is erased. A tear could have been added via makeup or digital effects, but Gondry and the crew waited until Carrey summoned up the real deal.[18] On the set Gondry also utilized a variety of tricks to coax genuine reactions from his actors. In Joel's first visit to Lacuna, Stan surprises Howard and Mary by hiding in the hallway. Gondry had pulled aside actor Mark Ruffalo, suggesting he jump out and surprise the unsuspecting actors. Their shocked response is authentic and unrehearsed.

The poignant circus parade was unplanned and unscripted. When Gondry heard the circus was in town, he rushed actors and crew down to witness the arrival of the Ringling Brothers Circus. As the elephants marched by, Gondry

Identity

pulled actress Kate Winslet from beside Jim Carrey. When Carrey turned around, he looked genuinely surprised and anxious. He was caught so far off guard by this unscripted moment that he yelled out "Kate" rather than "Clementine." Gondry kept his actors off balance in order to capture authentic moments on-screen. It is far too easy for gifted actors like Carrey to pull from a preestablished bag of thespian tricks. *Eternal Sunshine* may be his finest performance because his comedic crutches were removed. Carrey acknowledges his connection with the psychological truth of Joel's character:

> I think that quick fixes are big for sure. I think that we're all erasing things every morning when we go to Starbucks. We're just like, "Ah, whatever, it can't come up again. Don't let it come up again," and that kind of thing. We suppress. We don't completely erase, but I think that we would in the moment. I think that we would definitely choose that a lot of times when we're on our knees screaming at God.[19]

The most overtly theological moment in *Eternal Sunshine* comes when Joel is on his knees, begging for the right to hold on to his memory. His change of heart (or mind) occurs on the ice, where he had experienced a moment of transcendence. After a magical evening under the stars, he had told Clementine, "I could die right now, Clem. I'm just—happy. I've never felt this before. I'm just exactly where I want to be." Joel's desire to eradicate a painful past proves too costly. Confronted by the loss of such romantic memories, he offers a heartfelt cry for mercy. He begs the Lacuna employees to cancel the procedure, to *not give him* what he originally asked for. It is a cry of regret. This prayer is not sent to heaven, but it is lifted above—from his unconscious state to the cloudy but conscious plane. Joel attempts to transcend his circumstances by any means necessary. The appeal is offered to the technicians rather than God, but science fails to listen.

Only the still small voice of Clementine provides Joel with a vestige of hope. She whispers, "Meet me in Montauk." This rendezvous plan has a heavenly air about it. Montauk stands as both their original meeting place and the sight of magic moments together—playing on a beach in the snow. While memories of their relationship from the city may be sullied, Montauk lingers on as a place of eternal discovery, their unsullied Garden of Eden. It is unclear where this whispered meeting point comes from. Throughout the film, the voice of Clementine is mostly filtered through Joel's memories. Yet this contingency plan is not rooted in a recollection. It is a wholly original suggestion. Is it what Clementine *might* have said? What Joel *wanted* to hear? Or is it a heartfelt cry from beyond their experience (so far)? The film ends with Joel and Clementine reunited in Montauk, playing on that snowy beach. Is this a glimpse of their future together on earth or in heaven, or is it some kind of inescapable, recurrent cycle? Wisely, Kaufman and Gondry preserve the mystery, leaving it up to the audience to follow their bliss.

Dueling Quotations

To talk about theology in a film where God is seemingly absent is a dicey proposition, yet that is the pervasive power of general revelation.[20] Movies mired in the complications of love invariably tread on theological ice. Mary offers Howard two quotations that echo eternal questions from philosophy and art. She has taken them out of context, from *Bartlett's Quotations*, yet her blatant effort to spark conversation or impress a learned man outlines competing approaches to life.

The quotation from Friedrich Nietzsche's *Beyond Good and Evil* (1885) can be read multiple ways. "Blessed are the forgetful, for they get the better even of their blunders," may undercut all our notions of self-improvement. The search for a totalizing truth is doomed, so we must move beyond categories of good or evil. In a life filled with tragedy, only the foolish can be truly wise. Yet Nietzsche's own embrace of the eternal recurrence suggests another reading.[21] He saw plenty of fools holding on to old fictions. He derided those who merely observed life from a cold, nihilistic distance. Instead, Nietzsche proposed an active embrace of life's tragic dimensions, a willingness to reinvent ourselves ad hominem and ad infinitum. The self-made "new philosophers" may not escape this world, but they will transcend it when they get in step with the eternal recurrence. Yet the placement of the Nietzsche quotation within *Eternal Sunshine* can also suggest a critique of Nietzsche's project. The new philosophy (or science) of Howard has gotten Mary nowhere. She is stuck, back in the same situation he supposedly corrected months ago. Self-actualization is an empty promise.

Mary's second quotation, from Alexander Pope's poem "Eloisa to Abelard," occupies pride of place, providing the title for Kaufman's story.

> How happy is the blameless Vestal's lot?
> The world forgetting, by the world forgot;
> Eternal sunshine of the spotless mind!
> Each pray'r accepted, and each wish resign'd.[22]

Identity

Pope's poem is based on a twelfth-century story of a tragic teacher-student romance. Heloise's (Eloisa's) secret marriage to her brilliant (and older) French teacher Abelard does not prevent her family from exacting a brutal revenge. Abelard is castrated and resigns himself (and Eloisa) to a monastic life of separation for the rest of their days. Their tortured correspondence informed tragedies from Shakespeare's *Romeo and Juliet* to Kaufman's *Being John Malkovich*. In *Malkovich*, a puppeteer reenacts Heloise and Abelard's story as a counterpoint to his own sexual longings. He is emotionally castrated, cut off from his feelings and desires. But the drama enacted by puppets in *Malkovich* takes a decidedly human form in *Eternal Sunshine*. What of these separated and emasculated lovers captivates so much of Kaufman's mind?

Probably no finer cry for a gracious memory loss has ever been uttered. Locked in a convent, Eloisa wants to forget her former lover, Abelard, to erase him from her past. Her unquenchable desire haunts her. Having loved and lost, she longs to obliterate her past. Like Joel and Clementine, Eloisa desperately wants a spotless mind. But is that prayer truly preferable? The poem expresses the tension between holy vows and sexual ecstasy. But Pope's verse can be interpreted in multiple ways. It could be a protest against social norms that took choice away from twelfth- (and Pope's eighteenth-) century women.[23] Eloisa's prayers can also be read as the triumph of romance over against chastity. While her physical options may be limited by social mores, her heart remains firmly committed to Abelard. You can separate the lovers physically, but their love remains just as passionate in spirit. Prayers and resignation to a life of chastity have not diminished Eloisa's insatiable desire for Abelard. She keeps the fire burning.

Maybe Kaufman appreciates the duplicity in Pope's poem (and Eloisa's mind). In her world, the sacred and sexual can coexist as complementary, even indivisible ideals. Likewise, Kaufman welcomes multiple interpretations of his work. When a reporter alerted him to the ambiguity that marked a postscreening discussion of *Eternal Sunshine*, he said, "That's the nicest thing I could hear. That's exactly what we were hoping for. And maybe at different times those people could have the opposite reaction." Kaufman continues, "That's what I want in my scripts. I want people to be able to have different experiences."[24] Some may find this disingenuous, an artistic equivocation. Yet perhaps Kaufman is simply challenging the either/or assumptions of twelfth-century France or Alexander Pope's eighteenth-century England or the modern world. What if Eloisa and Abelard were given a false choice between sex and religion, the divine or the worldly? *Eternal Sunshine* criticizes both a Nietzschean "will to power" and a romanticized idyll. The social and religious foolishness that condemned Eloisa and Abelard to a life apart has been replaced by an equally misguided scientific method. Romeo and Juliet didn't need to die. Joel and Clementine may not have a perfect relationship, but those moments on ice or on the beach come awfully close. In these memorable passages, divine and earthly loves merge into a timeless, transcendent reality—an eternal kiss.

Reinventing the Romantic Comedy

Eternal Sunshine deconstructs the will they/won't they, either/or conventions of romantic comedy. My wife's disappointment with the film was rooted in her expectations of what makes a good date movie. *Eternal Sunshine* gives us the pleasure of romantic pursuit but then unravels it. It moves from bliss to breakup, subverting the expected trajectory of Hollywood convention. So which version is true? People meet and fall in love? Or *Eternal Sunshine*'s second half of the equation: people meet, fall in love, fall out of love, and eventually make a choice to remain in relationship? As we will see, the Bible affirms the spark of romance, the trials of life, and the wisdom of sticking together, learning to appreciate the gift of companionship and family. *Eternal Sunshine*'s revelatory power resides in its ability to mix the bitter and the sweet, to document not just a blossoming romance but a long-term relationship.

From the opening line, *Eternal Sunshine* takes on romanticized versions of the dating game. Joel considers Valentine's Day "a holiday invented by greeting card companies to make you feel like crap." Romantic comedies seem to have had the same effect on Charlie Kaufman. He recalls:

> Movies about romances are almost always about people and their obstacles in meeting. Once they meet, everything, it's assumed, is going to be great. Of course, in real life, we know that . . . nothing's ever great. So, you know, I feel really kind of hurt by those movies. Growing up, I felt they hurt me because I then had expectations of the world that I was never able to realize.[25]

One can imagine how Kaufman felt about the fanciful Parisian romance of *Amelie* (2001, IMDb #31). It is a love letter to the Montmartre of postcards, a throwback to innocence, daydreams, and movie magic. From its full French title to the snappy voice-over narrator, *Le Fabuleux destin d'Amélie Poulain* announces itself as a fable. French director Jean-Pierre Jeunet bathes his idealized Paris in lush reds and greens. The bistros sparkle with life. Yann Tierson's *chansons* on the sound track are delightful. *Amelie* is an unabashed valentine to an unforgettable city and a captivating young woman.

As Amelie (Audrey Tautou) gradually works her way into her neighbor's graces, she also charms cynical moviegoers. Amelie engages in acts of kindness, from returning a box of childhood mementos to staging photos of her father's gnome on a trip around the world. She also gives sight to the blind, describing the vibrant Parisian street life in brilliant detail. But Amelie harbors a secret: a lack of affection from her father. She turns to her imagination as an escape. Within the Two Windmills Café, she is shy and expresses herself tentatively. When she discovers Nino (Matthieu Kassovitz) collecting discarded photos from a booth, Amelie engages in her most creative games yet. *Amelie* is relentlessly sunny, upbeat, and joyous, an unapologetic escape from life's drudgery. Within the decidedly masculine universe of the IMDb, Amelie rose to number seven on female viewers' list of the top movies.[26] IMDb rater Carmen-d from Norway writes, "It makes an unemotional person like me want to cry, want to smile and it succeeds! I can't help but to have a silly smile on my face, a feeling of love all over my body, something no other movie can make me feel. Does love exist? Is life beautiful? After I have seen this film I must definitely say YES!"[27] Jilske from Belgium wrote, "Never before has a movie INFLUENCED my life in such a way. . . . This movie is for everyone who understands passion or who has lost his/her childhood somewhere along the way. If you love art and music, sunshine and poetry then you are qualified for seeing this movie; be warned though . . . this movie can change your life (and maybe . . . it will ;-)!"[28] Amelie also captivated plenty of men on the IMDb. Composer Mike called it the "best gift from France since the Statue of Liberty."[29] It is the highest rated romantic comedy of all time, a stirring tribute to our enduring hunger for fantasy. Consider the deliriously romantic *Amelie* as the anti-Kaufman.

Yet rather than discount *Eternal Sunshine* as an antiromantic comedy, I am inclined to associate it with Stanley Cavell's notion of the comedy of remarriage.[30] In his study of films from Hollywood's golden era of the thirties and forties, Cavell finds a focus on the threat of divorce rather than the promise of marriage. Screwball classics like *It Happened One Night* (1934, IMDb #133) and *The Philadelphia Story* (1940, IMDb #178) put their lovers through rigorous emotional tests. The central tension involves skepticism, deciding whether those we know too well can be trusted anew. In a reflection of their progressive era, the women tend to demand the right to an education or equality. Yet the comedy of remarriage may also reflect what wasn't happening. They arose at a time when marriages rarely ended in divorce. Films like *Bringing Up Baby* (1938,

Audrey Tautou serves up a rosy cinematic romance in *Amelie*. © 2001 by Miramax.

IMDb #232) or *The Lady Eve* (1941) expressed what couldn't be said or done. The ambiguous endings that define the best comedies of remarriage left audiences with a shocking level of ambivalence. Nervous laughter resulted.

Perhaps in an era marked by noncommitment or divorce, the comedy of remarriage offers remarkable resonance. Sociologist Zygmunt Bauman describes the fragmentary and discontinuous nature of postmodern relationships. Our transitory ways enable us to evade moral responsibility, leading to "disengagement and commitment-avoidance."[31] Recent romances honored among the IMDb's top films reflect our cultural cold feet. Richard Linklater's *Before Sunset* (2004, IMDb #190) is rooted in regrets. The central tension resides in *what ifs*. As a sequel to his earlier *Before Sunrise* (1995), Linklater and his actor-collaborators Ethan Hawke and Julie Delpy capitalize on the nine years that passed between films. In both movies the setting is Europe and the plot is essentially a long, rambling conversation. Jesse and Celine philosophize and flirt on the banks of the Seine, toying with notions of chance, fate, and finding monsieur or mademoiselle "right." Audiences that pulled for them in *Before Sunrise* can return to Jesse and Celine's story informed by their own regrets and *what ifs*.

Identity

What is the key difference between the two films? The younger, idealized portrait of *Before Sunrise* is burnished by Jesse's troubled marriage in *Before Sunset*. Jesse's "would have, could have, should have" is matched by the midlife crises creeping up on Linklater's target audience. Impulsive love has been replaced by a lack of a pulse. Things that didn't happen nine years ago now find a ripe and opportune moment in *Before Sunset*. As in *Amelie*, Paris provides a romantic backdrop, loaded with possibilities. As Celine dances to the intoxicating sound of Nina Simone, a divorce (or certainly a doubt) enters Jesse's mind. A child at home complicates the situation as well. Will he follow through on the action he failed to take as a young man? Time has taught Jesse to act decisively, without regret. But before anything indelible happens, Linklater fades to black. Viewers fill in the blanks and wait for the three-quel.

Walk the Line (2005, IMDb #197) also deals with looking outside marriage. Like Jesse in *Before Sunset*, Johnny Cash is stuck in a relationship that is not working. His wife doesn't understand his music or his demons. On the road and onstage, Cash (Joaquin Phoenix) discovers a true companion in June Carter (Academy Award–winner Reese Witherspoon). She has been branded with the stigma of divorce and had her fitness as a mother and as a Christian questioned. Together, the two outcasts, Johnny and June, sing their finest songs. But June has reasons to be reluctant. Having loved and lost, she is guarded and cautious about getting involved with the haunted "Man in Black." Johnny must overcome his addiction to pills before June will consent to marriage. Will his dangerous "ring of fire" consume her? June remains steadfast in waiting on John. Her parents offer emotional support. Johnny must grow up, overcome old grudges, and put away childish things before they're married. Cash must decide what he is most committed to—June or his pills. In a decidedly Hollywood ending, he kicks all habits and makes the right choice. Johnny proposes and June accepts onstage, before an adoring audience. Cold feet are conquered when Johnny finally goes cold turkey.

Both movies dance around issues of infidelity. *Before Sunrise* and *Walk the Line* suggest that true romance transcends commitments to wives, children, or social convention. They are emblematic of an era in which true love seems so elusive that people are advised to grasp it wherever it can be found. Personal satisfaction trumps marital vows when ethics begin with "authenticity to self" rather than "commitment to biblical expectations." Interestingly, both films suggest it may arrive only later in life, when enough wisdom has been gained to recognize what a precious and rare gift an enduring relationship can be. As filmgoers are getting married later in life, so movies are featuring comedies of remarriage, delayed marriage, and nonmarriage. Young romance has been replaced by older, wiser, battle-tested love.

In the captivating comedy *Juno* (2007), a young woman is forced to deal with the demands of adulthood. Juno MacGuff has skipped romance altogether, ending up pregnant via a single, spontaneous sexual encounter with her friend Paulie Bleeker. Teen boredom leads to comic complications. Rising star Ellen Page portrays Juno as confident and worldly wise. But as the movie unfolds, we recognize how much vulnerability lurks under her hip, witty surface. She has so many mixed feelings about the baby's father, the awkward but earnest Bleeker. Should Juno express her true feelings? Should she abort the baby? Or endure the scorn associated with teen parenthood?

Juno's decision is forged outside a clinic. A classmate, Su-Chin, holds a sign and shouts, "All babies want to be borned." The simple notion that a fetus has fingernails slows down Juno. Her decision to bring the baby to term resulted in plenty of appreciation from pro-life factions. Yet the film also points out how many adults remain unprepared for parenting. The seemingly perfect, adoptive couple, Mark and Vanessa, have very different attitudes toward Juno's baby. As the birth approaches, Mark reveals just how adolescent his fantasies of rock stardom remain. The birth of Juno's baby leads to Mark and Vanessa's divorce. *Juno* suggests that when it comes to romance, we often get ahead of ourselves. Even though they invert the established order (sex before marriage, pregnancy before commitment), Juno and Bleeker manage to find each other in the end.

Eternal Sunshine begins with mutual attraction, but its plot thickens with a breakup. Joel's pain and confusion drives the story line. Director Michel Gondry considers Joel's final, failed attempt to reconcile with Clementine the saddest scene in the movie. It is about a couple (or at least half of the couple) trying to work out their differences. As such, it is not about falling in love but about what happens after the final credits roll in traditional romantic comedies. When two people find each other, the story (and challenge) is only beginning. Charlie Kaufman explains, "I was interested in trying to write a movie about a relationship rather than a romance. I wasn't interested in it being romantic. I was interested in finding something true to me, with all the struggle and all the dysfunction. . . . I wanted to write what I knew from my own experience."[32] Can such an admittedly subjective undertaking acquire universal application and appeal? The particulars of Kaufman's experience also find ample parallels in biblical texts. They resonate in the lives of viewers. By tapping into the reality of his life, Kaufman has portrayed our lives. His distinction between romance and relationship is echoed in the (often overlooked) Wisdom literature from the Bible. Perhaps

Joel and Clementine's alternately joyous and tortured relationship can open our understanding of the Song of Songs and Ecclesiastes.

Songs of Innocence

Love is a canvas furnished by Nature and embroidered by imagination.

Voltaire

No book of the Bible captures the rapturous nature of young love better than the Song of Songs. In the first verse it is attributed to King Solomon, although the reference is made in the third person rather than as an authorship claim. Ongoing scholarly debate about "the Canticles of Wisdom" has prevented a consensus on its origins. It features a remarkably strong and assertive young woman. The voice of this woman in Song of Songs is so singular that some have suggested its authorship could be female.[33] It reaffirms the image of God as male and female set forth in Genesis 1 and 2. The Canticles also counterbalance all the patriarchy that followed Genesis 3 by celebrating a reciprocal love between equals. The woman's curse of Genesis 3:16 ("your desire will be for your husband") is contrasted by the mutuality of Song of Songs 7:10 ("I belong to my lover, and his desire is for me").[34] Like Eloisa (or even Clementine), the woman unapologetically relishes her passion for her lover.

Song of Songs celebrates the thrill of the romantic chase; how exhilarating a dating and mating process can be. But it subverts poetry in the ancient Near East (and classic Western notions of romance) by making the woman equally aggressive.[35] Clementine and Joel's dance on the train platform in Montauk echoes the wandering in the garden of young lovers in Song of Songs. The pleasure is in the pursuit. The Canticles also capture the impatience that marks a blossoming romance. Like Joel and Clementine, the lovers in Song of Songs cannot wait for their next rendezvous. At the end of their first encounter, Clementine offers Joel an unapologetic order, "I would like you to call me." As soon as Joel enters his house, he calls. The "Beloved" in Song of Songs says, "All night long on my bed I looked for the one my heart loves; I looked for him but did not find him. I will get up now and go about the city, through its streets and squares; I will search for the one my heart loves" (Song 3:1–2). This is a remarkably assertive woman for the ancient world. Like Hollywood's earliest romantic comedies, the man and woman in Song of Songs exist on equal footing. They both acknowledge their desires and find delight in each other's presence. The lovers' relationship can be described as mutual possession, found in the repeated phrase, "My lover is mine and I am his." It is a romantic paean to *we*.

The open sexuality of Song of Songs has made it a problematic text. Noted Jewish Rabbi Akiba praised the Song of Songs as "the Holy of Holies" among the Hebrew Wisdom literature.[36] It was read as an allegory for God's love for Israel, yet it virtually ignores God as a character. Pledges are made to gazelles or does in an overtly naturalistic theology. Attempts to unify Song of Songs into a cohesive whole or find a coherent plot result in frustration. Some scholars have suggested the text may be the script for a lost drama, missing vital instructions or act breaks. Others have attempted to read it as an ancient wedding rite, although no additional sources from the ancient Hebrew world corroborate. Scholars Ariel and Chana Bloch suggest the easiest way to reconcile the disparate strands of poems and speeches is to read it as a poetic unity. "It makes no sense to judge lyric poetry by the standards of logical discourse, requiring a systematic progression from A to B to C and thence to a conclusion, with every link soldered firmly into place as some exegetes do. . . . Apparently the biblical poets had a more flexible notion of unity and structure than many scholars have recognized."[37] The Song of Songs offers poetic vignettes, snapshots of a relationship. Like *Eternal Sunshine*, it offers fleeting glimpses, poetic moments from a rapturous relationship isolated in time. Elizabeth Huwiler suggests, "These idiosyncrasies draw the audience into the text and into the confusion and false confidence of young love much more effectively than a neatly wrapped-up plot or a tightly structured outline could ever do."[38] What an apt summary of both Song of Songs and *Eternal Sunshine*.

Song of Songs celebrates the joy of sex without the necessity of childbearing. Allegorical interpretations of the text arose as an effort to redeem the absence of God language and shore up the silence regarding children. Building on Jewish interpretations that equated the lovers with God and Israel, early Christian scholars like Origen connected the lovers to Christ and his bride, the church. Gregory of Nyssa offered a mystical emphasis on contemplation, detaching the senses from matter until our souls are united with God. In the medieval era, the Canticles became a guide to mystic communion and divine love. Song of Songs became the most copied and widely disseminated book of the Bible.[39] So why has it fallen out of contemporary sermons and everyday use? Perhaps our hypersexualized age has made the Christian community reluctant to embrace such an earthy text. Its Hebraic blending of the sacred and the sexual challenges a rational, dualistic faith. Jürgen Moltmann suggests we think of the Father, Son, and Holy Spirit as an erotic community of love. He would reclaim the word *erotic* as a passionate participation in the beautiful. So the interpenetration of the Trinity (the *perichoresis*) is physical and spiritual, earthly and transcendent, a movement into each other. This mutual indwelling is, above all else, poetically beautiful.[40] Yet the affirmation of physical pleasure and the material world in the Song of Songs cannot be explained away as allegory. Like Pope's Eloisa and Abelard, Song of Songs explores both the power of physical attraction and the mystery of divine love.

Perhaps the relational tensions dominating our postmodern context can help us recover the holistic wisdom that secured a place in the canon for Song of Songs. The Canticles acknowledge both love's playfulness (see 2:1–3) and its pain (see 3:1). It is a risky but rewarding adventure. Song of Songs unites the sensual and the spiritual, embracing them as indivisible. To reduce *Eternal Sunshine* to neurological impulses may cause us to miss its theological possibilities. Isn't love much more than biology? Sex as solely physical satisfaction leaves both partners in the relationship wanting. Yet an overly spiritualized faith may cause us to miss the insights embedded in *Before Sunset* or *Walk the Line*. Aren't there destructive marriages that people of faith and conscience should flee? Haven't thousands of divorced Christians experienced God's grace in second marriages? I would suggest that careful reflection on postmodern romances like *Eternal Sunshine* may unlock our appreciation of overlooked passages of the Bible. Can these movies ignite the Spirit's revelatory actions?

For example, Song of Songs revels in description. It reminds us that the immanent creation (things) is often the only way to talk about eternal or transcendent notions (feelings). But to contemporary ears, the metaphors in Song of Songs can feel so comic or foreign (breasts like fawns?) that we miss the author's intent. Like a designer catalog, the Canticles list all the attributes of the lovers and their bodies. As we might make lists of likes and dislikes about potential spouses, the lovers in Song of Songs create their own top-ten reasons they're so infatuated. But the poetic metaphors are mixed in a creative manner. References to gardens, wine, and animals commingle with military imagery (devoted to the woman!). She is a tower whose neck could carry the shields of a thousand warriors (Song 4:4). The closest contemporary equivalent is a freestyle rap song, where loose associations and comedic wordplay are meant to entertain and enlighten. As *Eternal Sunshine* shuffles the random images from Joel's childhood, so the lovers in Song of Songs have "hair like goats" and "temples like pomegranates." The visual collages of *Eternal Sunshine* cinematographer Ellen Kuras and editor Valdis Oskarsdottir are matched by the cut-and-paste poetics of the narrator of Song of Songs. (All are gifted women!) They concentrate on the details of our daily life in an effort to affirm the enduring (and ethereal) power of love.

Setting is also important in Song of Songs. The lovers connect each other to their surroundings. Eyes are like "pools of Heshbon"; noses are like "towers in Lebanon." Joel and Clementine link their love to Montauk. Their dramatic good-bye occurs amid the crumbling house where they first found each other. Everyday objects also serve as convenient metaphors in Song of Songs. Spices, perfumes, and fabrics become reference points for the Beloved. Joel and Clementine also have collected a treasure trove of mementos from their relationship. Production design—from props to sets to clothing to makeup—contribute vital information about where Joel and Clementine have been together. Their physical environment is littered with notes, photos, and art projects, like their potato people. To remove Joel's memory of Clementine is to extract everything he ever associated with her, including his childhood experience of Huckleberry Hound. Mementos also cannot be replicated apart from their original environment. To Joel, Clementine is a "Tangerine." Patrick offers a pale imitation, trying to rename her "Tomato." *Eternal Sunshine* and Song of Songs remind us of the importance of place—our garden, your apartment, our stuff—to authentic loving relationships. In a materialistic era, perhaps we need to rediscover the power of things to mediate matters of the Spirit.

Songs of Experience

Yet the innocent, early infatuation of the lovers eventually fades. Joel and Clementine's frolicking on the ice does not last. Charlie Kaufman wants to tell us the rest of the story—what happens *after* couples fall in love. My wife entered the theater expecting a joyous Song of Songs. *Eternal Sunshine* offered a more seasoned take on life, closer to the alternative wisdom of Ecclesiastes. If the Song of Songs comes from a young woman, Ecclesiastes springs from a weary old teacher identified in the original Hebrew as "Qohelet." He looks back on life and declares, "Everything is meaningless." The vanity of vanities that Qohelet bemoans matches Joel's disdain for Valentine's Day. When Clementine's impetuous life force proves incompatible with Joel's dogged cynicism, he embraces his darker leanings. Charlie Kaufman's worldview sympathizes with Joel (and Qohelet). They are tired of false hopes and disappointments. They've seen enough fake smiles and heard enough broken promises. Life has no meaning, no pattern, and no guarantees other than death (and maybe taxes). Perhaps the human experience

Identity

is so painful that we must avoid getting involved with others. *Eternal Sunshine* and Ecclesiastes can be (mis)read as a call to despair. Don't risk relationships because you're bound to get hurt. Stay home. Lock the door. Shut out the fallen world and its vain temptations.

But both Ecclesiastes and *Eternal Sunshine* expect audiences to look closer, to push past the initial provocation. Scholar Elizabeth Huwiler says, "Ecclesiastes states more emphatically and more consistently than any other biblical book that human access to truth and knowledge is limited."[41] Like *Eternal Sunshine*, it obscures and obfuscates, not out of cloying cleverness, but to question our sense of certainty. Huwiler adds, "Like many postmodern texts, Ecclesiastes seems in ways to be a puzzle. . . . It is as though Qohelet wants the reader to struggle to figure out a complicated puzzle to which there is, after all, no solution."[42] Ecclesiastes and *Eternal Sunshine* play tricks on their smart audiences, exploiting their probing attention. The ascetic tone that starts Ecclesiastes does not necessarily match the lesson. Only on second viewing do we recognize Joel and Clementine's playful first meeting as a bittersweet reconciliation.[43] The storytellers' enigmatic methods are the message.

Ecclesiastes and *Eternal Sunshine* can be seen as fatalistic, but a more apt description is *resigned*. Given the complications of life and the raft of inevitable disappointments, what pleasures can we take away? Qohelet and Kaufman offer dour paradoxes, full of hard-won hope. Life may be a meaningless series of vanities, but Qohelet urges his readers to enjoy the wine and love their wives every short and transitory day. *Eternal Sunshine* challenges us to treasure the precious moments in time, staring at the stars with our lovers beside us. Isn't this sufficient consolation? Like Qohelet, Clementine reminds all of us that the clock is ticking: "This is it Joel. It's going to be gone soon. . . . What do we do?" Joel offers practical wisdom: "Enjoy it." God may seem distant and remote; at times, meaning remains elusive. But embrace what's before you; love the one you're with, not out of Epicurean revelry, but as an act of worship—a profound appreciation for the simple gifts the Creator offers: wine, food, family (see Eccles. 9:7–10). Only as Joel begins to lose those sensations does he realize how precious such consolations can be.

I am not suggesting that Charlie Kaufman read the Song of Songs or Ecclesiastes as inspiration for *Eternal Sunshine*. Yet Kaufman deals with haunting existential questions of whether we're alone in the universe. His angst-ridden yet slightly hopeful responses stand up alongside the similarly paradoxical biblical Wisdom tradition. His distant (or even nonexistent) God connects with his Hebraic religious tradition and its rigorous emphasis on ethics (just like

Ecclesiastes and Song of Songs). I am suggesting that a close reading of *Eternal Sunshine* might reawaken our neglect of potent but underexplored biblical passages like Song of Songs. Our wearying life experiences that resonate with *Eternal Sunshine* may find fresh connections in Ecclesiastes. The lightbulbs that flick on in Joel's head (and audiences' hearts) have ample precursors in Song of Songs and Ecclesiastes. Perhaps the waking up that accompanies our viewing of *Eternal Sunshine* can continue in a close reading of Scripture. Forgotten books of the Bible may burn anew after the Spirit speaks to us. Ecclesiastes and the Canticles fulfill the labels assigned by medieval biblical commentators as "two dangerous books."

Good News for Postmodern Skeptics

The hard-won wisdom of Qohelet finds its finest expression in Joel and Clementine's awkward hallway conversation that concludes *Eternal Sunshine*. Mary's return of their tapes creates a mental and emotional crisis they cannot ignore. As their Lacuna cassettes play, Clementine and Joel ponder their future. Charlie Kaufman admits to spending the most time rewriting this penultimate scene, desperate to get it right. He says, "I wanted to make dialogue unnecessary."[44] The threat of sentimentality lurks over all romantic comedies, even *Eternal Sunshine*. Gondry and Kaufman went to great lengths to avoid it, admitting, "We always felt we were being manipulative."[45] So how to earn a hard-won happiness? Joel must deal with his tendency to idolize Clementine or turn her into an idealized concept. As she admits, "I'm not perfect," he responds, "I don't see anything I don't like about you." Yet the tape betrays him. He says, "I love your hair," at the same time his voice recalls, "I hate your hair." He must embrace equal parts of love and hate for Clementine, and she must renounce her commitment to spontaneity and freedom: "I'll get bored with you and feel trapped because that's what happens to me." Her maturity will arrive when she's learned to stick with things (and people). Christopher Orr of *The New Republic* summarizes the transcendent depths of their dilemma:

> At its core, *Eternal Sunshine* is about the need for atonement and redemption. "Freed" from the memory of their painful breakup, Joel and Clementine can no longer forgive nor ask forgiveness for past hurts received or inflicted, and can reconcile neither with one another nor with themselves. Their past together is like a frayed nerve that leads nowhere, the phantom limb of the amputee. No matter how many times they wander in the footsteps of their lost memories they can never recapture them. It is only through Fate or God's grace or True Love—or, for the

more literal-minded, a glitch in Lacuna's process—that they are given a second chance to make themselves whole. These are admirably big themes.[46]

At the conclusion of the movie, Joel and Clementine offer not grandiose promises but humble acknowledgments. Rather than turn an "I don't" into an "I do," Joel and Clementine summon up a simple, "Okay." Essentially, he admits, "I, Joel, will accept that you, Clementine, are not perfect." Her de facto confession: "I, Clementine, will get bored with you, Joel, but I shall not run when I feel trapped." New life begins in acknowledging their past disappointments and renouncing their future expectations. Freedom is not constantly running away from things (such as commitment). Their mutual *okay*s are about staying together despite the evidence. The Bible may define faith as "the substance of things hoped for, the evidence of things not seen" (Heb. 11:1 KJV), but Joel and Clementine take an even bigger leap of faith—*perseverance in the face of the things they have seen*. This is the opposite of blind faith; it is faith with eyes wide open.

This is good news for postmodern skeptics. No matter how many times we may have been burned by bad relationships, we need not despair. We can develop eyes to see the transcendent moments that remain. Amid our considerable pain, God has still given us life as a gift. The theology of Qohelet suggests, "There is a possibility of trying to live faithfully, of working out one's role in creation, even when God is experienced as distant."[47] Despite the risks, audiences responded to *Eternal Sunshine*'s challenges with revelatory enthusiasm. Daryl from Illinois wrote, "I left the theatre wanting to be a little more spontaneous and take chances more often. Experiences are what make life worth living. You should treasure them, both good and bad, as they make you the person you are today." Cat from North Carolina reflected, "After viewing *Eternal Sunshine*, I fell in love with life all over again. I've never been so moved. It rekindled a spark in my soul that I've been missing for a while."[48] Even Kaufman was surprised by the results of his artistic experiment: "I think it could have failed in any number of ways that it didn't. And I think it's fine that it would have. But it wouldn't have been as pleasing if it did. When you're going out into territory that you're not certain of, that's always a possibility. But you have to accept that as a possibility or you can't do anything interesting. Looking back on it. I think, 'Oh good, it worked.'"[49] Like most enduring art, *Eternal Sunshine* transcends its authors' hopes and intentions. The Spirit moves beyond our wildest imagination.

For a screenwriter who eschews warm and fuzzy life lessons, Charlie Kaufman offers a remarkably hopeful conclusion. Perhaps his early tendencies toward despair have been chastened by the love of a wife and the gift of children—Ecclesiastes' lessons realized. He is mellowing in all the right ways. The mind games of *Being John Malkovich* have found focus in *Eternal Sunshine*. Sure, love can drive you crazy. We may even want to erase all our painful memories of failed relationships. But careful reflection on our past can result in hard-won wisdom. Song of Songs is about acting on our impulses, and plenty of us need to learn how to seek out and embrace life's pleasures, to affirm the physical world. Yet love is more than sex. It is for Song of Songs too! Many of the descriptions have to do with intangible qualities. Ecclesiastes is written from the end of life, when things (literally) aren't working. It looks back not with longing but with appreciation for the precious moments with our loved ones that endure.

Eternal Sunshine concludes with Beck's cover of the Korgis's 1980 hit, "Everybody's Got to Learn Sometime." The simple lyric offers two challenges with one result:

> Change your heart, look around you.
> Change your heart, it will astound you.[50]

For those who have given up on the possibility of love (or the potential of movies), *Eternal Sunshine* recommends a change of heart. The results echo the mysterious move of the Spirit—"it will astound you." The eternal sunshine promised by Lacuna Inc.'s blank slate proves to be a lie. But that doesn't mean we quit searching for eternity or sunshine. Beck sings, "I need your lovin', like the sunshine." Eternal sunshine does not arrive via memory loss or pain-free living but by embracing the complexity of life. Just like the sunshine, we all need God's physical and emotional, sacred and eternal lovin'.

Part 2

Community

Cain spoke to Abel his brother.
And when they were in the field,
Cain rose up against his brother Abel and killed him.

Then the Lord said to Cain,
"Where is Abel your brother?"

He said, "I do not know;
am I my brother's keeper?"

And the Lord said, "What have you done?
The voice of your brother's blood is
crying to me from the ground."

Genesis 4:8–10 ESV

4

Crashing into the Ensemble Drama

Communities in Crisis

Hotel Rwanda (2004, IMDb #59)

Crash (2004, IMDb #107)

Mystic River (2003, IMDb #180)

Little Miss Sunshine (2006, IMDb #234)

United 93 (2006, IMDb #238)

> Cowboys are special with their own brand of misery,
> from being alone too long.
>
> Willie Nelson[1]

Alone on the Range

Whenever Willie Nelson sang, "My Heroes Have Always Been Cowboys," I happily joined the chorus. I practiced my hero worship through the rough-riding films of John Wayne and Clint Eastwood. Old westerns dominated the afternoon matinees playing on my parents' television. I escaped my surroundings with visions of the Wild West. Cinematic cowboys lived close to nature, exploring vast, open plains, a picture of freedom. They also got to wear cool outfits, shoot big guns, and live above the law. I admired John Wayne's "True Grit"—his ability to rescue a community in crisis.

In spaghetti westerns like *Per qualche dollaro in più* (*For a Few Dollars More*, IMDb #134), Clint Eastwood rides into town as a man with no name. He lets his gun do the talking, taking out the bad guys who threaten a burgeoning town. Cowboys dispensed rough justice.[2] They took on some personal buckshot but escaped comparatively unscathed. With order restored, they were free to move on, to ride into the sunset in search of an elusive peace. I related to the outsider who keeps short accounts. I longed to blow into town, win a young woman's heart, solve a crisis, and move on.

But I never listened closely to the poetic words of Willie Nelson's song. It begins with romanticized visions of a high-riding cowboy but shifts into the patterns of a "modern-day drifter." Willie advises us not to "hold onto nothin' too long." His cowboy suggests you "take what you need from the ladies, then leave them, with the words of a sad country song." Not exactly a sparkling model of fidelity. By the second verse such selfishness has turned to misery, "from being alone too long." Cowboys "could die from the cold in the arms of a nightmare." What an ugly ending! I loved the illusion of freedom but failed to consider the costs of isolation. Cowboys may ride off into the sunset, but they die alone, cut off from community. "Home on the range" may also mean "alone on the range." It could take months for a cowboy's death to be noticed. No wonder Willie Nelson also sang, "Mamas Don't Let Your Babies Grow Up to Be Cowboys."[3] How much has a cowboy's commitment to rugged independence and autonomy cost him?

Somehow, the movies failed to communicate the rest of the story. They presented an idealized version of the cowboy life that overlooked the genuine sadness that accompanies lone rangers. Maybe the cowboy myth was more tragic than heroic. To its credit, *Brokeback Mountain* (2005) portrays just how sad the cowboy life can be (regardless of sexual orientation). By the end of the film, Ennis Del Mar rots alone in his modest mobile home. His daughter's efforts to reach out to him before her wedding are rejected. His freedom has been preserved, but he has missed the events and connections that make life rich and rewarding. Like the Man with No Name, Ennis will ride into the twilight of life alone, clinging to what might have been.

I still struggle with my affection for the cowboy myth. Something about the Lone Ranger appeals to my wanderlust. Despite the clear call to join together as a Christian community, I have struggled mightily with the reality of church life. I entered the fellowship of believers with such high hopes and such a superficial survey of Paul's letters that the amount of backbiting, infighting, and positioning shocked me. The temptation was to go it alone, to follow Christ into the wilderness. I didn't need anyone beyond "my Savior and me." Like my Hollywood heroes, I would occasionally saunter into a troubled community, offer a few key shots (of wisdom), and move on. But the problem with all those movies is that the test of true community begins only at the end, when the surrogate sheriff leaves. Will the townspeople rally? Will they forge a long-term peace and prosperity? Has civilization triumphed, or have the forces of disunity been kept at bay only for another day (when the gunslinger is not around)?

From MySpace to Sacred Space

The death of the Hollywood western has been accompanied by the rise of the ensemble drama. Stories about leaving a town have been replaced by complex meditations on how we navigate community. We are vacillating between the autonomy we've been offered and our gnawing desire for connection.

Our conflicting emotions regarding individual freedoms and social responsibility are reflected on the Internet. Is our wired world more connected than ever? Or have we isolated ourselves even further through electronic communication? The World Wide Web allows us to find people with common interests on the other side of the globe. Pop culture serves as the shorthand for adding online friends. At places like www.facebook.com we forge networks around shared classes, experiences, and interests. Groups can be created and joined with a single click. Those networks of relationships are simultaneously virtual and real.

MySpace demonstrates our competing desires to stand apart from others *and* add more and more friends. We have an opportunity to gauge our popularity, to rank others, and to add them to our list of "favorites." MySpace can turn into an online competition. (It is called MySpace rather than OurSpace!) But it also brings people together across great distances, reuniting old friends and forging new networks. Is it a convenient way to manage relationships, to keep others at a comfortable and virtual distance? Or can MySpace lead to a greater understanding of shared space and interconnectivity? The best ensemble films invite us into a shared space, filled with mutual respect and cooperation, properly understood as *God's space*.[4]

Quentin Tarantino's *Pulp Fiction* (1994, IMDb #8) sparked a wave of ensemble films that depend on interlocking stories. Tarantino preserved the quirks of individual characters while arguing for the overlapping nature of humanity. We may think we are alone, but our common needs and place under divine providence suggest otherwise. Perhaps the ensemble drama has exploded on-screen at precisely the moment when we need it. Despite greater proximity to different peoples and cultures, we are in danger of talking past one another, devolving into a *Babel* (2006). With communities in crisis, many have found the movies serve as a helpful corrective to our romanticized visions of the Lone Ranger. *Little Miss Sunshine* (2006, IMDb #234) enables us to laugh at the absurdities of family, to come together despite considerable eccentricities. A haunting film like *Mystic River* (2003, IMDb #180) demonstrates the corrosive effects of community secrets. It deals with the complications that arise from those closest to us. Is family a tragedy or a comedy? We will also consider our call to the Christian family. What can the church learn from ensemble dramas?

The second half of this chapter will discuss communities in crisis, specifically Los Angeles, Rwanda, and post-9/11 America. These places were torn apart by violence, forced to rebuild in an era laden with distrust. If it is difficult to live with our loved ones, what happens when we encounter *the other*? How do we deal with people from different cultures, who speak different languages, and who practice different religions? Kenneth Ross of the Human Rights Watch described the new tribalism: "The explosion of communal violence is the paramount issue facing the human rights movement today. And containing the abuses committed in the name of ethnic or religious groups will be our foremost challenge for years to come."[5] Filmmakers have found such challenges ripe for drama. Will they also provide a place for revelatory insights?

Crash (2004, IMDb #107) is a meditation on the American experiment. What was once a melting pot is more like a mash up, a clash of cultures that don't want to blend in. *Crash* shreds our veneer of respectability to expose a raging racism underneath. It asks the same question Rodney King posed to a burning Los Angeles in 1992: "Can we all get along?"

Hotel Rwanda (2004, IMDb #59) chronicles the horrific genocide of a decade earlier. As Hutus slaughter Tutsis, the international community, including the United Nations' "peacekeepers," watches from the sidelines. One man rises to the occasion and becomes a Rwandan "Schindler."

The shattering events of September 11, 2001, are re-created with jarring accuracy in *United 93* (2006, IMDb #238). It rises above the politics surrounding that horrible day by putting viewers inside a doomed plane. Capitalizing on a cast of unknown actors, *United 93* portrays the courageous acts of a few people who sacrificed their lives to save many others.

These three ensemble dramas mine our recent past and, in the process, portray the dark side of humanity. What kind of violence occurs when we break the ties that bind us as people? Can we affirm our individual characteristics and differences and still live within a shared communal space? The American cowboy myth may prove to be a particularly damaging approach to international relations. Croatian theologian Miroslav Volf serves as a helpful discussion partner. In his acclaimed book *Exclusion and Embrace*, he challenges us to move past social arrangements to our role as social agents. He writes, "Instead of reflecting on the kind of society we ought to create in order to accommodate individual or communal heterogeneity, I will explore *what kind of selves we need to be* in order to live in harmony with others."[6] Here, too, is the focus of these movies. They restate the question posed by God to Abel, "Where is your brother?" (cf. Gen. 4:9). The finest ensemble films demonstrate what it means to fulfill the challenge to "love your neighbor as yourself" (cf. Lev. 19:18). They offer contemporary meditations on Jesus's parable of the Good Samaritan (see Luke 10:25–37). To a culture hung on ethnic or religious differences, Jesus offers a tangible test—three divergent examples of community. Will we pass by a person in need, looking away from one who has been beaten by robbers and left for dead? Or will we dare to care, bending down to get involved in healing and restoration? The best ensemble dramas echo Jesus's question, "Which of these three do you think was a neighbor?" (Luke 10:36).

Ensemble dramas are rooted in characters' choices. They deal with the fragile links of community, through a variety of combinations and permutations. Ensemble films serve up a menu of options, across the breadth of the human experience. Their interlocking stories demonstrate how connected we are to one another. As such, they reflect the trinitarian roots of reality. God said, "Let *us* make man in *our* image" (Gen. 1:26, emphasis added). It was never about one God making one person. Rather, a communitarian God created Adam, and the initial diagnosis remains true: "It is not good for man to be alone" (Gen. 2:18). We were made to be together, to relate to one another. Like the Father, Son, and Holy Spirit, ensemble dramas unfold as tripartite stories about complementary gifts.

Life's Rich Pageant

The ensemble drama traces its roots to the crosscutting editing techniques pioneered by D. W. Griffith. He taught filmmakers how to intercut two stories, building tension between good guys and bad guys racing toward the same goal. The early silent films kept the number of characters and their dramatic ambitions simple. Over time, Griffith's plots and intentions grew in complexity. In *Intolerance* (1916), Griffith chronicled four eras of human history united by a common theme, humanity's intolerance toward each other. From the life of Christ, through the Babylonian Empire, to the persecution of the French Huguenots, right up to Victorian social reformers' condemnation of an unfit mother, Griffith jumps from scene to scene, era to era. He tinted each section with a unique color scheme, offering viewers the same visual shorthand as the recent ensemble story *Traffic* (2000).

As films came to employ synchronized sound, Hollywood turned to Broadway playwrights for dialogue. The ensemble drama shifted from historical epic to soap opera. MGM's *Grand Hotel* (1932) and *Dinner at Eight* (1933) dealt with the vagaries of love within a single setting. Life's rich pageant was reflected in the wealthy clientele traipsing through the Grand Hotel or invited to dinner. With stables of movie stars under contract to a particular studio (in this case Metro Goldwyn Mayer), the ensemble drama was much easier to coordinate than today's era of free agency. Stars could be gathered under one roof (or boat or plane). Such frothy ensemble comedies continue to appeal to moviegoers in search of humanity (and escape).

A second type of ensemble film deals with the question, "Who done it?" A large and intriguing list of suspects makes a better mystery. French director Jean Renoir defined the darker version of these tangled romances in *The Rules of the Game* (1939). While love still drives the varied protagonists, murder drives the plot. It satirizes the European idle rich, pointing out how savage the game of love can be. Agatha Christie perfected the ensemble murder mystery in countless plays, and more recently it has been revived in *Gosford Park* (2001). This movie highlights the difference in class, as the guests' and servants' lives come to overlap in surprising ways. They proved that both actors and audiences remain drawn to the human surprises evident in ensemble dramas.

Beyond love and mystery, a third type of ensemble story deals with family—especially wacky families populated by eccentric uncles and crazy aunts. It taps into our first experience of community, trying to navigate relationships with parents and siblings. Zany families drive Frank Capra's *You Can't Take It with You* (1938). It mines the same premarital comic vein of the embarrassing family in *Meet the Parents* (2000).

Indie hit *Little Miss Sunshine* (2006) builds on Capra's legacy with a family of lovable losers, offering both originality and preciousness. *Little Miss Sunshine's* unexpected box office success proved that audience appetite for cute kids and quirky grandpas remains intact. It also straddled a precarious line between savage satire and endearing family comedy. Many were moved by the way love triumphed despite intergenerational differences. MatthewinSydney wrote, "As the film started I wasn't so sure about it. All the characters . . . seemed to be written as being amusingly quirky in a predictable indie-comedy way. But as the movie went on it became easier to warm to them."[7] By packing an eccentric clan into the confined space of a Volkswagen van, first-time filmmakers Jonathan Dayton and Valerie Faris ratchet up the family's craziness several notches. All of the sparks generated by being together are magnified by confined spaces. With nowhere to run (like behind a teenager's bedroom door), the challenge of being a multigenerational family is writ large. The dark comedy also features a tangible (and highly satirical) target, the Little Miss Sunshine pageant. These are the hallmarks of ensemble pics—a clearly defined group united in a particular place to achieve a measurable goal. With all the dramatic elements in place, the story can wander down the trails created by character quirks without coming off the rails.

In *Little Miss Sunshine*, comedy trumped dysfunction. A radiant child brought disparate adults together. It provides therapists with ample examples of how family dynamics play out.[8] Yet *Little Miss Sunshine*'s stinging barbs proved too pointed for some. While many howled at Olive's competitive striptease routine (taught by her bawdy grandpa), just as many could not laugh at such exploitation of a seven-year-old. IMDb user Ark-Flash from Canada commented on the "sicko grandpa": "If he isn't dead, he should be locked up. . . . Although it was nice of her family to stick up for her, the subject matter was very inappropriate."[9] For some viewers, eccentric crosses over into offensive. Olive's innocence brings the family together, but at what price unity? We may recognize their madness as being similar to our own but question whether such satire ennobles or merely unmasks. Is wearing a "Jesus was wrong" T-shirt a little too easy (and unsupported) a gag? Ensemble family stories may make us wince, but they will ultimately renew our commitment to each other. *Little Miss Sunshine* represents how far we've moved from the lovable kooks of Frank Capra to dangerous dysfunction. Has our view of community (or at least family) shifted from warm to hostile, from quaint to manic? Or have we finally owned up to the legitimate challenges of community? In *Little Miss Sunshine*, a flawed but authentic community is held up as true family. Life is not a beauty contest; perfection is not the goal. Can we remain committed to each other despite our significant flaws and differences? Genuine disagreements could be the beginning of wisdom (and love). These are the simple, revelatory reminders offered by independent film.

Unity amid Diversity

Greek tragedies were united in time, place, and action. The stories took place in one location, on a single day. They followed a single hero, befallen by a tragic flaw. So how to bring together multiple protagonists on multiple stages? What unites a story without an obvious center? Screenwriter Linda Cowgill discusses the writer's limited options in creating an ensemble film.[10] She notes three ways a filmmaker can retain the unity of enduring drama: First, an ensemble story can be *united by time*. Films may be set in one day, one week, or one era. Second, the ensemble drama is often *united within a particular place*. From jurors in a packed courtroom to customers in a barbershop, tight confines ramp up dramatic and comedic tension. Third, Cowgill suggests ensemble stories can also be *united around a common goal*. A disparate group must come together to accomplish a task, from protecting the village to executing a heist. The group's success depends on pooled talents and shared expertise.

Like the apostle Paul's comparison of the human body to the body of Christ, the ensemble pic depends on the brains, brawn, or bravery of each character to be complete. Paul challenges the burgeoning church to see itself as one body with many parts. Yet each performs a valuable task. The church is an irreducible whole: "Each member belongs to all the others" (Rom. 12:5). Our shared baptism in the Holy Spirit breaks through potential cultural or class barriers between Jews and Greeks, slaves or free (1 Cor. 12:12–13). But Miroslav Volf notes how God affirms rather than erases our differences: "The resurrected Christ . . . is not a spiritual refuge from pluralizing corporeality, a pure spiritual space into which only the undifferentiated sameness of a universal essence is admitted. Rather, baptism into Christ creates a people as the differentiated body of Christ. Bodily inscribed differences are brought together, not removed."[11] In similar ways, the best ensemble films often draw on the human family, with all races and cultures represented. The community is strengthened by their complementary differences. While ministers may be reluctant to compare the gifts of pastor, prophet, or teacher to safecracker, document forger, or getaway driver, most filmgoers appreciate the communal aspects of the well-planned heist film. It demonstrates how much we need one another's unique gifts.

The Bible unfolds like an ensemble drama. It contains way too many characters. Whole chapters are long lists of casts and clans (see the genealogies in the first chapter of Numbers or Matthew). They are hard to keep straight. There's not enough screen time to truly develop each and every person, but the central biblical narratives, like the exodus out of Egypt and the nativity of Jesus, are loaded with interesting supporting characters. Hollywood has gravitated toward them in films from *The Ten Commandments* (1956) to *The Nativity Story* (2006). Yet a close inspection of the biblical text reveals just how scant some character information can be. In the Gospel of Matthew, Mary's husband, Joseph, is described simply as "a righteous man" (Matt. 1:19). His character is revealed through his actions rather than his biography. The choice he makes not to shame Mary, to respond to a dream, and to honor his commitment reveal plenty. The Gospel of Luke introduces Mary's cousin Elizabeth and her husband, Zechariah, to the nativity story yet does not refer to them in later chapters. They arrive on the scene at a historic point in time and their contribution to God's story (while significant) is finished. Perhaps understanding our supporting (rather than starring) role in God's theo-drama can reframe our understanding of church life. We are just one face (more than an extra, less than the lead) in a great cloud of witnesses. Our job is to support the director's vision rather than impose our own notions of what might make a better script. Our prayers and practices must unite with the rousing gospel song. When the saints go marching in, we want to be in that number; part of the parade, a member of the band, not the drum major.

The real, ongoing ensemble dramas in the Bible concern the formation of God's collective people. What distinguishes the church from the ensemble drama is God's search for us. The divine protagonist writes the screenplay, builds the set, and casts the drama.[12] While Abraham, Isaac, and Jacob form the bedrock of Israel, a succession of faithful and evil kings form the backdrop of the story. The monarchs serve as surrogates, representing the rising and falling faithfulness of God's people. The New Testament equivalent to the refining of Israel is the formation of the church. The New Testament tracks Jesus's initial call to "follow me" through the foundation of faith communities in Rome, Corinth, and Galatia. While Jesus explains his radical notions of God's kingdom, his twelve closest confidants bicker and fight. This motley crew succumbs to competitiveness, jealousy, infighting, and backbiting, yet their blown assignments become an occasion for personal growth. Only after their leader leaves the scene do they rise to the occasion. The community rallies in the book of Acts, finally showing the heroism modeled by their Master. False prophets, persecution, infighting, and moral failure challenge their resolve. Paul's inclusive vision of the church causes even more soul searching. But the ragtag team gathered around Jesus finally begins to show their skills. With preaching, teaching, and healing, the early church becomes the band of brothers and sisters Jesus envisioned.

As a historical story, the formation of the church invites a certain amount of nostalgia—a looking back with longing on better days. It is easy to romanticize the choices made by Peter, Paul, James, and John. The ideals set forth by Paul can become a kind of tyranny, an unattainable perfection. The rose-colored tint of more recent ensemble dramas illustrates how rarified we can make our backward glances. Consider the golden glow attached to nostalgia pictures like *American Graffiti* (1973), *Diner* (1982), and *Stand by Me* (1986, IMDb #151). They look back on a bygone era with longing, offering a snapshot of a generation before the sixties divided the American consciousness into competing camps. In each film, a group of close friends are passing into adulthood, moving from innocence to experience. *Return of the Secaucus Seven* (1980) and *The Big Chill* (1983) look back from the other end of the sixties, wondering what happened to the idealism that fueled youthful dreams. In each case, the ensemble drama attempts to boil the shared experiences of an era into a small group of people.

Whether talking about the call of the apostle Paul or the lofty visions of sixties radicals, idealism regarding communal possibilities creates its own problems. When we read Paul's admonitions toward the churches in Corinth, Galatia, and Ephesus without grasping the stark human drama lying behind it, we do the current Christian community a grave disservice. The cast of bickering characters who fought both in Jesus's presence and in Paul's young churches should give us great comfort the next time we encounter debate and dissent within a church setting. We have always been petty and triumphalist and self-serving, even while Jesus was teaching. We cannot cast too golden a glow on our forbearers, trying desperately to recruit the good old days of the early church or the 1950s. The real challenge to community starts in the disillusionment occasioned after the 1960s. Only after our ideals fail can we begin to call ourselves a people. As Bonhoeffer writes in *Life Together*: "The existence of any Christian life together depends on whether it succeeds at the right time in bringing out the ability to distinguish between a human ideal and God's reality, between spiritual and human community. The life or death of a Christian community is determined by whether it achieves sober wisdom on this point as soon as possible."[13] So are we starting to sober up in a time of community crisis? Or will the call to perfection plunge us further into anger, disillusionment, and distance?

The Festering Power of Secrets

What happens when those empowered to protect the community injure and exploit the powerless? Child abuse represents the ultimate in communal break-down. It is a complete perversion of Jesus's call: "Let the little children come to me"

(Matt. 19:14). Documentaries like *Twist of Faith* (2004) and *Deliver Us from Evil* (2006) chronicle the layers of lies that covered up priests' crimes. Roman Catholic dioceses in southern California have settled abuse claims for almost one *billion* dollars. Yet no price can be put on the innocence lost, the damage done behind the cloak of a collar. In *Magnolia* (1999, IMDb #175), Paul Thomas Anderson wrestles with the biblical concept of the sins of the father being visited on their children.[14] The film concludes with a rain of frogs that pours out mercy across Los Angeles. Yet it stops short in the case of Jimmy Gator. Anderson declared that Jimmy's abuse of his daughter Claudia placed him beyond redemption:

> It's the first time when I've been able, at the end of a film, to hate one of my char-acters. There is truly a sense of moral judgment at work with this character. I can't even let him kill himself at the end—he's got to burn. And that's what he deserves. I wanted it to be really clear that with this character, I'm saying "No." No to any kind of forgiveness for him.[15]

Child molesters are the new lepers—the most socially unacceptable of char-acters. In November 2006, California passed Proposition 83, which prohibited sexual offenders from living within two thousand feet of any school or parks where children regularly gather.[16] In the dark drama, *Little Children* (2006), the appearance of a convicted child abuser at a public pool creates a panic. While parents play sexual games with each other, they extend no grace or forgiveness to the child molester.

Mystic River (2003, IMDb #180) starts with a sickening example of child abuse. Three friends play in the street, writing their names in freshly poured concrete. A policeman interrupts them and insists they get in his car. While Jimmy and Sean resist, Dave, the third friend, goes along for the ride. A cop assigned to protect children becomes an unexpected conduit of torture and abuse. In just a few scenes we experience all the isolation and powerlessness that will haunt Dave and the friends who abandoned him. And the lives of all three will bear psychic scars of this random and tragic event. *Mystic River* revolves around the uniting and dividing that accompanies that haunting experience. As the child abuse unleashes an inescapable curse, *Mystic River* descends to the depths of the darkest Shakespearean drama.

Based on Dennis Lehane's novel, *Mystic River* portrays life amid Boston's Irish working class.[17] Jimmy (Sean Penn) grows up to become a kingpin in the com-munity, the neighborhood tough guy who owns a "legitimate" convenience store. Sean (Kevin Bacon) channels his memories into becoming a good cop, righting the wrongs he witnessed as a child. Dave (Tim Robbins) is barely functional as an adult, still haunted by nightmares of an incident from over twenty years ago. When Jimmy's beloved daughter, Katie, is murdered, he unleashes a torrent of rage. Jimmy embarks on a path of vigilante justice, despite Sean's pleas to let the police handle it. While Jimmy tries to solve Katie's murder, Dave engages in his own long-term revenge, seeking out the man who robbed him of his childhood innocence years before.

The sins of the fathers have definitely passed on to their wives and children. When Dave comes home covered in blood, his wife, Celeste (Marcia Gay Harden), takes his secret to an enraged Jimmy, demonstrating a perverted sense of loyalty. As the undisputed neighborhood tough, Jimmy confronts the confused and weakened Dave down by the river. He says, "We bury our sins here, Dave. We wash them clean." Yet Jimmy's bloodletting is sacrifice without redemption; it is revealed as empty and misguided, a rush to judgment. At the conclusion of the film, Jimmy's wife, Annabeth (Laura Linney), offers a chilling speech to justify all kinds of malfeasance. She reveals a calculation that makes Lady MacBeth seem sunny in comparison. Nobody escapes *Mystic River* unscathed. A wave of sin borne thirty years earlier comes home to roost.

The other major character under Clint Eastwood's steady direction is the Mystic River itself. It serves as a silent witness to a community in crisis. The story unfolds on the wrong side of town, or at least the less glamorous side of the river. While the Charles River offers picturesque views, the Mystic River is where the blue-collar community of Charlestown forms tight bonds to survive. What happens when those ties are broken? *Mystic River* deals with the banality and everydayness of evil. It demonstrates how betrayed or frayed friendships can unravel years later. Not standing by one another for even one seemingly insignificant moment can unleash a harvest of hate. In *Mystic River*, secrets and denials fester and grow into a malignant attack that undermines community. Are we our brothers' and sisters' keepers? Absolutely.

Mystic River unfolds in a slow, magisterial pace. Director Clint Eastwood trusts his top-notch cast to deliver the goods. As street tough Jimmy, Sean Penn earned the Oscar for Best Actor. Playing the squirrelly adult Dave, Tim Robbins was honored as Best Supporting Actor. Both performers offer haunting portraits of deep-seated pain. As the third friend, Sean, Kevin Bacon brings a more stoic and maybe even more important distance to the proceedings. While Jimmy becomes a ball of fury and Dave a bag of nerves, Sean seeks to do the right thing as a "good" cop. He shudders at the nightmare that continues to haunt them, saying, "Sometimes I think we are still kids, and all this is just a dream." At the end of the film, Jimmy seems to get away with murder. Sean more than suspects the cause of Dave's death, yet he lets Jimmy off with a mock gun gesture.

What are we to make of this unsettling ending? Movie critic David Sterritt praised, "This kind of quiet ambiguity, avoiding easy answers to complex human conflicts, is all too rare in American movies."[18] Yet to audiences hungry for justice, *Mystic River* arrives as an exercise in frustration. An IMDb user from Japan wondered:

> How can a movie that validates violence, murder, selfishness, lack of responsibility and consequences, be given any awards of any kind???? What kind of society are we, if we can become so dazzled by Clint Eastwood and his chosen actors that we miss the gaping hole where the film's moral center should be???? Or rather than absence, the film's moral center is one that is so amoral that it should be equally impossible to miss.[19]

Mark Greene, a moviegoer, shares the outrage, writing from Hong Kong:

> Call me simple, but . . . it appears to condone the killing of the character played by Tim Robbins in a sort of, "Well, he's been all messed up since he was raped and molested as a kid, anyway, so doing him in does everyone—especially him—a big favor." Excuse me, but I think that's a terribly brutal message to send.[20]

So what kind of message is author Dennis Lehane or filmmaker Clint Eastwood sending? Posting his IMDb review from Sweden, Mattias Petersson recommended a second viewing:

> The trick is not to watch this as a crime-drama. Rather it's a movie about behavioral patterns, about humans. What they are capable of and what dictates their actions. There are huge amounts of sadness and melancholy to this story. Of people unable to break out of the path it seems life has chosen for them.[21]

A viewer in Glasgow, Scotland, goes even further, suggesting, "The message is clear. You should never be surprised by what people are capable of, regardless of how they may appear."[22] Finally, a *Mystic River* fan in Nepal offered this recent assessment:

> The question's not about justice. . . . We should be thankful that many worse things never happen to us. It [the movie] succeeds on creating tragedy and importing fate into American film, a trait which has been lacking, given the ethos of self-creation, and free will. Here, instead, the gods intervene, to give up the killer, to punish a man [Robbins as Dave] that was more worthy of heaven, and perhaps this was the happy end, to have his sin absolved by the Mystic.[23]

Those beyond our American shores seem best at pointing out the problems of American independence and self-creation. The three boys should have stuck together and defended each other against abuse. But rather than uniting as neighbors, Jimmy and Sean abandon Dave. He is beaten and robbed of his childhood. Do Sean and Jimmy dress his wounds? No. Instead Dave becomes a sacrificial lamb, slaughtered by the sins of others.

Mystic River demonstrates how minor choices have major consequences. By choosing to live as a community in denial, the tight-knit people of Charlestown become a murderous den of thieves. Perhaps Jimmy says it best: "Ever think how one little choice can change a person's life?" *Mystic River* is a study of where wrong choices lead. Community begins with acknowledging our sin, confessing our shortcomings, admitting our faults.

Preparing for Disappointment

I appreciate the high standards for Christian community set by early church leaders. Peter calls us "a chosen people, a royal priesthood, a holy nation" (1 Pet. 2:9). Paul identifies us as "Christ's ambassadors" (2 Cor. 5:20) and "God's workmanship, created in Christ Jesus to do good works" (Eph. 2:10). The call to be a peculiar people distinguished by acts of service and sacrifice compels me.[24] In an era of conformity, the Christian community can provide a compelling alternative, living as "resident aliens" distinct from this world.[25] So why have we recently been known for hypocrisy and cover-up?

The failings of high-profile evangelicals like Ted Haggard arose when he cut himself off from community and accountability. He tried to go it alone. Or at least he considered his needs as separate from his congregation. Communities united around perfection rather than sin may actually foster situations like Haggard's moral crisis. Perhaps we need to reread Jesus's call to "be ye perfect" (see Matt. 5:48) as a profound and comedic overstatement, a dare to stop taking up an impossible task. Does Jesus laugh (or cry) at our fruitless efforts to still fulfill the full letter of the law? When evangelical leaders cannot find safe people with whom to share their struggles, then perhaps we need to write a new social contract. Do we need to recover the freeing power of confession? Perhaps we can begin by confessing our ongoing perfectionism.

Yet in the Catholic community, where confession remains a core value, the brotherhood of priests chose to cover up sin rather than pursue genuine restoration. They sided with perpetrators rather than victims. Surely Jesus weeps for them all. But by reassigning priests known to have a penchant for sexual molestation, the archbishops of Boston and Los Angeles exposed hundreds more to abuse and pain. They eventually cost their beloved church millions of dollars in settlements.[26] Archdioceses in Tucson; Portland; Spokane; and Davenport, Iowa, have declared bankruptcy.[27] Such dire financial straits were preceded by a disturbing spiritual bankruptcy. The human cost will never be known.

The conspiracy of evil plaguing the Catholic Church arose from a culture of denial. Priests put institutional concerns ahead of the parishioners they sought to serve. *Mystic River* offers an opportunity to enter into theological dialogue, to unmask (or reveal) our shortcomings. As in *Mystic River*, too many archdioceses became a community agreeing to look the other way. Such blatant disregard for the truth added even more insult to the injuries of those molested. The millions of dollars awarded to victims cannot restore the innocence or faith lost. Neither the Protestant model of perfectionism nor the Catholic example of corporate blinders is to be celebrated. Should despair rule the day? What does a genuine, transforming community look like? A cautionary tale like *Mystic River* prompts us to reflect, to recover overlooked revelations from God.

In 2 Corinthians 4:2, the apostle Paul says, "We have renounced the shameful things that one hides; we refuse to practice the cunning or to falsify God's word; but by the open statement of the truth we commend ourselves to the conscience of everyone in the sight of God" (RSV). Miroslav Volf takes Paul's statement as an opportunity to recover the relationship between facts and actions, words and deeds. The biblical testimony makes it clear that truth sustains a community, while deception destroys it. Volf puts it this way: "There can be no truth between people without the will to embrace the other. . . . Inversely, the will to embrace cannot be sustained and will not result in an actual embrace if truth does not reign."[28] But our understanding of truth telling must be grounded in our lived reality.

Dietrich Bonhoeffer's *Life Together* offers a strong corrective to either the idealized or institutionalized version of community: "Every human wish dream that is injected into the Christian community is a hindrance to genuine community and must be banished if genuine community is to survive. He who loves his dream of a community more than the Christian community itself becomes a destroyer of the latter, even though his personal intentions may be ever so honest and earnest and sacrificial."[29] Well-meaning preachers may have destroyed their ministry by trying to insulate it from their personal sin. Well-intentioned bishops and priests, dedicated to protecting the bride of Christ, sullied the Catholic Church by worshiping an ideal rather than administering a broken reality. Yet Bonhoeffer does not let disillusionment devolve into defeat. Authentic community can begin only when we abandon our idealized assumptions: "The sooner this shock of disillusionment comes to an individual and to a community the better for both. A community which cannot bear and cannot survive such a crisis, which insists upon keeping its illusion when it should be shattered, permanently loses in that moment the promise of Christian community."[30] The real test occurs when John Wayne rides into the sunset, when the people have to fend for themselves without a charismatic leader. Will the community bond together or collapse into chaos?

The Christian community has lived with the tension, tending to withdraw from the world in times of crisis. Yet the missional moment in the postmodern world suggests we must embrace that which threatens us. Feeling attacked by pluralism, relativism, and postmodernism, some will call us to circle the wagons, to retreat to safety with people we assume we can trust. Some Christian leaders will challenge us to reach out to deeper waters, inviting others onto the raft even as we worry about being swamped. What vision of church and community will prosper in our emerging world? Probably whichever one proceeds with the firmest grasp on reality. Bonhoeffer's call is to self-awareness, to acknowledge our limitations as the ground of Christian being. The family united in brokenness stands the best chance of survival.

Community in Crisis: The City of the Angels

In 1991 I moved to Los Angeles to work on my Master of Divinity degree at Fuller Theological Seminary. My wife and I had just gotten married, and we set up our first apartment in Pasadena, just north of the Fuller campus. We took advantage of the sunny skies, embarking on all kinds of tourist excursions to the beaches, mountains, and Hollywood. We also ventured into the amazing array of subcultures populating Los Angeles. We ate sushi in Little Tokyo, dim sum in Chinatown, and *tortas* in East Los Angeles. We went to Artesia for Indian curry and Westminster for a taste of Little Saigon. How encouraging to see Koreatown spring up alongside South Central, to find Armenians in Glendale next to Filipinos in Eagle Rock. It was a blissful honeymoon, exactly the kind of year off recommended in the Old Testament for newlyweds. Deuteronomy 24:5 insists, "If a man has recently married, he must not be sent to war or have any other duty laid on him. For one year he is to be free to stay at home and bring happiness to the wife he has married."

Back in North Carolina I had been engaged in a form of war, working with inner-city teens through urban Young Life. Few things were as daunting as restoring hope to teens who honestly did not expect to live past age twenty. We partnered with Progressive Baptist Church, a local congregation led by Reverend Charles Mack, offering an after-school tutoring program right across the street from a public housing project. Despite the best efforts of numerous volunteers, we buried far too many young men in Charlotte, cut down before their lives and potential blossomed. We came to Southern California looking for a respite from urban warfare.

When we smelled smoke outside our Pasadena apartment on April 29, 1992, we suspected brush fires in the San Gabriel Mountains. But an overt war had returned to urban America, in the wake of the not-guilty verdict for police officers who pummeled Rodney King. The black community in South Los Angeles erupted with protest in the form of fires, robbery, and unrest. The city burned for three days. Even in the suburbs of Pasadena, the scent of civic uproar demanded a response. Four days after the uprising began, some semblance of calm returned. On Saturday, May 2, my wife and I headed toward downtown Los Angeles, eager to help clean-up efforts. We entered a war zone, responding to a minister's invitation to start shoveling the shattered glass and smoldering debris.

Many speculated on what went wrong. Soul-searching newspaper editorials revealed years of resentment in the black community going back to the Watts Riots of 1965. Many thought allegations of police brutality sanctioned by Police Chief Daryl Gates had finally caught up to the Los Angeles Police Department. The videotape of officers beating Rodney King told a clear story in the court of public opinion. But when justice failed to serve Rodney King, an already frayed social fabric snapped.

Perhaps much of the violence and loss of life could have been avoided had we heeded the prescient films that emerged prior to the Rodney King beating. Spike Lee challenged viewers to *Do the Right Thing* (1989) on a simmering day in Bedford-Stuyvesant. It is one of the most complex and complete portraits of race relations ever captured on film. Spike Lee's best film was inspired by a real incident in 1986, in which a young black man was chased into oncoming traffic by a gang of ten white men in Howard Beach, New York. The timeliness of *Do the Right Thing* was sadly confirmed when another group of whites armed with baseball bats and guns murdered an innocent Yusef Hawkins in Brooklyn's Bensonhurst neighborhood in August 1989. In both cases, the white killers were sentenced to prison time, preserving a sense of justice in New York courts (and relative peace in the neighborhoods).

As the rebuilding began after the uprising in Los Angeles, a coalition gathered by Fuller Seminary worked to find common ground in our splintered community. While we could not agree about the roots of the rebellion or the path to reconciliation, we could unite around our shared stories of Los Angeles captured in the movies. The inaugural City of the Angels Film Fest was held at the Directors Guild in October 1994.[31] It was offered as a gift to the city, a place to discuss where we've been and where we are headed. Films screened ranged from backward glances like *Chinatown* (1974, IMDb #43) to dystopian futures like *Blade Runner* (1982, IMDb #95). Each screening was followed by a panel discussion, focused not only on the film, but also on its implications for our city. *Grand Canyon* (1991) opened with a poignant speech from a noble truck driver: "This ain't the way it's supposed to be . . . everything's supposed to be different than what it is here."[32] We all nodded in agreement with such a heartbreaking and accurate assessment. Fifteen years later, resentments in Los Angeles resurfaced in *Crash*.

A Crash Course in Race Relations

As drugs were to *Traffic* (2000) (or oil to *Syriana* [2005], or human trafficking to *Trade* [2007]), so racism is to *Crash* (2005). It explores a complex, multilayered problem through interlocking stories and characters. As a modestly budgeted independent film, it arrived without much fanfare. This ferocious ensemble film snuck up on viewers (and Academy Award voters) in the summer of 2005. While *Do the Right Thing* did a better job wrestling with race and *Magnolia* offered a more complex portrait of Los Angeles, *Crash* exceeded all three of them in unexpected Oscar acclaim. It became the little social injustice film that could.

Paul Haggis's directorial debut contains memorable moments filled with both outrage and healing. It shows the reasons for white fear, as a district attorney and his wife are carjacked. This opening confrontation serves as Haggis's own starting point, the impetus behind the plot. He said, "There was an instance in 1991 in which my car was jacked and I just kept wondering about these two kids who'd stuck a gun in my face and stolen my car." The incident occurred near his home, and so he and his wife had the locks changed that evening. As a writer, Haggis's mind swam with possibilities. "I said to myself, 'What if the guy changing the locks was Hispanic, with gang tattoos and baggy pants?' How would I have felt about that?"[33] Ten years after that traumatic event (and two months after 9/11), Haggis began writing the script with Bobby Moresco. With the perspective of

Coming face-to-face with our racism in Paul Haggis's Oscar-winning film *Crash*. © 2004 by Lions Gate Films.

time and place (Haggis is a native of Canada), Haggis crafted his personal brush with violence into a portrait of a raging Los Angeles circa 2005.

Thankfully, Haggis doesn't deal exclusively with white fear. *Crash* is a mini United Nations where *everyone* has racist tendencies. *Crash* reveals the injustices of being stopped for DWB—"driving while black." The racist actions of LAPD cops like Officer John Ryan (Matt Dillon) snap viewers back to the days of Daryl Gates's police force. *Crash* also takes on the subtle but significant racism inherent in television broadcasting, where stereotypes serve as a shortcut to easy laughs. We understand why rage builds in an otherwise successful TV producer (Terrence Howard). Topping all the issues pertinent to Los Angeles is a subplot rooted in post-9/11 fears. A Persian father struggles to protect his family and his livelihood in a world prejudiced against Arabs. He nearly commits a deadly snap judgment. Racism doesn't bubble beneath the surface in *Crash*; it is the surface, the substance, the animus behind everyone's thoughts and actions.

As the animosity ratchets up, so does the need for redemption. An IMDb user from California named Rai recalls, "I could literally feel my rage at some of the characters forming to a fever pitch. The fear and hatred I was confronting wasn't just on the screen, but in the pit of my stomach. And in one absolutely brilliant moment I was literally sobbing at the expectation of horror unfolding, only to be cathartically released in a most unexpected way."[34] A car crash brings a racist cop (Matt Dillon) and his victim (Thandie Newton) face-to-face in the most intimate and inescapable way. Viewers come to understand how the failure of the social system to care for an elderly white man can breed his policeman son's hatred of all things black. Those who claim to be above the fray are revealed as just as quick tempered and capable of deceit. Who pulls the trigger too quickly? The "good" cop played by Ryan Phillippe. Who saves the suburban housewife (Sandra Bullock) from her misery? Her Latino maid becomes a Good Samaritan. Great needs are met by great ironies. By the end of *Crash*, the stereotypes we've formed of the characters must now be reversed.

Yet despite lovely individual moments, *Crash* feels too simplistic and too convenient. It reduces people to their racism. When black youths (Ludacris and Larenz Tate) complain about being profiled by restaurateurs, not only do they admit to being poor tippers, but they immediately pull out guns to commit a carjacking. Paul Haggis makes sure voters get *the point* by offering no time and no distance between contradictory statements and practices. Despite plenty of praise from IMDb users, others called *Crash* "trash"[35] and found it "contrived, manipulative, preachy, and simpleminded," referring to it as "Racism for Dummies."[36] It often condescends toward the audience, underlining things with the subtlety of a sledgehammer (and opening itself to charges of stereotyping and racism itself). While overly dependent on coincidence and drawn way too broadly, *Crash*'s primary contribution may be in simply fueling an important conversation.

Crash's most memorable scenes argue for a providential interconnectivity; we are never alone in our aloneness. When the Persian shopkeeper seeks revenge, a cloak of protection saves a young locksmith (Michael Pena) and his daughter. It could be perceived as a miracle of divine intervention, but ultimately, we are shown the wisdom of loading blanks into our weapons. Next time we respond too quickly or too heatedly, we may save more than our own lives by firing blanks rather than bullets. While the film announces car crashes as the central metaphor (and in the dramatic life-saving, soul-saving action of the most racist cop), the subtext bringing the stories together is Christmas. A cool-headed cop (Ryan Phillippe) provides a frustrated husband (Terrence Howard) with a way out of his self-created mess against a backdrop of Christmas decorations. A divine grace has protected both of them from pulling triggers and unraveling their lives. Even in Los Angeles, the driest urban center in America, a white

Christmas proves possible. The snowflakes are ambiguous, perhaps connected more to the embers of a burning car than a mercy falling from the sky.

Director Paul Haggis backs off any overt social or religious interpretations of *Crash*. Asked if there was a supernatural element in the film, like the cloak, he responded, "I wanted to tease people with that but I don't think so. There are elements of fate—it's like when I get too big for my boots and the gods come along and smack me upside the head." The revelations in *Crash* are decidedly general, never connected to a particular deity. Haggis admits some revelatory intention to test the audience: "We really believe we know who we are but we don't—not until we're tested. That's what I was exploring." He wants to provoke a response, but he backs off any truth claims. Haggis concludes, "I'm actually not trying to say anything. I don't think it's our place to say anything. My job is to ask questions and make films but I like to write about things I don't have the answers for. With *Crash*, I didn't have the answers to any of these questions."[37] Given the overt (and important) nature of the theme, Haggis's response seems remarkably unenlightening.

So where do we find answers? Can film provide more than a disturbance to our psyche? Can the Spirit work through our fumblings in the dark? Absolutely! What do the demands of community require? Haggis seems to have violated the spirit of community by ripping a scab off a historical event without offering a healing balm. Instead of dressing the wound, he offers merely window dressing. The biblical prophet Jeremiah asked for a healing balm for his people: "Is there no balm in Gilead? Is there no physician there? Why then is there no healing for the wound of my people?" (Jer. 8:22). Jesus's parables may have provoked questions in his audience, but he didn't tell them as mere riddles. Christ promoted genuine healing and unity, modeled in his relationship to the Father. In the Gospel of John he offered a prayer: "I have given them the glory that you gave me, that they may be one as we are one: I in them and you in me." Diversity need not divide us. Jesus's disciples have a profound calling to overcome differences of race, class, and gender. The Son asks the Father, "May they be brought to complete unity to let the world know that you sent me and have loved them even as you have loved me" (John 17:22–23).

Community in Crisis: Postcommunist Europe and Rwanda

With the fall of the Berlin Wall in 1989, the authoritarian yoke of communism was removed. Freedom reigned in the Czech Republic, in Russia, in a unified

Germany. Hope, promise, and optimism washed over Eastern Europe. Croatians, Slovenians, and Serbians dreamed of independence. Yet the collapse of the central state also awakened new uncertainties. The break up of Yugoslavia unleashed long simmering ethnic and religious tensions. New tribalism and horrific barbarism resulted. Croatian theologian Miroslav Volf locates much of the conflict in the deadly "politics of purity." Whenever we start blaming our problems on "the other," war and genocide are soon to follow. Just as Nazi Germany dreamed of pure Aryan blood, Serbians sought to cleanse their land of all "non-Serbian intruders." Volf summarizes the insidious rationale for genocide: "The origin and the goal, the inside and the outside, everything must be pure: plurality and heterogeneity must give way to homogeneity and unity. One people, one culture, one language, one book, one goal; what does not fall under this all-encompassing 'one' is ambivalent, polluting, and dangerous."[38] Whether such "noble goals" are enforced by totalitarian regimes or renegade armies, their fruits are horrific. Balkanization embodies the worst side of community: the use of our solidarity to take on a demonized "them."[39]

In April 1994, the politics of purity resulted in the senseless deaths of eight hundred thousand Rwandans. The historic roots of the conflict lay in Belgian colonists dividing and conquering Rwanda. To subjugate the Africans, the Belgians introduced the concept of "the other." They divided Rwandans into two tribes, Hutus and Tutsis. The roots of the Rwandan genocide were sown in a game of blame. Belgians placed Tutsis in an arbitrary position of power over the Hutus. When the Belgians left, the Hutus began pointing to the Tutsis as the source of their problems. Hutu generals offered a bloodthirsty call to stamp out the Tutsis like cockroaches. The assumptions were the same as those in the Balkans—"Once we remove them, then we will have peace and prosperity."

Yet Volf points out how Jesus located the problem of sin within, rather than outside, us. In Mark 7:15, Jesus cuts through our desire to blame the other for our failings. There is nothing outside us that can defile us. A misplaced hunger for spiritual purity can become a dangerous, religiously justified, political pogrom.

Hotel Rwanda (IMDb #59) presents a haunting, firsthand biography about this contemporary travesty. Yet it distributes the blame for genocide across the spectrum. It asks us all to consider God's question to Cain, "Where is your brother?" As Abel's blood cried to God from the ground, the bodies strewn across Rwanda demand a response.

While Americans were arguing about patients' right to die (see the next chapter), an African nation was engaged in genocide that was met with Western indifference. How can we pour so much energy into debates about dying *we can't agree on* while ignoring countless deaths in Rwanda that we unanimously agree *should have* and *could have been avoided*? *Hotel Rwanda* shames us (after the fact) into putting our ethics into action. It is a simple, direct, and uncontestable plea for saving lives through courageous acts.

Hotel Rwanda introduces us to the creative heroism of Paul Rusesabagina (Don Cheadle). As manager of a luxury hotel in the Rwandan capital of Kigali, Rusesabagina has perfected the art of hospitality. He woos guests and curries favors from government officials with lobster, Scotch, and Cuban cigars. Paul stays out of politics, committing himself to *style*. When his gardener is arrested, Paul's wife, Tatiana (Sophie Okonedo), insists, "We must do something." Paul retorts, "He's not family. Family is all that matters." Hear the echoes of Cain's abdication of responsibility for Abel: "Am I my brother's keeper?" Yet when the Rwandan president's plane is shot down under mysterious circumstances, the nation plunges into a ghoulish civil war. Long-standing hatred between the rival Hutu and Tutsi tribes is unleashed. As the radio reports bark, "Cut the tall trees," the bloodthirsty Hutu militia (the Interahamwe) slices unsuspecting Tutsis into pieces. Suddenly, Paul Rusesabagina has more family, in more need, than he ever imagined.

As with Oskar Schindler in *Schindler's List* (1993, IMDb #7), Rusesabagina becomes an unlikely hero, buying the freedom of friends and relatives, making room for refugees in the Hotel Mille Collines. He plays games with names, numbers, passports, and guest lists in an effort to thwart the Hutu generals. Like Schindler, he also resorts to bribery to save lives, violating one ethical principle for a much greater good. As in the maddening comedy *No Man's Land* (2004), the United Nations adopts the position of peacekeepers rather than peacemakers. They honestly don't want to get involved in this prickly situation. Yet Paul acts swiftly, converting his luxury hotel into a safe house for refugees escorted by UN Colonel Oliver (Nick Nolte). When French and Belgian soldiers arrive, the Rwandans holed up in the hotel think they are being rescued from the slaughter. Colonel Oliver delivers the haunting news that the army has only arrived to evacuate Westerners. Oliver tells Paul a brutal truth: "The West, all the super-powers . . . they think you're dirt. They think you're dumb. You're worthless." While Catholic priests and nuns protest such indifference, Rusesabagina and a host of Rwandan children are left to fend for themselves. Racism, both within and without, undoes Rwanda.

Hotel Rwanda uncovers the lip service we pay to equal rights and justice. It demonstrates in dramatic fashion how politics trumps principles. The script, initiated by Keir Pearson and polished by director Terry George, cribs from newsreel documentation of the events of April 1994. It includes US State Department spokesperson Christine Shelly's careful choice of words to describe the conflict as just "*acts* of genocide." The United States and the international community were able to distance themselves ever so slightly from the civil war by such word games. Yet the haunting question remains, "How many acts of genocide does it take to make genocide?" Are we our brothers' and sisters' keepers? It is estimated that 800,000 people were murdered in one hundred days.[40] Why didn't President Clinton or the United Nations intervene?

In October 1993, eighteen US soldiers had been killed in Somalia. (That botched mission became the riveting war movie *Black Hawk Down* [2001].) When the Rwandan crisis arose six months later, the Clinton administration wasn't willing to risk more US lives (or political capital) on Rwanda. How could Americans afford such indifference? The people clinging to life in the Hotel Mille Collines didn't vote in US elections. They were distant (and therefore ignorable) neighbors. Senate Minority Leader Bob Dole did not offer any compassionate conservatism either. He told *Face the Nation*, "The Americans are out, and as far as I'm concerned, that ought to be the end of it." *Hotel Rwanda* challenges such myopia, offering parallels to the Good Samaritan. As Paul instructs the refugees to call their influential friends, "We must shame them into sending help."

Hotel Rwanda also exposes the false roots of our prejudices. The seeds of Rwanda's civil war were planted by Belgian conquerors. In an effort to consolidate their power, colonial Belgium separated Rwanda into two tribes. Ethnic identity cards were introduced in 1926.[41] In *Hotel Rwanda*, a journalist recounts the process: "They picked people . . . those with thinner noses, lighter skin . . . the Belgians used the Tutsis to run the country. Then, when they left, they left the power to the Hutus. And of course, the Hutus took revenge on the elite Tutsis for years of repression." Yet *Hotel Rwanda* points out how arbitrary such distinctions by appearances have become. Paul and his wife, Tatiana, come from different tribes; each represents *the other*. But their children represent the blending of the tribes, extending the apostle Paul's bold claim that in Christ, "There is neither Jew nor Greek, slave nor free, male nor female," Hutu nor Tutsi (Gal. 3:28; Col. 3:11). By the end of the film, Rusesabagina has expanded our definition of global family, answering the question, "Where is my brother?" He lives today in Belgium, with his wife, four children, and two orphaned nieces they adopted.

This small film made an unexpected impression, garnering Academy Award nominations for acting and screenwriting (although it was overlooked for Best Picture). Perhaps *Hotel Rwanda*'s prime place on the IMDb's list (#59) offers some

Learning to live with the other. A Hutu and a Tutsi united by marriage in *Hotel Rwanda*. © 2004 by Lions Gate Films and United Artists.

consolation to the cast and crew. *Hotel Rwanda* began as a passionate, personal project for aspiring screenwriter Keir Pearson. Pearson heard about the heroism of Paul Rusesabagina in 1999, just as he finished film school at New York University. After a year of research, Pearson traveled to Rwanda to meet Paul and see the grave sites of thousands of victims. When Pearson returned home to write the script, he felt "an overwhelming responsibility toward the survivors I had met, especially Paul."[42] Irish director Terry George had also been intrigued by modern Africa for some time. He noted, "The sheer scale of that continent's suffering—its poverty, wealth, beauty, and horror—moved and excited me like no other topic." Following his tour of the mass burial sites, George wrote through tear-stained eyes, "I promise to tell the story of the genocide to the world."[43] George fulfilled his vow, acting on his commitments with financial sacrifice and risk. Lead actor Don Cheadle got involved because "Rwanda was an incredibly under-reported, under-noticed event in the world's history. This is a great example of how fear caught up with prejudice. Human beings in the proper setting will do things that are unimaginable."[44] Paul Rusesabagina resisted attempts to canonize him: "What I did was normal. . . . When did the day arrive when not to kill is considered heroic? All I did was carry out my duties and responsibilities."

Duties and *responsibilities* are basic words with huge implications. *Hotel Rwanda* ties together several strands of this broad survey of recent movies and their meaning. It stresses the importance of understanding history. It celebrates heroism and serves as a living memorial, challenging us to "never forget." It demonstrates how horribly a community, fueled by prejudice, can behave. It posits an ethical dilemma. Yet it does all this in a straightforward fashion. No camera tricks, no playing with time, no self-reflexivity. Does that make it a throwback to an earlier era of humane dramas—solid stories told in a respectful manner? Perhaps *Hotel Rwanda* anticipates a new sincerity, a hunger for unadorned authenticity and genuine community. In a confusing era, the Spirit can still speak through "old-fashioned" films.

The Real Test

As the filmmakers responded to Paul's compelling story by taking action, so viewers seem to be genuinely moved by *Hotel Rwanda* to initiate change. On the IMDb, ksapmorgan admits: "After watching this movie last night in the privacy of my own home, I was left sorry and embarrassed. Embarrassed by the fact that in 1994 I was well old enough to have paid more attention to events going on in the world around me. . . . I am so glad I saw this movie so that now I personally can be more aware of similar tragedies going on in the world around me today!"[45] Rakesh Thind writes from England, "Please see this and let it inspire you as it did me—to try to cultivate selfless actions."[46] Posting as a "resident of Planet Earth," Anhedonia says, "I would like to believe that we learn from history and the more powerful western nations will always come to the aid of oppressed people everywhere. But we're doing little in Darfur."[47]

Yet not everyone was enamored by the story. Some found its telescoping of the facts as too much "Hollywoodization" and recommended the harrowing documentary about UN commander Romeo Dallaire, *Shake Hands with the Devil* (2004), as a more compelling alternative.[48] Others critiqued *Hotel Rwanda*'s screenplay as obvious. Attila the Pooh from Ireland found, "There are no rounded characters, only mouthpieces of the humanitarian message that the writers are trying to convey."[49]

While grateful his story has been told, Rusesabagina questions how many lessons have really been learned. The *general revelations* available in *Hotel Rwanda* haven't necessarily resulted in transformed lives. He says, "We Rwandans still refuse to call evil by its name. It is always to do with 'the other.' The Hutus will tell you a history that favors their side; the Tutsi do the same. To me, we are all guilty. . . . We need to sit around a table together—Hutus and Tutsi—and negotiate the future."[50] Community begins in accepting responsibility (whether for Catholic priests who molested children, Hutus who murdered Tutsis, or those who failed to intervene in either situation). The parable of the Good Samaritan (Luke 10:25–37) suggests that indifferent spectatorship is not an option. Director Terry George concludes, "When we start realizing that it's worthwhile to go in and rescue people, to stop these sorts of humanitarian crises going on, then I think the world will be a much better place."[51] The real test of a film's lasting impact occurs after the story has been told. What happens when the cinematic spotlight no longer shines on Rwanda?

A decade after the genocide, Rwanda has rallied behind a new president, Paul Kagame. The countless number of war crimes overwhelmed their court system, but local people's courts, called *gacaca*, have arisen to mete out justice. The tribal councils weigh the contrition of the criminals; those demonstrating regret via observable actions have been met with mercy. Rick and Kay Warren of Saddleback Church in Lake Forest, California, have redirected the spotlight focused on their celebrity toward Rwanda. Warren considers the success of his best-selling book *The Purpose-Driven Life* (2002) as a prelude to his true calling—tackling the debilitating giants of spiritual lostness, corrupt leadership, global poverty, illiteracy, and AIDS. Rwanda has become the focal point for Saddleback's P.E.A.C.E. plan.[52] It challenges churches in the affluent West to partner with churches in the impoverished two-thirds world for mutual benefit. Warren believes that if the first Protestant Reformation was about creeds, the next Reformation will be driven by deeds. Communities must be united by faith in action (see James 2:14–26).

Opportunities to respond to crises will not cease. As the genocide in Rwanda subsided, civil wars expanded in Sierra Leone and Uganda. Children in northern Uganda were dragged into war by the misnamed "Lord's Resistance Army." Grassroots documentaries like *Invisible Children* (2006) and *War/Dance* (2007) have raised awareness and funds for the "night commuters" in Uganda still searching for a safe place to sleep. A decade after Rwanda erupted in violence, fighting broke out in the Darfur region of Sudan between the Islamic fundamentalist militia Janjaweed and Black Muslim farmers. The human rights abuses are chronicled in two feature documentaries from 2007, *The Devil Came on Horseback* and *Darfur Now*. It is estimated that two hundred thousand people have been killed and 2.5 million refugees displaced since 2003. Yet it took the United Nations three years to develop a peacekeeping force in the region, which the Sudanese government has blocked. Don Cheadle joined a coalition of celebrities who traveled to the region, bringing the spotlight of the international press with them. Cheadle's simple pledge: "Not on our watch."[53] The fight to stop the fighting continues.

Community in Crisis: September 11, 2001

While we may dismiss these crises as "local conflicts" outside our sphere of influence, the shocking realities of geopolitical terror hit home on September 11, 2001. Words can barely contain the horror that accompanied the collapse of the World Trade Center. *United 93* (2006) is equally tough to discuss with any manner of objectivity or dispassion. Yet director Paul Greengrass pulled off a cinematic miracle, making *United 93* more personal than political. It is a straightforward account of how events unfolded within the doomed (and largely forgotten) flight. As destruction at the Pentagon was overwhelmed by images from Ground Zero in New York City, so Flight 93's plunge into a Pennsylvania cornfield has been overshadowed by more dramatic footage elsewhere.

In *United 93*, the action rotates between the plane, NORAD, air traffic control, and the FAA. Greengrass cast real pilots and controllers alongside his unknown cast, enabling the audience to focus on the characters and their plight. Their relative anonymity places the emphasis on their collective response rather than individual heroism. There are no lone rangers on flight 93. They forge a plan *together*, summoning strength in *unity*. *Film Comment*'s Gavin Smith rightly salutes the filmmakers' remarkable restraint, calling *United 93* "an anti-spectacle."[54] Greengrass extends empathy to both the victims and the hijackers.

The handheld camera work keeps the audience off balance and gives *United 93* an intense documentary feel. The editing, performances, and music create considerable suspense despite the foregone outcome.[55] His faith in both the actors and the audience results in the rarest of cinematic experiences—genuine catharsis. On the IMDb, pwhitmar said, "When this film was over a silence hung over the theater unlike any I had ever heard. My eyes watered as I left the hall, and I said a quick prayer as I exited; simply in honor of all the people who died on September 11th."[56] Saraemiller1 describes a similar experience at a screening in Texas:

> When it ended, I've never seen a more still theater. You could hear people breathing as they pulled themselves together. This is something that happened to our nation, and while it shouldn't take a movie to make people remember, maybe it does. Maybe we have forgotten or chosen to ignore what happened that day, falling to politics and quick to accuse people who didn't prevent it. Maybe we are against this movie because it makes us uncomfortable, as all meaningful things should. Who knows? Not I.[57]

One of the more illuminating sequences juxtaposes prayers uttered on both sides, in English and in Arabic. What could have been a flag-raising battle cry, "Let's roll," instead becomes an understated tribute to everyday heroes. The passengers rally and sacrifice their lives for the sake of others. Their uphill climb toward the cockpit involves grit and determination equal to any war scene ever staged. The passengers' courage comes from connecting themselves to a larger story: the targets on the ground. Flight 93 missed its target because a brave and otherwise anonymous community stepped up to save lives.

United 93 serves as a stirring memorial to people who are already too easily overlooked. We remember the twin towers that collapsed but forget the blood crying out from a field in Pennsylvania. Too many Americans fail to recall that bombs in London and Madrid also brought down innocent bystanders. While we neglect to count the deaths of Iraqi civilians in the war on terror, God hears the blood crying from the desert sand. *United 93* dignifies the deaths of common, everyday people, putting a name and a face to each fragile, fallen life. IMDb user Spydamang describes his revelatory encounter: "Paul Greengrass's 'United 93' is not only the most powerful and real film I've ever seen, it's one that will stick with me for an eternity. I think it should be a requirement that every person should watch this film, because it will change your outlook on life, much like *Schindler's List* should have done."[58] Isn't that the power and purpose of the most enduring art? Yet many potential filmgoers avoided the film. Perhaps the events of 9/11 still felt too close; we weren't ready to process so much pain. *United 93* serves as a fitting memorial whenever we are ready to address such a haunting event. The filmmakers have guaranteed that the lives lost on the fourth, "forgotten" flight of September 11, 2001, will be remembered. Community sometimes requires sacrificial actions, even unto death.

Wrestling the Cowboy Myth to the Ground

What do these four films about communities in crisis suggest? How do we view *the other*? What kind of responsibility do we have when *others* suffer?

The United States of America was built on the cowboy myth. Historians have traced our self-reliance, independence, and sense of manifest destiny to our understanding of the frontier as a wilderness to be tamed.[59] From Teddy Roosevelt to John F. Kennedy, presidents have spoken of new frontiers. The tough talk and cowboy imagery of Ronald Reagan and George W. Bush on their ranches created fans in America and alienation in Europe and beyond.[60] The phrase "cowboy up" came to symbolize more than just shaking off the dust after a rough rodeo ride. After getting knocked down on September 11, 2001, Americans sang, "When the goin' gets tough . . . Boy you better cowboy up." But the United States' continuing interest in new lands and boundless frontiers has led to the darker side of the cowboy myth—economic expansion and global intervention (which not all of our neighbors have appreciated). We've been greeted as liberators and derided as infidels. Like a John Wayne character, we've acted heroically (and unilaterally), striding into conflicts without much backup. Like a Clint Eastwood character, we've also shot first and explained afterward.

What works in westerns doesn't always translate into enduring foreign policy. Our foreign policy administrators use the term *collateral damage* to marginalize those who die via our violence. Yet in an increasingly wired world, such enlightened self-interest seems shortsighted. We're slowly coming to see ourselves as part of a region (from North America to the Americas). While the United States may view itself as the world's police officer (an ennobled cowboy), those on the receiving end of our intentions see our behavior as aggressive and imperial (more like a corrupt sheriff). I'll grant to our prayerful leaders how difficult it is to know when to intervene and when to withdraw. But what is our calling as people of faith? Where should our primary citizenship reside? Have we acted "alone on the range" when Christ calls us to pledge allegiance to his kingdom?

We have ample reasons to ride solo. Global cooperation takes time. It can be unpredictable and doesn't always work out as planned. Visions of international unity have often failed to deliver on their promises. The League of Nations, founded in the wake of World War I, could not keep the Axis forces of Nazi Germany and Fascist Italy at bay. The United Nations arose from the ashes of World War II. While a true third world war has yet to materialize, the UN's peacekeeping forces have been viewed with suspicion from all sides. While some consider the United Nations a sign of the apocalypse, others support its ongoing work to secure human rights around the globe. Its Millennium Development Goals have served as a tangible benchmark for waging a global war on poverty (irrespective of borders) through 2015. Yet as the ensemble dramas discussed in this chapter show, the limited success of United Nations' policy suggests that our idealized visions of a global community may need reassessment. A rosy "brotherhood of man" looks just as elusive as the lone cowboy riding the range.

In times of crisis, we are all confronted with the ethical choices faced by Paul Rusesabagina in *Hotel Rwanda*. He presents a different kind of cowboy. In the face of international cowardice and indifference, he rose to the occasion, not with a gun, but with the gift of diplomacy. He charmed those who sought to murder his countrymen and women. Besieged by racism and violence, he formed a makeshift community, united in their suffering.

Jürgen Moltmann associates such solidarity with Christ on the cross. In that sacrificial act, Christ identifies God with the victims of violence and the victims with God "so that they are put under God's protection and with him are given the rights of which they have been deprived."[61] The passengers on *United 93* rally in a similar fashion, choosing to go down with the plane for the sake of others. *Hotel Rwanda* demonstrates that the best of community can overcome the worst tribalism. Only when we follow our convictions with appropriate actions do our ethics make a difference. *Crash* challenges viewers to admit our weaknesses and get beyond our delusions regarding race. It is not somebody else's fault or problem. *No Man's Land* offers a fragile hope for Bosnia and Serbia. If comedy can be found amid such atrocious genocide, then perhaps there are possibilities for a humble new beginning. We must reunite beliefs with practices. The ensemble drama asks, "Who is my neighbor?" Where can we find models of community that include *the other* and welcome the stranger?

Created for Community

We remain desperate to be connected despite repeated disappointments. Regardless of the ample reasons to abandon community, we continue to form governments, join clubs, plant churches. What drives our restless longing for community? Jürgen Moltmann appeals to the Holy Trinity of Father, Son, and Spirit as the ultimate reality. The Godhead is relational, an eternal conversation between God the Father, Christ the Son, and the sustaining Holy Spirit. Reality is not a dialectical debate between competing forces. Instead, our source is three-sided, a multilayered, multilevel community of faith. Moltmann writes:

> The triune God is a God in community, rich in inner and outward relationships. It is of Him only that we can say "God is love," for love is not solitary, but joins those who are different, and distinguishes those who are joined. If "the Father, the Son, and the Holy Spirit" are joined together through eternal love, then their one-ness is in their *concord* with each other. They form their own unique divine community through their self-giving to one another.[62]

Our notions of family, of church, of community start with the mutuality found in the Trinity.

In the Trinity we see three distinct persons retaining their individual characteristics. In such a relationship, personhood is not abolished but realized. Genuine community does not erase differences but celebrates the gifts we bring to the conversation. We freely give and freely receive. But how do the many become one? The mystery of the Trinity is embodied in the church.[63] We come as individuals with particular backgrounds and talents, but collectively we form something much greater, a community of remarkable breadth and diversity. What allows us to claim that we are united in Christ? The Holy Spirit, who animates our being and fans our faith into flame, interpenetrates the Christian community. Unity in the Spirit is an internal reality that works *through* our physical or cultural differences. Ancient Christian theologians referred to this mutual interpenetration within the Trinity as *perichoresis*.

To those who question whether the Trinity is more a theological concept than a biblical notion, Moltmann cites two foundational Christian prayers. In 2 Corinthians 13:14, Paul quotes the early Christian benediction, "The grace of our Lord Jesus Christ, and the love of God, and the fellowship of the Holy Spirit be with you all."[64] This does not represent a hierarchy but rather the experience that characterizes most Christian fellowship. What begins with the grace imparted via Christ allows us to feel embraced by God the Father and then enjoy the fellowship with other believers, rooted in the Holy Spirit. Church unity comes not from our common humanity but from the presence of the Spirit in us. Jesus offers hope for his community, the church, in the Gospel of John 17:21. Jesus prays, "That they may all be one; even as thou, Father, art in me, and I in thee, that they also may be in us, so that the world may believe that thou hast sent me" (RSV).[65] The mysterious, mutual indwelling of "Father in me and I in thee" is the *perichoretic* ground of Christian unity. The unity of God's people begins with the unity embodied in the Trinity and mediated by the Spirit. Moltmann saw this concept reflected in the posters of a 1986 conference of Latin American leaders in Trinidade, Brazil, which proclaimed, "The Trinity is the Best Community."[66] An interior, spiritual unity cuts through our external differences, making many individuals into one body.

The notion of the silent cowboy alone on the range has withered. A new concern for community has arisen in its place. Filmmakers around the world have repeatedly emphasized our connections (despite our differences). The realities of racism, classism, and sin are substantial impediments to the call to community. Our penchant for disengagement and for distancing ourselves from conflicts can stifle our hunger to join something beyond ourselves. Yet the bonds of family, nation, tribe, and creed keep calling us back.

As we saw in *Mystic River*, perhaps the greatest threat to community is secrets. Covering up our worst inclinations threatens authentic relationships. Only when we are willing to be fully revealed can we be fully healed. The call to Christian community is a call to reveal ourselves as God revealed himself in Christ. He became vulnerable and open to disappointment. Yet the love of Christ transcended the betrayals that hounded him unto death. We also must learn to embrace *the other*. The Christian community does not erase our differences. It unites individuals around the body of Christ. The Holy Spirit invites us into dynamic relationship with the Godhead, the Holy Three in One. As we study the nature of God, we may come to realize the challenges and wonders that await those who eschew the Lone Ranger instinct. Movies have reminded us that we are not alone, that we must join life's rich pageant whether in family (*Little Miss Sunshine*) or across races (*Crash*), tribes (*Hotel Rwanda*), cultures (*No Man's Land*), or ideologies (*United 93*). The Trinity of Father, Son, and Holy Spirit demonstrates that we are at our God-given best when we are most open to community. The ancient church father, Irenaeus, envisioned the Son and the Spirit as the long arms of the Father who made us and embraces us, drawing us into their holy community.[67] May our arms reflect the arms of God, reaching out in love, drawing the other near.

5

Talk to Her (and Him and Us)

Everyday Ethics

Million Dollar Baby (2004, IMDb #78)

Hable con ella (*Talk to Her*, 2002, IMDb #209)

> Searching for the truth the way God designed it,
> The truth is I might drown before I find it.
>
> Bob Dylan, "Need a Woman"[1]

What united the five Oscar nominees for Best Picture of 2005? *Brokeback Mountain*, *Good Night and Good Luck*, *Capote*, *Munich*, and *Crash* tend to be smaller in scale than typical Academy Award contenders, rooted more in character than spectacle. These independent-minded movies wrestle with important choices we all face in our contemporary context. They are about communities confronted by ethical dilemmas. The *Washington Post* noted the trend toward substance with a front-page story, "And This Year's Oscar Goes to Social Issues."[2] The article debates whether the nominees were initiating or reflecting a genuine cultural shift. Do these provocative films mirror current political tensions? Is Hollywood honoring filmmakers who embody their interests? Or is there a latent catch-up to the traumatic events of 9/11? Are films just starting to wrestle with the ethical implications prompted by that communal crisis?

In October 2006, Fuller Seminary's Reel Spirituality Institute hosted a conference focused on these five films. "Morality Bites" dealt with the ethical questions emerging from the 2005 Oscar nominees. Our discussions found that each film highlighted the tension between the individual versus the community. *Capote* chronicles the rise of the new journalism, when the reporter became more important than the story itself. *Good Night and Good Luck* demonstrates how a newsroom (the crew of CBS's *See It Now*) stands together to resist the demagoguery of Senator Joseph McCarthy's communist witch hunts. *Brokeback Mountain* takes on the myth of the American cowboy, "alone on the range." Will two loners find love amid the isolated backdrop of the American West? *Munich* shows what happens to a nation in mourning and grief following the 1972 Olympics. Responding to terrorism with acts of retribution may not bring about the justice Israel seeks. *Crash* tackles the issue of isolation and community head-on. It asks whether we crash into each other just so we can feel something. We all need community despite our persistent efforts to resist it.

Each of the contenders for Best Picture revolved around potent ethical dilemmas. Eponymous subject Truman Capote was challenged by killer Perry Smith to tell the truth. In the most chilling scene, Capote lies to a person who had considered him a trusted friend. *Good Night and Good Luck* questions the whole nature of journalism. It encourages audiences to follow Edward R. Murrow's example, standing up to those who would seek to obscure the truth with political grandstanding. Often overlooked in the broader debates about *Brokeback Mountain* was the issue of adultery. Unattainable homosexual love was held up as the tragic core of the story. But what about the women and children who suffered as well? For Americans, personal happiness (being true to ourselves) has emerged as a higher moral calling than commitment to spouse or children. *Munich* wonders if an eye-for-an-eye justice results in anything other than blindness for all. *Crash* exposed our latent racism with the subtlety of a sledgehammer.

Do these painful truths offer enough common ground to forge a new ethical framework? Despite disparate subjects, the Oscar-nominated films explored the results of lying and cheating. They demonstrated the cost of retribution and the folly of fools. They echo the cautionary aphorisms found in Proverbs. The finest postmodern movies mine the ethics of everyday life: general revelation as a daily discipline. Practical wisdom serves as an essential hedge against self-destruction. This chapter will explore the questions posed by two Oscar-winning dramas:

Million Dollar Baby and *Talk to Her*. They both wrestle with the key question, "Who is my brother or sister?" They both turn to the same place for an answer—to a beloved woman, suffering through paralysis in a hospital bed. But what does she say? What do their complex ethical dilemmas suggest to us?

Institutionalized Ethics Tumble

Small movies about big ethical questions have emerged from an institutional vacuum. Crippling moral crises have beset traditional defenders of ethics like the church and the state. The cynicism that followed the Nixon administration's Watergate scandal (and the Reagan administration's Iran-gate or Bill Clinton's Monica-gate) has reduced politics to fodder for comedians' late-night monologues. My introduction to the Christian community came via a front-row seat to 1987's PTL scandal. While serving as a youth minister in Charlotte, North Carolina, my daily news was overwhelmed by the allegations against televangelist Jim Bakker and the mascara-stained tears of his wife, Tammy Faye.[3] The sordid details surrounding the collapse of their PTL (Praise the Lord) Club and the first Christian theme park (Heritage USA) were followed shortly thereafter by another televangelist confession of sexual indiscretion. The past peccadilloes of Jim Bakker, Jimmy Swaggart, and assorted other Pentecostal preachers were reawakened by Ted Haggard's reluctant confession in 2006. Haggard's simultaneous campaign to ban gay marriage in Colorado while engaging in a three-year affair with a gay prostitute undermined the Religious Right's grandstanding (even though a gay marriage ban was passed by voters). Just to ensure that hypocrisy isn't solely a Protestant issue, the cover-up associated with the Catholic Church and its pedophile priests sealed the church's inability to claim any moral high ground.[4]

The aura surrounding Wall Street as the solution to all our woes came crashing down with the Enron scandal (along with the retirement savings of so many unsuspecting employees). The "smartest guys in the room" proved to be simply the slickest, most deceptive guys on the NASDAQ.[5] Even journalism, created to report on the abuse of power, resorted to lies and deception to boost readership. The fraudulent reporting of Stephen Glass for *The New Republic* fueled his meteoric rise and fall.[6] The august *New York Times* admitted it hadn't done due diligence with compromised journalist Jayson Blair.[7] The shady ethics and high stakes maneuvering behind *60 Minutes* suggested by *The Insider* (1999) took poisonous root in an effort to undermine President Bush's 2004 reelection.[8]

Reporters' heads rolled at *60 Minutes* for using fabricated documents in a story about Bush's service in the National Guard.[9] While Fox News may have celebrated the egg on CBS's face, the fall of journalism breeds cynicism in us all.

Nearly a thousand years ago, the French Estates General brought together the competing interests of the royalty, the church, and the commoners. This tripartite power structure became a model for British parliament and the diet of the Holy Roman Empire. While the top-down power of royalty eventually tumbled in democratic revolutions, the top-down ethics of the church remained in place—until now. Each of the three estates has tumbled. With the "Fourth Estate" of journalism unraveling, where can people turn for ethical integrity? The absurd "truthiness" of *The Colbert Show* offers a sane response to such maddening and widespread obfuscations.[10] We choose to laugh rather than cry, but will we slip into detached irony? How can we rebuild ethical standards amid so much ugliness? As unlikely as it may sound, Hollywood has stepped into the breach, trying to serve as watchdog and whistle-blower. The trend continued at the 2008 Oscars, as films about integrity (*Michael Clayton*) and character (*Juno*) were nominated for Best Picture. In *There Will Be Blood* and *No Country for Old Men*, we saw the bloody wages of sin. *Atonement* demonstrated how a single lie can fester and unravel relationships. Our best efforts to save ourselves, to atone for our sins, fall short. We may try to write a new ending for our lives, but we're caught short by our ethical failings."[11] We may discount Hollywood's insights, but serious artists are eager to inspire communities and broker ethical reform.

From Aesthetics to Ethics

Many have rightly derided the collapse of ethical standards. Postmodernism has been blamed for the "truth decay" that undermines our institutions.[12] Ambitious calls for a renewal of "total truth" have been met with best-selling enthusiasm in some Christian circles.[13] They offer a sound, reasonable approach to placing ethics and values on the same plane as scientific facts. Yet, these sincere and sometimes brilliant efforts to rebuild ethics on a dismantled epistemological foundation are bound to end in frustration. How do we forge an ethical framework in a time of shifting notions of right and wrong?

In searching for meaning within movies, we follow theological trails blazed by Hans Urs von Balthasar. Writing in post–World War II Europe, Balthasar saw the signs of ethical collapse but traced the downfall to something other than the decay of truth. Balthasar mourned the death of beauty. Perhaps the implosion of ethical standards stems from an ignorance regarding what makes goodness attractive. Balthasar suggested:

> In a world that no longer has enough confidence in itself to affirm the beautiful, the proofs of the truth have lost their cogency. In other words, syllogisms may still dutifully clatter away like rotary presses or computers which infallibly spew out an exact number of answers by the minute. But the logic of these answers is itself a mechanism which no longer captivates anyone.[14]

Balthasar believed that those who sneer at beauty would eventually stop praying and have a hard time loving. He anticipated our loss of faith but suggested that beauty (or aesthetics) could lead to the resurrection of transcendental virtues as an act of "mysterious vengeance." Could virtuous, onscreen heroism revive our standards and restore our hope? Might fictional characters inspire us to choose wisely and to behave beautifully?

Departing from the Enlightenment notion of dogma driving ethics, Balthasar reversed the hermeneutics, suggesting that beauty can lead us to goodness and truth. In *The Glory of the Lord*, he wrote:

> We believe that what is beautiful in this world—being spirit as it makes its appearance—possesses a total dimension that also calls for moral decision. If this is so, then from the beautiful the way must also lead into the religious dimension which itself includes humanity's definitive answer to the question about God and, indeed, our answer to the question God poses to *us*.[15]

Balthasar worked from aesthetics to ethics to metaphysics. While he acknowledged the dangers of aesthetic theology, he celebrated a discipleship forged with eyes wide open. The community could rely on divine revelation to drive theological aesthetics. Has the storytelling of the entertainment industry stepped into the hole created by the crash of our storied institutions? People's hunger for shaping stories and moral role models arrived on the unlikely shores of the cineplex.

The best dramas help us process life's most vexing moral quandaries. *Million Dollar Baby* (2004, IMDb #78) raises relevant issues of life and death, suffering and relief. What does compassion look like when medical science can sustain a body but torture a soul? Who has the right to play God with another person's life? Iconoclastic Spanish director Pedro Almodóvar also confronts the ethics of euthanasia in *Talk to Her* (2002, IMDb #209). But Almodóvar also rearranges our understanding of gender roles, caregiving, and healing. By combining stalking and sainthood, Almodóvar challenges us to rearrange our ethics in our postinstitutional era. *Talk to Her* celebrates art and beauty as sustaining comfort amid tragedy. Both films find wisdom in the trials of women, echoing the decidedly feminine personification of wisdom in Proverbs 8. Whether united by fate, tragedy, or divine intervention, these dramas present multiple perspectives on current problems. While some may consider a list of options as relativizing, audiences are finding such complexity comforting in a world of confusion. Our established institutions disappointed us with unreflective, prechewed conclusions. But our cinematic (and online) communities dive into lively debates prompted by ethically driven dramas.[16]

The tension between individual rights and communal standards continues to rage, but each ethical tradition borrows its principles from earlier eras. We face the enormous challenge of forging a social ethic amid a profound insistence on people's claims of autonomy. "Because I say so" has been replaced by "as long as you don't hurt others." Yet neither seems satisfactory to navigate our current ethical questions. With our institutions in ruins, will we devolve into all kinds of personal or regional "little" wars, demonizing the other? Or can our institutions be renewed, forging a fresh set of ethical lenses that recognize postmodern realities? The humiliation of our top-down institutions could and should create a rare air of humility. The possibility of waiting on God and listening to others offers unprecedented possibilities for the Spirit. Revelation arises in teachable moments, when we have eyes to see and ears to hear.

An Underdog with a Powerful Punch

Million Dollar Baby is a small movie about huge choices. With Hollywood increasingly turning to blockbusters for box office relief, *Million Dollar Baby* represents a remarkable alternative. Like boxing trainer Frankie Dunn (Clint Eastwood), the movie is dark, quiet, and introspective. Like its haggard narrator, Eddie "Scrap Iron" Dupris (Morgan Freeman), it takes its time, works the ring, making sure its punches land with jarring ferocity. Like its feisty protagonist, Maggie Fitzgerald (Hilary Swank), *Million Dollar Baby* became an unexpected, award-winning champion. It earned Oscars for Best Picture, Best Director (Eastwood), Best Actress (Swank), and Best Supporting Actor (Freeman) and a place on the IMDb's list of all-time classics (#78).

Based on the short stories of F. X. Toole (the pen name of boxing veteran Jerry Boyd), *Million Dollar Baby* fuses three stories into one devastating package. The boxing ring binds Frankie, Maggie, and Eddie together, but it also unravels their

Maggie Fitzgerald (Hilary Swank) ready to take on all challenges, early in *Million Dollar Baby*. © 2004 by Warner Brothers.

hopes and dreams. The action rotates between a gym, a boxing ring, and, finally, a hospital room. These highly confining spaces swallow up the protagonists. Screenwriter Paul Haggis (of *Crash* fame) focuses on the fragility of human relationships and the choices and regrets that haunt us. Ghosts from the past, whether acknowledged or not, loom in *Million Dollar Baby*'s dark shadows. Director Clint Eastwood and ace cinematographer Tom Stern allow the screen to go remarkably black. It recalls the smoky black-and-white images of the classic boxing films. We see the literal darkness that dogs Frankie, Maggie, and Eddie. Eastwood's spare jazz score underlines their loneliness and isolation. Like the best boxers, it is stripped to pure muscle—lean and potent.

Million Dollar Baby builds on the time-honored Hollywood tradition of the boxing picture. From *Body and Soul* (1947) to *Raging Bull* (1980, IMDb #68), the best boxing movies deal with lowlifes, back alleys, and the shady ethics of the fight game. But they also document the dogged determination of underdogs like Terry Malloy, in *On the Waterfront* (1954, IMDb #89), or *Rocky* (1976). Borrowing a page from the gritty, indie film *Girlfight* (2000), *Million Dollar Baby* subverts expectations by following the dreams of a woman boxer. Maggie's first battle is against prejudice. She wants to be trained, but Frankie must overcome his own objections to seeing women in the ring. He repeatedly declares, "I don't train girls." But as a determined woman, Maggie refuses to take *no* for an answer. As narrator, Scrap adds sage insights like, "All fighters are pig-headed some way or another . . . if you can beat the last bit out of them, they ain't fighters at all." Her painful, "trailer-trash" upbringing has made Maggie a born fighter, desperate for a shot at glory. Eddie defines the allure of boxing as "the magic of risking everything for a dream that nobody sees but you." Slowly but surely, she wins over Frankie and starts boxing.

Frankie's primary lesson to Maggie is: "Protect yourself at all times." He has seen too many fighters struck down in their prime, including Scrap. Yes, he could have been a contender. Now Eddie is burdened by a glass eye as a reminder of Frankie's neglect (and his own inability to protect himself). Frankie is also haunted by questions about his estranged daughter. His letters to her are returned unopened. Where is she? Is she safe and protected? Frankie becomes more than a trainer to Maggie. Given her sordid roots, Maggie comes to see Frankie, her boss, as family. Driving to a fight, she says, "I ain't got no one else but you." He nicknames her *Mo cuishle*, Irish for "my darling, my blood." This surrogate family plays a key role in the denouement, as Maggie's inability to heed Frankie's basic rule, "protect yourself," becomes her undoing. She is knocked down and out by the cheapest of shots, a late punch. She leaves the ring on a stretcher, paralyzed by a spinal cord injury.

Blindsided

Like Maggie, audiences were blindsided by her unexpected paralysis. *Million Dollar Baby* doesn't announce itself as an ethical dilemma. The poster never suggested that viewers would see a rumination on patients' right to die. Yet *Million Dollar Baby* hinted at its strong moral underpinnings through one key setting. Throughout the film, Frankie spends a surprising amount of his time in church. (I recognized the location as St. Mark's Catholic Church in Venice, California, near my home.) He brings questions about the Trinity to his priest. Frankie wonders, "Is it sort of like Snap, Crackle, and Pop, all rolled into one big box?" Is Frankie playing theological games, engaging in cute hypothetical scenarios? What does he seek in church? Father Horvak notes, "Frankie, I've seen you at Mass almost every day for twenty-three years. The only person who comes to church that much is the kind who can't forgive himself for something." We see Frankie's pain regarding his distant daughter. What happened to his marriage? Did Frankie walk away? Did his wife leave? Now, with Maggie in the hospital on life support, her body emaciating, Frankie faces an even greater moral crisis involving his surrogate daughter, Maggie.

Paralyzed from the neck down, Maggie, the scrappy fighter, wants to die. She bites her tongue in an effort to bleed to death. That takes bravery and courage, but such fatalism seems to contradict her earlier determination in the ring. How can a true boxer throw in the towel? Maggie gives her rationale: "I can't be like this, Frankie. Not after what I've done. I've seen the world. People chanted my name. . . . I got what I needed. I got it all. Don't let 'em keep taking it away from me. Don't let me lie here 'til I can't hear those people chanting no more." Frankie can't imagine pulling the plug on her ventilator, yet he blames himself for putting her in this regrettable position. When Maggie was knocked out by a late blow, she crashed into the stool that Frankie had placed in the corner of the ring. Her suffering becomes his suffering. He tells his priest, "By keeping her alive, I'm killing her." His guilt drives him toward honoring her plea for a mercy killing. But the priest dismisses the possibility of Frankie's intervention: "You step aside, Frankie. You leave her with God." Frankie spars with the priest, turning the official church position around: "She's not asking for God's help. She's asking for mine." *Million Dollar Baby* outlines the eternal stakes when the priest declares, "Forget about God or heaven or hell. If you do this thing, you'll be lost. Somewhere so deep, you'll never find yourself again." This crucial scene ends with Frankie's resolve, "I think I did it already." Frankie returns to the hospital and engages in a mercy killing. He walks out of the hospital alone, never to return.

Real-Life Relevance

The thorny ethical questions posed by *Million Dollar Baby* took on haunting relevance in the real-life case of Terri Schiavo. In 1990, twenty-six-year-old Terri Schiavo collapsed in her Florida home and the oxygen supply was cut off to her brain. Terri's husband, Michael, and her parents, Bob and Mary Schindler, worked together toward Terri's rehabilitation until a medical malpractice suit in 1993. A jury awarded Michael Schiavo $1.3 million, with $700,000 to be placed in a trust fund to cover Terri's therapy and medical treatment.[17] As in *Million Dollar Baby*, a tragic accident became a strange occasion for financial opportunism. Relatives started fighting over money before the loved one was even deceased. Financial settlements brought out our pettiest instincts.

From the time of the settlement, competing versions of Terri Schiavo's wishes emerged, pitting the once united family at odds during *twelve years* of legal battles. To Terri's parents (and their supporters), Michael Schiavo had become a villain, reneging on his initial commitments to care for her regardless of the circumstances. Terri's situation illustrated criminal neglect—from doctors who failed to rediagnose her, to judges who refused to protect her. To Michael Schiavo (and his camp), Terri's life (and suffering) had been prolonged by senseless court battles that ignored her right to die. Among the issues being debated—whether Terri was in a persistent vegetative state, whether she had ever expressed end-of-life wishes, and whether her Roman Catholic faith would have precluded anything other than a natural death.

The urgency of her case was heightened by Michael's petition to remove Terri's feeding tube in 1998. Seven years of legal petitions and maneuvers followed. Among the most contentious pieces of evidence were conflicting doctors' testimonies and video of Terri and her mother that either (1) demonstrated Terri's responsiveness or (2) confirmed her vegetative state. Following Florida Judge George Greer's court order, Terri's feeding tube was removed for a second time on October 15, 2003. The Florida legislature passed Terri's Law, empowering Governor Jeb Bush to order her feeding tube reinserted.[18] More appeals followed until Judge Greer's order on March 18, 2005, to remove the feeding tube. President George W. Bush and congressional Republicans attempted to get the Schiavo case turned over to federal jurisdiction, but the Supreme Court declined to demand a judicial review. Terri's final days became a media circus. She died on March 31, 2005, five days after receiving Last Rites and a final Eucharist (and one month after *Million Dollar Baby* won the Oscar as Best Picture).[19]

The real-life Terri and the fictional Maggie both became unexpected pawns in a political battle regarding human rights to life or death. *Million Dollar Baby* stepped into the messy moral morass regarding euthanasia. It prompted vigorous critiques from conservatives like Rush Limbaugh and Michael Medved and was defended by standard bearers from the left like Frank Rich and Maureen Dowd.[20] The United States Conference of Catholic Bishops praised the film's performances but deemed it "morally offensive." The disability community was reminded of earlier fights against Clint Eastwood over his handicapped inaccessible restaurant in Northern California. A Web site and documentary attacked the "Million Dollar Bigot" for suggesting that death is preferable to disability.[21] Could the road to assisted suicide lead to eugenics and the elimination of all who require special or extraordinary care? The story is still being written.

The Online Debate

The divergent and voluminous responses to the film on the IMDb (over nine hundred posted reviews) demonstrate how timely and loaded the issue remains. Many dismissed *Million Dollar Baby* as a calculated work with a Hollywood liberal ax to grind. Alistair Deacon thought, "This movie is total rubbish. In classic Hollywood tradition, the film focuses on a chic subject and a chic controversy—women's boxing and 'mercy' killing of the disabled. Unfortunately, the film has nothing to say about either."[22] Movieguy1021 from "Anywhere, USA," said, "*Million Dollar Baby* is propaganda by the baby-killing liberals. As is every movie dealing with a controversial issue, especially ones made by those ultra-liberal people at Warner Bros. and that staunch Democrat Clint Eastwood."[23] (Note to Movieguy1021—Eastwood is actually one of the rare registered Republicans in Hollywood, although he has claimed his leanings as Libertarian, telling *Playboy*, in his view, "Everyone leaves everyone alone.")[24] Others begged audiences to leave their politics aside, to enter into the story without bias. HollywoodAM proposed an art-first approach: "Liberal, conservative, democrat, republican: shut up. . . . Try understanding these characters, put yourself in their position. It may not change your mind, and it may not adhere to your morals, but you're not paying to see your film. When you watch a movie, you don't have to share or adapt to the film's point of view in order to enjoy it."[25] Filmmakers may hope that viewers enter into the theater with an open mind, but sometimes personal experience and convictions cannot be set aside.

Many in the disabled community were legitimately offended by the fatalism in *Million Dollar Baby*. IMDb user mbrent711 responded from personal experience:

> In the end, the movie proves to be a cheap political statement, and sends a terrible message in the process. I was paralyzed from the shoulders down at age 18. I'm not on a ventilator as Swank's character is, but I am totally dependent on others for feeding, dressing, etc. . . . This movie just perpetuates the myth that sustaining such an injury leads to a meaningless life. Swank can choose between school and death, and she chooses death. Thank you for setting the disabled community back a few more years. . . . What have I done differently? I've gone to college, lived on my own, and work as a respected journalist in the community. Where is the story about someone like me?[26]

It is tough to argue with his impassioned response. How would you feel if a film invalidated your decision to fight and live? For organizations like the Life Rolls On Foundation (www.liferollson.org), *Million Dollar Baby* arrived as an affront to their very existence. While they search for a cure for paralysis (and even take people with spinal cord injuries surfing), Maggie Fitzgerald gives up the fight.

So what to make of those who were legitimately challenged and moved by the movie? Ivanhoe Vargas from Jersey City said, "What could have been a feminist's answer to *Rocky* becomes something different, revelatory." He called it "visual poetry that unfolds into a tight tapestry which by the end of the film will have stirred many emotions with nary a manipulative hand in sight."[27] Darren DeBari thought, "The film is about the triumph of the human spirit, the emotional world we try to hide from that eventually sucks us all in, our compassionate hearts, and the difficult decisions we face when it comes to those we care about. It's about friendship, trust, and the bonds of the heart that are unavoidable. It is a true masterpiece."[28] Were Mbrent and Darren seeing the same movie?

Million Dollar Baby worked best for those willing to enter into the pathos and particular choices given to the characters within the movie. Yes, Maggie probably would not have needed Frankie's help to end her life given today's patients' rights. Yes, she should have received psychological support to cope with her accident. But in this one small world involving these particular characters, Frankie has to make a choice as to how he will respond to Maggie's request. They are tortured by two equally painful options. Dramatic resonance results from our willingness to enter into their dilemma. IronboundFW admits:

> The reason I loved this movie is because it forced me to come to terms with myself. ... When I left the film, I did not like or respect myself as a person, because I found myself siding with Hillary Swank's character. Like her, I am a strong individual when I want something, but when dealt a bad hand I am positively sure that I would make the same choices she did. That realization has been gnawing at me for three weeks since I saw this film. This film stays with you, it keeps you up at night, it makes you think, it makes you re-evaluate your choices.[29]

For that viewer, *Million Dollar Baby* operated on a soulful level, prompting genuine reflection and self-analysis. The revelatory refining process demands that we set aside our assumptions. We must be willing to see and hear and receive. FilmSnobby suggested that such moral complexity threatens all kinds of preconceptions.

> If you feel secure in your dogmas—religious, philosophical, or otherwise—then *Million Dollar Baby* is bound to be an upsetting experience for you. The most devastating, artistically sublime scene in the film occurs when Clint's Frankie confronts his priest. ... The priest, horrified at Frankie's raw pain, can only mouth Church

dogma before scuttling out of the camera's frame, far away from the unanswerable darkness sitting beside him. The movie has ensured that the priest's answers—that is to say, moral generalities—are meaningless within an individual context. THIS is the heart of what the film is about.[30]

What a telling statement! It identifies the central tension behind all the controversies as "moral generalities" versus "individual context." What happens when broad community standards are challenged by particular cases? How do we negotiate the messy middle where biblical principles are sometimes strained to fit? Many may be uncomfortable with the notion of situational ethics. It is much easier to embrace an overriding systematic or institutional approach to complex problems. As pastors and practitioners, we may know where we stand and what we think, but we can't possibly have imagined every scenario within God's colorful kingdom. Just when we think we have biblical ethics figured out, God (life, humanity) will always throw us a curveball. We may face a sudden death, an unforeseen temptation, a choice between two goods (or even more haunting, between equally regrettable evils). In an interview with *Film Comment*, Clint Eastwood acknowledges the gap between our preestablished positions and life's heart-rending realities:

> When the tragedy happens, it becomes the toughest fight he'll ever go through, that anyone could go through. And where it leads—there's no answer to it. Nobody knows what they'd do in that situation. There's no way to predispose that. You could say, does that mean you believe in euthanasia? Not necessarily. But who knows? It's a supposition unless you've been put in that position.[31]

Whatever our assumptions about life, the school of hard knocks offers a potent test of our true mettle.

Have we become content to paint situations with a single brush, when the endless variations of humanity affirm the wonder of God and the mystery of life? In moving from the particulars of special revelation to general ethical guidelines, have we absolutized what God had intended to be particular? The ongoing debates that arise around biblical ethics encompass the Jewish roots of the Christian faith. The rabbinical tradition wrestles with endless *what if* scenarios. Ancient texts are constantly reexamined in light of ongoing ethical dilemmas. The canon becomes a lived reality, a midrash negotiated under God's direction by each generation. Perhaps our ethical dilemmas can be sorted out by a recovery of the practical, Jewish roots of our faith. The biblical Proverbs arise from a careful study of the text of life.

A Practical Theology

In *Million Dollar Baby*, Frankie is presented with an ethical choice. What does wisdom look like in such a terrible situation? Old Testament scholar David Hubbard suggests that Proverbs "sees experience as a means of revelation . . . it brings us insight gained from personal and social experience, often at considerable pain."[32] Having proposed all types of hypothetical theological questions to his parish priest, Frankie now faces an all-too-real scenario. While written to give knowledge and discretion to the young (Prov. 1:4), the collection of proverbs takes on added resonance for someone like Frankie at the end of his life. Having already lost his biological daughter, Frankie has a choice in how to love and care for his adopted daughter, Maggie. Proverbs contrasts those who fear the Lord with fools who despise wisdom and discipline (see Prov. 1:7). Having dispensed his collected wisdom to a host of boxers, Frankie finds himself also reliving a nightmare from early in his career. Maggie's injury awakens Frankie's fears and regrets regarding Scrap as well. So what has experience taught him?

While some may attempt to turn the Proverbs into a comprehensive ethical system, real wisdom comes from recognizing the limits of the Proverbs. The longer Frankie lives, the more exceptions he has seen, even to his own rules. Maggie challenged his assumptions about women boxers. Now her accident threatens to undermine Frankie's Catholic theology. David Hubbard reminds us that the Proverbs "overstate and oversimplify, they carry no fine print, no footnotes, no lists of exceptions." So what should Frankie do with Maggie's exceptional scenario? He may long for an easy answer, a clear directive from God, but "we cannot use Proverbs like subway tokens, guaranteed to open the turnstile every time. They are guidelines, not mechanical formulas."[33] Knowing when and where to apply biblical truths constitutes genuine wisdom. This is the realm of practical theology, where we reconcile what we've read or heard with what we've witnessed. Real wisdom acknowledges the sovereignty of God, leaving ample room to be surprised or corrected, for "many are the plans in a man's heart, but it is the LORD's purpose that prevails" (Prov. 19:21).

Some may consider the words *practical theology* an oxymoron. What could be less practical than pontificating about God? Yet the roots of theology are found in the gray areas of life. Our questions fuel our search for meaning. God meets us in times of great need and crisis. And when the Almighty fails to respond in what we might consider a timely manner, our theological problems are only amplified. When the outer envelope of church dogma comes up against the inner envelope of lived realities, practical theology steps into the gap to negotiate a fragile, but viable, peace. The Enlightenment notion of universal categories and overriding ethics has collapsed in a postmodern era of exceptions. Rather than entering into a top-down discussion of ultimate truth, many of us prefer to navigate the ongoing tension between beliefs and practices, understanding and interpretation. We do not want to disregard the powerful testimony of the Bible, but we seek to draw on special *and* general revelation, the Word proclaimed read alongside the text of life.

Don Browning's *Fundamental Practical Theology* weighs the history of church theology and dogma against the concrete demands of real-world situations. It echoes John Wesley's fourfold source of theology, which factors in church tradition, biblical precedent, reason, and experience. Browning renews Wesley's language, updating our understanding of *tradition* as "community of memory," the principles and practices handed down across the centuries. But he also recognizes the dynamic process of change that informs our evolving ethics. Browning writes: "When inherited interpretations and practices seem to be breaking down, practical reason tries to reconstruct both its picture of the world and its more concrete practices. The overall dynamic of practical reason is a broad scale interpretive and re-interpretive process."[34] Our biblical text remains sacred even as our interpretive method evolves. Browning's practical theology encourages us to merge the outer envelope of wisdom we have been handed with the inner core of experience. It turns faith into a dynamic process rather than an accomplished event. Browning deals with the basic questions, "What should we do?" and "How should we live?" They echo God's question that anchors this part of our story, "Where is your brother (or sister)?" Browning weighs God's creation and redemption of the world against practical concerns of everyday life, fully respecting and animating both concrete realities.

In *Million Dollar Baby*, Frankie's years in church are challenged by an excruciating choice before him. He longs to unite what Maggie's request seems to divide. The terrible choice echoes God's call to Abraham to sacrifice Isaac (see Gen. 22:1–19). What parent would willingly take his or her child's life? Imagine the horrors that gripped Abraham (and Isaac!) as he bound his son and pulled out a knife. Frankie faces an equally vexing choice rooted in considerable pain. While the priest stands outside Frankie's experience with dogma, he's left wrestling with his inner demons alone (or only with his friend Scrap). But where is God in this situation? Surely he sits beside Frankie and Maggie in their tears and anguish. As Abraham wrestled with the ethics of sacrificing his son, surely God wept over the death of Jesus. Christ also experienced a tortured decision in the Garden of Gethsemane to accept death. Jesus sides with all those who suffer. So how should we walk beside people in crisis? How do we help people bridge the gap between beliefs and practices, ideals and realities?

Theologian Ray Anderson suggests that ministry precedes theology. In *The Shape of Practical Theology*, he presents a host of vexing scenarios similar to the case of Terri Schiavo (or even Maggie Fitzgerald).[35] His case studies are not merely academic exercises, but real-life dilemmas that arose within his own ministry context. Anderson expands on Browning's theological method, bringing Christ firmly into the center of our experience. To the question, "What would Jesus do? (WWJD)," Anderson adds, "What *is* Jesus doing?" What thoughts, actions, and responses does our living Lord have for us today? In the book of Acts we see Jesus's disciples changing their minds under the promptings of the Holy Spirit. As a hungry Peter prays in Acts 11, he receives a vision of a large sheet covered with a meal that is considered ceremonially unclean. But the voice of the Lord corrects him, "Do not call anything impure that God has made clean" (v. 9). The exclusive ways of the Jewish Christian community are altered *after* the resurrection. The Spirit prompts Peter to lead an inclusive church. As the disciples had to remain open to correction of their accepted dogmas, so today's Christians must be open to shifts in theology and practice. The revelation of Jesus is still being unveiled by the Holy Spirit on a host of ethical dilemmas *not outlined* by the Bible.

It may prove helpful to think of the Bible as more of a compass than a map. It is not about fixed points but a journey of faith, both as individuals and as a community. If the general scriptural guideline is "Choose Life" (see Deut. 30:19), *Million Dollar Baby* asks an important follow-up question: "What is life?" It wonders, "Isn't life more than biology?" Frankie thinks that perhaps "it is morally wrong to prolong the body and kill the Spirit." He's searching for a life-affirming choice to terminate a life. Perhaps he would be helped by Jürgen Moltmann's efforts to reunite *spirituality* and *vitality*. In *The Spirit of Life*, Moltmann writes: "In this world, with its modern 'sickness unto death,' true spirituality will be the restoration of the love for life—that is to say, vitality. The full and unreserved 'yes' to life, and the full and unreserved love for the living are the first experiences of God's Spirit, which is not for nothing called *fons vitae*, the well of life."[36] Maggie's suffering is as much spiritual as physical. She has lost her love of life, her fighting spirit; she has said *no*. Can the alleviation of suffering constitute the most compassionate response? This is new ethical terrain introduced by scientific breakthroughs. Now that we can extend life beyond consciousness, many legitimately wonder what constitutes "life." They have seen science rob people of dignity even while preserving their heartbeat. Have Christians reduced life to biology at the very instant that the broader culture might be affirming the Spirit? Might God be revealing himself through the dilemmas presented in *Million Dollar Baby*?

Despite our seeming surety about what constitutes "life," philosopher Nancey Murphy traces how the Christian understanding of humanity has adapted over time. In *Bodies and Souls, or Spirited Bodies?* Murphy discusses four theories of human nature that have held sway. Some consider life pure "physicalism or materialism." Others lean toward dualism, as in "body and soul" or "mind and body." A third theory divides human life into the tripartite: body, soul, and spirit. Murphy calls the fourth view "idealistic monism," basically life as strictly spiritual or mental. While most Christians vacillate between the second or third option, Murphy finds that the Bible fails to settle any arguments. She concludes that "the biblical authors, especially the New Testament authors, wrote within the context of a wide variety of views, probably as diverse as in our own day, but did not take a clear stand on one theory or another."[37] The Bible may be broadly pro-life, but it fails to clarify whether Maggie is merely a body in pain, a soul trapped in a bad body, or a Spirit longing for release. For Murphy, the New Testament authors attest that humans are psychophysical unities, that eternal life is staked on bodily resurrection, and that humans are understood in terms of their relationships to the community of believers and especially to God.

Staying alive used to be sufficient struggle unto itself. Doctors were viewed as warriors, engaged in a fight for life. Suffering and death were viewed as the ultimate evil to be resisted by any means necessary. Yet the Christian tradition argues otherwise. Death is just another rite in an ongoing saga. Christian mystics turned suffering into a virtue. The preparation for death can become a meditation of profound significance. The rising science of gerontology considers aging an art to be mastered. Too many have felt abused by the health-care system, dehumanized by doctors who have been reduced to technicians. William F. May suggests we need to recover medicine's more holistic call as healer.[38] In *The Physician's Covenant*, May urges doctors to view themselves as "covenanters." They enter into a pact with the patient and their extended family to offer care with a sense of fidelity that transcends the considerable pressure exerted by insurance companies and hospital beds. Doctors must give aid to the sick and dying out of giftedness rather than obligation, retaining humanity rather than reducing it.

At the same time, the unilateral nature of Maggie and Frankie's decision poses a threat to our notions of community. They uphold their own personal covenant but flaunt the larger social fabric. It too easily embraces our notion of the heroic, autonomous individual. *Million Dollar Baby* conflates the right to die with assisted suicide. Like many ethical debates, it privileges one system (our *rights* from social contracts) over another (the *consequences* of utilitarianism). Both systems arose as rational alternatives to integrated Christian ethics. In *Million Dollar Baby*, Maggie's individual rights take precedence over her family's objections. The movie makes the family members such grotesque and unsympathetic characters that audiences will never consider *their* feelings. But what of community standards that could easily prosecute Frankie for murder? The legal questions are just beginning as the movie ends. While *Million Dollar Baby* was collecting Academy Awards, the Supreme Court was hearing a case on physician-assisted suicide in Oregon. Does Oregon's Death with Dignity law represent a change in community standards that other states will follow? Forty-nine states have numerous debates ahead. Surely we must humbly seek the wisdom of God found in Scripture, community, and tradition. Yet *Million Dollar Baby* offers Frankie and Maggie an easy heroism, isolated from others. Their actions affect them and them alone. Why doesn't the movie explore a more communal discernment, with doctors, psychologists, and therapists weighing in?

The Winning Choice?

The moral of Frankie and Maggie's story is hinted at by the sign on the wall of the gym: "Winners are simply willing to do what losers won't." The implication is clear: "pulling Maggie's plug" represents a horrible but winning choice. While Frankie and Maggie were undoubtedly traumatized by her paralysis, is their dual exit a winners' response? The "happy" ending of the film draws on the poetic vision of William Butler Yeats:

> I will arise and go now, and go to Innisfree
> And a small cabin build there, of clay and wattles made:
> Nine bean-rows will I have there, a hive for the honeybee,
> And live alone in the bee-loud glade.
> And I shall have some peace there, for peace comes dropping slow.[39]

Yet isn't that a rather singular and selfish version of peace? Frankie will never reconnect with his long-lost daughter if he retreats to a little cabin in the woods. Peace may be desirable, but does it count in isolation? Maggie's hunger to hold on to the glory of her past foregoes an even more inspiring future. What of

Community

Maggie's many fans? Wouldn't they rally around a fallen champion? Couldn't she generate even more cheers for daring to carry on despite her accident? She misses an opportunity to prove her true mettle, to inspire others in a profoundly different way. Frankie and Maggie also ignore the miraculous, ruling out both potential advances in medicine and divine intervention.

Perhaps any analysis that reduces our choices to winning and losing reduces the complexity of life. Maggie has won fights and lost a great battle to walk again. The juxtaposition of those two divergent experiences makes for a sublime tale. It is beautiful and ugly, inspiring and depressing at the same time. But the ability to hold those two paradoxes in tension, to embrace both aspects of Frankie and Maggie and Scrap's life, constitutes enduring aesthetic beauty. The power of the film resides in its ability to provoke discussion and raise ethical issues. To attack its morality is to salute its power. It pushes so hard on our assumptions in such surprising and unexpected ways that it opens our hearts and minds to truly hear the voice of God. This is general revelation in action.

In our overly politicized era, we need a rather strong tonic to challenge our convictions. *Million Dollar Baby* delivers a devastating punch in the gut powerful enough to knock us out or maybe wake us up. While the politicians and courts rule on assisted suicide and the right to die, those of us lying in the hospital beds or serving as caregivers need to wake up to our responsibility—to make an active and informed choice, to get into the ring and take a swing at life in all its darkness, perplexity, and possibility. We may admire or revile Frankie. We may salute Maggie's boxing but regret her decision to throw in the towel. But we will not soon forget them and their dilemma. Revelation comes even amid or because of this critique. We can hear God in a variety of ways, even among those with whom we disagree.

Talk to Her (and Him and Them)

Pedro Almodóvar's *Hable con ella* (*Talk to Her*, 2002) represents an even more complex take on the new ethical horizons prompted by medical breakthroughs. It presents two examples of life-threatening paralysis. What *Million Dollar Baby* turns into a third-act surprise, *Talk to Her* (IMDb #209) takes as a starting point. Frankie's tortured isolation is countered by the shared struggle in *Talk to Her*. It is about two men finding community in their mutual experience caring for a paralyzed lover. Yet as an avowed provocateur, the Spanish filmmaker Pedro

Almodóvar challenges our preestablished notions of love, relationships, and life. He inverts our expectation regarding gender roles and merges molestation with the miraculous. If *Million Dollar Baby* explores one question with great depth and feeling, *Talk to Her* tackles the overwhelming questions of how we should live and love and die with an audacious mix of style and substance. It blends dance and life, fantasy and reality into an intoxicating and unforgettable artistic stew. Almodóvar became the unexpected winner of the 2003 Oscar for Best Original Screenplay for *Hable con ella*.

Almodóvar introduces his characters and their backstories in a roundabout manner. We know they are suffering before we know why. How their stories are told is as important as the stories themselves. Marco (Dario Grandinetti) is a virile but sensitive journalist who is well acquainted with grief. While pining for the one that got away, Marco meets Lydia, a bullfighter also getting over a breakup. Marco's lothario is contrasted with Benigno (Javier Camera), an effete male nurse. Benigno is obsessed with a ballet student named Alicia. Dance serves as Marco and Benigno's first connection. Benigno notices Marco's tears flowing at a performance of German choreographer Pina Bausch's *Café Muller*—a paean to female suffering. Months later, they meet again at El Bosque, a private hospital. Marco's *torera* Lydia (Rosario Flores) has been gored by a bull and is in a coma. Benigno has become the primary caregiver for the object of his affections, Alicia (Leonar Watling), who is also comatose due to an accident. Benigno becomes Marco's teacher, imploring him to talk to her, to continue his conversations with Lydia as if she were responsive.

Hable con ella is about two men learning to communicate. As an openly gay filmmaker, Almodóvar may have been expected to have his male protagonists develop sexual feelings for each other. But Almodóvar uses our assumptions about him to challenge our understanding of gender roles and relationships. The first barrier to communication is our own prejudices; we cannot hear God if we are unwilling to listen. Revelation often begins with surprising reversals.

Film critic Carrie Rickey suggests the men in *Talk to Her* may be more asleep than Lydia and Alicia. She considers it "a powerfully moving film about men who think they want to lose themselves in their women, then they are startled to realize that they're the ones who have been comatose."[40] Marco has the appearance of control, but he's still obsessing over a lost love. Benigno has manufactured an entire relationship with a woman who barely knows he exists. His love is completely one-sided and delusional. Benigno even manufactures a mental condition to visit Alicia at her psychiatrist father's office. Flipping the biblical story, in *Talk to Her*, the paralytic women provide the healing power that enables the men to rise and walk (cf. Mark 2:1–12).

As in *Million Dollar Baby*, paralyzed women become the occasion for masculine transformation. Their suffering becomes a teachable moment, a chance for men to choose wisdom. In contrast to the biblical warnings against ladies of smooth words (Prov. 2:16–19) or sultry beauty (Prov. 6:25–29), the women in *Talk to Her* and *Million Dollar Baby* are nearly silent. The films could be read as an antifeminist fantasy, the chance to silence the female voice. Yet the women cry out even from their hospital beds. Their value is recognized only in retrospect, after they're nearly gone. Like Dame Wisdom in Proverbs 8, the women in Eastwood and Almodóvar's movies demonstrate that "wisdom is more precious than rubies, and nothing you desire can compare with her" (Prov. 8:11). To hard-headed men they whisper, "I love those who love me, and those who seek me find me" (Prov. 8:17). With countless hours to contemplate their worth, the grieving men by their bedsides discover, "My fruit is better than fine gold;

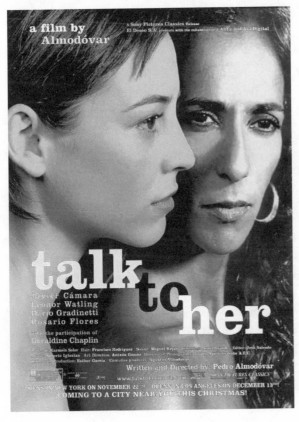

Dame wisdom personified as strong, silent, and suffering in Pedro Almodóvar's Oscar-winning screenplay for *Hable con ella*. © 2002 by Sony Pictures.

what I yield surpasses choice silver" (Prov. 8:19). Wisdom transcends time; she was with God in the beginning "when he set the heavens in place" (Prov. 8:27). After months at the hospital, the mourning men discover that "Blessed is the man who listens to me, watching daily in my doors, waiting at my doorway. For whoever finds me finds life" (Prov. 8:34–35). This is the power of Dame Wisdom even on her deathbed.

Marco and Benigno's awakening mirrors the audience's own revelations. In making Lydia a female bullfighter, Almodóvar tweaks one of Spain's most sacred institutions. Lydia has her own contradictions. She can stand defiantly before the most masculine of symbols, the bull, yet panics at the sight of a snake. Marco seems like the ultimate female fantasy, a voracious lover who weeps openly. But Marco refuses to let Lydia wear the pants in their relationship. He wants her to be needy, to need him. Marco refuses to listen to Lydia's true feelings (until she is in a coma).

Viewers may assume that Benigno, the sensitive male nurse, is homosexual. His devotion to his deceased mother awakens all kinds of stereotypes regarding "mama's boys." We expect him to hit on Marco. But Benigno uses such social assumptions to his advantage, gaining almost total control of Alicia's care (and body). Benigno constantly touches, rubs, and massages Alicia. He also massages her with words of love and encouragement—another side of female fantasies. Yet his true sexual feelings are masked. His name suggests he is an unlikely threat, "Benign." Yet he comes to be revealed as the nicest rapist you'd ever want to meet. Almodóvar challenges us to look closer, to judge characters not by their orientations (or our assumptions) but by their actions. Benigno emerges as a wise fool, a stone-faced comedian dispensing sage advice on what women want.

While offering his characters a wide berth, Almodóvar offers plenty of judgment toward the actions of certain institutions. As in many of his more outrageous films, Almodóvar launches satirical barbs against the Catholic Church. When Lydia's sister lights a candle in remembrance, she asks if anyone read about nuns being raped by priests in Africa. Marco considers that a change prompted by the AIDS epidemic—"The priests used to rape the local women instead." Two more people chime in, suggesting that not all priests are like that, "Some of them are pedophiles instead." Ouch. Almodóvar doesn't seem bothered by all the sexual acting out, just the church's attempts to cover it up. Like Jesus, he is angered most by hypocrisy. Yet Almodóvar doesn't limit his outrage to the church. He also mocks science and medicine, confronting the inhumanity of our therapeutic culture. What happens when institutions fail to perform their valuable functions? How do we renew (or resist) institutions that have forgotten their mission? Almodóvar starts by airing their dirty laundry, revealing hidden secrets.

A Twisted Case

Like *Million Dollar Baby*, *Talk to Her* mines contemporary issues of medical ethics. But Almodóvar drew on cases that pushed well past the debates about whether Terri Schiavo should have a feeding tube. He recalled three surprising examples drawn from real life. Almodóvar was intrigued by photos of an American woman rising from sixteen years in a coma. He noted, "Her awakening contradicted everything that science says about such cases."[41] Almodóvar also heard about a girl in New York City who had been in a coma for nine years before giving birth. The orderly who raped her was caught, but Almodóvar was intrigued by the notion that a body pronounced clinically dead could beget life. His third source involved a girl in Romania, presumed dead, who was raped by the night watchman in a morgue. Thanks to his unsolicited harassment, she came to life, snapping out of her catalepsy. While the rapist was sent to prison, the girl's family was grateful for his life-saving assault. Almodóvar calls it, "One of those miracles of human nature which I don't think the Pope would like very much."[42] Where some see perversity, Almodóvar sees humor—and a story.

Almodóvar depicts Benigno's rape of Alicia in the most outrageous way possible. He breaks from the narrative entirely, inserting a faux silent film titled *Amante Menguante* (*The Shrinking Lover*). Silent movies have served as a connection point between Benigno and Alicia. Her interest thus becomes his obsession. So he narrates the outrageous tale of a beautiful scientist and the little man who loves her. Almodóvar elevates the female form to unprecedented grandeur. The scientist's breasts become literal mountains for the little lover to climb. And where must this miniature explorer hide from intruders? In the ultimate furry cave—his lover's vagina! Almodóvar turns his set decorator loose to create the largest prop to ever celebrate the birth canal. Nothing in *Talk to Her* could prepare viewers for this unexpected journey that merges Spanish surrealism and Oedipal nightmares with the humor of Woody Allen. Even when it is seen, this self-contained black-and-white short may not be believed. Stephanie Zacharek of Salon.com notes, "He has always loved to drop shockers like water balloons from a terrace—his characters, more often ruled by their hearts than their heads, often behave in ways that we can't wholly approve of."[43] Yet it gets viewers past a painful plot point with broad humor and unparalleled style.

Not everyone could accept Benigno's rape as an act of devotion. Among IMDb users, Abigail17 from North Carolina found it pitiful and depressing, concluding, "My overall impression of the film is one of disgust! Yuck. I feel like I wasted not only $5 and 2 hours, but need a shower."[44] In a post titled, "Can't Get Past Society's Views," theman5 from Miami admits, "I don't know why this movie is among the top 250. . . . Basically, if you feel that what a character does can make you upset because it is outside of society's norms, then don't watch the movie."[45] But what if society's norms are changing? How will we navigate uncomfortable but unavoidable situations? Almodóvar takes viewers down a twisted but ultimately rewarding road.

As in *Million Dollar Baby*, viewers must get beyond the provocation. A certain amount of cinematic faith is involved, offering Almodóvar room to move us. Danisaley from the United Kingdom found that *Talk to Her*

> left me more questioning my moral perceptions, I felt like my conscience had been troubled. Days later I was still thinking back on it, trying to come to grips with the concluding sensation I was left with. Then when you find out that he rapes the girl, you're left feeling completely bemused by the whole situation. You know you should be feeling disgusted, sickened and angered by what he has done, but instead you just pity him, feel real empathy, compassion and just sorry for the whole situation. Because you know that what he did he did out of love for her, and he felt that those feelings were being reciprocated by her. This film really makes you meditate on how you perceive such extremely moral right and wrongs.[46]

Most film viewers recognized Almodóvar's story as blatantly button pushing. They refused to dismiss it due to outrageousness and found more provocative principles lurking beneath the taboo subject matter. Jono-73 from the United Kingdom suggests that "Almodóvar is attempting to make rape emotionally acceptable," but finds that "the film's exquisite monstrosity lies not in Benigno's act but in Almodóvar's conclusion: Coldness kills women, true love brings them back to life. Benigno's 'act of love' lies somewhere between rape and necrophilia and yet Almodóvar does get away with it."[47] *Getting away with it* recurs as a key theme in his expressive oeuvre. Stephanie Zacharek believes, "Almodóvar movies, at their best, are all about the uselessness of either approval or disapproval as tools to help us get through life."[48] This could cause some justifiable sense of social alarm. Without any ethical glue to bind us together, are we reduced to a sea of free agents, floating aimlessly in our own moral confusion?

Beauty amid Tragedy

Talk to Her replaces conventional ethics with a very active communal discernment. The legal system remains to intervene, but it may not be able to weigh elusive motives like love or devotion. *Hable con ella* is fueled by acts of beauty that are recognized only in hindsight. Almodóvar takes the long view of Benigno's relationship with Alicia. Benigno may end up in jail, reviled by society, but Marco seems to know better. Through prison glass, Benigno and Marco grow closer than ever before. Tragedy arises because Benigno does not get to appreciate the life-giving power of his seemingly selfish act. The real beauty remains hidden, veiled, only to be revealed in due time.

What small comforts we have amid suffering often involve beautiful paintings, music, movement, or films. Almodóvar says, "I think that situations which involve moments of unexpected, extraordinary beauty can bring tears to your eyes, tears which have more to do with pain than pleasure. Tears which fill the place in our eyes of those who are absent."[49] His solution to social problems is *empathy via beauty*. By learning to see and hear and appreciate art, we may come to see and appreciate and embrace others. To the legal system or medical profession, this may seem idealistic or nonsensical, but Almodóvar's film defies logic. It asks viewers to enter into a painful scenario with an open heart and mind. It also reflects the theological presuppositions of Hans Urs von Balthasar.

The art of seeing (which Balthasar calls "the theory of vision") precedes the logic of ethics. Only when we perceive God and his activity in the world (manifested in the Incarnation) can we respond by aspiring to resemble such divine activity (what Balthasar calls "the theory of rapture").[50] For Balthasar, the object of our gaze, the most beautiful sight is Christ incarnate. He emphasizes the power of Jesus's image to transform us. Seeing Jesus clearly will alter our behavior. Balthasar finds this process outlined in 2 Corinthians 3:17–18. For Paul, the Spirit of the Lord grants freedom. And when we see the Lord's glory, we are transformed into Christlikeness. Almodóvar's emphasis on the transforming beauty follows the same principle. When we've failed to see the beauty in others or creation, we've failed to act. Marco (and the viewers) must learn to see things Benigno's way. Almodóvar uplifts Benigno as the ultimate example of rapturous love.

Benigno's story of *The Shrinking Lover* underscores the movie's theme of talking to her and him and them and us. A short film becomes a story within a story about the power of stories. Yet Almodóvar resists all the self-referential games that could come with such postmodern problems. He has learned to respect the medium of movies as a liberating art with revelatory potential. Almodóvar invites us to get swept up in his miraculous story of healing *as a means of* healing. He just happens to wrap it within the transgressive role model of a rapist. Does this kind of scandal preclude the truth contained within the characters' hearts and minds? Almodóvar dares us not to limit the power of God to work through any means.

Despite his anti-institutional, antichurch leanings, Almodóvar creates with a strong sense of biblical inversions. As God chose Moses the stutterer as liberator of Israel, so Almodóvar relies on the unassuming Benigno to bring Alicia back to consciousness. As a boy like David defeats a giant like Goliath, so Almodóvar has proven that the Spanish film industry can compete (and win!) on Hollywood's stage, the Academy Awards. Jesus repeatedly placed unlikely heroes at the center of his parables, from overlooked widows to despised Samaritans. Like a host of biblical prophets, Benigno stands out as a holy fool, dismissed by society but celebrated by God.

Almodóvar ends *Talk to Her* with a surprising affirmation of the miraculous. Alicia is revived by childbirth. A mother is healed by having a child. Two miracles emerge from Benigno's tragic life. David Sterritt of the *Christian Science Monitor* notes that many movies feature "manufactured miracles, cooked up special effects in fantasies we're not meant to confuse with the real world." Alicia's recovery "is not a miracle in the strict sense, since it is generated by human love rather than religious faith. But that doesn't stop it from being as moving as anything on screen this year."[51] Benigno's life also continues in the revived Marco. At the end of the film, Marco returns to the Pina Bausch ballet as a changed man. Ella Taylor of *LA Weekly* notes, "The dance of suffering gives way to a more hopeful number, sexy and sublimely conciliatory—another example of art's power to heal the pain of living."[52] *Talk to Her* has rearranged our traditional social and ethical framework. It subverts viewers' expectations and challenges our notions of love.

Pedro Almodóvar presents a stalker saint and resensitized lothario as proof that anything can happen and anyone can change. He believes in the possibilities of miracles, from a life-giving rape to men who learn to listen. Almodóvar unsettles us in an effort to pull us together, to make us better caregivers and more vivid life-livers. As with *Million Dollar Baby*, the offensiveness of the story has proven off-putting for some, for whom the beauty remains stillborn. But for others, the movie proves revelatory. Women on the brink of death challenge men to dig deeper, to take a risk and choose wisely. The films reawaken the everyday ethics (and power of Dame Wisdom) found in Proverbs.

I am challenged by Almodóvar's openness to the spirit of creativity. As Christians struggle to hold on to fading moral influence, filmmakers have stepped into the ethical void. With nothing but empathy as their guide, Clint Eastwood and Pedro Almodóvar have approximated Jesus's method of offering solidarity to the suffering. *Million Dollar Baby* and *Hable con ella* are messy films for a messy world. They unfold in unexpected ways, creating ethical conundrums most of us have never considered. As such, they provide excellent case studies in practical theology. They take us back to the Jewish roots of our faith, to the situational ethics of Proverbs. While we may debate their conclusions, we must appreciate the revelatory gifts they offer. At a time when our ethical moorings are up for grabs, *Million Dollar Baby* and *Hable con ella* offer beautiful pictures of broken people struggling for answers—practical theology for today's audiences. Are we our brothers' and sisters' keepers? Absolutely.

Part 3

History

Then I saw a new heaven and a new earth,
for the first heaven and the first earth had passed away,
and the sea was no more.
And I saw the holy city, new Jerusalem,
coming down out of heaven from God,
prepared as a bride adorned for her husband.

And I heard a loud voice from the throne saying,
"Behold, the dwelling place of God is with man.
He will dwell with them, and they will be his people,
and God himself will be with them as their God.

He will wipe away every tear from their eyes,
and death shall be no more,
neither shall there be mourning
nor crying
nor pain anymore,
for the former things have passed away."

And he who was seated on the throne said,
"Behold, I am making all things new."

Revelation 21:1–5 ESV

6

Finding Neverland
Nostalgia and Imagination in History

Der Untergang (*The Downfall*, 2004, IMDb #45)
The Pianist (2002, IMDb #47)
Gladiator (2000, IMDb #135)
Finding Neverland (2004, IMDb #172)
Cinderella Man (2005, IMDb #187)

Day after day the wind blows away the pages of our calendars, our newspapers, and our political regimes, and we glide along the stream of time without any spiritual framework, without a memory, without a judgment, carried about by "all winds of doctrine" on the current of history. Now we ought to react vigorously against this slackness—this tendency to drift. If we are to live in this world we need to know it far more profoundly; we need to rediscover the meaning of events, and the spiritual framework which our contemporaries have lost.

Jacques Ellul, *Presence of the Kingdom*[1]

Back to the Garden

I've always been a collector. It began with baseball cards but soon expanded to include football cards, basketball cards, even hockey cards. The rise of pop culture compounded my collecting. Soon cards featuring *Star Wars*, *Planet of the Apes*, and television's *Welcome Back Kotter* were added to my cramped closet. Hand-me-downs from my parents expanded my holdings to include coins, stamps, and postcards. By the time I hit adolescence, my interests widened to records. The rise of compact discs made my old long-playing albums obsolete, and now MP3s have supplanted my CDs. But I'm still a collector, a completist, and a lover of stuff—especially old stuff. Why? What about the past so appeals to me? Is it a way to preserve my childhood, to prolong a sense of innocence? Or is it more of a hedge against the onslaught of adulthood, a staving off of maturity? Flipping through faded mementos snaps me back to the garden, or at least to the comfort of my boyhood home. Suddenly I'm ten years old again, and the wonder of childhood returns. Has an attachment to the past arrested my development or fueled my imagination by keeping me young at heart? What lies behind my nostalgic impulse?

When the future is uncertain, nothing comforts quite like the past. History offers a sense of certainty. There is comfort in knowing we existed. Places were visited, things happened, and we have the photos, mementos, or baseball cards to prove it. Our nostalgic present often reveals more about where we are than where we've been. Anxiety about our current surroundings can make us pine for even lamentable prior circumstances. As the Israelites wandered in the desert, they looked back to Egypt with longing. During the exodus, they grumbled against Moses's leadership, questioning his wisdom. The slavery of their past looked rosy compared to the uncertainty of tomorrow.

What fuels our current interest in all things past? Frederic Jameson suggests our nostalgia for the present corresponds to our lack of faith in the future.[2] We look back because we are afraid to move forward. In Jameson's estimation, we have lost all hope or imagination and therefore content ourselves with recycling recent history. He criticizes our substitution of style for substance, where the "1930s-ness" or "1950s-ness" of fashion passes for authenticity. Such shorthand shortchanges us, substituting poses for personhood, but perhaps there is more at work. A backward glance, no matter how limited the historical distance, is always a twofold process. We want to figure out "How did we get here?" and "How do we get out?"—two more shades of God's question to Adam in the Garden of Eden, "Where are you?" We retrace our steps to find our next tentative step. To move forward, we desperately need a renewed faith and a revived imagination. Rather than going back to the garden, maybe we need to set aside space for a new garden.

Bob Dylan asked us how it feels to be on our own with no direction home.[3] Forty years later his questions still resonate. Have we lost our sense of home? Where did we come from? We all seem to have some sense of a better place, a safer place, an earlier place. Even if we didn't particularly like our childhood, we still embark on a search for Neverland, for a mythical land where we never get old, where every pain is salved, where our hunger is truly satisfied. This idyllic home seems to be back *there*, somewhere in the forest, in the mist, in the past. Joni Mitchell provided a poetic counterpoint to Dylan's vision with her own paean to the sixties generation in "Woodstock." In her Edenic vision, the children of God converged on Max Yeager's farm in an effort "to get ourselves back to the garden."[4] Why do we have such a strong desire to get back to the garden, to our roots? Where is that goal, that place, the destination? Why do we feel like we have "no direction home"?

Our unprecedented mobility gives us the ability to reinvent ourselves in new cities and new jobs. But as we distance ourselves from our past, we may end up more *unknown* than ever. We try on new personas but rumble around like rootless rolling stones. Like Joni Mitchell (who didn't attend Woodstock), we sing the praises of places we've never been and pine for eras we never witnessed. We experience the isolation of exile amid our considerable comforts. When we don't know where we're headed, where do we turn for guidance? We keep looking at the past for a way out, a sense of direction. We sense that we came from something better; we were created for something more. For a rootless or rudderless culture, history provides an important baseline. Perhaps a survey of history in film will provide a window into what ails (or at least concerns) us. History can offer valuable perspective. What are we looking for in the past? Do we seek forgotten virtues, lessons learned, and keys to the future?

This chapter will turn to recent historical epics in an effort to discover general revelations. What might God be revealing about our present circumstances through films focused on the past? We will contrast the valor of Maximus in *Gladiator* (IMDb #135) with the cowardice of Hitler in *Der Untergang* (IMDb #45). The warm sepia tones attached to *Cinderella Man* (IMDb #187) are undone by the grim, colorless reality of *The Pianist* (IMDb #47). Two recent films rising on the IMDb list, *Letters from Iwo Jima* and *Das Leben der Anderen* (*The Lives of Others*) desaturate their colors even more intensely. They take us inside the minds of men called to a death and a duty that betray their best instincts. How should an individual respond to the orders of a corrupt state? Whether our backward glances are filled with nostalgia (*Cinderella Man*) or horror (*The Pianist*), we all seem to be searching for Neverland. Yet *Finding Neverland* (IMDb #172) involves facing, rather than escaping, reality. It is a journey into the dark abyss of children losing their parents. Given painful pasts, it takes a considerable artistic and spiritual imagination to envision a future.

Dressing Up

Whenever Hollywood producers long for an Oscar, they dig into the history books. Historical epics offer prime opportunities for accolades in cinematography, art direction, costume design, and makeup, and they create an attractive escape for actors and audiences. Whether riding along with *Ben-Hur* (1959, IMDb #119) in a thrilling chariot race, traipsing across the desert on a camel with *Lawrence of Arabia* (1962, IMDb #28), or following a foolish officer into constructing *The Bridge on the River Kwai* (1957, IMDb # 52), blockbuster epics are prime Oscar bait. Actors love to dress up and try on period fashion and foreign accents. Biopics offer plum roles from ruthless generals like *Patton* (1970, IMDb #162) to peaceful leaders like *Gandhi* (1982, IMDb #138). Set decorators scour flea markets for antiques to surround *The Queen* (2006). Composers mine the vast riches of classical music to reintroduce sounds from forgotten eras. Audiences are drawn to the splendor and the pageantry of majestic castles and historic battles. Epic dramas appeal to viewers of both sexes, whether in a stuffy British drawing room or on a sweeping field of knights in armor. They recall eras of greatness, allowing us to reclaim lost glories (even if only for two hours in the dark).

Historian David Lowenthal declared, "The past is a foreign country." He added with humorous insight, "Nostalgia has made it 'the foreign country with the healthiest tourist trade of all.'"[5] England serves as the movies' primary tourist destination. Refined manners and a sense of decorum make the British Empire seem like a noble conqueror worth recovering (particularly for the white Anglo Saxon diaspora). Her Majesty's palace is somehow associated with home. With a wealth of fine novels and a surfeit of antiques, the Brits have perfected the art of nostalgia. The National Trust protects, preserves, and conserves castles and gardens to prop up the heritage industry. Their restoration efforts create convenient (and profitable) movie locations. From *A Room with a View* (1985) to *Howard's End* (1992), the distinguished filmmaking team of Merchant and Ivory turned the British costume drama into their personal brand.[6]

Costume dramas provide us with perspective—a chance to marvel at others' mistakes or perhaps appreciate how far we've come. Yet the best period pieces add important commentary or resonance with our contemporary challenges. Jane Austen's novels made a surprising recent comeback as movie material. *Sense and Sensibility* (1995), *Emma* (1996), and *Pride and Prejudice* (2005) suggested that the pain and promise of love translates across the centuries. They brought back the lost art of genuine sexual tension. Victories for chaste heroines may have echoed the resurgent interest in sexual abstinence. Suddenly, "true love waits" in the movies. Biographies like *Elizabeth* (1998) and *The Queen* (2006) raised viewer appreciation for even the chilliest of royals. They revealed a heart beating within "ice queens." Each offers an imaginative take on Queen Elizabeth's private thoughts. They turn suppression and restraint into an art.

The masculine side of costume drama gets bloodier. Repression is replaced by aggression. Ancient virtues of loyalty, valor, and courage translate easily to a present era still longing for leadership. The heroism of William Wallace in *Braveheart* (1995, IMDb #90) may cause us to summon conviction to face our current battles. *Saving Private Ryan* (1998, IMDb #64) salutes the bravery of anonymous young soldiers on the beaches of Normandy. Even *The Motorcycle Diaries* (2004) offers a glimpse into the character formation of eventual revolutionary Che Guevara. But not all historical dramas are about bravery and role models. In *The Aviator* (2005) we may recognize our own foibles in Howard Hughes's reclusive hubris. In *There Will Be Blood* (2007), the unchecked greed of Daniel Plainview leads to his downfall. Paul Thomas Anderson's operatic film contrasts America's two great enterprises: oil and religion. Both industries are at their worst when they're consuming the most. The same overreaching can undo proud cultures and result in fallen empires, as in Mel Gibson's bloody chronicle of Mayan decline, *Apocalypto* (2006).

Movies about the past reveal plenty about today. But what does the paucity of recent historical dramas on the IMDb's top films suggest? Is history dead, or do we warm only to a particular kind of nostalgia? Are we managing our present challenges with such acuity that we haven't needed historical perspective, or does our ignorance or indifference toward history underline our cultural hubris? Perhaps we're too busy making history to learn from history. Yet the postmodern movement has caused us to reexamine our past, to question our conclusions.

The field of film studies has exploded with books on memory, history, and nostalgia.[7] Scholars are asking core questions like: What is the relationship of history to our present context? Is history a valuable treasure trove of certain lessons learned? Were the right morals drawn from those stories? Does the historical case need to be reopened and rewritten from the perspective of the powerless rather than the powerful? Localized and personal histories are emerging that challenge the facts of history. The stories of ordinary people have awakened seemingly dead, or at least closed, histories.

The heroism embodied by survivors of *The Killing Fields* (1984, IMDb #247) brought the overlooked struggles of Cambodia to a global audience. *Glory* (1989, IMDb #163) told the neglected story of black soldiers serving in the Civil War. *Forrest Gump* (1994, IMDb #85) offers a peek into the past through the experience of an extremely simple man. It plays games with technology, mixing Forrest into archival footage of John F. Kennedy. But the film merely skims the surface, providing a greatest hits version of the facts, reduced to Forrest's bumper sticker, "Shit Happens." The history of the underdogs, of those who lost the wars or suffered under the brutal regimes, is just being unearthed. Yet vast segments of today's students seem dismissive of ancient history as old news. Are we blind to our own errors, marching into tomorrow with no appreciation for the past?

The biographies that connect with today's audiences transcend their age, taking on timeless relevance. They have a prophetic urgency that shakes up our indifference. They connect the dots between where we've been and where we're headed in such compelling and original ways that they cannot be ignored. They do not get bogged down in debates about historical accuracy. The filmmakers' creative speculation allows them to leap over traditional notions of what "based on a true story" might mean. What kind of prophetic imagination is necessary to open our ahistorical eyes? What costume dramas resonate with postmodern moviegoers? At the top of IMDb's list are *Gladiator* (2000), *The Pianist* (2002), *Der Untergang* (*The Downfall*, 2004), *Finding Neverland* (2004), and *Cinderella Man* (2005). What do these films have in common? What differences emerge in their attitudes toward history? What does their ongoing resonance suggest about what Svetlana Boym has called "the future of nostalgia"?[8]

An Incurable Disease

Nostalgia began as a sickness. In 1688 Swiss doctor Johannes Hofer coined the term to describe the longing for home that afflicted soldiers fighting abroad. It combined two Greek concepts: *nostos*, meaning "to return home," and *algos* connoting "pain."[9] Nostalgia was seen as a sign of patriotic commitment, an attachment to a beloved homeland. What began in the brains of Hofer's patients soon spread to soldiers' bones. Their "longing for home exhausted the 'vital spirits,' causing nausea, loss of appetite, pathological changes in the lungs, brain inflammation, cardiac arrests, high fever, as well as marasmus and a propensity for suicide."[10] The steady stream of bullets aimed at their heads only heightened soldiers' hunger for their hometowns! Once Hofer's thesis gained wider acceptance in the medical community, so did the instances of the disease. Nostalgia became a strategic defense for petrified soldiers eager to avoid the battlefield. When a trip home failed to eradicate the soldiers' symptoms, doctors questioned the physical roots of the malady. Maybe nostalgia is more mental than physical—a state of mind rather than a disease rooted in place.

In 1798 Immanuel Kant began to note the difference between returning to a place and returning to a time.[11] Soldiers didn't just want to come back home, they wanted to turn back the clock and reclaim innocence lost. This kind of disease has no cure because time cannot be reversed. What's past is past. Nostalgia isn't a physical malady but a psychological fixation on a kinder, gentler era. The elusive nature of nostalgia gives it ongoing power and appeal. Nostalgia will remain permanently unsatisfying, an unrequited love. Perhaps my attachment to baseball cards is a means of bracketing my past, fixing my childhood in time. I may grow older, but my cards, toys, and music remain timeless—"Forever 80s."

Nostalgia arises from loss. Having tasted triumph, we long to reclaim the glory of an earlier time. The establishment of Jerusalem erased the Hebrews' bitterness toward the arduous journey out of Egypt. Israel entered a golden era of unparalleled prosperity under King David. David's son Solomon oversaw the completion of the temple. But the glories of a united kingdom proved short-lived. When the kingdom of Judah began falling to the Babylonians in 597 BC, a heavy dose of nostalgia washed over those who were exiled. "By the waters of Babylon," the Judean exiles sat down and wept when they remembered Zion (Ps. 137:1 ESV). Their identity was connected to a particular place. Their faith was connected to the temple, to a physical space. Urban historian Dolores Hayden calls this phenomenon "the power of place."[12] But the dislocation occasioned by exile was physical *and* spiritual. The Israelites were heartsick and homesick, longing for faded glory. Such traumatic events can arrest our development, locking exiles into a permanent fixation on the past.

The psychological theories of Sigmund Freud find a creative expression in Marcel Proust's *Remembrance of Things Past*.[13] Proust demonstrates how memory becomes a form of defense, a chosen distraction to deal with the pain of our past (and present). Proust takes one hundred pages to recount the wonders of Swann's childhood possessions and place. Swann (and Proust) is more in search of lost time than the love of Odette. Nothing snaps him back to the wonders of childhood faster than a *petite madeleine* dipped in tea. Like the smell of grandma's cookies in the oven, our senses transport us to the safe places and pleasures of the past. (Martha Stewart made millions selling us idealized kitchens—and childhoods!) The top prices paid for toys, comic books, and baseball cards from the sixties, seventies, and eighties suggest that many will spend their adulthood reassembling their rooms to look as they did at age seven. What would Proust (or Freud) make of these obsessions? What pain are we avoiding via memory? Is the West in exile? Are we pining for a former era, fixated on the good ol' days? Or is nostalgia a genuine, God-given consolation in a troubled world?

For those who didn't enjoy an earlier era, nostalgia holds minimal appeal. Black Americans do not wish to return to the pre–Civil Rights era of the 1950s. Reverend Martin Luther King Jr. suggested that "the ultimate measure of a man is not where he stands in moments of comfort and convenience but where he stands at times of challenge and controversy." Rosa Parks kept her seat on the bus in Montgomery, Alabama, because she couldn't tolerate the racist past for another day. She was tired of feeling tired. An oppressed people tends to look toward a future day of reckoning, an impending release, a promised land to come. The apocalyptic literature of the Bible comforted the underclass who served under bloody regimes. Stories of the coming judgment for the rich and repressive served as salve for the oppressed. Today's science fiction may function in a similar way.

Nostalgia is the song of a formerly powerful people. Consider the mournful lament of Psalm 137. The Israelites wept by the rivers of Babylon when they remembered their former glory in Zion. The Japanese call a fond remembrance of things past *natsukashii*. Recent efforts to reclaim their imperial legacy suggest a longing for past glory. "If only we could go back, before World War II, when we were a strong people, a united nation." Those previously in power long to return to positions of comfort and prestige. Progressive scholar Linda Hutcheon notes the ideology embedded within nostalgia.[14] It has an inherent conservatism, a holding on to the past (whether for right-wing regimes or even by the most progressive Marxists). Imperial nostalgia makes domination of others look quaint. Films like *A Passage to India* (1984) cover up British racism toward India with proper manners and the search for a good cup of tea. Nostalgia can arise from a hunger for former glory or the fear of our future, but it always arises from people who are literally "out of time," who want to be somewhere else. That sense of displacement can be physical, mental, or spiritual, but the idealized past that fuels the nostalgic imagination is rooted in a present discontent (or disconnect).

History

Russell Crowe: Man out of Time

Acclaimed actor Russell Crowe has been our most powerful "man out of time." From the bruising physicality of Maximus in *Gladiator* (2000) to steering the HMS Surprise as Captain "Lucky Jack" Aubrey in *Master and Commander* (2003) to boxer James J. Braddock in *Cinderella Man* (2005), Crowe dons the mantle of historical figures with considerable aplomb. Born in New Zealand and raised in Australia, Crowe comes across as a manly man, a throwback to earlier eras of empire. Crowe's characters fight for noble causes, taking viewers back to a time when wars were more easily justified. In *Gladiator*, the evil machinations of Commodus give former General Maximus ample reasons for revenge. Maximus fights on behalf of his family and the fallen emperor, Marcus Aurelius. He also takes up arms to defend Lucilla from her brother Commodus's incestuous advances. We want Commodus defeated and the primacy of the Roman Senate restored. Nostalgia drives Maximus; he wants to see Rome returned to its former glory. The Oscar-winning picture has enough allusions to history that audiences can enter into the Roman Colosseum without questioning the story's veracity. It offers the spectacle and splendor we expect from historical epics: lavish costumes, detailed palaces, thousands of (digital) extras. These sword-and-sandal pictures appeal to (primarily) a white male audience, eager to reassert their cultural dominance.[15] Director Ridley Scott makes the flashbacks to Maximus's murdered family especially poignant. The gladiator's hand floats among the wheat fields of his home. Maximus wants revenge, but he mostly longs to find his deceased family amid the Elysian Fields.

Gladiator (IMDb #135) is a libertarian fantasy. Maximus did not want to fight; he wanted to live in peace on the family farm. But after being sold into slavery, he must fight for his life, for his freedom, for the opportunity to enter the ring with Commodus. His war is more personal than political. IMDb user Addie-7 got involved in his struggle: "The creation of a truly heroic character in a pivotal role is a classical and, unfortunately, out of date device. It requires an actor who can not only convince you that his character possesses a heroic and noble nature, but who can also make you care terribly about what happens to this hero. Crowe does both. The viewer loves and admires his Maximus, and agonizes with him in his travails."[16] Maximus fits into a long tradition of reluctant warriors. They take up arms because others strike the first blow. Like America in World War II, they attack only after they are provoked. The inscription on the flagpole of the new National World War II Memorial in Washington DC could serve as Maximus's message: "Americans came to liberate, not to conquer, to restore freedom and to end tyranny."[17] But this "man of peace" can also take down emperors and tigers! Eldakim writes on IMDb, "It actually inspired me to be something greater. I felt the need to achieve and become what truly defines a man. . . . A man has to be responsible and patient, and this man just does that. If I have to pick a single most influential person besides Jesus, I'd still go with Maximus. What he did in the movie was truly outstanding and I wish that he was an actual person in history."[18] Such absurdly high praise!

The equivocating heroes of *Troy* (2004), *Kingdom of Heaven* (2004), and *Alexander* (2004) failed to capture the affections of *Gladiator*'s audience. Viewers didn't necessarily want to see sword-and-sandal epics; they wanted to follow unabashed heroes into battle. Achilles and Hector have a stirring face-off at the conclusion of *Troy*, but the cowardice of Paris (and Orlando Bloom's weak performance) undercuts the heroism intended in his killing of Achilles. It is a tragedy without purpose. The same unbearable lightness of being hampers *The Kingdom of Heaven*. Orlando Bloom cannot fill the considerable shoes of Balian or his crusader father, Gregory of Ibelin. While Oliver Stone may have aspired to offer a more complete portrait of the complex *Alexander the Great*, the resulting feature offered no nostalgic satisfaction whatsoever. Alexander's affection for his boyhood friend Hephaestion echoes our contemporary discussion of sexuality and politics, but to what end? It may be historically accurate to portray an ancient world where bisexuality was the norm, but to ignore the current politicized context proved costly for the filmmakers. Colin Farrell's bushy blond wig didn't help either. Epic battles and sweeping vistas are not sufficient to repeat movie history (of *Gladiator*). Nostalgia is connected more to a psychic space rather than a historical place.

The most enduring historical epics portray heroism through noble causes and courage under fire. The movie *300* (2007) turned the Spartans into rock-ribbed superheroes. Protagonists can have doubts, fears, and questions, but audiences long for just wars. We don't want to question motives or manhood. Such a postmodern problem belongs in our present moment. Whether done in the video game style of *300* or the drab tones of *Letters from Iwo Jima* (2007), viewers don't want to undercut the glorious past. We want Maximus not minimus. We long for old-fashioned heroes who fight for what is right.

Knocked Out

So what happened to *Cinderella Man* (IMDb #187)? It offers Russell Crowe as a man of the people, boxer James J. Braddock, fighting on behalf of his family amid America's Great Depression. Renee Zellwegger plays Braddock's long-suffering wife, Mae, forced to water down the milk for their three children. The Braddocks never give up in the face of the considerable odds against Jim's comeback. Despite reviewers' enthusiasm and the rapturous ratings on the IMDb, the $88 million production of *Cinderella Man* stopped at $61 million at the US box office. Did the creative team behind the Oscar-winning *Beautiful Mind* (2001) miss the cultural zeitgeist? Is the costume drama dead? What was this boxing story missing?

Cinderella Man began as a blatant response to the events of September 11, 2001. Universal Studio executives had gathered to hear the insights of futurist Watts Wacker. He told the execs that in the post-9/11 world, people want meaning. Studio head Stacy Snider recalls, "Before 9/11, the movie seemed to many of us less timely, less relevant. It seemed more timely and relevant after 9/11 because it is a story about America getting up off its feet after being knocked out."[19] Marc Schmuger, Universal's sharpest in-house prognosticator, considered *Cinderella Man* "irresistible populism," especially given the Academy Award–winning team of director Ron Howard, producer Brian Grazer, screenwriter Akiva Goldsman, and star Russell Crowe. The marketing campaign connected the film to our post-9/11 context: "When America was on its knees, he brought us to our feet." More than mining nostalgia, Universal boxed it up and sold it by the hour.

Critics acknowledged their bias against such blatantly heartwarming stories. We may have seen one too many *Rocky*'s, the underdog boxer battling the odds to become world champion. Manohla Dargis of the *New York Times* wrote, "*Cinderella Man* is a shamefully ingratiating old-fashioned weepie."[20] Rene Rodriguez of the *Miami Herald* called *Cinderella Man* "an awfully square movie." Yet he offered a backhanded compliment: "This is an utterly predictable, thoroughly manipulative, and thunderously obvious movie. I wouldn't change a frame of it."[21] Against the backdrop of our cynical age, Roger Ebert found the earnestness of James J. Braddock refreshing:

> *Cinderella Man* is a terrific boxing picture, but there's no great need for another one. The need it fills is for a full-length portrait of a good man. Most serious movies live in a world of cynicism and irony, and most good-hearted movie characters live in bad movies. Here is a movie where a good man prevails in a world where every day is an invitation to despair, where resentment would seem fully justified, where doing the right thing seems almost gratuitous, because nobody is looking and nobody cares.[22]

Cinderella Man won its initial bout with the critics. Universal hoped to build audience interest via such positive word of mouth. Only three days after the film opened, Russell Crowe was in New York on a media tour to promote the movie when he was arrested for tossing a telephone at a desk clerk at the Mercer Hotel—neither heroic nor inspiring! Perhaps Crowe's stirring on-screen portrait of decency and goodness was undercut by his offscreen antics.

Unfortunately, *Cinderella Man*'s box office returns were already down for the count prior to Crowe's arrest. So the question remains: why was *Cinderella Man* not embraced by the broad movie-going public? Some suggested that a serious picture shouldn't have opened in the summer. As a sepia-toned Oscar contender, *Cinderella Man* belonged in the amber premieres of autumn. But the problems of audience disconnect run deeper than the wrong season. Like another Depression era underdog story, *Seabiscuit* (2003), *Cinderella Man* is more admired for its intentions than loved for its resonance. IMDb reviewer Chris Docker from Scotland suggests, "This is classic American-style hero creation and worship and, on the face of it, healthy enough. So why the doubts? . . . Compare it with European cinema and it all seems very full of absolutes. The heroes don't have any failings. . . . Much as I admire the use of role models, I somehow wonder if more human heroes aren't sometimes called for."[23] Flagrant-Baronessa from Sweden saluted *Cinderella Man* as a well-crafted and often-entertaining film, "but it is extremely standard, safe, predictable, logical, been-there-done-that—there are no puzzling detours, twists, or unusual character developments. Sure, it is grounded as a reality-based biography but there is NO flair. . . . You've seen it all before."[24] *Cinderella Man* may also have suffered in comparison to another boxing picture. IMDb rater ignatiusloyala noted, "When there was *Million Dollar Baby* already last year, *Cinderella Man* doesn't seem fresh."[25] Perhaps the parallels between getting off the mat during the Great Depression and rising from the rubble of the World Trade Center were overestimated. Even during the volatility of our stock markets, we still have unparalleled wealth. We got knocked down on 9/11 for being more like the neighborhood bully than a scrawny underdog. Maybe James J. Braddock's victory over preening champion Max Baer failed to rouse us because we couldn't recognize ourselves in the comeback role. It is hard to embrace a David versus Goliath story when we're the giant. We want to see ourselves as the desk clerk struck by a petulant star. But we may be closer to Russell Crowe, a spoiled actor, than we care to admit.

Our nostalgic need is not for championships but for innocence. Americans don't need to turn back the clock to a time when "we're number one!" We're still number one. No, we need to get back to an era when our reasons for fighting were pure, our motives unquestioned. We don't need surrogate boxers to win unlikely victories for us; we need a time machine that restores blamelessness. We long for moral clarity, but we cannot erase all the variables we know. The road to incorruptibility must wrestle with the faded glory in our historical closet—World War II.

The Ongoing War

> Who controls the past, controls the future; who controls the present, controls the past.
>
> George Orwell, *1984*[26]

What continues to make World War II the filmmakers' war of choice? Does it represent the last moment the West was united around a common cause? Are the moral choices so clear as to be comfortable? Our nostalgia for World War II suggests an acknowledgment of failure (or at least confusion) since then. We don't need to be reminded of our embarrassment in Vietnam. Perhaps the apparent clarity of World War II provides an important corrective to our sense of false certainty in Iraq. Yet the specter of Hitler and the Holocaust raises ongoing red flags about our (in)humanity. What lessons can be gleaned by remembering? Why do filmmakers feel the need to tell stories of "the greatest generation"? Where will our nostalgia end?

Historians generally want at least fifty years of distance before analyzing the past. It takes time to sort out fact from feelings, intitial impressions from lasting impact. In the mid nineties, interest in World War II thus reached epic proportions. The shift between memory and history reached a critical mass. Director Steven Spielberg's Shoah Foundation committed to recording the eyewitness stories of the Holocaust survivors before they perished, so we might never forget what happened. His *Schindler's List* (1993, IMDb #7) re-created concentration-camp horrors like never before. The stark black-and-white photography captured the bleakness of the dire situation. Yet Oskar Schindler's commitment to saving as many people as possible reminded us that courage and conscience could make a difference. Spielberg concluded the film with a living link to history, taking the survivors or their offspring from Schindler's real-life list to visit his grave atop Mount Zion in Israel. The imaginative and the historical met in a documentary moment before the survivors and their memories were lost.

Maurice Halbwachs offers the foundational take on this dynamic social process in *The Collective Memory*.[27] Halbwachs suggests that history begins only when the collective memory and shared traditions of a generation or community start to fade. As the individuals who form the collective die, historians step in as archivists to record the memories (like the Shoah Foundation and their march against time to get interviews on film). Building on the foundational notions of Plato, Halbwachs shows little enthusiasm for written history. He prefers the "living text" of memory. Historians strive for an objectivity rooted in the highly subjective experience of those within the community. The facts emerge by comparing and contrasting the eyewitness accounts. Over time, conclusions are drawn and the particulars become generalized. Philosopher Paul Ricoeur expanded on Halbwachs's sociological take on memory and history. He found room for individuals' memory within (or alongside) the collective memory. Near the end of his distinguished life, Ricoeur concluded:

> True testimony is oral. It is therefore a living voice. Once it is written and only then, it becomes a document. And at this moment it becomes part of an archive. But the very fact of the archive constitutes a neutralization of the living voice, which lines up voluntary testimonies, themselves given from presence to presence. . . . In this sense, history begins only with the confrontation with and between testimonies, and, in particular, with testimonies that were reduced to silence by archivization.[28]

The explosion of World War II films at the end of the twentieth century offers a study in what Ricoeur calls "the historiographical operation." History forms as we support, refine, or refute the collective memory. The various controversies arising amid cinematic histories and biographies reflect the ongoing tension between memory and history, oral testimony and written archives.

Among the recent films on World War II to press people's buttons was *La Vita è bella* (*Life Is Beautiful*, 1997, IMDb #82). Filmmaker and star Roberto Benigni dared to find humor amid concentration camps. Guido's ability to make his wife and son smile right up to his own demise struck some as overly sentimental and exploitive—the Holocaust made palatable. Film critic Jonathan Rosenbaum snapped, "The hero's slapstick behavior to the everyday realities of the camps borders on the nauseating."[29] Richard Schickel of *Time* magazine called *Life Is Beautiful* a "fascist fable" that must be resisted. Schickel lamented the death of concentration camp survivors and the accompanying rise in Holocaust deniers. He wrote, "In this climate, turning even a small corner of this century's central horror into feel-good popular entertainment is abhorrent."[30]

Benigni's imaginative leaps behind barbed wire were seen as too much, too soon, yet audiences laughed and cried, embracing the hope emerging from the rubble. *Life Is Beautiful* burst into the IMDb's Top 100 list and became America's highest-grossing foreign language film of all time.[31] Hollywood rewarded Benigni with an Oscar as Best Actor. So was *La Vita è bella* ugly and irresponsible or poetic and profound?

The controversy surrounding *Life Is Beautiful* raises key questions about property and propriety. Historical films (especially comedic ones) wade into issues of representation and responsibility. By adding a nostalgic glow to concentration camps, Benigni may have trivialized what he sought to redeem. The relationship between memory and imagination, history and fiction is tenuous and loaded with political land mines. Paul Ricoeur moves the discussion past polarization in his final book, *Memory, History, Forgetting*.[32] This thick volume starts with the traditional opposition of memory and imagination. Is memory a subcategory of the ever-unreliable imagination? Or does the image that comes to mind stand apart as the outcome of a conscious act of remembering? Ricoeur traces the dueling tensions back to Plato and Aristotle, proposing a blended approach to the phenomenology of memory and imagination. What some will consider Benigni's betrayal of memory, others will praise as a transcendent reimagination of a historic event. Both arguments miss the more important point embedded in Ricoeur's argument. It is not memory versus imagination but their complementary roles in our history making. For some, *Life Is Beautiful* moved too quickly past their vow to "never forget" the horror. For others who have no direct experience of the Holocaust, *Life Is Beautiful* worked as an imaginative fable that offered up an emotional victory over the dark forces behind the Shoah. It shifted the Holocaust from frozen memory or fixed idol into dynamic moments of ongoing reconciliation. The past became present—the time and place where the Spirit meets us.

In *Flags of Our Fathers* and *Letters from Iwo Jima* (both from 2006), Clint Eastwood presents two sides of the same brutal battle in the Pacific. The harrowing films demonstrate the importance of our postmodern emphasis on our "situatedness": where we sit determines what we see. Eastwood's companion movies document the horrors of war both on the ground and within the Japanese tunnels. They are among the darkest movies (both in their cinematography and outlook) exploring what many remember as a celebratory war. Both films question the nationalism of leaders that gets us into conflicts that everyday soldiers are forced to fight.

Flags of Our Fathers explores the real, complicated story behind the famous photograph of the American flag hoisted atop Iwo Jima. It concentrates on the selling of the war back home. Adam Beach gave a haunting performance as the Native American soldier Ira Hayes who falls into the cracks between a patriotic image of war and the actual lives lost on the island. Unfortunately, the cynical tone of Paul Haggis's screenplay robbed *Flags* of too much humanity. *Letters from Iwo Jima* takes the same remote island location but puts the camera on the other side of the fighting. Eastwood takes us inside the dark caves, where General Kuribayashi (Ken Watanabe) struggles to rally his beleaguered troops despite their certain death. It contrasts the Japanese concept of honor with the American notion of heroism. The poignant letters written by soldiers, such as Saigo to his pregnant wife back home, stand in contrast to the grim reality. Thus, the historical gaps in the record take so long to sort out. While American audiences balked at the subtitles, Japanese filmgoers flocked to the humanizing *Letters from Iwo Jima*. IMDb user sford-20 exemplifies Eastwood's hope at bridging the cultural/historical divide:

> I'm American, my wife is Japanese. Together, we've visited and cried together at the A-bomb Dome in Hiroshima, and again at the Arizona Memorial in Hawaii. I have relatives who fought in the Pacific, she also has family who fought in the war and who lived in Hiroshima. I have two sons now serving in the US Marines. Together my wife and I watched and enjoyed both movies. . . . We may be from different cultures, eat different food, speak different languages, pray to God differently, but we all have things in common. We all live, love, want to be loved, and we dream about and long for peace. And, sometimes we are called to serve and pay for the opportunity.[33]

We cannot cling to nostalgia if we hope to find common ground. We must acknowledge our mutual losses if we hope to move forward. *Letters from Iwo Jima* evokes an empathy that fulfills Jesus's challenging call to "love your enemies and pray for those who persecute you" (Matt. 5:44).

Playing to Live

Two European films already emerging as enduring classics look at the quieter side of the war. They take place beyond the battlefield, in the personal demons that threaten to undo us. *The Pianist* (IMDb #47) and *Der Untergang* (*The Downfall*, IMDb #45) are harrowing descents into hell, with two very different responses to unbearable surroundings. They force audiences to confront the worst aspects of human behavior, to stare into the dark. How much evil are we capable of? How much can we tolerate? How do we muster the courage to continue in the face of wartime atrocities? *The Pianist* and *Downfall* put audiences through the wringer as a wake-up call. Elie Wiesel describes this important work of remembering: "The memory of death will serve as a shield against death."[34] These powerful films offer impassioned and personal cries of "Never Again!"

The Pianist takes place within the walls of the Warsaw ghetto. It tells the true story of accomplished musician, Wladyslaw Szpilman. The Nazi occupation moves him from concert halls to bombed-out buildings. He becomes an eyewitness to the Warsaw Ghetto Uprising, a living testimony to the compelling need to resist evil. Yet Szpilman never resorts to the heroism we expect in war movies. He never takes up arms, leads a resistance, or takes a bullet for others. As Szpilman, Adrian Brody vanishes within the role, his white pallor and thin frame mirroring the tattered remains of Warsaw. He must make himself invisible in order to survive. *The Pianist* represents a rare instance when passivity in a title character works. We cheer for him to vanish, to go unnoticed. By the conclusion of the film, Szpilman and the city are barely standing.

Director Roman Polanski drew from his own childhood memories of World War II in Poland. He pours a sense of desperation into every muted frame. The little details of a father dividing a caramel into six pieces for his family ring true. When German soldiers toss an old man in a wheelchair off a balcony because he failed to stand at their appearance, the insanity of the Nazis is telescoped into a single, maddening scene. Polanski honors his fallen comrades with this paean to his Polish heritage. Szpilman stands in as a surrogate for Polanski, an artist seeking to play a sad song on behalf of a fallen people. They are both living witnesses to what happened in Warsaw. *The Pianist* surprised Oscar prognosticators by winning well-deserved honors for Best Actor, Best Adapted Screenplay, and Best Director. (Its laughable loss to *Chicago* as Best Picture will be avenged by *The Pianist's* enduring power and impact.) *The Pianist* proved that the lessons of World War II and the need to remember the Holocaust endure a decade after *Schindler's List*.

The nostalgia impulse in *The Pianist* arises from the use of music. Szpilman's entire being is rooted in song, especially the evocative work of Polish composer Frederic Chopin. Chopin's innovations came from the room he left for poetic, personal expression. Szpilman brings soulfulness to Chopin's compositions for solo piano. In simply touching an abandoned instrument, Szpilman can feel the rhythm in his hands. To deprive him of this source of comfort and solace is truly dehumanizing. The scene in which Szpilman discovers an upright piano in his latest safe house affirms the sustaining power of art. Szpilman's private recital drives all the horrors of his reality away. Just as the sounds of opera waft over the prisoners in *The Shawshank Redemption*, so music lifts Szpilman out of his grim circumstances, transforming him into a picture of contentment. As an audience, we panic that he will be discovered—until Polanski reveals that Szpilman's impromptu concert is in his head. He plays above the keys, hearing Chopin in his mind. This revelatory moment brings us simultaneous relief and delight. We are transported into the pianist's revelry. This demonstrates the concurrent power of music and memories. We replay our favorite tunes in our minds whenever we desperately need them.

When a Nazi officer discovers him hiding in an attic and asks him to "play something," Szpilman embarks on what he must have believed to be his final concert. Szpilman plays a defiant hymn to life, carving out a heavenly artistic space. After watching Nazis behave like animals, we finally discover what separates humanity from bestial behavior—music; beautiful, haunting music. It also becomes a uniting, life-saving passion. As a fellow music fan, Captain Hosenfeld becomes his unexpected savior, a "good" Nazi who provides food and clothing. In a dramatic reversal, Szpilman has gone from living to play to playing to live.

The Pianist also raises troubling questions about a world that operates so randomly. A wrong question can result in a girl's instant death. Why do the innocent suffer? Why do some survive and others tumble? Can faith be retained in a time when so many prayers appear unheard? *The Pianist* suggests that the Holocaust is less of a burnt offering than a Shoah—a random catastrophe that destroys all notions of faith or order. Szpilman survives through sheer happenstance, a random act of mercy that is not extended to other equally innocent victims. Is he protected by providence? Divine mercy is mediated through another person. The grace extended by a Nazi officer suggests that individuals can still make a difference even amid the most trying circumstances. Even within genocide, people can demonstrate redemptive qualities. Good people can wear bad uniforms. The universe may appear capricious; God may seem absent. But we still retain a choice in how to respond—offering a coat of comfort or a cold shoulder of death. History asks us to choose wisely.

Humanizing Monsters

Der Untergang (*The Downfall*, 2004) drills even further down into World War II, taking viewers inside Adolph Hitler's bunker as the Russians march on

Berlin. Claustrophobia and cyanide capsules loom large as Hitler's entourage considers their limited options. An air of apocalyptic dread looms over the proceedings. The sounds of bombs bursting shatter any delusions of security within the bunker. How to respond to certain defeat? Most of the Nazis choose suicide. *Der Untergang* (IMDb #45) is based on books by historian Joachim Fest and the memoirs of Traudl Junge, Hitler's secretary at the fall of the Third Reich. Junge narrates *Downfall*, offering glimpses of Hitler's inner circle, including Eva Braun, Heinrich Himmler, and Joseph Goebbels (and his family). It is a long, harrowing film framed by the question of forgiveness. An aged Traudl Junge looks back and wonders, "How can I forgive myself?" Will the global community forgive the Nazis? What kind of grace would be sufficient to cover their heinous crimes?

Controversy dogged this German production, along with accusations that it was sympathetic to the Nazis. Director Oliver Hirschbiegel employs a documentary style that immediately draws audiences into the human drama. Bruno Ganz's performance as a haggard Hitler conveys both the magnetism and mania that fueled his insane plans. His kindness toward his dog, his secretary, and his wife contradicts our perceived notions of Hitler as a monster. Yet he continues to hold on to delusions of grandeur that the war might still be won. He rails against his general's incompetence, "I never attended an academy and yet I conquered Europe all by myself!" As his dream of a thousand-year reich dies, Hitler weeps.

Some have questioned Hirschbiegel's decision to play the "Crucifixus" from Johann Sebastian Bach's *Mass in B Minor* during Hitler's time of silent contemplation. Is the director trying to draw parallels between the deaths of Hitler and Jesus? Viewers must give the filmmaker more credit than that. If anything, the use of Bach's "Crucifixus" puts us inside Hitler's delusion, his own sense of self-importance and (false) messiahship. His disdain for the German people who have failed him illustrates Hitler's megalomaniacal focus. He blames others for his death, pointing fingers at the Nazis' collapse: "There is no compassion for traitors." Hitler didn't come to rescue a people but to build a personal empire—the very antipathy of Jesus's crucifixion. Hirschbiegel uses irony for revelatory purposes: "For them who have ears to hear" (see Matt. 13:9–17).

The supporting characters in *Downfall* demonstrate moments of humanity and delusion as well. While the Russians invade, Eva Braun throws a birthday party for Hitler, trying to dance the inevitable away. Traudl Junge joins Eva for walking the dog or sharing a cigarette. Magda Goebbels poisons her six children with frightening dispassion yet begs the Führer not to commit suicide. She is a true believer in the Nazi vision even through her submission to a firing squad. Humanizing the people behind such atrocities doesn't necessarily make them sympathetic. Instead it reminds us how conspiracies of evil grow, one indifferent "Yes, Fuhrer" at a time. Zygmaut Bauman notes that the Holocaust "was accompanied not by the uproar of emotions, but the dead silence of unconcern."[35]

This echoes Jesus's illuminating tale of the Good Samaritan (and the indifferent predecessors). Who is our neighbor and when should we get involved? Miroslav Volf describes the process of rationalization: "I go about my business . . . I start to view horror and my implication in it as normalcy. I reason: the road from Jerusalem to Jericho will always be littered by people beaten and left half-dead; I can pass—I must pass—by each without much concern. The indifference that made the prophecy, takes care also of its fulfillment."[36] *Der Untergang* puts us inside Hitler's circle and questions how we would respond given similar circumstances. Would we become sheep following a magnetic and maniacal shepherd? Or would we rally as a voice of conscience, rising up to oppose evil?

An equally painful but underreported scar on German history drives the 2006 Oscar winner for Best Foreign Film, *Das Leben der Anderen* (*The Lives of Others*). Set in communist East Germany during the 1980s, *The Lives of Others* re-creates an oppressive era with a drab, grey color palette. It follows the transformation of Stasi agent Gerd Weisler as he spies on playwright George Dreyman and Dreyman's girlfriend, Christa Maria Sieland. The artists' passionate, hidden lives prove so compelling that Weisler jeopardizes his own career to protect them. The movie demonstrates the power of beauty to transform even the most hardened heart.

The Lives of Others shows how a corrupt regime maintains power—through threats and intimidation. Secrets obtained through wiretaps are used to enforce allegiance. When a blacklisted writer abandons hope and commits suicide, the playwright Dreyman is compelled to action. While Dreyman plays a stirring "Sonata for a Good Man" on the piano downstairs, Weisler listens in upstairs. The cold, clinical Weisler finds himself reduced to tears. How can he betray such pure beauty? Weisler begins to engage in small acts of civil disobedience, siding with the artists against their oppressors. Free will reigns even under the most oppressive governments. Weisler's new life becomes a beautiful song despite tragic circumstances.

First-time filmmaker Florian Henckel von Donnersmarck displays remarkable control of his material, parceling out one subtle plot twist after another. His parents endured the oppressive policies of East Germany. Their fear fueled von Donnersmarck's imagination. He turns a story of invasive voyeurism into one of the most humane dramas in cinematic history. What was the secret of his success? Von Donnersmarck asks himself basic questions when directing a scene: "'Is this image as I conceived it? Do I find it beautiful? Do I find it truthful? Does the way that these actors are performing convince me or does it feel like a lie? If it feels like a lie, what element feels untrue? Can I name it?' That really isn't much of a craft—it's using your own perception. It's like forgetting everything that you've learned and trying to see if you find it convincing."[37] Von Donnersmarck trusts his actors to capture the truth of the scene, often without the use of dialogue. The late actor Ulrich Muhe delivers a remarkably still performance as Weisler. We sense how torturous conditions have threatened his soul. His gradual awakening is a palpable portrait of redemption.

IMDb users were initially mystified that *The Lives of Others* upset *Pan's Labyrinth* for the Academy Award for Best Foreign Film. They wondered, "Why haven't I heard anything about this film?"[38] After seeing it, an IMDb reviewer exclaimed, "This should be seen in every country and its merits trumpeted from the skies."[39] Like the Stasi agents, *The Lives of Others* sneaks up on audiences, demanding meticulous attention to detail. Its rewards await patient viewers. *The Lives of Others* also offers a challenging notion to those hoping to engage in lifestyle evangelism. Far too often in religious communities we attempt to put our best face forward, witnessing to others through positive attitudes and platitudes. But what if people could see and study our private selves, outside religious settings? Would we be embarrassed by our behavior? Would it be considered unChristian?[40] In *The Lives of Others*, the beautiful actions of a playwright and an actress transform a Stasi spy. Their authentic witness unknowingly transforms a lonely man and the lives of many others.

Downfall and *The Lives of Others* serve as both reminders and warnings. They force Germans to face their sordid history. From Nazi collaborators to Stasi spies in East Berlin, the German people must own their complicity in national evil. But by humanizing butchers, these films put the temptations of evil on a universal plane. We all have the capacity to spy or kill, even mothers who put ideology above their children. The framing device in *Downfall* provided by the narrator, Traudl Junge, counterbalances this grim reality. Hitler's real-life secretary reflects on what she witnessed, "I assured myself with the thought of not being personally guilty. And that I didn't know anything about the enormous scale of it [the concentration camps, the final solution, etc.]." But her encounter with the youthful face of Nazi resistor Sophie Scholl's memorial wakes her up.[41] Junge concludes, "And at that moment I actually realized that a young age isn't an excuse. And that it might have been possible to get to know things." *Der Untergang* and *Das*

Leben der Anderen can be viewed cynically, as an effort to expiate German guilt. Junge was young and easily duped; therefore, she (and by extension, Germany) should be excused. Stasi agents like Weisler were simply doing what they were told. Unreflective viewers may think, "Beneath their frosty exterior, they were innocent and sweet." Understandably, attempts to escape blame still enrage the victims and survivors of the atrocities. But *Downfall* and *The Lives of Others* can also be appreciated as cautionary tales. They dare audiences to question their leaders, to follow their conscience, to remain ever vigilant.

Memory and Imagination

> Exegesis is the progressive returning of everything history has formed, back to the original Light.
>
> Alois Gugler[42]

Finding Neverland (2004) opened in theaters almost exactly one hundred years after J. M. Barrie's enchanting *Peter Pan* revolutionized British theater. This gentle and genteel film provided a perfect antidote to our war-ravaged era; its simple message—"believe." The groundbreaking frivolity of *Peter Pan* rewrote the rules of onstage propriety, introducing playfulness into a stuffy art form. Both the original play and the historical drama behind it are about the wonders of childhood and the power of belief. They offer a fanciful world full of fairies and flight. But *Finding Neverland* (IMDb #172) is also about dashed dreams and dealing with grief. It demonstrates our need for new eyes amid innocence lost. Director Marc Forster's movie doesn't merely mourn a vanishing childhood with a melancholic nostalgia; it literally takes us back to the garden, bringing the magic of childhood to even the most jaded filmgoer. *Finding Neverland* allows us to slip into the original Peter Pan's shoes. We share his pain, shed his tears, and understand his rage, until we are all transformed by the magical storytelling of James M. Barrie. *Finding Neverland* is equal parts biography, historical drama, and childhood fantasy. It embraces the power of art to transform our circumstances.

Finding Neverland springs from the real-life relationship of acclaimed British playwright James Barrie with Sylvia Llewelyn Davies and her five children. It is set amid the "belle epoque," the last innocent era before World War I shredded notions of civility. Wrestling with writer's block (and the lofty expectations that accompany success), Barrie finds comfort and inspiration in Sylvia's children,

James M. Barrie of Peter Pan fame challenges Sylvia Llewelyn Davies and her boys to rediscover their childhood imagination. *Finding Neverland.* © 2004 by Miramax.

especially the enigmatic Peter. They cross paths in London's Kensington Park. Within minutes, Barrie is dancing with his sheep dog, entertaining the children and impressing Sylvia. Barrie's childlike (or childish) approach to life becomes a foil for Peter's world-weary perspective. While Barrie challenges the Davies boys to see his dog as a dancing bear, Peter protests, "This is absurd. He's just a dog." Barrie calls *just* a "horrible, candle-snuffing word" and lays down the film's central thesis: "With those eyes, my bonnie lad, I'm afraid you'll never see it. However with just a wee bit of imagination, I can turn around right now and see the great bear, Porthos." Producer Richard Gladstein says, "That line is really the quintessential part of the movie. . . . It's really about giving a child back his childhood."[43] The filmmakers transport viewers inside Barrie's mind—from a dog in the park to a dancing circus bear.

Finding Neverland is based on a stage play inspired by real-life events. That means the story fudges facts, turning Sylvia into a widow well before her time and conflating the five Davies children into four boys. *Finding Neverland* addresses allegations of impropriety between Barrie and the children in a single scene, but it never deals with the ominous question of whether Barrie was a pedophile. In real life, the death of Barrie's older brother, David, in a skating accident traumatized their mother. James stopped growing both physically and emotionally, locked into eternal youth. *Neverland* director Marc Forster describes Barrie as more asexual than predatory.[44] The movie (and Barrie's life) became about playing games, about escaping to childhood rather than fixating on youth.

While the movie ends on a hopeful note, the biographies of the boys were much darker. The Llewelyn Davies boys grew up to tragic lives—George died in World War I, Michael drowned at Oxford, and Peter, who came to call *Peter Pan* "that terrible masterpiece," committed suicide at age sixty-three. *Finding Neverland* could have been as troubling as the war films we reviewed, but the filmmakers chose to portray how imagination can overcome daunting circumstances.[45] The harsh reality behind (or beyond) the film spoiled the experience for *New Yorker* film critic Anthony Lane. He reviews the facts of history, rather than the film, concluding:

> The effect of "Peter Pan" was like that of those iron bars on the hero's family home; it is a kind of prison drama played onstage as a slice of festive cheer, and it locked the Llewellyn Davies [sic] boys into the garden of pre-puberty. . . . In making the five the tinder for Peter Pan, he [Barrie] treated them as ideal spirits made flesh and no child should be freighted with such an embarrassing burden.[46]

Lane's imagination was disabled by Barrie's biography. He couldn't forgive the man for what he had wrought. The facts of Barrie's sordid case trumped any artistry arising from the history.

As in the reaction to *Life Is Beautiful*, for some, the politics of history ruined the movie-going experience. While remembering past wrongs may serve as a protective against future abuses, the victims of history cannot be healed by the memories themselves. Theologian Miroslav Volf suggests that "the *means* of healing is the *interpretive* work a person does with memory."[47] Barrie may not have recounted things accurately because his memory had already transformed his painful past into a creative future. Producer Richard Gladstein insists *Finding Neverland* was never intended as a biopic: "It would have deprived us as filmmakers of using our own imagination when you're making a film about imagination."[48] A biography of Barrie *should have* taken liberties. *Finding Neverland* isn't about recounting the facts but about transforming and redeeming history for today.

Johnny Depp conveys a genuine sense of wonder and glee as Barrie. He masters Barrie's Scottish brogue and yet plays a convincing pirate (just prior to his masterful creation of Captain Jack Sparrow in *Pirates of the Caribbean*). Kate

Winslet brings a grace and beauty to her role as Sylvia. Her silent suffering is mirrored in the frustrations of Barrie's wife, Mary (played by Radha Mitchell). The social pressures of turn-of-the-century England serve as the villain. As Sylvia's class-conscious mother, Julie Christie embodies social conformity. Amid such acclaimed actors, child actor Freddie Highmore wins our hearts as Peter. His rage at the loss of his father (and the creeping sickness of his mother) comes roaring out when he destroys a playhouse. As he smashes stage props and shreds a play, he screams, "Stop lying to me! I'm sick of grown-ups lying to me. All you do is teach me to make up stupid stories. I'm not blind. I won't be made a fool." He wants reality, not fantasy. Barrie waits patiently for Peter's tantrum to end. They are complementary characters: the adult who refuses to grow up and the child who has experienced too much, too soon.

Cinderella Man aspired to offer audiences comfort after 9/11. But while James Braddock rises via strength and determination, J. M. Barrie and Peter overcome their losses via imagination. *Finding Neverland* is about learning to play again. As Barrie, Johnny Depp carries toys into almost every scene. He teaches the boys to fly kites, to portray pirates, to howl like cowboys and Indians in the woods. The film echoes Jesus's challenge to become like children to enter God's kingdom (see Matt. 18:3). Childlikeness is the province of artists, those who never stopped playing with paint and clay and fiction.[49] As Barrie frets over public response to Peter Pan, he comes up with a foolproof way to soften his audience: he reserves twenty-five seats for children from a local orphanage. The cinematic idea came from producer Richard Gladstein. He had noted Barrie's instructions to the actors in the original production of *Peter Pan*. The only adornment the cast needed to bring with them to the theater was a child's outlook. In *Finding Neverland*, we literally see the play through children's eyes. The film becomes a test of viewers' imaginations.

Finding Neverland also confronts the specter of death. Marc Forster admits, "Pretty much all my work—from *Everything Put Together* on—is concerned, in one way or another, with death."[50] Three deaths rocked Forster before he directed *Monster's Ball* (2001): "There was a three-month period when my father, my brother (to suicide) and my grandmother all died. So I understand how something like that changes you in the way you see life and the way you do things."[51] The apparent randomness and fragility of life seeps through *Finding Neverland*. It seems cruel (or at least manipulative) that children who have already lost a father (offscreen) must now face the loss of their beloved mother. But children often bear the brunt of war, poverty, or disease. Memorials for 9/11 focused on the victims, but what of the survivors—the widows, widowers, and orphans? How do they process their grief? Sylvia puts on a brave face, but James tells her, "You can't go on pretending." She insists, "We need to go on pretending until the end—with you." In one of the more touching scenes of recent cinematic history, the cast and crew continue pretending with Sylvia. If she's too ill to attend the play, then they bring the show to her. What a demonstration of our calling as Christians. In the book of Genesis, our Creator would not rest until we had seen the wonder of his show. The incarnation of Christ demonstrates how far God would go to bring the story to us. To those who haven't seen or heard, *we bring the story to them*—out of love.

And what a production Barrie and company mount! *Finding Neverland* director Marc Forster and his team break the fourth wall, literally opening up the Davies's house. They create a Neverland without digital effects; just old-fashioned movie magic—props, costumes, makeup, lighting. Tinkerbell drinks poisoned medicine to save Peter Pan's life. She can be revived only if the children believe in fairies. Peter challenges them, "If you believe, clap your hands." The most cynical character, Sylvia's mother, leads the applause. Reality and fantasy merge as Sylvia enters into her backyard and the play. Neverland has become a tangible world, as fairies, sprites, and animals welcome Sylvia. The paradise lost by the Davies family has now been found. In entering Neverland, Sylvia literally gets back to the garden. She is suddenly robed in splendor, dressed for an eternal dance. Sylvia joins the heavenly pageant where lions lie down with lambs—a peaceable kingdom full of mystery and wonder. And the audience weeps, overcome by beauty. Shameless manipulation? Absolutely. Well-deserved tears? Definitely.

The audience reactions posted on the IMDb tell the story. *Finding Neverland* works as an old-fashioned family film. It satisfies our basic craving for nostalgia. Sapphira Gratz from Tampa, Florida, writes, "This movie gets my highest rating because it is everything that most movies today are NOT! It's so sweet, innocent, and pure that I can see where some critics find fault because they are used to a movie being filthy and sensational."[52] But it is about much more than turning back the clock. *Finding Neverland* stares an ugly reality in the face and transforms it, for those who have ears to hear or eyes to see. Marcin Kukuczka writes from Cieszyn, Poland, "Skeptical people will probably find it strange; realists will treat it as a nice fairy tale for kids; materialists will see no benefit in what the movie shows, particularly in what James does. Yet, all people who perceive the world through heart and their dreams through imagination and faith will absolutely love it."[53] *Neverland* cuts through even the most hardened heart. Naoum from Thessaloniki, Greece, admits, "The movie had a very touching almost healing effect on me with me actually bursting into tears. That hasn't happened in years (well almost), me being a grown-up male and all that. So, those who have forgotten the magic of being a child and of the fairies that guide them in their every step should let this movie remind them of the magic they lost on their way to adulthood."[54]

So, all other trauma aside, why do we cry in *Finding Neverland*? Is it the beauty of the garden? The fulfillment of a long-held vision? A viewer in India writes: "When the screen went white with a small black 'The End' written subtly in the middle, I felt the tear which tried four times in the past one and half hours to roll on my cheek, finally did so. But I didn't feel what it was for: grief, joy or nostalgia. Whatever it is, 'Finding Neverland' touched me like no other movie I saw this year did. And I don't think I know why."[55] The complexity of reactions mirrors my own conflicted reasons for obsessing over baseball cards: grief, joy, and nostalgia. *Finding Neverland* brackets the grim realities of adulthood with the wonder of childhood. In Peter Davies, audiences see their cynical selves born anew. Ciprian Cucu, a filmgoer from Romania, admired the ultimate questions flowing through Neverland. Cucu posts:

> It's the oldest question in the book. . . . What is the meaning of life? Is it to be rich? Is it to be famous? To climb up your social status? Or can we just live the day, enjoy every moment, try to inspire others without any interest in our well-being and in the consequences? This is what this movie has been about, for me. About being different. About not wanting what everybody wants, not seeing what everybody sees or wants to see, not being afraid to act childish and in some ways stupid, letting go of one's imagination and allowing one's self to dream. . . . And it makes me wonder if we have any imagination left.[56]

Finding Neverland satisfies all the nostalgia we've come to expect from a costume drama. It has impeccable sets, lush costumes, and expert accents. Yet it doesn't end as a museum piece. It blends genres, giving us history and fantasy—painful reality transformed by imagination.

Finding Neverland poses one final test—a tear-inducing assault on our ossified hearts. After Sylvia's funeral, Barrie finds Peter sitting on a park bench, his feet unable to reach the ground. The true test of Barrie's effectiveness as surrogate father arrives only after Sylvia is gone. Peter asks all the right questions, the ones that have never been given a satisfactory answer. He wants to know, "But why did she have to die?" James gives the only honest response possible: "I don't know, boy." He offers fond remembrances of her. But to this dark, grim reality, Barrie adds an imaginative promise: "She went to Neverland, and you can visit her anytime you like if you just go there yourself. How? By believing, Peter. Just believe." Peter's imagination is put to the test. Has it been restored, or has the psychic damage of death killed it? Freddie Highmore, as Peter, summons up a moment of pure, piercing vision. He sheds a tear just as he declares, "I can see her." His vision has been restored. His childhood transformed.

A Theology of Imagination

J. M. Barrie describes an imaginary place where Peter can visit his mother. He can carry his pain and air his legitimate questions in Neverland. Barrie demonstrates the power of imagination to help us see beyond our circumstances. To a grieving boy, a vision of Neverland offered just enough hope to carry on. This is the power of the prophetic imagination (and general revelation) in action: to restore hope to a defeated people. By the rivers of Babylon, the Israelites sat down and wept when they remembered Zion. They should have. When the temple was burned down and the holy city of Jerusalem destroyed in 587 BC, life as Judah knew it ended. Grief is understandable, natural, the right response to catastrophe. But sitting in darkness need not be the end of the story. The Hebrews had to learn how to believe again. There were plenty of reasons not to hope, not to trust. But the road to recovery begins by acknowledging our pain by staring into the dark.

In *Hopeful Imagination*, Old Testament scholar Walter Brueggemann insists we must relinquish in order to receive. Judah "had to let go of the old world of king and temple that God had now taken from it. It had to receive from God's hand a new world which it did not believe possible and which was not the one it would have preferred or chosen."[57] As a people in exile, Israel had to acknowledge the disaster that befell them before they could imagine a future. Brueggemann demonstrates the insight of the Old Testament prophets he has committed to studying. He argues, "The loss of authority for the dynasty and temple in Jerusalem is analogous to the loss of certainty, dominance and legitimacy in our own time. In both cases, the relinquishment is heavy and costly."[58] What glorious visions of the past have we idealized (or idolized)? What might God be asking us to relinquish before we receive?

The connections between Israel in exile and America after 9/11 are prescient. Our sense of security has been breached, our confidence shaken. In an effort to reorder our world, many of us have understandably turned back the clock for comfort. We long for a world without terrorism and the war in Iraq. Yet mere nostalgia, without transformative imagination, cannot provide substantive solace. It is a Band-Aid at best, an attempt to keep the hounds of our contemporary hell at bay. Didn't the same fear of the future fuel the terrorists' attacks? We cannot bomb our way back to the Stone Age. Pluralism and cultural collisions are an inevitable part of our wired world. Until we are ready to own our part in the global misunderstandings regarding our American empire, we will be bound by the nostalgia of our enemies and ourselves.

We have studied historical epics and costume dramas as a means of understanding our present darkness. Backward glances often reflect anxiety regarding the basic question, "Where are we?" So what general revelations have these historical films offered? *Gladiator* reveals our eternal longing for heroes, dedicated to noble causes, fighting for freedom. Like Maximus, we dream of Elysian Fields where there will be no more war. *The Pianist* and *Downfall* remind us of the need to be ever vigilant. We must remember what evil humanity is capable of unleashing. The collapse of the Twin Towers was our stark reminder. *Cinderella Man* was designed to comfort a beaten-down people, but the circumstances have shifted. We are no longer the underdog trying to climb off the mat. Can we adopt an attitude of humility, a teachable posture that allows us to receive God's revelations? What can we learn from observing *The Lives of Others*?

Finding Neverland lets go of what *Cinderella Man* held on to. Peter offers a model for relinquishing control (by accepting his parents' death) and then receiving a new vision for a world he's never imagined (without his parents). Perhaps the Davies family's second loss was easier than the first. They had no strength to stand on. If they hadn't acknowledged their father's death, then their mother's death would have been a definite nail in the first coffin. Did post-9/11 America really acknowledge our loss? Did we engage in genuine grief? Or did we gloss over the pain by striking back? We never relinquished our power, confessed our brokenness. That is why we cannot see, cannot envision our future. We may have idolized and ossified our anguish, using it as the foundation for the wrong war.

It is early enough in our collective memory to revisit 9/11. Remember the worldwide compassion that greeted America? Remember the solidarity we felt from all corners of the globe? Our delusion of power was shattered, and in our grief, we found brothers and sisters in unlikely places. They shared our suffering; they had already been there many times before. The prophetic imagination would help us understand where we went wrong and then paint a portrait of who we might become. A theology of imagination remembers. A theology of imagination embraces history. A theology of imagination vows to never forget, not the sins of others, but the lessons we've learned. Without imagination, we may be doomed to live a life of nostalgic fantasy. What could be worse than never finding Neverland? Chasing it for eternity.

Imagination can lead to false memories and mistaken histories. Films like *Downfall* and *The Pianist* help us to remember crucial events. But an idolization of the past, a fixation on our legitimate grief can also destroy us. Historical epics must not offer a mere escape. *Cinderella Man* paints such a rosy portrait of heroism that we're inclined to dismiss it. The best costume dramas allow us to enter into others' dilemmas, to observe their choices, to ponder our own circumstances. Biopics built to last honor the collective memory, guard against historical amnesia, but also include a hard-won hope for the future. In *Finding Neverland*, memory and imagination merge, turning history into opportunity. Only as we relinquish our obsession with the past can we receive a new word, a new image, a divine revelation—a walk in the eternal garden.

Spirited Away by Fantasy

Tending the Garden

Sen to Chihiro no kamikakushi (*Spirited Away*, 2001, IMDb #51)

The Incredibles (2004, IMDb #97)

Finding Nemo (2003, IMDb #109)

V for Vendetta (2005, IMDb #116)

Wo hu cang long (*Crouching Tiger, Hidden Dragon*, 2000, IMDb #125)

Ying xiong (*Hero*, 2002, IMDb #168)

Shrek (2001, IMDb #183)

Big Fish (2003, IMDb #186)

El Laberinto del fauno (*Pan's Labyrinth*, 2006, IMDb #188)

Wallace & Gromit in The Curse of the Were-Rabbit (2005, IMDb #200)

Monsters, Inc. (2001, IMDb #221)

Pirates of the Caribbean: Curse of the Black Pearl (2003, IMDb #225)

The idea of God as an omniscient, omnipotent being, who moreover loves us, is one of the most daring creations of fantastic literature. All the same, I would prefer that the idea of God belonged to realistic literature.

Juan Luis Borges[1]

I oppose simplifying the world for children. The fact of the matter is that children know, somehow they intuit and deeply understand the complexity of the world we live in. So, I would suggest that you not underestimate children.

Hayao Miyazaki[2]

I have a profound respect and interest in all things Japanese, from sumo to sushi. When I graduated from college, I went to Tokyo to teach English and help found a new church, Tokorozawa Christian Fellowship. I was captivated by Japan's accelerated culture. The pace of rush hour, when millions of Tokyo commuters are literally crammed onto trains, is dizzying. From bullet trains to cell phones, the Japanese are always perfecting faster ways to transport information (and themselves). Their emphasis on smaller-is-better technology arises from their island setting. With 120 million people sharing a habitable area the size of Rhode Island, it is easy to see why saving space is valued in Japan.

The Japanese ability to cram advanced technology into tighter packages has brought them considerable affluence. In the wake of their wealth, they have turned to shopping, fashion, and design as the ultimate forms of self-expression. Their mastery of niche marketing shows in their obsession with *manga*. As I rode the subway in Tokyo, I noticed people of all ages passing time in the same way—reading comic books—from the sweet to the hypersexual. People from eight to eighty were diving into *manga* aimed at schoolgirls, teen boys, housewives, and businessmen. *Manga* comprise 50 percent of book and magazine sales in Japan! The interest in comics crosses over into anime, with ninety animated television programs airing every week, "from family dramas to violent cyber stuff to totally *kawaii*, or cute, kids' stuff."[3] To the Japanese, anime is a universal art that transcends age or interests. And the undisputed master of Japanese anime remains Hayao Miyazaki.

Miyazaki and his Studio Ghibli have created a series of hand-drawn animated films unparalleled in their artistry. His labor-intensive projects take viewers into forbidden or vanished worlds. Growing up in the specter of World War II (born in 1941), Miyazaki developed a lifelong fascination with old Europe. His settings range from enchanted forests (*Mononoke-hime, Princess Mononoke,* 1997, IMDb #113) to haunted ruins (*Howl's Moving Castle,* 2004). His youthful protagonists coexist with pigs, wolves, and other friendly animals. Miyazaki presents a robust, natural world worth protecting. His most widely seen and critically acclaimed project is *Sen to Chihiro no kamikakushi* (*Spirited Away,* 2001, IMDb #51). Miyazaki suggests that success may have spoiled Japan. *Spirited Away* critiques consumerism and awakens interest in forgotten gods. It is among the most original, invigorating, and perplexing films I have ever experienced.

How can an animated movie for kids have such a profound effect on my rather jaded heart and mind?

J. K. Rowling's *Harry Potter* series and C. S. Lewis's *Chronicles of Narnia* have brought magic and fantasy back to the movies. Pixar's innovative, digital animation has produced a string of commercial hits that drew critical raves. When *Shrek* was awarded the first Oscar for Best Animated Film in 2001, children's movies had officially grown up. *The Lord of the Rings: Return of the King* (2003) built on such precedence by becoming the first fantasy film to win an Academy Award for Best Picture. While computers and technology animated these movies, they have also reenchanted our world, reintroducing us to the wonders of nature. Why were fantasy films so often dismissed as kids' stuff? Why have they experienced a new maturity, being embraced by audiences of all ages? Perhaps we need to recover the childlike sense of wonder that Jesus celebrated. The proliferation of fantasy films reflects the rise of general revelation and a growing hunger for shaping stories among kids of all ages.

In this chapter we will trace the history of fairy tales, from oral tradition to celebrated children's classics. We will also trace the growing acceptance of fantasy films as a legitimate art form. What does the embrace of cinematic fantasies by the IMDb reveal about our desires, our dreams, and our disappointments? In an ugly world, fantasies offer hope and escape, a way to bracket chaotic surroundings. The finest fantasies take evil seriously, portraying the monsters that haunt us with surprising ferocity. They also can provide a prophetic corrective. Science fiction offers visions of the future in efforts to influence the present. What does the enchanted world of fantasy tell us about our endangered environment? Fantasy films help us connect eschatology and ecology. I will also suggest that the best fantasy films circumvent our problems of memory by constructing a timeless place that approximates how things ought to be. Fully realized fantasies can empower the Christian community to reestablish the essential link between the beginning (Gen. 1) and end (Rev. 22) of our epic story.

From Wicked Witch to Fairest of Them All

> The history of fairy-stories is probably more complex than the physical history of the human race, and as complex as the history of human language. All three things: independent invention, inheritance, and diffusion, have evidently played their part in producing the intricate web of Story. It is now beyond all skill but that of the elves to unravel it.
>
> J. R. R. Tolkien, "On Fairy-Stories"[4]

Fairy tale did not enter the Oxford English Dictionary until 1750. It was defined as: (a) a tale about fairies or a fairy legend, (b) an unreal or incredible story, and (c) a falsehood. Such suspect origins set fairy tales and fantasy films on a long road to respectability. The Greeks had their myths, the Persians had *Arabian Nights*, but Western literature had been largely bereft of *recorded* fairy tales. Children's stories were primarily an oral tradition until French authors like Madame d'Aulnoy (*Goldilocks*, 1697) and Charles Perrault (*Tales of Mother Goose*, 1697) wrote them down. Perrault's fairy tales provided Walt Disney with *Cinderella* and *Sleeping Beauty*. Jeanne-Marie Leprince de Beaumont abridged an earlier version of *La Belle et la bête* (*Beauty and the Beast*, 1756). *Grimm's Fairy Tales* (1812) introduced *Hansel and Gretel*, while Scandinavia's Hans Christian Andersen contributed *The Little Mermaid* (1836) and *The Emperor's New Clothes* (1837). Publishers like Andrew Lang began collecting the stories across cultures. Scholars like Antti Aarne, Stith Thompson, and Vladimir Propp organized folk-tales into a broad typology.[5] They found divine rewards and punishments fall on persecuted maidens and cursed princes across languages and contexts. Yet the age of Enlightenment eventually (and literally) chopped down enchanted forests everywhere. Can the fairy tale be updated and saved?

Shrek (2001, IMDb #183) acknowledges the gap between the fairy tales we have heard and the harsh world we encounter. It begins with the familiar refrain, "Once upon a time." An ogre reads about a princess locked in a castle guarded by a fire-breathing dragon. Brave knights are vanquished in their efforts to rescue her. She awaits her true love's kiss. Sitting in an outhouse, Shrek shreds the page and laughs; "Like that's ever gonna happen." *Shrek* addresses our incredulity, our tendency to dismiss fairy tales as mere fantasy.

Shrek springs from William Steig's 1990 children's book.[6] It tosses fairy tales into a postmodern blender and reimagines them for a cynical age. *Shrek* follows the familiar trail of a knight's journey to rescue a princess. But in *Shrek*, the knight is a monster and his faithful squire is a wise-cracking donkey. What has crowded the enchanted forest and pushed our reluctant ogre into action? The unimaginative Lord Farquaad has banished fairy tales from his kingdom. He doesn't want lively characters like the Three Blind Mice, the Seven Dwarfs, or the Big Bad Wolf to contrast with (and thereby highlight) his boring personality. (Surely ministers also know how easily kids can captivate congregations during baptisms or children's sermons.) *Shrek* comments on the blandness that arises from a world without myth or magic. Farquaad expresses the sentiments of an Enlightenment era that reduced nature to a science and creativity to an enterprise. His Duloc castle may appear perfect, but it lacks the animating spirit of imagination supplied by fairy tales—consider it dull.

Shrek tears down the conventions of fairy tales in order to rebuild them. It sends up the traditional morals of fairy tales in an effort to redefine beauty and love (while still offering plenty of comic relief). As DreamWorks's first breakout hit, *Shrek* satirizes all things Disney, including Princess Fiona's devastating duet with an unfortunate bluebird. It also manages to pull off the ultimate postmodern trick by juggling irony and sincerity, keeping adults laughing and kids entertained. *Shrek* proves that there's plenty of life remaining in fairy tales. As a huge hit with audiences and critics, *Shrek* demonstrated that even the hardest hearts still long to be rescued, to live happily ever after in a land of enchantment. Mine does!

The Yellow Brick Road to Respectability

You have to write the book that wants to be written. And if the book will be too difficult for grown-ups, then you write it for children.

Madeleine L'Engle, *Walking on Water*[7]

Fantasy films have not always been so prevalent or profitable. Where did fantasy films come from? What distinguishes the memorable from the forgettable? Walt Disney brought early respectability to the fantasy genre with the first animated feature, *Snow White and the Seven Dwarfs* (1937). Based on a Grimm fairy tale, *Snow White* offered a cautionary tale about the lure of sin and the destructive power of vanity. Through a jealous queen, we see how the desire to possess beauty can turn us into ugly creatures. The Edenic forest setting of Snow White and her seven friends is contrasted with a corrupt monarchy. *Snow White* also shows how temptation can be disguised. A poison apple is offered as a shortcut to success: "One bite, and all your dreams come true."[8] Only a kiss of pure love can wake Snow White from her poison-induced slumber. Ministers of the era recognized the biblical parallels: "It is the retelling of truth as basic as sin and salvation. It might even tempt one to a sermon."[9] Yet it also avoids any particular religious expressions, setting up what Mark Pinsky has described as "The Gospel according to Disney." *Snow White* points out the lure of temptation but places faith in faith, upholding the magic of wishing. In describing the Disney universe, Tony Campolo says, "It's not what you believe in that makes the difference, it's the believing that makes the difference."[10]

Despite his well-documented personal faults, Disney never condescended toward his audience.[11] He treated kids with respect, refusing to simplify their world. In a 1962 interview, Disney told *Guideposts*:

> Children are people, and they should have to reach to learn about things, to understand things, just as adults have to reach if they want to grow in mental stature. Life is composed of light and shadows, and we would be untruthful, insincere and saccharine if we tried to pretend there were no shadows. Most things are good, and they are the strongest things; but there are evil things, too, and you are not doing a child a favor by trying to shield him from reality. The important thing is to teach a child that good can always triumph over evil, and that is what our pictures attempt to do.[12]

The most enduring fantasies suggest real choices and high stakes. They may be allegorical, but they always attempt to be honest about how the world works. Many children's first exposure to overt evil has come via Disney. From wicked stepmothers to Cruella de Vil, Disney movies do not shy away from depicting villains who should be feared. The witch and her poison apple haunted Snow White (and me). Disney stories identify evil and greed as the source of the world's problems, while offering a rather unspecific solution—"just believe."

The Wicked Witch of the West in *The Wizard of Oz* (IMDb #91) terrified me even more. Her green skin and flying monkeys nearly scarred me for life! The Technicolor splendor of *The Wizard of Oz* was beset by production problems. Audiences gave it a cool reception in 1939, initially turning it into a money loser.[13] Perhaps the message, "There's no place like home," failed to resonate with a country at peace. Only over time, through annual screenings on television, did the story of Dorothy and her trip down the Yellow Brick Road take on classic status. Like all good fairy tales, it held up under the weight of repetition. The best judges of fantasy films aren't necessarily adults or critics but the target audience of children. While many may be tempted to soften the edges of Grimm's Fairy Tales, kids want (and need) the dark truths embodied in seemingly sunny stories.

Jean Cocteau's *La Belle et la bête* (*Beauty and the Beast*, 1946, IMDb #182) has also grown in acceptance and reception over the years. The lush costumes, dreamy cinematography, and steamy performances hold up half a century later. The special effects that Cocteau achieved *in camera*, long before digital FX, continue to captivate. (Disney's 1991 animated, musical version of the classic fairy tale borrowed Cocteau's magical arms as candelabras.) But *La Belle et la bête* endures because of its sense of menace and mystery. The Beast is an animal capable of killing; we see his mouth dripping with blood after feasting on a stag. Belle's love for him is never safe. (This echoes C. S. Lewis's description in *Narnia* of Aslan the Lion as not safe, but good.) Belle must risk her life to free the Beast from the spell that binds him. Perhaps our ghastly behavior in the twentieth century has enabled us to recognize the beast within us. We desperately need a beauty to tame our savage instincts. Christ risked his life to free us from our spell.

Resisting Evil

For fairy tales to work, *evil must be taken seriously*. Fantasy must mirror our world's ambiguity, mystery, and danger. J. R. R. Tolkien refers to this as the "perilous realm." There *are* poison apples and berries and mushrooms in the forest. The Wicked Witch of the West fuels children's nightmares because kidnapping remains a legitimate fear (for parents as well). A wise person doesn't fall for the queen's fair appearance. Children (of all ages) must learn to see *through* nature, to discover the genuine dangers hiding beneath facades. Acclaimed author Frederick Buechner notes, "Not only does evil come disguised in the world of the fairy tale but often good does too."[14] The Wizard seems ferocious, but he's really benevolent. The Cowardly Lion turns out to be brave. Belle learns how to tame the savage Beast. Buechner explains, "Maybe above all they are tales about transformation where all creatures are revealed in the end as what they truly are."[15] Genuine revelation arrives when we see the true nature of people and things.

In *Pan's Labyrinth* (*El Laberinto del fauno*, IMDb #188), eleven-year-old Ofelia confronts monsters in two realms. When her mother remarries a *capitan* in Fascist Spain, Ofelia is transported to a world of violence, torture, and abuse. She escapes to a fantasy world of fairies and fauns that appears equally menacing. While her brutal stepfather, Vidal, focuses solely on the baby boy residing in her ailing mother's womb, Ofelia explores the labyrinth in the dark woods nearby. A slippery faun gives her three tasks necessary to reclaim her true nature, as princess of the underworld. Ofelia recovers a key vomited up by a massive, slimy frog. She sneaks into the frightening chambers of the Pale Man. His skin hangs from his body, a sign of rot. The stigmata in his hands hold the Pale Man's eyes. He is a devourer of children. Yet her stepfather proves to be equally monstrous, torturing members of the Republican resistance and revealing his machismo in his utter disregard for the health of Ofelia's mother. *Pan's Labyrinth* becomes a bloody nightmare of a fairy tale, collapsing the distance between the Spanish Civil War and Ofelia's imagination.

Courageous Ofelia confronts the Pale Man (and the Fascists) in Guillermo del Toro's dark and haunting fantasy, *Pan's Labyrinth.* © 2006 by Picturehouse.

Mexican director Guillermo del Toro admits his violent fantasy is not for children. Del Toro embraces the dark aspects of his tale: "This fairy world has a grimy edge to it. Even the fairies are meat eaters! I wanted all the creatures to have an air of menace. Fantasy is not an escape for Ofelia but it is a dark refuge. There is something vaguely embryonic about all the magic environments because I believe that fairy tales are ultimately about two things: facing the dragon or climbing to our world inside."[16] The dragon in *Pan's Labyrinth* is Capitan Vidal, a cold-blooded sadist who spends an inordinate amount of time staring into a mirror. Del Toro considers him the embodiment of evil: "For me, fascism is a representation of the ultimate horror and it is, in this sense, an ideal concept through which to tell a fairy tale aimed at adults. Because fascism is first and foremost a form of perversion of innocence, and thus of childhood."[17] Consider the parallels between del Toro's contempt for Fascists and the indignation behind Jesus's directive, "Let the little children come to me" (Luke 18:16). He warns his disciples, "Do not hinder them," for the kingdom of God belongs to them. Those who would pervert, devour, or separate children from Jesus face an incomparable wrath.

To navigate *Pan's Labyrinth* (and life's twists and turns), Ofelia must gain wisdom and discernment. Her three tests in the fantasy realm become a means of dealing with the real horrors of civil war. She fails some initial trials, awakening the Pale Man from his slumber. The faun is definitely an elusive character, both captivating and menacing. Can he be trusted? Ofelia finds models of resistance in the housekeeper, Mercedes, and the local physician, Dr. Ferreiro. They aid the Republican soldiers hiding in the woods in subtle and (mostly) undetectable ways. Ofelia discovers that evil can and must be resisted.

Del Torro, despite his torturous Catholic upbringing, ends *Pan's Labyrinth* with remarkably Christian imagery and choices. The faun proves to be a trustworthy companion, drawing Ofelia (and her baby brother) into the labyrinth with Vidal in hot pursuit. During her final test, Ofelia chooses to sacrifice her own life rather than her baby brother's. Del Toro affirms her brave decision:

> [Ofelia] dies *at peace* with what she did. She's the only character in the film who decides not to enact any violence. Not to take any lives. Even the doctor takes a life. But the only one who chooses, "I will not take any life because I own only mine," that's the character who survives, spiritually. The fascist dies the loneliest death you could ever experience and the girl. . . . I'm reminded of the quote by Kierkegaard that said, "The tyrant's rule ends with his death. The martyr's rule begins with it."[18]

Pan's Labyrinth concludes with a heavenly vision, as Ofelia is ushered into her father and mother's presence. Ofelia stands before a royal court and takes her place as princess. She may have perished on earth, martyred for resisting evil, but in another world she is crowned with glory. Del Toro considers *Pan's Labyrinth* a Rorschach test: "If you view it and you don't believe, you'll view the movie as, 'Oh, it was all in her head.' If you view it as a believer, you'll see clearly where I stand, which is it [the fantasy realm] is real. My last image in the movie is an objective little white flower blooming in a dead tree with the bug watching it. So . . ."[19] We may suffer under tyrants. We may be tortured to death. But their initial victory need not be equated with ultimate defeat. As monsters are unmasked, revelation begins. We must learn to see with Ofelia's eyes, resisting evil and anticipating an eternal reward.

Why does Jesus challenge his followers to turn and enter his kingdom "like little children" (Matt. 18:3)? We often focus on their innocence, but we should also affirm their wisdom and courage. Perhaps children are the best judges of fantasy because they haven't developed filters to hide their longings and sublimate their desires. In Jungian analysis, the fascination with the darkness can be seen as a shadow longing for the beautiful. Scary wizards and dark princes make safety and rest that much more appealing. Kids like Dorothy know something is off with the Wicked Witch, even if they can't put their little fingers on it. They would take Belle's risk, entering an enchanted castle to free the prisoner within. Ofelia is willing to die to save her baby brother. These are models of courage under fire, not innocence removed from the world.

In dismissing fantasy films as *childish*, are we missing something profound about the nature of God and the character of his kingdom? Children have an innocence we need to recover if the divine is to be revealed (or received). But in fantasy films, young protagonists must also resist forces that seek to compromise or even destroy them. Guillermo del Toro salutes Ofelia's courage in *Pan's Labyrinth*:

> Blind obedience castrates, negates, hides, and destroys what makes us human. On the other hand, instinct and disobedience will always point you in a direction that should be natural, should be organic to the world. So I think that disobedience is a virtue and blind obedience is a sin. . . . You choose to be destructive or you choose to be all encompassing and love-giving. Each choice defines who we are, no matter what the reason behind it is.[20]

This assessment gives me great hope for my strong-willed offspring. Rather than breaking the will of our children, perhaps we need to affirm their desire for understanding. When we cannot explain why things are twisted, tortured, or wrong, perhaps we need to join with children in their incredulity and outrage. What kind of insight can children's fantasies help us recover? As in *Pan's Labyrinth*, we may all have to undergo the same painful process of learning to discern before we can experience genuine revelation. The kingdom comes to those who become like children; glory arrives for those who learn to resist the evil and recognize the good—just like Ofelia.

Reclaiming Movie Magic

Enduring fantasy films not only present legitimate dangers, but they also imagine a faraway place where we all long to live. They appeal to our longing for an Edenic ideal. However, the magic inherent in folktales often causes us to dismiss or ignore such longings as idylls. J. R. R. Tolkien distinguished between "fairy tales" and "fairy stories." He tried to rescue the notion of *magic*, suggesting fairies aren't needed to create a fairy story. Tolkien embraced magic, "but it is magic of a peculiar mood and power, at the furthest pole from the vulgar devices of the laborious, scientific, or magician."[21] He moved fantasy beyond the allegorical, taking it outside the realm of our world as we've experienced it.

He didn't propose a supernatural earth but a separate, self-contained universe, "a secondary world." Such otherworldly fantasies are equal parts warning and hope, a meditation on dystopia balanced by a vision of utopia. As such, fantasy films are often dependent on technical breakthroughs. Directors' visions may exceed their ability (or budget) to create it on-screen. The advent of digital technology has made the creation of *secondary worlds* and *movie magic* more feasible than ever.

Fantasy films reenchant the world through production design. They offer a peek inside another world (what Tolkien calls a "subcreation"). It is not created God's way, ex nihilo (out of nothing), but reflects things we recognize from this world. Their kingdoms have warriors and horses and queens. These subcreations may be set in the past, in the future, or in a timeless, parallel universe. The illusion begins with lavish attention to detail in costume, makeup, and sets. Production designers create (or rather re-create) a world through rigorous research and fanciful sketches. They give us ancient and magical worlds as we've imagined them. The advent of computer-generated imagery (CGI) increases the tools available to realize directors' and production designers' visions. Producer Jon Boorstin suggests that all films must pass a visual test, appealing to the audience's voyeuristic eye.[22] We scan the screen for anachronisms, searching for reasons to dismiss the filmmaker's vision. We surrender our hearts only to films that satisfy our mind's eye by constructing a believable world.

Visionary director Tim Burton loves to create fantasy worlds. *Big Fish* (2003, IMDb #186) confronts the skeptic inside each of us. Burton clearly relished the opportunity to construct a magical version of the South, complete with witches, giants, and an enchanted forest. Yet the film plays such mythology as straight, or at least as sincere in our hero's eyes. In Burton's fanciful film, a son's commitment to logic confronts his father's tall tales. Will Bloom returns home to visit his dying father, Ed. He wants the real story. But Will's efforts are frustrated by dad's adherence to "fish stories." The film takes dad's side in the debate. Far-fetched accounts of gentle giants and werewolves as circus ringmasters are held up as true. It also celebrates the power of love, seen in Ed's relentless wooing of his eventual bride, Sandra. (Consider the similarities to Jesus's tireless wooing of his bride, the church—the Bible ends with a wedding!) Burton casts our sympathies with Ed. We root against the rationalist and cheer for the absurdist storyteller. *Big Fish* assaults our cynicism; it challenges those who would drain the world of magic and mythology to reconsider.

Big Fish is also meant to console. As Will faces the end of his father's life, he (and we) must consider what matters. Is life only what can be seen or measured?

Can love truly transcend our limitations? Can our modest life story connect to a larger story or tradition? Tim Burton stops short of making any grand, overarching claims. In the end, *Big Fish* affirms the power of storytelling to animate our lives. It celebrates the importance of a dying art. We need fantasy to narrate and navigate our world, to face death with dignity.

Fantasy films are dependent on movie magic, from traditional stunts to CGI. The rousing fight scenes that animate adventure films like *Wo hu cang long* (*Crouching Tiger, Hidden Dragon*, 2000, IMDb #125), *Ying xiong* (*Hero*, IMDb #168), and *Pirates of the Caribbean: The Curse of the Black Pearl* (IMDb #225) defy logic or physics. They appeal to the child in all of us. Viewers swooned along with the bending bamboo groves in *Crouching Tiger, Hidden Dragon*. Director Ang Lee created a classy, upscale take on the Chinese Wuxia tradition. Wuxia novels blend elements of magic and martial arts, wizards and warriors, to create a distinctively Eastern fairy tale. But Ang Lee gives this low-budget genre the grand treatment it richly deserves. Dramatic mainland Chinese locations range from lush waterfalls in the Yellow Mountains to the massive Gobi Desert.

Crouching Tiger contrasts the maturity of Mu Bai (Chow Yun-Fat) and Shu Lien (Michelle Yeoh) with the impetuous youth of Jen Yu (Ziyi Zhang). Their pursuit of the enchanted Green Destiny sword becomes an occasion for master-disciple training sessions that rival the *Star Wars* trilogy. A fiery upstart tests the ancient codes; she must learn to play by the Wudan rules. The trio engage in ludicrous but balletic duels across forests, rooftops, and pools. The "wire fu" techniques of master fight choreographer Yuen Woo Ping combine martial arts and elaborate harnesses into a seamless, breathtaking whole. He uses the latest technology to elevate ancient arts. As in the moral of the story, Ping's individual achievement is ultimately underplayed for larger purposes. Global audiences were swept away by the sheer magic of *Crouching Tiger*, making it the first foreign film to earn over $100 million in America.

Set in feudal China, *Hero* (2002) follows the exploits of a swordsman called Nameless. As played by Jet Li, our nameless protagonist borrows a persona from Clint Eastwood's westerns. The nameless hero takes down three assassins aimed at the king of Qin. He is summoned to the king's court and recounts his tales in flashback. (Of course, he also has a hidden motive.) The assassins' mythological roots are revealed in their poetic names, translated from Mandarin as Sky, Broken Sword, and Flying Snow. In *Hero*, each epic battle corresponds to a different color or season (of life). Director Zhang Yimou juggles the stories with such acrobatic grace that we come to accept walking on water as utterly plausible. Yimou counterpoints the action with the sounds of steel, creating a musical symphony with swords. A ferocious duel between Flying Snow (Maggie Cheung) and Moon (Ziyi Zhang) among falling yellow leaves is breathtakingly beautiful. The engineering required to fly the actors across the screen is magical. From *The Matrix* to *Kill Bill*, wire fu has crossed over from Hong Kong to the world.

We also marvel at the stunts and digitized swordplay in *Pirates of the Caribbean: The Curse of the Black Pearl* (2003). Johnny Depp's spirited portrayal of Jack Sparrow won audiences over, but the visual effects added an extra *wow* factor. *Pirates* blends a ghost story with a rollicking adventure. Whenever the moonlight hits them, the pirates morph into skeletons with convincing ease. *Pirates* also offers surprisingly sacrificial heroism amid the swashbuckling.

The central premise of *Pirates of the Caribbean* resonates with the Christian story. The pirates are a form of living dead. Barbossa describes their lamentable condition: "For too long I've been parched of thirst and unable to quench it. Too long I've been starving to death and haven't died. I feel nothing." Cursed by their greed, the pirates can be freed only by the blood of one man (or his son). Their freedom will be bought for a price, which must be paid in full by the complete restoration of a treasure. Only a blood sacrifice can reverse the pirates' curse. In the final sword fight when Barbossa pierces Jack, his curse is revealed. We no longer notice the effects but Jack's pluck and courage. We end up caring for the skeletal pirates, understanding the depths of their longing. I was moved by their newfound freedom, touched by the captives' release. In the finest fantasy films, special effects serve the story and enhance the mystery. The reversal of the pirates' curse becomes a transcendent moment of true movie magic.

Filmmakers are dependent on technical possibilities to realize their visions. Has the Spirit of God's creativity also been unleashed by emerging technologies? General revelation may be tied to the recovery of imagination—an ability to dream God-sized visions. Consider the future expressed by the apostle Paul in Romans:

> I consider that our present sufferings are not worth comparing with the glory that will be revealed in us. The creation waits in eager expectation for the sons of God to be revealed. For the creation was subjected to frustration, not by its own choice, but by the will of the one who subjected it, in hope that the creation itself will be liberated from its bondage to decay and brought into the glorious freedom of the children of God. (Rom. 8:18–21)

What a long view, animated by an ability to imagine a brighter tomorrow. Those silly battles with swords may approximate a much greater battle for the soul of creation itself. As we develop the ability to not only imagine but also depict heroes walking on water, are we getting closer to realizing Christ's heroic future for his church? The digital technology driving fantasy may be helping us recover the hopeful vision that emboldened early Christians.

A Fragile Future

Perhaps the most *fantastic* triumphs of production design and movie magic are reserved for science fiction. Each new advance in cinematic technology has sparked another wave of adaptation. The fanciful visions of Jules Verne and H. G. Wells have repeatedly inspired cinematic sci-fi. Verne's book *20,000 Leagues Under the Sea* (1870) imagined a future where submarines probed the ocean depths. Each era of technical breakthroughs led Captain Nemo and the Nautilus on to new cinematic treatments (in 1907, 1916, 1954, 1969, and most recently as a 1997 television movie).

Science fiction often reflects the tone and politics of its era, alternating optimism with pessimism. In *The Shape of Things to Come* (novel 1933, film 1936), H. G. Wells anticipated World War II. He recognized that our wars often drag on so long that by the end, no one can even remember why they started. Yet Wells also offered a utopian vision of a day when a world council of scientists reconstructs society. Wells thought civilization would be perfected when we follow truly enlightened leaders. Theologian Jürgen Moltmann notes such misplaced faith in a manufactured future.

> As long as the industrial system was being built up, objective progress therefore enjoyed the magic of transcendence. It promised to overcome man's dependence on nature, to fulfill human longings, to conquer economic alienation and even to bring about the kingdom of peace, politically. But modern post-industrial planned society de-futurizes this type of transcendent future.[23]

Visions of human progress vanished in the ashes of Auschwitz and Hiroshima. Our advanced technologies had only yielded new ways of killing.

Recently, science fiction has offered visions of dystopia. In *The Matrix* trilogy, the earth has been scorched by nuclear holocaust. A virtual reality covers the ugly truth—we have nearly destroyed ourselves. Machines rule our world, reducing humanity to an energy source. *The Matrix* (1999, IMDb #34) generated immense devotion by combining the look and ideas of anime with Hong Kong wire fu. It also interwove core philosophical questions about the meaning of life and our choice to engage or disengage. Viewers gladly took the red pill, following Neo down the rabbit hole. Along the way, we learned how to free our minds, bend spoons, and lean back in bullet time. Andy and Larry Wachowski were hailed as visionaries who could expand our thinking.[24]

The 2003 sequels, *The Matrix Reloaded* and *The Matrix Revolutions*, dissipated the rapturous reception accorded to *The Matrix*. The CGI was even more accomplished, but the novelty had worn off. Rather than satisfying fans' longing for blood, Andy and Larry Wachowski concluded the series with a surprisingly peaceful vision. Neo may have defeated Agent Smith, but violence was rejected as the answer. The Wachowskis suggested that we can ensure a bright future only if we stop waging war against (and with) machines. Only when we embrace technology will we find a lasting peace. Yet initial *Matrix* fans largely rejected their vision.

Perhaps after so many thrilling battle scenes, the Wachowskis' eschatology seemed too easy. Neo and Trinity lay down their arms (and lives), yet viewers felt far from saved. Have we become so attracted and inured to violence that we cannot imagine a peaceful ending? Have the upside-down values of God's kingdom become "foolishness" to audiences so baptized by bloody visions they reject alternatives? (See 1 Cor. 1:18–27.) Perhaps Neo's renunciation of power looked too weak to viewers accustomed to power moves. As Christ's death defied expectations of the Messiah, so Neo and Trinity's sacrificial actions failed to satisfy an audience looking for a more traditional Hollywood-style revolution.

V for Violence?

Why has there been a paucity of recent science fiction films reaching the IMDb's Top 250? Did the innovation of *The Matrix* scare off aspirants to the sci-fi throne? Did the flameout of *Reloaded* and *Revolutions* give studio executives (and filmmakers) cold feet? Perhaps we have simply lost faith in the future. (Remember our discussion of nostalgia?) Jürgen Moltmann points out how personalizing history into an existential choice (taking *The Matrix*'s blue or red pill) fails to satisfy. (Remember the failures in *Memento* and *Eternal Sunshine*?) Moltmann finds that "the personalistic understanding of future as potentiality of existence is just as much a product of the cleft in the modern mind as the objectifying of the future in the automatic progress of society."[25] Despite our alleged autonomy, we are not alone. Sometimes choices are foisted on us (*Crash*ing into our isolation, creating communities in crisis). The seemingly unprovoked nature of the 9/11 attacks or America's invasion of Iraq push things past the personal. I may choose to practice peace in my community, but what happens when someone else drops a bomb on my world? To those dissatisfied with their vision of a personalized and peaceful future from *The Matrix Revolutions*, the Wachowski brothers offered a more violent alternative—*V for Vendetta*.

The Wachowski brothers' screenplay for *V for Vendetta* (2005, IMDb #116) contained enough contemporary parallels and sonic booms to satiate hardcore fanboys' tastes. It rocketed to a place in the IMDb pantheon despite limited box-office success. Alan Moore and David Lloyd created the graphic novel *V for Vendetta* as a commentary on Margaret Thatcher's administration in 1980s England.[26] Moore rehabilitated the legacy of Guy Fawkes and the Gunpowder Plot, turning terrorism into the ultimate act of patriotism. The Wachowskis adapted Moore's story of an anarchist taking down a fascist government that has tortured and abused him. The film transforms V into a reluctant freedom fighter who indoctrinates an orphan named Evey Hammond. The Wachowski brothers placed the action in the near future of 2020. V's assault on a repressive regime now echoes post-9/11 America and Britain. V challenges Evey (and viewers) to protect their civil liberties, to resist all efforts to suppress dissent. In settings that echo Abu Ghraib, V even tortures Evey in an effort to free her from fear. First-time director James McTeigue demonstrates everything he learned working as first assistant director on *The Matrix* trilogy. *V for Vendetta* contains virtuoso action sequences and thrilling special effects. But the heart of the movie resides in V's unapologetically revolutionary ideas.

V for Vendetta is not subtle. The Wachowskis follow Flannery O'Connor's advice: to the hard of hearing they shout, to the almost blind they draw large figures. V delivers lengthy speeches about "government fearing the people." Hidden behind a laconic Guy Fawkes mask, V forces Evey (and audiences) to follow his alliterative logic as he reverses the "voracious violation of volition." Playing V, Hugo Weaving brings a surprising humanity to the victimized angel of vengeance. Weaving demonstrates the same cool resolve he brought portraying Agent Smith in *The Matrix* movies. As Evey, Natalie Portman is stripped down to a shaved head. She comes to represent a cross between pure innocence and a paramilitary time bomb trained to explode. V's nemesis is Chancellor Sutler (played by John Hurt). The Chancellor dominates the people via the media, stirring up fear by telling bald-faced lies. V abandons all efforts to reason with such vice—"the only verdict is vengeance." He adopts the only "sensible" strategy, rallying the masses and blowing up Parliament.

While some may dismiss *V for Vendetta* for advocating anarchy, it also offers insight into terrorists' rationale, demonstrating how little may separate freedom fighters from Al-Qaeda. Where we sit determines what we see. To Catholics being oppressed by the Protestant King James I, Guy Fawkes is remembered as a religious martyr rather than a traitor. V also attempts to rewrite the official version of history. As a victim of a violent government (and a failed army science experiment), V has ample reasons for the chip on his chemically altered shoulder. He gives the young Evey an education about her government and her past. *V for Vendetta* also offers a strong argument for preserving art history. V has created a storehouse for all manner of masterpieces, serving as conservator of revolutionary ideas. He entrusts this trove of culture to Evey Hammond—the new Eve. Can art and beauty save humanity? Not in this movie.

V for Vendetta also contains a large dose of antireligious rhetoric, through posters that proclaim "Strength=Unity, Unity=Faith." Rather than affirming the religious roots of Guy Fawkes's rebellion, the Wachowskis seem to equate all religion with oppression. They anticipate the best-selling books of "the new atheists" like Richard Dawkins and Sam Harris.[27] We all recognize that religion has sometimes been manipulated for political purposes; when the church starts to serve the state, bad things are bound to follow. Dietrich Bonhoeffer witnessed and opposed such compromises in Hitler's Germany (even unto death). As a native Croatian, Miroslav Volf experienced religious wars in the Balkans and the oppression of Tito's Yugoslavia. V's critique has validity. It finds echoes in the eschatology of Jürgen Moltmann: "The magic of true transcendence is inherent in the future if that future promises something qualitatively new, which stimulates people to change the 'system' of the present radically; and if in this future something different can be expected which will lead to the altering of the foundations of the present, antagonistic condition of immanence."[28] This is the creation groaning for release in Romans 8:22–25. We know something is wrong. Christians and atheists both long to usher in a new world where justice prevails.

In *The Matrix* and *V for Vendetta*, the Wachowski brothers actively challenge the system. They have no tolerance for the status quo. Yet they have not offered a viable alternative to our present antagonism. For all of its provocative ideas, *V for Vendetta* reinforces the cycle it seeks to break. V's call to oppose oppressive regimes applies more concretely in the Middle East than in middle America. Who more actively oppresses women and dissidents? The Wachowskis point V's finger at England and America rather than at Arab despots. *V for Vendetta* validates violence when one is on the right side. But isn't that what wars are always about—competing interpretations and a commitment to being right?

When differences cannot be hammered out with talk, we take out hammers. Who determines who is right? Where is the ultimate trump card—in V's hand or the will of the people?

David Lloyd, the illustrator of the *V for Vendetta* comic, ultimately places responsibility on the people who elect villains like Hitler. We get the politicians we deserve. Lloyd laments:

> People are constantly voting for governments that they shouldn't vote for, and that's because they don't take responsibility. They turn a blind eye to things that happen that they shouldn't turn a blind eye to, and that is how people come to power who shouldn't be in power. People don't vote for their ideals any more, they vote for what the government is going to put in their pocket.[29]

Unfortunately, such democratic ideals can easily be lost amid V's stylish violence. *V for Vendetta* ends up just as preachy as the religions and regimes it seeks to replace. As a true anarchist, V destroys in order to save. This violent resolution resonated more with fans of the original *Matrix* than the peaceful conclusion of *Matrix Revolutions*.

Time will tell which vision endures. What seems prescient today may seem pedantic tomorrow. In an effort to comment on our contemporary context, science fiction can miss the timeless quality that animates the finest fantasy films. Filmmakers too eager to preach may miss the voice of God (just like ministers). Is that why the Bible suggests "a little child shall lead them" (Isa. 11:6)? Revelation comes to those with the patience to wait, watch, and observe. How do we recover a sense of humility and wonder? We turn to the most childish genre—animation.

The Animator's Eye

> Animation can explain whatever the mind of man can conceive. This facility makes it the most versatile and explicit means of communication yet devised for quick mass appreciation.
>
> Walt Disney

Animation is a strange and magnificent art. It is one of the ultimate deceptions, offering only "the illusion of life."[30] To take pen and paper (ink and cel, keyboard and rotoscope) and make characters live, move, and have being is a profound act of hubris (and genius). Frank Thomas and Ollie Johnston, two of the "Nine Old Men" who formed Disney's original animation team, recognized

History

their grand folly: "For some presumptuous reason, man feels the need to create something of his own that appears to be living, that has an inner strength, a vitality, a separate identity—something that speaks with authority—a creation that gives the illusion of life."[31] The Christian community will trace that need back to the Garden of Eden, to our creation in the image of our Creator God. We've been drawing, designing, and painting ever since the original Animator gave us breath. We cannot create life ex nihilo, out of nothing. But we've been given plenty of tools and materials to work with as a consolation. So how can a two-dimensional image offer such depth of feeling, emotion, and verisimilitude?

Animation is a craft that is perfected through careful observation of nature. Like Adam in the Garden of Eden, Disney animators studied the movement of lions, tigers, or bears before attempting to draw (or name) them. It is a scientific art, breaking life down below the surface, to bone structure and musculature. Animators must understand how a wing works before they can make Tinker Bell fly. Animation merges science and art, seeing and being. Nick Park, creator of Wallace and Gromit, describes himself as "an observer, quiet and contemplative"—essential virtues for an Oscar-winning animator.[32]

Animation requires incredible patience. The illusion of motion is created one frame at a time. Consider the years of meticulous craft behind Aardman Animations's *Wallace & Gromit in The Curse of the Were-Rabbit* (2005, IMDb #200). Nick Park molds his comedy out of clay, adjusting his characters ever so slightly for each frame. It takes twenty-four frames to create a single second of screen time! Park's understated Anglican faith shines through in his craft. He says, "They're born out of clay, these characters. You have your hands on them every frame of the way, tweaking them. There's a directness about it. It's not just moving them, you're resculpting them, teasing the character out of the clay, and that direct contact gives the characters extra humanity, I think."[33] Loving attention to character also enhances the comedy. How brave (or foolish) to construct a Claymation story dependent on so much physical humor. But the slight changes in Gromit's deadpan expression offer profound comedic enjoyment. Wallace and Gromit remain an understated pleasure probably because it is easier to raise an eyebrow than resort to Claymation pratfalls. The humor in *Wallace & Gromit* is also defiantly British—quirky, dry, and slightly obtuse.

Wallace and Gromit's feature film debut is rooted in the ancient folktales of lycanthropy—the transformation of a human into a wolf (or beast). It plays on childhood fears of scary monsters, but the stakes never get uglier than protecting prizewinning vegetables in the garden. (Evidently, in England that could constitute a national crisis!) *The Curse of the Were-Rabbit* is a comedic riff on the conventions of horror movies. It demonstrates what happens when we become too possessive. It also continues Aardman's streak of vegetarian, animal-friendly fare (from the Oscar-winning short, *Creature Comforts* to *Chicken Run*). Wallace and Gromit share a bond that goes deeper than owner and pet. They are true partners, complementing Wallace's far-flung sense of invention with Gromit's ability to solve the problems Wallace creates. Nick Park's attention to detail, from the wallpaper to the cheese, also offer profound visual pleasures. The complexity of Wallace and Gromit's chase scenes deepen our appreciation for the planning and patience necessary to create it. In a digital world, Claymation remains a handmade art. Nick Park's love for his characters, his cheese, and his Creator shine through each hilarious moment.

What irony that despite the manic pace of their movies, animators cannot be in a hurry to get things moving. Animation is incremental by definition. But when rendered effectively, it not only mimics life but awakens our eyes to how things talk, work, and behave. An effective animated picture will sharpen our senses; when we emerge from a darkened room, we will see with more clarity.

Perhaps the art of animation can reawaken our own religious practices. Ancient Christian traditions such as centering prayer can sharpen our spiritual senses. Learning to pray through (not to) icons can open up a whole new window onto the thin line separating us from the saints across history. When we slow down long enough to walk through a prayer labyrinth, we enter a more mystical time. Animators are patient observers, attentive to miniscule movements. In the ancient practice of *lectio divina*, we meditate on Scripture long enough, with enough repetition, that it slowly saturates our souls. We begin to notice the subtle interplay of particular words or phrases. We give the Spirit room to breathe with us and in us. We may begin to see and hear God with more clarity and consistency when we focus on objects or things, not because we worship objects, but because an image can sometimes focus our easily distracted minds. I am challenged to engage in what scholar-activist Ched Meyers has called "Theological Animation."[34] He admires the joy and freedom found in the animator's art. Cartoonists portray an idealized world as it could or should be. Animators begin with the creative act of Genesis 1 and 2 but offer a hopeful vision echoed in Revelation 21 and 22. Their art can serve as comfort and consolation between the already and the not yet. As animators bring life to their creations, so perhaps the creative Spirit of God can reanimate a dormant or unimaginative faith.

Pixar: Reviving the Spirit of Disney

> I do what I do in life because of Walt Disney—his films and his theme park and his characters and his joy in entertaining. The emotional feeling that his creations gave me is something that I want to turn around and give to others.
>
> John Lasseter of Pixar Animation Studio[35]

Few filmmakers can claim the winning streak of John Lasseter and the team at Pixar Animation. Beginning with *Toy Story* (1995, IMDb #171), Pixar has reeled off an impressive list of critical and commercial triumphs, including *Monsters, Inc.* (2001, IMDb #221), *Finding Nemo* (2003, IMDb #109), *The Incredibles* (2004, IMDb #97), and *Ratatouille* (2007). They are all comfortably ensconced in the IMDb's all-time Top 250, praised for their humor and imagination. As critic Peter Rainer said of *Finding Nemo*, "It has what the most heartfelt Disney animated features used to have: rapturous imagery matched with real wit."[36] Pixar has single-handedly kept the Disney animation legacy alive (while simultaneously undermining hand-drawn art). Team Pixar merges breakthroughs in digital technology with old-fashioned virtues like character and craft. So what is the secret of Pixar's success? They treat audiences with the utmost respect, bringing intelligence and compassion to something previously dismissed as insignificant.

Their animated adventures work on multiple levels, appealing to viewers of all ages. The best Pixar films begin with genuine childhood (or parental) phobias, gradually turning those fears into laughter. *Monsters, Inc.* deals with furry creatures hiding in kids' closets. It begins with echoes of our ongoing energy crises, by giving children credit for the imaginative fuel—fear. A scream of fright is a force of nature (but not necessarily to be harnessed). *Monsters, Inc.* anticipated the manufacturing of fear that became a growth industry after 9/11. Ultimately, it humanizes the monsters, finding fears lurking in their (adult) closets as well.

Finding Nemo is a delightful father-and-son story about overcoming the odds despite the memory impairments of their comedic assistant, Dory. It is a story of survival and beauty. *Nemo* puts the possessive love of a Prodigal Father into action, seeking out his captured son. On their arduous journey to a joyous reunion, father and son each enlist the cooperation of a community—one captive, one free. While its message of unstoppable love triumphs in the end, *Nemo* entertains adults and frightens big and little kids with sharks' anonymous meetings and dentist-office nightmares.

Finding Nemo also celebrates the wonders of the ocean, transporting viewers to Australia's Great Barrier Reef. It does not shy away from depictions of anglerfish and jellyfish who threaten Nemo's dad, Marlin. Yet who can forget the exhilaration of the turtles riding the East Australian Current? The beauty of the sea serves as its own rationale for environmental protection. Director Andrew Stanton and his team of animators demonstrate their love and respect for nature in every frame.

The Incredibles is not only the longest Pixar movie but also the most complex in both plot and politics. The Parr family tries to keep their superhero talents under wraps. Bob Parr still pines for his heroic past as Mr. Incredible. His wife, Helen (the former Elastigirl), appears content to raise their three children. But Bob's combination nostalgia–midlife crisis jeopardizes his safety and snaps the family into action. Only when he admits, "I'm not strong enough," does his real power become evident.

Director Brad Bird celebrates his love for retro style but launches Pixar into the world of action adventure. *The Incredibles* lampoons our litigious ways, which mitigates risk (and greatness). Bob has become a claims specialist for the insurance industry that has robbed him of his vitality. Bird rails against a society that shaves the creative edges of our kids to insist on mediocrity for all. *The Incredibles* also satirizes the fanboys who place demands on their entertainment, like Mr. Incredible's nemesis, Syndrome. How can we heal the breach between demanding audiences and lowering standards? *The Incredibles* rises above Pixar's competition as their most grown-up cartoon yet. It paradoxically celebrates individuality and family, aspirations and humility.

Bird continued his affirmation of artistic expression in *Ratatouille* (2007). It trades on classic tropes of the country mouse lost in the big city of Paris. To become a chef, Remy must overcome human bias against rats in the kitchen. His family isn't too keen on Remy abandoning his modest roots either. But Remy takes the promises of his guardian angel, Anton Gusteau, quite literally, believing "Anyone can cook"—even a rat! He channels his culinary skills through an awkward human named Linguini. Unfortunately, Linguini proves that not everyone can cook. *Ratatouille* questions false promises parents have made to kids who may *not* master anything they attempt. (Consider St. Paul's reminder in Romans 12:3, "Do not think of yourselves more highly than you ought" [KJV].) Yet Remy's aspirations cut through the snobbery that can stifle self-expression. (Revel in the glorious notion from Psalm 8:5, "For thou hast made him a little lower than the angels, and hast crowned him with glory and honor.") Brad Bird pokes fun at food critics and the pretense of the French Michelin Guide. Food

History

from the heart wins over even the most selective palettes. With *Ratatouille*, Pixar serves up a tasty dish.

So what unites Pixar's critical and commercial triumphs? They have recovered the secrets of Walt Disney's success, combining compelling characters, corporate teamwork, and emerging technology into a seamless whole. Lasseter recognizes, "Building great characters is the most important thing in the movies. We know someday the technology will be far beyond *Toy Story* and *A Bug's Life*. . . . But Buzz and Woody live on in people's minds. And that's what we want—movies that live on."[37] Joe Ranft, the voice (and animator) behind Heimlich in *A Bug's Life*, offers this advice: "Try to draw something that connects with people. Whether it's an individual character that you're trying to find the expression of, or the character of the environment. How does it feel? What does it evoke in others? Is it funny, sad, beautiful, irritating, claustrophobic, invigorating? Work on creating expressive drawings—drawings that feel like they're alive."[38] The mice in *Ratatouille* passed the smell taste of picky pet owners. As an admitted rat owner, IMDb user Igenlode Wordsmith appreciated the way "Pixar ha[s] captured their scamper and their funny trundling walk, their habit of carrying things with their chins raised, their athletic climbing abilities and above all their superb sense of smell; if anyone could design a new dish for a restaurant simply by sniffing it, it would probably be a rat."[39] What a challenge to make a rat heroic!

The task of the animator is nothing less than breathing life (inspiration) into flat characters. Lasseter and Pixar have recovered the origins of animation. They respect the art form and understand its unique calling. Lasseter explains, "Chuck Jones, one of my mentors (and the creator of the Road Runner and Wile E. Coyote), always had a term that I believe: 'Animation is a gift word.' You can't call yourself an animator, that's something for other people to say that you are."[40] In other words, animation is an art that takes time. It is rooted in the careful observation of nature and the relentless pursuit of artistic perfection. As a Christian, Pete Docter, director of *Monsters, Inc.*, acknowledges the spiritual nature of their work. He told *Radix* magazine, "Bringing something to life that is really just a bunch of squares and wedges is like mimicking God. . . . On the computer it's a bunch of digital information, but it doesn't really exist anywhere except in the mind of the artist who puts it together, so I guess it's a desire to 'play God' and all that."[41] The Pixar team creates whole new worlds using a seemingly impersonal tool, the computer. They are a living example of how technology can be humanized. (Perhaps the hopeful vision of *The Matrix Revolutions* will yet be vindicated.)

Do not presume that Pixar's success resides in their embrace of new technology (out with hand-drawn animation, in with computers). Pixar has resisted the temptation to let technology drive their creativity. Instead, they have chosen to tell stories that correspond to their technological limitations.[42] They started with *Toy Story* when digital animation still exhibited a plastic feeling. With *Monsters, Inc.*, Sully's hairy body presented a problem to be solved. *Finding Nemo* began as an experiment with light, trying to capture the translucent quality of fish under water. In each case, they succeeded. *The Incredibles* arrived only when Pixar felt that digital technology could finally tackle humanity in a believable and compelling manner. They started with toy stories and monsters not out of a desire for marketing tie-ins but because the medium wasn't ready for humans. (They happened to sell a few toys en route.) At no point have they rested on technology as the answer to their problems. Instead, the Pixar team pushed themselves toward creative solutions to vexing problems, harnessing the computer's potential to serve their vision.

It is almost inconceivable that something as previously *disposable* as cartoons for children would cross into the realm of high art. Yet Pixar's films were celebrated with a 2005 retrospective at the Museum of Modern Art in New York City. Roberta Smith, art critic for the *New York Times*, salutes their accomplishments: "Pixar's innovation is ultimately primarily formal and stylistic. It brought a new and startling degree of spatial illusion and sculptural reality to animation, and, as we all know, illusion is an exciting, many-splendored thing. To see the characters and objects in 'Toy Story' move, or more often careen, through space for the first time was thrilling." She connects the dots across art history, linking Pixar to old masters. Smith says, "You can imagine the Italians of the Renaissance experiencing a similar delight upon seeing the cleanly defined box of illusionist space created by Masaccio's, Pollaiuolo's and Raphael's progressively more assured deployments of linear perspective."[43] Pixar may not have broken new ground in regard to story, but these masters of a new medium meld classic animation techniques to burgeoning technology.

What Would Walt Be?

Pixar has dusted off and rehabilitated the tattered legacy of Walt Disney. John Lasseter's childhood wish to become an animator coincided with Disney's creation of a character animation program at the California Institute of Arts. Established by Walt and Roy Disney in 1961, CalArts was the first college to offer degrees in both visual and performing arts.[44] Lasseter's classmates at CalArts included future filmmakers Tim Burton (*Corpse Bride*), Brad Bird (*The Incredibles*), and John Musker (*Aladdin*). At CalArts, Lasseter thrived under the tutelage of veteran Disney animators. He recalls, "I finally realized that I wasn't the only one with this geeky love for animation. We could come out of the closet now. And all of us had the same dream: to work at Disney one day."[45]

Lasseter fulfilled his dream, working his way up from the Jungle Cruise at Disneyland to the animation department at the studio. But his visionary instincts were frustrated by a now-institutionalized Disney Studios. The powers that be did not want to hear new ideas or consider new technologies like computer animation. Employees were expected to fit into the Disney machine.

Shrek's fractured fairy tale could have been a prime moment of payback for Lasseter. DreamWorks's animated triumph was fueled by another Disney castoff. Jeffrey Katzenberg cofounded DreamWorks to rival and ultimately undermine his old boss at Disney, Michael Eisner. The animus (as opposed to *anemos*) in their relationship spills over into *Shrek*'s satirical take on Lord Farquaad's presumptuous playground. Duloc is a kingdom ruled by rules. Puppets sing out the regulations with surprising cheer: "Stay in line; we'll get along fine; Duloc is a perfect place." This is the antithesis of creativity, individuality, and all that makes humans human. It is a kingdom drained of all magic.

Lasseter could have ended up crushed by the Disney animation factory. Thankfully for all of us, he found a creative home in the Bay Area, working for George Lucas's special effects group. In 1986 Steve Jobs, of Apple Computer fame, purchased Lucas's computer graphics company and rechristened it "Pixar."[46] After ten years of short films, commercials, and experimentation, Lasseter made *Toy Story*, which became an "overnight" sensation (and a financial boon for their distributor, Disney). In the ultimate irony, Lasseter returned to the Disney Studios as a conquering hero. When Disney purchased Pixar in 2006 for somewhere north of $7 billion, Lasseter took over the creative reins of Walt's legacy and the animation studio that had failed to catch his youthful vision.

Pixar's success stands as a testament to teamwork. Lasseter offers technical and creative challenges to his collaborators. They are all salaried employees, called on to make each movie better. Pixar culls collective wisdom (and humor). They've practiced art as a team sport, allowing everyone's muscles and talents to flex. Lasseter explains the corporate ethos that has kept such star employees as Andrew Stanton on board: "Pixar is a studio of pioneers.

And that's why a lot of people work here; they love doing something new that's never been done before. . . . They love to be challenged. They love for me to come to them and say, 'We don't know how to do this. Here, figure it out.' And they live for that. It's much harder work that way, but that's what drives us."[47]

As a comparatively small boutique, Pixar's corporate culture harkens back to Disney's original creative vision. Disney biographer Neal Gabler defines the difference in terms of core questions. While the Walt Disney Company was paralyzed by the question of "What would Walt do?" the Pixar team got busy figuring out "What would Walt be?"[48] Rather than merely preserving a noble past, they followed Disney's innovative ethos. Walt's followers at Pixar incorporated his spirit instead of bottling his legacy. Could this simple revelation revolutionize our faith practices? Has the Christian community in the West become a bloated Disney rather than a responsive, focused creative team? Have we become more interested in protecting a brand and preserving market share than serving the public?[49] When Jesus gazed at the crowds, he had compassion on them. He saw them as harassed and helpless, like sheep without a shepherd (see Mark 6:34). Perhaps we have been too busy minding our store to feed hungry, desperate sheep.

John Lasseter and company have recaptured the spirit that animated Walt Disney. Biographer Neal Gabler reveals the secret behind Walt's magic:

> Whatever Disney contributed in terms of technology, the element that made even his early animations superior was the sense of anima in them—the spirit. Walt Disney never thought of his characters as moving drawings. He saw them as living, feeling, thinking creatures, which is why he believed audiences responded to them. The technologies he advocated were simply ways to enhance the anima.[50]

Pixar has taken the animator's calling seriously. They have harnessed new technologies in an effort to breathe life into ideas. What used to be two-dimensional cartoons have become three-dimensional worlds. Despite their unprecedented success, the Pixar team remains grounded by a respect for their audience. Lasseter describes his sense of calling: "I believe in the nobility of entertaining people, and I take great, great pride that people are willing to give me two or three hours out of their busy lives. I don't want anyone to feel they wasted any of their time or money to see one of our films or ride one of our rides or go see one of our shows."[51] What would Walt do? Stand and cheer as a proud father to creative sons and daughters. They expanded a beloved field by actively cultivating the garden today.

But What Are They Teaching Kids?

Pixar's revelatory power may reside more in how they achieve their films than what their stories communicate. Thematically, the Pixar films are not necessarily triumphs of originality. Friendship, hard work, perseverance, and family are held up as enduring virtues. Individual achievement can accomplish only so much; community enables us to overcome our biggest obstacles. Pixar movies blend American values and the Judeo-Christian tradition into something resembling the gospel according to Disney. While the movies like *Toy Story* or *Monsters, Inc.* may hint at chaos lurking in kids' bedrooms, they ultimately reinforce a suburban status quo. God is a distant deity, cheering us on as we pursue our dreams.

The Pixar philosophy echoes the beliefs of America's teenagers, tracked by sociologist Christian Smith and his team at the National Study of Youth and Religion.[52] They found adolescents are more influenced by their parents' faith than previously anticipated. At the same time, those religious beliefs are more diffuse than imagined. Perhaps we've all been sprinkled with more of Disney's pixie dust than we realized. Smith and his research team describe this emerging belief system as "moralistic therapeutic deism." God is good but distant. Our task is to feel good about ourselves and follow a broad but malleable moral landscape. Smith concludes, "The language, and therefore experience, of Trinity, holiness, sin, grace, justification, sanctification, church, Eucharist, and heaven and hell appear, among most Christian teenagers in the United States at the very least, to be supplanted by the language of happiness, niceness, and an earned heavenly reward."[53] We have embraced entertainment as a rite and lauded Pixar's characters as moral exemplars. Perhaps Pixar's films are better at spreading joy and gaining respect than engendering belief. Cute films are no substitute for true religion. Pixar's lasting contribution may be in how they mastered technology rather than what they did with it. The journey of the Pixar team, the creative community that Lasseter has assembled, serves as its own reward.

Master Miyazaki

When John Lasseter and the Pixar animation team are experiencing a creative block, they turn to Hayao Miyazaki's lush, hand-drawn films for inspiration. Lasseter has used his considerable pull at Disney to bring Miyazaki's films to America and a global audience. The one caveat that Miyazaki and Studio Ghibli demanded in their negotiations—no cuts or alterations. Disney may dub an English language sound track, but they cannot change a frame of Miyazaki's vision. The original, uncut *Sen to Chihiro no kamikakushi* (*Spirited Away*) won the 2003 Academy Award for Best Animated Film. It also dominated critic's lists, topping Metacritic's aggregate list of not just the best animated feature, but the best-reviewed film of 2002.[54] What makes *Spirited Away* so captivating to even the toughest audiences? Miyazaki's visual imagination is utterly transporting—a perfect blend of the fantastic and the credible. *Spirited Away* presents selfish humans who are forced to work with the gods to restore themselves and the environment around them. It brings audiences back to the wonder of childhood and the beauty of the natural world. This cautionary tale suggests we must remember who we are and where we've come from before it is too late.

Miyazaki brings a grandfatherly wisdom to *Spirited Away*. It starts with the anxieties of Chihiro, a ten-year-old girl moving to a new neighborhood. She appears somewhat spoiled, complaining about leaving her school friends behind. Miyazaki says, "The most important thing for me in making this movie was to persuade the 10-year-olds that this movie was for them. I wanted them to be able to recognize themselves in the characters. I think I would like them to leave the movie theater with a sense of humility about the complexity and difficulties of the world we live in."[55] En route to their new home, Chihiro's parents take a wrong turn. Dad refuses to ask for directions and tries to find a shortcut. Chihiro spots broken shrines at the foot of a dilapidated *tori* gate. Are they a nod to an ancient past or a hint of things to come? The family ends up lost in the woods. The wind blows her parents toward an abandoned theme park. Chihiro resists, but the wind pulls her into a fantastic adventure. Miyazaki insists, "I do think we need fantasy. For those who are in their powerless childhood, when they feel helpless, fantasy has something to give them: relief."[56]

The old Japanese amusement park has echoes of an abandoned Disneyland, but it was actually inspired by real-life Tokyo park, *Tatemoneon*, dedicated to Western-influenced architecture. Miyazaki expresses a genuine affection for emblems and architecture of a bygone era. During an interview in Old Tokyo's *Tatemoneon*, he said, "I feel nostalgic here, especially when I stand here alone in the evening, near closing time, and the sun is setting—tears well up in my eyes (laughs). . . . I think we have forgotten the life, the buildings, and the streets we used to have not so long ago. . . . Everyone thinks our problems today are the big problems we have for the first time in the world. But I think we just aren't used to them."[57] So Miyazaki's sense of loss is quite palpable, his nostalgia sincere.

Problems arise when Chihiro's parents spot some food. With no owner in sight, they help themselves to the banquet before them. When Chihiro questions the wisdom of digging in, her parents dismiss her. Mom says, "Don't worry about it—we can pay them [the owners] when they get back." Dad points to his cash and credit cards as sufficient insurance. Their confidence resides in their wealth. But when the parents are transformed into pigs, no credit card can help them. Chihiro tries to wake from this nightmare, but it proves all too real. Consumption becomes a major theme in *Spirited Away*. From a big, oversized baby to an engorged spirit named No Face, *Spirited Away* is packed with characters putting on the pounds. They have no self-imposed limits; they are just devolving into a bag of appetitive desires. Miyazaki places the blame for overconsumption squarely on adults. They are so busy gorging themselves that they fail to hear their children's cries. He notes, "There are too many things around us to relieve our unsatisfied hearts and boredom. This is the fault of adults; it's adults who are in the wrong shape. Children are just mirrors, so no wonder they are in the wrong shape."[58] Chihiro must overcome the selfishness both around and within her.

What has turned Chihiro's parents into pigs? How can she help reverse their curse? Her new companion, Haku, advises her to munch on a berry because, "Unless you eat something from this world, you'll disappear." Chihiro must

Hayao Miyazaki critiques Japanese consumer culture when Chihiro's parents become pigs in *Spirited Away*. © 2001 by Walt Disney Pictures.

learn and practice ancient spiritual truths, becoming grounded in the natural world. Haku directs her toward a bizarre bathhouse reserved for spirits. She is instructed to humbly ask for work. Perhaps the mighty and mysterious sorceress Yubaba will take pity on her and her parents. Chihiro must conquer her initial fears. When she is helped by a literal spider-man named Kamaji, she forgets to say, "Thank you." Her retraining may take time.

How does Yubaba rule the bathhouse employees? She steals their identity. Yubaba pockets a few crucial Japanese *kanji* (symbols) from Chihiro's name, rechristening her "Sen." Haku advises her, "You'll never find your way home if you don't remember [your name]." Miyazaki makes conscious allusions to the historical amnesia plaguing Japan. He diagnoses the problem: "I believe that children's souls are the inheritors of historical memory from previous generations. It's just that as they grow older and experience the everyday world that memory sinks lower and lower. I feel I need to make a film that reaches down to that level. If I could do that I would die happy."[59] As in *Memento* and *Eternal Sunshine*, the loss of memory has grave consequences. We must remember our true names and nature if we hope to escape our crippling circumstances.

Restoring an Enchanted World

Miyazaki places the answers within the imaginative spirits who gather at the *onsen*. He says, "For me, a bath house is a mysterious place in town. . . . Japanese gods go there to rest for a few days, then return home saying they wished they could stay for a little while longer. . . . I was thinking that it's tough being a Japanese god today."[60] In a disenchanted world, where would a god go for a little rest and relaxation? Miyazaki affirms ancient or forgotten Shinto traditions. Shinto was co-opted for political purposes during World War II. Miyazaki tries to awaken beliefs from the premodern era, when "Shrine Shinto understood the whole of life, including both humans and nature, as creative and life giving." He recalls, "In my grandparents' time . . . it was believed that spirits [*kami*] existed everywhere—in trees, rivers, insects, wells, anything. My generation does not believe this, but I like the idea that we should all treasure everything because spirits might exist there, and we should treasure everything because there is a kind of life to every-thing."[61] Shinto's eight million gods offer Miyazaki ample room to flex his creative muscles. Trees, bushes, and birds become locations for the divine. A radish god bears a striking resemblance to a sumo wrestler. A stink god resembles a river of flowing waste. Miyazaki makes pantheism appear real and appealing.

Sen begins to learn the value of hard work. She cleans a massive tub reserved for the dirtiest guests. While Yubaba and the guests flee from the stink god, Sen steps up, willing to take on the challenge. While the toxic stench threatens to undo the staff (it even ruins the purity of the white rice), Sen dives in, trying to solve the stink god's problems. To truly experience the vital power residing within nature, a person must cleanse his or her heart and mind (called a *kokoro* in Japanese).[62] As a precious herbal formula washes over the guest, Sen notices an appendage sticking out of the stink god. She yanks on the arm or handle with all her might. With grit and determination, Sen and her fellow workers dislodge the bicycle that has dammed up all manner of refuse within the god. Years of garbage and neglect come pouring out. A majestic and pure river god emerges from the muck. He mutters in appreciation, "It feels good" (translated as "well done" in English). Sen has cleansed the *kokoro* of the *kami* river god and, by extension, herself.

Drawing on a childhood memory, Miyazaki summons all his artistic talent to animate this memorable scene. Like Sen, he digs deep within, discovering untapped reservoirs of hospitality and imagination. This is animation at its finest—transporting viewers to unseen worlds, revealing the genuine evils lurking beneath the surface, but offering triumph through heroic actions. Miyazaki's commitment to the environment shines through in the restoration of the river god. Miyazaki aspires to nothing less than the recovery of awe toward nature. But he doesn't cast blame for the polluting of the river god. He says, "When you talk about plants, or an ecological system or forest, things are very easy if you decide that bad people ruined it. But that's not what humans have been doing. It's not bad people who are destroying forests. Hard-working people have been doing it."[63] Environmental crises arise from our collective indifference. Miyazaki longs for a recovery of the sacredness of life:

> In the past, humans hesitated when they took lives, even non-human lives. But society had changed, and they no longer felt that way. As humans grew stronger, I think that we became quite arrogant, losing the sorrow of "we have no other choice." I think that is the essence of human civilization, we have the desire to become rich without limit, by taking the lives of other creatures. . . . And it leads to the idea that the world is not just for humans, but for all life, and humans are allowed to live in a corner of the world.[64]

His films hark back to a premodern era when humanity did not place itself above or apart from nature. He recovers the pantheistic impulses of Shintoism. Miyazaki doesn't necessarily offer a tangible solution but allows viewers to wrestle with the questions. He concludes, "When we recognize that even living humbly destroys nature, we don't know what to do. And I think that unless we put ourselves in the place where we don't know what to do and start from there, we cannot think about environmental issues or issues concerning nature."[65] Miyazaki wants to leave his Japanese viewers vexed and perplexed. Yet his critique extends to the entire modernist project. Christians in the West are called to question the West's consumption. General revelation starts by disturbing our status quo.

Reception and Remembering

So how have Hayao Miyazaki's extravagant visions been received? *Spirited Away* broke box office records in Japan. IMDb ratings have been equally rapturous. Danherb writes from Germany, "Seldom have I seen a movie full of such boundless fantasy, incredible beauty and opulent pictures."[66] Tomimt from Finland appreciated its nuances: "Not your typical Disney cartoon. And that is a compliment. No ready chewed, easy to point up moral codes, but more real grip from things. A line between good and bad is a very vague line."[67] Glen Wang posts from Malaysia, praising Miyazaki for showing "the innocence, the bizarre, the horror and the wondrous revelation that the main protagonist (Chihiro) sees, feels and experiences throughout her spiritual journey."[68] What many received as sublime, others called "inane," "unwatchable bilge," "muddled," "nonsensical," and "gibberish."[69] There are plenty of cultural gaps that must be bridged to *get* the film. *Spirited Away* doesn't follow the traditional plot and structure we're accustomed to in Western myths, and Miyazaki doesn't identify characters as good or evil. He operates on a different level, drawing out of a sense of compulsion or calling. His concern for the vanishing values of Japan is genuine. He insists, "You can't measure the success of a picture on how many tickets it sells. You can only measure it in how many hearts it changes."[70] Despite his personal pessimism, Miyazaki draws as a person of boundless hope, eager to change hearts and minds.

Sen continues to face plenty of obstacles after she has seemingly learned her lessons. She attracts attention she doesn't necessarily want. Haku approaches in the form of a flying dragon. He is bloodied, injured by Yubaba's spell. Yubaba's twin sister steals the big baby, and No Face will eat himself into oblivion if Sen doesn't acknowledge him. What absurd plot points to discuss! Yet the effect of the film is mesmerizing. Sen takes her friends on a train trip to the country. They glide over the water in a magical train as *Spirited Away* moves toward remembering, restoring, and reuniting.

History

Sen and her friends must learn responsibility and the rewards of hard work. The spoiled big baby figures out how to stand up on his own. No Face discovers a craft and finds his purpose when he feels useful. And Sen remembers her real name, Chihiro. But how will she free her friend Haku from his current incarnation as a dragon? Miyazaki's films feature scenes of freedom and flight. His father worked in an airplane parts factory, so Miyazaki always associates flying with feelings of home.[71] Chihiro takes to the skies, enjoying an invigorating ride on Haku's back. Only in the air, free from the constraints of her situation, does Chihiro recall her connection to Haku. She remembers falling into the Kohaku River when she was young. The "Haku" river carried her safely to the shore—Haku's true name revealed! Yubaba's spell over him is broken! Her power is undercut by remembering rightly. The moral of Miyazaki's story slips in: "Nothing that happens is ever forgotten, even if you can't remember it." Those who have forgotten their roots, who have become cut off from nature, end up lost and adrift, living under a spell. But for those who can connect to something larger, who see themselves within a much larger history of humanity in relation to nature, restoration awaits. Chihiro has reacquired her name and clarified her vision. She can now identify her parents (even as pigs). Chihiro helps her friends and parents throw off their shackles and restore their humanity. They have all moved from selfishness to sacrifice, from sulking to sincerity.

Miyazaki comes to his films as a pessimist, admitting, "I know the world is heading in a bad direction." Yet he continues to draw, working at a furious pace. "If, as artists, we try to tap into that soul level—if we say that life is worth living and the world is worth living in—then something good might come of it."[72] *Spirited Away* affirms a Shinto perspective that gods animate nature and insists we must reconnect with both. How might this vision inform my own faith? What is an appropriate theological response to such an animated, life-giving vision?

Neo-Paganism or Panentheism?

> When thou sendest forth thy Spirit, they are created; and thou renewest the face of the ground.
>
> Psalm 104:30 RSV

In *The Pagan Temptation* (1987), philosopher Thomas Molnar suggests that an overly rationalistic faith has resulted in the recent rise of neo-paganism. While the inherent reasonableness of Christianity is one of its strongest (and earliest) features in displacing paganism, we must resist the temptation to completely desacralize the world. In attacking the mythic elements of others' religion, Christianity made science possible. But a deification of science threatens to undermine Christianity and allow for the resurgence of pagan religions, particularly the Asian varieties exhibited in Hayao Miyazaki's *Spirited Away*. Molnar laments:

> Christianity did not pay sufficient attention to this need for the nourishment that nature provides to the soul, and it consequently yielded such preoccupations to rationalists and scientists, who took from nature its mysteries. . . . The desacralization of nature by Christianity necessarily led to a similar desacralization, or "disciplining," of the imagination, something that the Christian religion could ill afford since nature, in the form of myth and symbol, was needed as a mediation toward the supernatural.[73]

The loss was felt not only by the pagan religions. "Joseph Campbell notes that when a civilization begins to reinterpret its mythology, the life goes out of it and temples become museums."[74] Europe is crowded with such cathedrals. Molnar describes the spiritual malaise gripping most of Western Christianity. "Old churches look like museums, new ones like factories. Priests and nuns look like busy bureaucrats, particularly since they hardly ever display signs of their sacred callings. Sermons, like newspaper editorials, deal with political, social and economic issues."[75] He sings a sad, demoralizing song: "Having desacralized the world around it, Christianity turned upon itself and desacralized, demythologized and desymbolized religion. It profaned the cult and the mystery while it injected a kind of lukewarm semi-Christianity, a mainly moralizing discourse, into institutions and public life."[76] Miyazaki found the same institutional malaise within Japan. Theologian Sallie McFague suggests, "The eighteenth-century individual, isolated from other people except through contracts and from nature except as the resource base from which to amass wealth, is false *according to the picture of reality in our time*."[77] We've already seen the cost of isolation in *Memento, Eternal Sunshine*, and *Crash*.

So are there signs of hope? General revelation, led by the Spirit, will arise despite religions' efforts to squelch it. We cannot abolish our mythical past. Our pagan rituals—from New Year's Eve to Groundhog Day—remain. To satisfy our hunger for a shaping story, Mircea Eliade suggests, "The cinema, that 'dream factory,' takes over and employs countless mythical motifs—the fight between hero and monster, initiatory combats and ordeals, paradigmatic figures and images (the maiden, the hero, the paradisal landscape, hell and so on)."[78] Movies have risen as a pagan alternative to a spiritless religion. Amid a profane world and a desacralized cosmos, this book has suggested that movies can provide a prophetic corrective. God will raise up unlikely outsiders to wake us from our slumber and indifference. Filmmakers are asking the same questions first posed by God: Why are we hiding? Who are our brother and sister? Can we imagine a better world?

If the Enlightenment era declared the death of God, the postmodern era has opened up the possibilities of gods lurking behind every tree or bush. In our renewed paganism, the question is not "Is there a God?" but "Which god?" Hayao Miyazaki presents an enchanted universe where gods hide behind every bush and take hot baths whenever they get a chance to relax. For the Christian, this can sound far too pantheistic. Yet perhaps we need to recover the *panentheistic* roots of our faith; not everything *as* God but God *in* everything. McFague posits, "We need to reconceive ourselves. . . . The postmodern picture sees us as part and parcel of the earth, not only dependent on it and its processes, but since we are high on the food chain, *radically* dependent."[79] Rather than dismissing Miyazaki's respect for nature as pantheistic, maybe we need to receive it as prophetic. McFague challenges us to worship God *through* nature, "by means of each being's uniqueness, each rock's concrete contours, each tree's particular form, each galaxy's unique constellation, God is glorified. The God whose glory is each creature fully alive revels in differences, not in sameness."[80] Miyazaki's vivid imaginary world equips us to appreciate God's precious creation.

We must recognize the glory of God residing in nature. We must develop eyes that see beauty and praise God in response. A restored appreciation for the environment can also animate our worship and devotional life. In his *Personal Narrative*, the stern reputation of Jonathan Edwards is belied by his rapturous encounter with the New Jersey countryside. Edwards writes, "God's excellency, his wisdom, his purity, his love, seemed to appear in every thing; in the sun, moon and stars; in the clouds, and blue sky; in the grass, flowers, trees; in the water, and nature."[81] He writes like an animator who has attended to nature with quiet, patient reflection. Perhaps Miyazaki's pantheistic approach to nature can help Christians recover a more holistic, orthodox perspective on God's creation.

We have lived far too long in the fallen world between Genesis 3 and Revelation 20. But what is the beginning and end of God's shaping story? A bizarre film like *Spirited Away* enhanced my understanding of Scripture. Surely the wages of sin and the damnation that result from biting forbidden fruit are major themes of special revelation. We lost our privileged position within the Garden of Eden for an apple. When we act like selfish pigs, we may get our wish (or something even worse). But as Chihiro restores the river god to its earlier glory, so the biblical story takes us back to the garden. The Bible begins and ends in a garden flowing with rivers of life. Our future does not reside in the sky but here, amid a new heaven and a new earth. The future of creation in Revelation 21 and 22 matches the birth of creation in Genesis 1 and 2. As Miyazaki suggests, what was once good will be good again—maybe even better. This is general revelation in action.

Too often our Christian apologetics start with the fall in Genesis 3 rather than the creation in Genesis 1. We have tried to work from problem to solution, emphasizing the judgment to come rather than the glory that awaits. We have communicated that humanity is sinful and the earth is going to burn. But our vision too frequently ends with Revelation 20, when the devil is cast into a lake of fire. This apocalyptic scene doesn't conclude the biblical story. Revelation 21 takes us back to the creation of Genesis 1, where the Spirit of God separated the sky from the sea, the heavens from the earth. We will not be transported out of this world but greeted by the descent of a new Jerusalem. In a flash of recognition, the world as we know it becomes secondary, as the primary world, the Holy City of God, arrives. In John's apocalyptic vision, "The dwelling of God is with men, and he will live with them" (Rev. 21:3). God promises to wipe away every tear and "To him who is thirsty I will give to drink without cost from the spring of the water of life" (Rev. 21:6). When we are fully satisfied, we won't be thinking about stealing a bite of forbidden fruit. This is a world that can animate our thinking, fuel our imaginations.

We may need to reread Scripture via *theological animation*. The Spirit may prompt us to renounce our exploitative habits, to reclaim our role as stewards of creation. We may even find ourselves agreeing with our critics. In an influential 1967 article for *Science* magazine, Lynn White was among the first to suggest that God's direction in Genesis 1:28 to "fill the earth and subdue it" had unleashed all kinds of ecological disasters.[82] White's critique has forced us to reexamine our own texts and traditions, to look closer at Scripture and nature. We may also find ourselves invited to join unlikely partners in creation care. Harvard biologist E. O. Wilson has written an open letter to an unnamed pastor in *The Creation: An Appeal to Save Life on Earth*.[83] While Wilson has abandoned his Southern Baptist roots for a remote deism, he invites Christians to join him in his love of nature and concern for the endangered environment. Our eschatology can find a partner in his ecology.

Thankfully, leading Christian theologians have attempted to reanimate our thinking in regard to fantasy and creation. Alistair McGrath combines his training in molecular biology and theology to heal the breach between Christianity and the natural world. He traces how a shortsighted Christian faith encouraged the domination and exploitation of nature, rather than our God-given role of tending and nurturing creation. Sallie McFague suggests dominion "sees the planet as a corporation or syndicate, as a collection of individual human beings drawn together to benefit its members by optimal use of natural resources."[84] Yet in Genesis 2 we are also appointed as stewards of creation, called to care for it. Tending the garden means seeing "the planet more like an organism or a community that survives and prospers through interrelationship and interdependence of its many parts, both human and nonhuman."[85] McFague and McGrath understand the dangers of pantheism and a romanticized view of nature, but they insist we must reenchant nature and recover our sense of wonder and respect for God's creation because "the beauty of the world thus reflects the beauty of God."[86] Miyazaki's animated visions can help us see things more clearly, to emerge from a darkened theater with our senses sharpened.

In *Spirited Away*, Haku and Chihiro had to remember who they were in relation to each other and the natural world. Well before Al Gore offered *An Inconvenient Truth* (2006) about global warming, Jürgen Moltmann was formulating "an ecological theology of nature" (1993). Moltmann suggests we must no longer view the earth as merely a subject to be studied or a resource to be mined. We do not reside atop a hierarchy of creation but join a highly relational "community of creation" initiated and embodied by Father, Son, and Holy Spirit. If God intends to dwell with us on earth, then we must make it as habitable, hospitable, and beautiful as possible. So as we exercise our creative gifts in production design, special effects, and animation, we may actually be participating in a dress rehearsal for coming glory. We are slowly remembering why we were created. We may need to adjust not only our relationship to nature but our understanding of God's place in the world. Moltmann explains: "An ecological doctrine of creation implies a new kind of thinking about God. The center of this thinking is no longer the distinction between God and the world. The center is the recognition of the presence of God in the world and the presence of the world in God."[87]

Miyazaki's universe may be overpopulated by gods, but the contemporary Christian worldview has overemphasized God's absence from the world. A reenchanted universe restores God's presence within creation and places humanity back into its proper place *tending* the garden rather than *pillaging* for gold. I deeply appreciate fantasy films because they give me a more complete picture of God. Heroism, bravery, sacrifice, and imagination are standard virtues in fantasy. Love triumphs over evil; truth defeats deception; tenacity overcomes obstacles. A clearer view of nature will offer a more robust understanding of God.

The Spirit of God that Jesus sends in the Acts of the Apostles was the same Spirit hovering over the waters in Genesis 1. The Spirit of creation and the Spirit of redemption are one. An overemphasis on creation as complete (and God as distant) led to deism. To place God solely on the earth, amid creation, led to pantheism. Moltmann suggests, "The Trinitarian concept of creation integrates the elements of truth in monotheism and pantheism."[88] It is both/and, the already and the not yet. If historical films deal with the *already* and science fiction anticipates the *not yet*, then perhaps fantasy films help us navigate the messy middle. Fantasy films imagine an idealized past, when knights defeated dragons and rescued damsels. Yet they also operate on a more transcendent plain, constructing secondary worlds that seem simultaneously ancient and eternal (*Crouching Tiger, Hidden Dragon*). The finest filmmakers can redefine the roles of men and women and rewrite classic fairy tales while retaining timeless truths (*Shrek*). We cope with the horrors of war by learning to unmask and resist evil (*Pan's Labyrinth*). Adults' newfound appreciation for fantasy film demonstrates that even digital technology can be used to rehumanize jaded audiences (the Pixar films). We can accomplish so much as a community united around a common task. Fantasy films are restoring our imagination, reminding us of the way things ought to (and someday will) be (*Spirited Away*).

People of faith and theologians in training must walk in the same confidence that the Spirit of God, who animated Genesis, will guide us toward the River of Life awaiting us in Revelation 22. The Apocalypse of John closes with a bottomless well, pouring forth a life-giving elixir. But this invitation is no mirage or magic trick. The wedding invitation extended by the Spirit and the bride in Revelation 22:17 is clear: "Whoever is thirsty, let him come; and whoever wishes, let him take the free gift of the water of life." Drink up—because this fantasy is reality.

8

Conclusion
Mnemonic Devices

The Lord of the Rings: The Return of the King (2003, IMDb #4)
The Lord of the Rings: The Fellowship of the Ring (2001, IMDb #14)
The Lord of the Rings: The Two Towers (2002, IMDb #20)

> Someday you will be loved.
>
> Death Cab for Cutie[1]

After reviewing forty-five films across hundreds of pages, what can we conclude? The most important movies reveal the following hard truths: We long for the past because we are fearful of the future. Despite our best efforts to mask our insecurities and to justify our darkest intentions, we are only fooling ourselves. We have forgotten who we are. We have lost our perspective. We are desperate for community but afraid to commit to each other. We have focused on the differences that divide us rather than the commonalities that unite us. Despite advances in science and technology, we are not certain what constitutes a human life. We do not know what to protect, what to preserve, where to turn for help when science or medicine fails us. We are fractured.

Environmentalist Bill McKibben declares that "every culture has its patholo-
gies, and ours is self-reliance."[2] The Bible calls our tragic condition "sin." While
we may debate the roots of our dilemma, like the *Pirates of the Caribbean*, we
are powerless to reverse our curse. Equally tragic is the theological divide that
has deepened our sense of disintegration. We have divided our heads from our
hearts, isolated our minds from our bodies. The physical has opposed the spiritual, pulling us away from God-given creation and community. This conclusion
will trace how the separation of special and general revelation has impoverished
our understanding of God and ourselves.

Despite all the evidence that life as we know it is fallen, confused, and bleak,
we still cling to hope. Human existence has a mysterious side, beyond logic and
reason. We long for fantasies. We seek a way out. We continue to dream of another world, an alternative universe where justice prevails, hunger is satisfied,
and peace reigns. It is a beautiful place, lush, relaxing, filled with color, diversity,
and splendor. This "Neverland" will never end.

Movies diagnose our problems and posit our futures. But filmmakers have
scant ideas about how to bridge the gap between our dreams and our realities.
General revelation tells us plenty about how we live, what we do to each other,
and what constitutes the human experience. Intimations of the divine, rumors
of a golden past, and hope for a bright tomorrow are laced throughout contemporary films. But general revelation cannot save us. The films we have surveyed
offer glimpses of sacrifice and models of redemption, but they lack the salvation
found in Christ alone. Can we connect what we have seen on-screen with what
has been revealed to us by our Creator God? Can our experience of the broken
world meet the suffering and risen Son of God? Can the Spirit lift us out of the
dark into the place we long to go?

In this conclusion we consider the theological history that has brought us to this
point. How did we get into a situation where our hearts long for love but our heads
actively resist it? Can faith and reason, doctrine and experience be reunited? We
cannot forge a future without an understanding of the past. How do we become
heroes, overcome our amnesia, and reunite with others? God lifts up outsiders,
from the margins of society, to communicate ancient truths in new ways.

Prophetic voices have always arisen from unlikely places. This book has suggested that today's most creative filmmakers, desperate to understand why things
are so broken, echo the heart and mind of the Creator God. Their haunting
questions to audiences are actually God's recurring questions to us. Why are
we hiding? Who is our neighbor? Can't we hear the sounds of our brothers' and
sisters' blood crying out for justice? Our cinematic dreams will also be fulfilled

in God's verdant promises for the future. As Death Cab for Cutie sings, "Someday you will be loved." There will be a better world, where wars cease, hunger is abated, and healing resides in the trees. We have an opportunity to join that divine project: to all who are thirsty, the Spirit and the Bride say, "Come—get started *today*" (see Rev. 22). The most timely, relevant, and haunting films resonate with the shaping story of Scripture: from the beauty of creation, through the tragedy of self-destruction, to the wonder of restoration. We don't need to chase the culture in search of relevance. Prayerful attention to today's art may help us reconnect with the timeless tale already entrusted to us.

I will conclude this study with the trilogy that tops the IMDb list of the top films of the twenty-first century, *The Lord of the Rings* (2001–3). Director Peter Jackson brought J. R. R. Tolkien's majestic adventure to the screen with loving care for a sacred trust. The *Rings* films address God's question that drove the first part of this book, "Where are you?" *The Lord of the Rings* is loaded with instances of people wrestling with themselves. The lure of the ring consumes those who do not have Frodo's resolve and resistance. In Gollum, we see a shell of Smeagal's former self; an obsession with the ring ("my precious") has robbed him of his humanity. Like Leonard in *Memento*, Gollum forgot who he used to be during his misguided quest. The *Rings* trilogy also explores God's second question to humanity, from Genesis 4:9: "Where is your brother?" Only as a fellowship of elves, dwarves, hobbits, and humans do the Company of Nine overcome the Dark Lord. Frodo can't complete the journey alone. In Samwise Gamgee we see the embodiment of loyalty, the greatest friend Frodo could ever imagine. All three films are about courage, community, and finding our place in a sacred drama. They are riddled with violence, greed, and deception. But as in the fantasy films we've studied, in the end they offer a hard-won hope, an opportunity to usher in a peaceable kingdom despite seemingly overwhelming circumstances.

What kind of theological resources need to be restored? We must recover our humanity, reconnect with our communities, and rediscover our role in a much larger story. We must reunite head and heart, thoughts and actions. We will not get there via determination; we need a renewed imagination. Most of all, we must remember where we've been in order to figure out where we are going. Whether in politics, film, or theology, democracy is predicated on an educated and responsible populace. Consider this conclusion an initial educational step. We must recount our sacred story, connecting the films we've reviewed to the gospel we've been given. May the general wisdom found in the best postmodern movies kiss the sweet sights of special revelation.

A Contentious Issue?

Perhaps the contentious nature of general revelation stems from its alleged scarcity within the special revelation of the Bible. Cases have been built *for or against* the power of general revelation, argued from select passages of the New Testament: John 1, Acts 14, Acts 17, and Romans 1–2. The light of humanity found in John 1, verses 4 and 9, has been read as either a statement of universal enlightenment, "light to every man was coming into the world," or as an affirmation that only the special revelation of Jesus ("the true light") grants life. Both sides in the debates regarding revelation have marshaled Acts 14:14–18 as evidence. When Paul heals a crippled man in Lystra, crowds rush to anoint him a god. A miracle leads to confusion rather than salvation. Yet moments later, Paul explains that God has showered Lystra with common grace: "He has shown kindness by giving you rain from heaven and crops in their seasons; he provides you with plenty of food and fills your hearts with joy" (v. 17). Even after this clarification, the crowd still wants to sacrifice to Paul rather than the God of grace. Passages like this have led some theologians to conclude, "No one has ever responded positively in his or her preconversion state to God through general revelation. To assert that individuals do, clearly contradicts biblical teaching."[3]

If Acts 14 creates debates about the power of creation, then Acts 17 fuels competing claims for creativity and culture. In Acts 17:23, Paul announces to the Athenians on Mars Hill, "What you worship as something unknown I am going to proclaim to you." Paul affirms their artistic expressions, stressing the relative nearness of God—"reach out for him and find him." His message also includes what would have been familiar quotations from popular Greek poets, Epimenides and Aratus. Those who find signs of life in general revelation draw potent conclusions. As Paul found a point of contact in the Athenians' art and poetry, so Christians are encouraged to comb today's Areopagus—pop culture—in search of opportunities to articulate the gospel.

Yet those who insist that general revelation has a limited impact and no salvific power highlight the verses that follow. Paul is not seen as conciliatory but frustrated. In Acts 17:30 Paul calls the Athenians' idol-making "ignorance." God commands all people to repent or be judged, and if the Athenians want proof of God's authority, Paul points to Jesus's resurrection. Some in the audience sneer at the mention of the resurrection. Others want to know more, and they end up following Paul and believing (in the resurrected Jesus). But the results, some argue, seem paltry in comparison to Peter's sermon on salvation history in Acts 4, where thousands repent and believe.

Is art inscribed to unknown gods or dedicated to Zeus evidence of a spiritual search or wrongheaded futility? Does God affirm the Athenians' art or condemn it as misguided? In the ancient world, the word *unknown* was synonymous with *ignorance*, so perhaps Paul is playing on words and slamming them. Yet the poets Paul points to are actually praising the Greek god Zeus. What a surprise! Paul doesn't just dignify their spiritual longings, he praises their art offered to a rival, false god. The intentions of an atheist like Philip Pullman in *His Dark Materials* or a movie like *The Golden Compass* still fall under the redemptive possibilities and purposes of God. Remember the insight of Joseph in Genesis 50:20: "As for you, you meant evil against me, but God meant it for good." Why are we still animated by so much fear instead of being animated by faith?

Many cite Romans 1 as evidence of the limits of general revelation. Romans 1:18–22 serves as the basis for natural theology. God's invisible qualities have been revealed via what has been made. But humanity's response to that general revelation reinforces the limits of natural theology. The truth of God was exchanged for a lie. People worshiped created things rather than the Creator (Rom. 1:25). All manner of perversion resulted. Yet this portrait of God bothers theologian Clark Pinnock. This passage also raises unsettling notions about God's revelation. Why would God give people just enough knowledge to condemn them but not enough to save them? Why can one learn from the created order that we are condemned but not that we can repent and be saved? Natural theology appears to be broad in scope but devoid of any salvific effect. Case closed.

Yet the judgment doled out on defiant humanity in Romans 1 turns out to be merely a set up for even starker news in Romans 2. The ignorance that follows in the wake of natural theology is minor compared to the hardheartedness that accompanies those who have received God's special revelation. The only thing worse than the senseless, faithless, heartless, and ruthless people of Romans 1 are the sincere, self-righteous, and hypocritical people condemned in Romans 2. General revelation may be ineffective in light of human sin, but it pales in comparison to the resistance that can accompany even God's special revelation. Many people who met Jesus decided not to follow him. Does that mean that the presence of Christ was not compelling? By no means! Rather, all forms of revelation are elusive and exceptional. We never know how or when the Spirit will move (or how blind we might be to the most beautiful evidence possible). Isn't that the mystery of faith? Isn't this why we can never rule out anyone or consider ourselves more highly than we ought?

My search for God began through the profane, unlikely means of Martin Scorsese's *Raging Bull* (1980). Thousands of IMDb users speak in rapturous terms about dark, twisted movies as miraculous, enlightening, and inspiring. So can't we reconcile the general revelation of God experienced via movies with the special revelation of Christ revealed in Scripture? Doesn't the same Spirit animate both theological categories? I want to recapture the spirit of Psalm 19, to embrace the general *and* the specific revelations of God, from an appreciation of nature to a passion for the law of the Lord.

Comparatively hidden verses unearthed by theologian Jürgen Moltmann energize me. His natural theology begins in the Old Testament with the Spirit in creation. The Spirit of God was moving over the face of the waters in Genesis 1:2. The *ruach* of Elohim was present in the original creative act. Moltmann insists that to understand the Hebrew word *ruach*, we must forget the word *spirit*.[4] Greek *pneuma*, Latin *spiritus*, and the German *geist/ghost* were conceived as antithesis to matter and body. They are inherently divisive, rooted in *otherness*. *Ruach* is not the antithesis of the material; it is much more *embodied*.

Ruach suggests God is a tempest, a storm, a force in body and soul, humanity and nature. The word *ruach* occurs 385 times in the Old Testament. The phrase *ruach Yahweh* is used twenty-seven times, including Exodus 14:21 and Ezekiel 13:13 and 36:26. In Exodus 15:8 it appears as an onomatopoeic word for *gale*, like the wind that divided the Red Sea. *Ruach* is the power to live in Ecclesiastes 3:21 and 12:7. God's breath blows in Psalm 31:5, Psalm 104:29, and Luke 23:46. *Breath* is a feminine word associated with God in Psalm 33:6. To experience Yahweh's breath is to occupy a large space, a broad place (Ps. 31:8; Job 36:16). God's Spirit gets involved in the anointing of kings (1 Sam. 10), in Nathan's prophecy to David (2 Sam. 7), and in the inward confessions of Psalms 51 and 139. This feminine side of God's Spirit shows up as Dame Wisdom in Proverbs 8 and Job 28. General revelation has many appearances in the Old Testament beyond Psalm 19, if one associates Yahweh's *ruach* with divine revelation.

This resonates with my own experience of God via movies. Creative people longing for inspiration are inherently (but perhaps unknowingly) on a search for God. Inspiration is the wind of God, which entrances, enthralls, and enraptures us. When we get *in the artistic groove* we rarely want to leave because the presence of God (whether acknowledged or not) is such a life-giving, life-sustaining creative force. We can't manufacture it; we can't manipulate it. God's wind blows mysteriously, but once we've experienced it, we desperately want more—not just in service of art but because of the incomparable high that accompanies God's *ruach*. Whether identified as a bright idea, a lightbulb, or listening to the muse, inspir(it)ation is the genesis of enduring art.

General versus Genuine Revelation

Psalm 19 suggests that God speaks through two complementary means: nature and the law. The heavens declare the glory of God; nature reveals the divine. The stars are a form of preaching; they speak volumes about the power of a colorful, Creator God. The psalmist refers to this creative God as "Elohim," the same broad, unspecific name for God used in Genesis. This divine revelation is global in scope, available to all. Like the most accessible family films, it is rated G for general audiences. But seeing does not necessarily lead to believing.[5] We are challenged to look *and* listen, to hear the Word of God in what we see. We must learn how to hear with our eyes.

What distinguishes *general* revelation from *genuine* revelation? We must not confuse the creation with the Creator. The psalmist takes on the sun worshipers of the ancient world, reminding them, "In the heavens he has pitched a tent for the sun." Sure, it is impressive, "like a bridegroom coming forth from his pavilion," or "like a champion rejoining to run his course" (Ps. 19:4–5), but one must not substitute the grandeur of the sun for the glory of God. Nature *points* to God; it is not God. General revelation without the gift of (in)sight can lead to misguided affections.

Others may miss the grandeur set before them altogether. Some look at the stars and shed a tear; others merely shrug. The general revelation of a brilliant sunset or a shooting star will not necessarily cure our blindness. Genuine, life-altering general revelation arrives as a gift from God, mediated by the Spirit. We have explored both the general revelation seen in nature and the genuine revelation that comes from *seeing through* nature, recognizing the Creator behind creation.

While most can understand these distinctions when discussing the natural world, things become much muddier when we turn from creation to creativity. We recognize the divine in a sunset, but what about in a painting of the same sunset? Has something been lost in translation? Or can art help us recover our sight, serving as another occasion for the Spirit to reveal profound and general truths about nature, humanity, and God?

Like Psalm 19, most art begins with the text of life. Artists offer us descriptive truth—what we know of the human experience and life here on earth. Their creativity is rooted in creation, celebrating the beauty and wonder around us while lamenting the wars, pain, and loss that bedevil us. General revelation and inspiration are available to all, yet only certain songs, stories, or films rise above a crowded field to become classics. Aesthetic judgments are colored by our cultural, educational, and even emotional contexts. Frank Burch Brown has noted the underdeveloped sense of taste and style within the Christian community.[6] Perhaps our art and music are often tacky because we haven't devoted enough time to aesthetics. Some will stare at a painting by Picasso and declare it something "my five-year-old could have painted." Others may turn art into a religion, idolizing painters and their paintings. I walk between those competing poles, offering an invitation to both sides.

To the artistically indifferent, I propose a more active engagement with entertainment. The finest films offer more than an escape from reality. Film-going (or rock concerts or even rock climbing) is laden with revelatory possibilities and potential glimpses of the divine. To dedicated film enthusiasts, I suggest that the good, true, and beautiful moments (the general revelation) found in enduring art are rooted in divine longing, creativity, and inspiration—*genuine revelation*. We must invite the Spirit into our forays, whether to the mountains or the movies. I advocate a sacramental approach to everyday life that can open us up to divine encounters.

Psalm 19 also celebrates the law of the Lord, the precepts of God handed down through specific and special times and places. The psalmist traces back such statues to Yahweh, the self-revealing God who spoke to Moses through the burning bush in Exodus 3. While the God of creation (Elohim) may be general, the God of the Ten Commandments (Yahweh) is associated with a particular people (the Hebrews). This special revelation (the law given by Yahweh to the Hebrews) began the canon of Scripture—eventually leading to the Bible and the incarnated Word of God in Jesus Christ. While the Gospels of Matthew, Mark, Luke, and John were addressed to specific audiences, taken together they offer potentially transforming news of God's love available to all.

Theologian Karl Barth distinguished between the actual and potential aspects of special revelation. Like the beauty of creation, the Word of God is a tangible reality—a text translated across the centuries. Yet its full, revelatory potential is often realized only when accompanied by the power of the Spirit. Words on a page take on life-changing force when the Spirit clarifies our hearing and sharpens our sight. For Barth, revelation begins and ends solely via God-initiated actions. For others, the revelatory power of general and special revelation depends on a mysterious blending of the Spirit's prompting and the audience's receptivity. Learning to see God through the general means of art and nature sharpens our ability to hear God revealed in Scripture. Likewise, when we invite the Spirit to speak through Scripture, we practice a spiritual discipline that should enhance our appreciation for the environment, the arts, and the global community.

Special revelation may be better understood as prescriptive rather than descriptive truth. It is more the province of preachers than artists. Filmmakers describe the problems to which ministers and theologians prescribe an answer. To some, this reduces general revelation to the role of warm-up act for the headliner to follow. They emphasize the second half of Psalm 19, how nature points to or is perfected by the law, concluding "natural theology is the vestibule of revealed theology."[7] General revelation establishes the existence of God and lays bare to humanity God's moral requirements. But should divine revelation be viewed as hierarchical, with the God of creation (Elohim) subjugated to the God of the law (Yahweh)? Aren't they the same God, communicating in two distinct but equally powerful ways? Some read the Old Testament as merely a preamble to the incarnation of Christ. Did the arrival of the Spirit trump previous manifestations of God? Absolutely not! General and special revelation are *complementary gifts* for navigating the complexities of life, for fueling our dreams, and for enduring our disappointments. Unfortunately, they are often placed in opposition, submitted to comparison and contrasts. What Psalm 19 joins together has been put asunder, reduced to competing columns. Some emphasize the otherworldly, transcendence of a Holy God (law), while others stress the immanent aspects of faith, God with us (creation).

This book suggests we cannot understand one without the other. A transcendent faith can end up divorced from experience. An immanent faith can prove too bound by what we can taste, touch, or measure. Like Death Cab for Cutie, I long to live where "soul meets body." Perhaps what we admire in movies stems from our finest, God-given intentions rather than our basest humanity. I am suggesting that movies can bridge the theological divide, demonstrating how general revelation mediated through art can deepen our understanding of the revealed Word of God found in Scripture. The IMDb provides a control group, a set of films by which to measure the postmodern condition. These are the artistic touchstones that have spoken the most poetically, majestically, and mysteriously about our plight and our possibilities. As the Spirit spoke through the stars in the sky, so God can communicate through cinematic stars.

A Theological Flashback

There is a time-honored tradition of allowing feelings to inform our facts about God. Unfortunately, the Christian community has nearly forgotten about it. In *Memento*, Leonard retains only the "facts" that support his case. Why didn't he listen to Teddy G., to those who offered an important corrective? Such one-sided, hardheadedness can create major blind spots (and result in Teddy's death). Our theological blinders have yielded what Robert K. Johnston has called "tidy doctrine but truncated experience."[8] The finest films help us recover the experiential aspects of faith.

During the scientific era of the Enlightenment, Friedrich Schleiermacher championed a faith rooted in feelings. The romantics' watchword became, "My experience is my proof." In stressing the aesthetic rather than the intellectual side of human nature, they focused on the sensual beauty of the natural world and the mysterious aspects of experience. God became the vital Spirit, immanent in all things, the creative *eros* in which everything moves and has its being. The romantic era inspired great art but untethered religion.

In a series of speeches *On Religion* in 1799, aimed at its "cultured despisers," Schleiermacher argued, "Man is first and foremost a feeling rather than a thinking being. Providentially excited by God, man possesses the intrinsic capacity to sense and taste the Infinite."[9] Theologian Bruce Demarest suggests that Schleiermacher leans toward pantheism and religious pluralism. I suspect *panentheism* is a more accurate perspective. God is both without and within our experience, transcendent *and* immanent. Schleiermacher clearly subsumed Scripture to the judgments of religious experience. Yet his was a valid theology of culture in its day, responding to the philosophical questions posed by Immanuel Kant and René Descartes.

The Enlightenment emphasis on individual experience indirectly led to a recovery of the feeling side of Christian faith. Quakers stressed inner and immediate revelation as the only sure and certain manifestation of a saving knowledge of God. The Puritans incorporated a threefold knowledge of God—via the natural light within, a rational reflection on the created order, and truth secured by faith reception of special revelation. They offered a combination of feelings, reason, and objective truth. Beginning with his transforming experience at Aldersgate, John Wesley introduced the notion of prevenient grace and offered a fresh call to sanctification.[10] His brother Charles Wesley composed rousing hymns that brought a vibrancy to worship that had been lost in the rush to prove the existence of God. Wesley's fourfold source of theology (Scripture, tradition, reason, experience) gave more room for general revelation than any previous theological system. The norming norm of Scripture was held up against church tradition. Both sources of knowledge were aided by reason and experience; our facts met our feelings.

Despite significant efforts to recover a holistic vision, Wesley still focused more on re-creation in Christ than the Spirit's work in creation. The Wesley brothers' dynamic theology was undercut by the antisupranaturalism initiated by the 1859 publication of Charles Darwin's *Origin of the Species* and Karl Marx's *Political Economy*. These two texts drove a wedge between the natural and the supernatural world, and theologians adjusted their methods accordingly. We've been arguing about the authority of Scripture on Darwin's terms ever since. The special revelation of the Bible would now be judged according to scientific principles.[11] The measurable became authoritative. Science trumped faith—or at least occupied a completely different sphere. Facts became real and faith became folly. This divorce precipitated a crisis. German theologian Karl Barth stepped in to heal the breach.

Karl Barth and Emil Brunner responded to the spirit in their age by rallying around special revelation. Barth and Brunner reframed the debate, shifting the emphasis from human reason and experience back to God. In building a theology on the self-revelation of God, Barth and Brunner changed the rules, taking the power away from scientists *and* poets. Divine revelation became the starting point of all theology—a first order statement rather than a second order deduction from reason or experience. Barth insisted that God could be known only via God, through his action and initiation. Natural or general revelation is the imprint of God on the works of creation. But that cannot be known without the definitive revelation of Jesus that opens our eyes to the structures of the world.[12] Barth considers a general knowledge of God by natural man an impossibility due to the total annihilation of the *imago Dei* through sin. For Barth, the hope of natural theology is an illusion. God cannot be appropriated—God appropriates us. No divine revelation is mediated "in reason, in conscience, in the emotions, in history, in nature, and in culture and its achievements and developments."[13] Scientific and historical research tells us nothing about God. Faith operates without reason—on Christ alone.

For Emil Brunner, like Barth, divine revelation is not identified with the Bible but transcends it. Revelation is personal—not a book or a doctrine, but God himself in his self-revelation within history in Jesus Christ. Brunner diverged with Barth on one key point, however. Brunner believed humanity's rationality and personality survived the fall, but the pristine condition of people's soul had been obliterated. Nevertheless, a point of contact with God remains. In their famous debates of 1934, Brunner sought to swing Barth back toward Calvin's notion of general revelation, to get back to a *theologia naturalis*.[14] Barth and "Neo-orthodoxy, in its original impulse, [were] anti-anthropological. . . . An anthropology could be theologically deduced, but there were no inductive possibilities *from* anthropology *to* theology."[15] Barth said "no" to any analogy of being—*analogia entis*—between God and man. Brunner proposed the possibility of the *Anknupfungspunkt*—the point of contact between God's revelation and man's situation. Brunner allowed for the possibility of rational truths to occur to humanity. We have plenty of gifts and potential, but the focus was still on man's lostness.

Despite Barth's appreciation of Mozart, fine tobacco, and the daily newspaper, the grim realities of World War I crushed his faith in human potential.[16] How could German theologians have affirmed the militarism and chauvinism of Bismark? They had confused theology with anthropology, studying humanity's ways to God rather than the proper flow of theology, from God alone. For Barth, history argued strongly against general revelation, with the dropping of the atom bomb and the postwar discoveries of the Holocaust offering confirmation that humanity is, first and foremost, barbarous.

Enlightenment claims of human autonomy required a rigorous trump card in the person of Christ. Barth thought a people obsessed with human progress needed to hear that there was *absolutely nothing* they could say, do, or initiate to secure their salvation. The first, last, and only word was Jesus. For Barth, if revelation is "wholly other" to the human spirit, then it remains "inexperienceable and hidden" producing a "permanent discontinuity between God's spirit and the spirit of human beings." In his universe, either revelation remains wholly other (and it is ineffective) or it correlates with human religious aspirations, in which case it seems less than revelation. Either revelation is beyond experience or experience is devoid of revelation.[17] H. D. McDonald identifies the damage resulting from such a false division. What happens when we cut ourselves off from the mysterious work of the Spirit? McDonald writes, "A Scripture without the Spirit makes for a fruitless faith, while the Spirit without the Scriptures gives an undisciplined faith. The one makes for a dead orthodoxy, the other for an unrestrained enthusiasm. The first gives lifelessness to the Church, the second license to the individual."[18] This is the spiritual schizophrenia that separated my transcendent experience of film from what I heard preached about God. How could I blend facts and feelings into a vibrant, holistic faith?

Jürgen Moltmann serves as my theological hero, bridging the theological chasm. He aimed to heal the false divide (dualism) created by the dialectical theology that preceded him. Moltmann finds the distinction between general revelation and special revelation misleading. There cannot be two theologies. "There is only one, because God is one."[19] For Moltmann, theology is not a battle between God's transcendence and immanence.

By setting up this antithesis between revelation and experience, Barth merely replaced the theological immanentism which he complained about with a theological transcendentalism. But the real phenomenon is to be found in God's immanence in human experience, and in the transcendence of human beings in God. . . . Anyone who stylizes revelation and experience into alternatives, ends up with revelations that cannot be experienced, and experiences without revelation.[20]

This was the tension handed to me in my initial exposure to Christianity. What I had experienced as a unity—God speaking through movies, music, and TV—was presented as a theological impossibility. The sacred could not emerge from the profane.

Hans Urs von Balthasar pushed past this dialectic by *combining* the insights of Barth and Schleiermacher, reuniting what we know with what we see. Balthasar asked:

Should we go the way of Karl Barth, who rediscovers the inner beauty of theology and revelation itself? Or (and this is perhaps implicitly included in Barth's position), may it not be that we have a real and inescapable obligation to probe the possibility of there being a genuine relationship between theological beauty and the beauty of the world and—in spite of all the dangers inherent in such an undertaking—to probe the feasibility of a genuine encounter between divine revelation and antiquity?[21]

The antiquity of this study is of extremely recent vintage. Some may question the "beauty" of the films we reviewed. They may feel we have left them "in the dark" of the movie theater. My efforts to highlight the accurate anthropology, the applications to ecclesiology, and the longing for a realized eschatology animating the films atop the IMDb list may have been in vain. But I trust that like fine wine, the most enduring films will age well, taking on more complexity and richness with time. Balthasar, Moltmann, and the movies moved me deeper into Scripture, nearer into God, and closer to the elusive integration of faith and experience.

Openness to God and the movement of the Spirit may threaten those who like their faith drawn and quartered. Yet Christ will accomplish his purposes with or without us. If God wants to use Martin Scorsese and *Raging Bull* to touch a moviegoer in Charlotte, North Carolina, then who am I to argue? If Jesus works through the digital magic of Peter Jackson in *The Lord of the Rings*, then I say, "When are you making *The Hobbit*?" If the Holy Spirit moves through *Hotel Rwanda* to break the Western world's heart for Africa, then I want to join Rick Warren's P.E.A.C.E. movement. The ways of God have always been mysterious, outside the box, progressive in their revelation. Try as we might to grasp the Spirit, she always seems to slip our fingers. I am comfortable playing catch-up, looking to the stars and the movies for signs of life.

A Timeless Story

> Fantasy is a natural human activity. It certainly does not destroy or even insult Reason; and it does not either blunt the appetite for, nor obscure the perception of, scientific verity. On the contrary. The keener and the clearer is the reason, the better fantasy will it make.
>
> J. R. R. Tolkien, "On Fairy-Stories"[22]

Once upon a time, in a galaxy far away, I joined an entire generation whose imagination was baptized by *Star Wars*. Fifteen years later, I followed in George Lucas's celebrated steps by enrolling at the University of Southern California's film school. Over and over, our entering class sang a familiar chorus: "When I saw *Star Wars*, I knew I wanted to be a filmmaker." A quarter century after the original *Star Wars*, another cinematic trilogy arose to enchant the next generation. As director of the film program at Biola University, I read the applications of hundreds of aspiring moviemakers. They repeat a familiar refrain, only the name of the movie has changed: "When I saw *The Lord of the Rings*, I knew I wanted to be a filmmaker."

Peter Jackson's rousing adaptation of J. R. R. Tolkien's *Rings* trilogy transported audiences. The story is deceptively simple, the action quite linear. A hobbit named Frodo Baggins engages in a long walk to toss a ring into the Cracks of Mount Doom. Most heroes' journeys involve the discovery of a pot of gold or buried treasure. *The Lord of the Rings* starts with the gold in hand and seeks to rebury the treasure. It is not about accumulating power or gathering possessions. Frodo is lifted up because of how much he willingly gives. He also learns that he cannot resist evil and temptation alone. He needs companions for the journey. Tolkien's epic tale undercuts almost every tenet of the American Dream. Lone rangers like poor, pitiful Gollum end up alone on the range. The challenges and temptations are so enormous it takes a village to bury a ring. So how did this seemingly mundane mission become a rousing, nine-hour adventure that rewards repeat viewing? A fellowship of craftsmen, led by their own barefooted "little person"— Peter Jackson—triumphed through teamwork, community, and cooperation.

While Peter Jackson received plenty of credit, *The Lord of the Rings* movies were truly a team effort. Consider the cumulative gifts of Jackson's collaborators,

Hobbits protect Frodo on all sides—now that's a *Fellowship of the Ring.* © 2001 by New Line Cinema and Warner Brothers Pictures.

like screenwriters Fran Walsh and Philippa Boyens. They satisfied both Tolkien's loyal fans and action film fanatics who rarely read a book. To conceptualize the look of the movies, Jackson hired artists Alan Lee and John Howe, who had created the first fully illustrated edition of *The Lord of the Rings* in 1991. Howe describes their contribution to the previsualization: "We tried to give depth to the design, so that you felt there was a history to it, that it wasn't just something that had been put together for the purposes of making a film but that these places had been developing for thousands of years."[23] *The Return of the King* won eleven highly deserved Academy Awards, including Oscars for Best Makeup, Best Costumes, and Best Art Decoration. The *Rings* trilogy also would not have been possible without the creatures, props, and effects created by New Zealand's Weta Workshop. Richard Taylor, director of Weta, recalled, "We have treated this entire project with a level of religious fervor. It has been a crusade, and I'm adamant that we have not been making a movie but creating a legacy."[24] Every aspect of postproduction, from editing, to sound effects, through musical score contributed to the masterful finished films. Even the New Zealand locations served as an inadvertent star (and subsequent tourist attraction).

The cooperation among the actors on-screen was mirrored offscreen. Sean Astin, who plays Sam, reflects on the bonds developed between the cast during the long shooting schedule. Astin remembers, "The Hobbits formed a core relationship. We ate together, we went to pubs together and we really hung out and did crazy things together. So we became friends, a loyal and earnest brotherhood."[25] The *Rings* trilogy stands as a testament to teamwork throughout an arduous production. Weta Workshop's Richard Taylor reflects on the crew's journey: "There are the houses that have been bought, the people that have got married, the children that have been born, the families that have grown: the beautiful tapestry of life that is the backdrop to the making of *The Lord of the Rings*."[26] Peter Jackson and his creative collaborators weave epic scale, dazzling digital effects, and high-stakes drama into a timeless story of communal courage. They practiced what their movies preach.

Rigorous attention to detail left audiences believing in elves, hobbits, dwarves, and wizards. Viewers' imaginations were ignited by the courage of Frodo, the loyalty of Sam, and the power of Gandalf. All three of the *Rings* films are ensconced within the IMDb's all-time Top 20. They attracted more votes (700,000), more capsule reviews (10,000), and higher ratings than any of their contemporary films. The devotion attached to *The Lord of the Rings* series is almost frightening in its intensity (perhaps surpassing even *Star Wars*). Among the praises flowing from fans on the IMDb include words like, "Breathtaking, unique, captivating, and enchanting."[27] Bonnie91 from Ventura, California, called *The Fellowship of the Ring*, "Not just a movie, but the Door to another Dimension." She expounds on her experience:

> I've never felt anything quite like what this epic evoked in me. It was akin to being a child again, with that tireless sense of wonder and enjoyment of each and every moment, maybe because as a child you are discovering your surroundings, and whatever age you are, when you watch *The Fellowship of the Ring* you are rendered in awe upon being introduced to the purity and beauty of Middle Earth and darkly enthralled by the majesty of Eisengard, Saruman, Sauron and all of their mighty malice.[28]

Jed Salazar from Boulder, Colorado, struggled to describe his viewing of the second movie:

> *The Two Towers* can only be explained in one word, beautiful. . . . This movie honestly moved me further than I thought any film could. I could see my face and the emotion I felt as I was watching this mammoth film. Peter Jackson has truly given us all a magnificent gift. This story has captivated my heart, and the

film has taken my breath away. There are no words that can express the greatness of this film.[29]

James Hitchcock from England adopts religious language to summarize his response to *The Return of the King*:

> I am, I admit, an unlikely convert to the religion of Tolkienism. I have never read the books, having, I thought, been put off them for life by the sort of obsessive freaks who read them when I was at school. . . . I also have never been a great admirer of the "sword and sorcery" school of fantasy writing or film-making; indeed, some of this genre (mostly those starring the current governor of California) struck me as being among the worst films ever made. . . . I have no doubt, however, that the trilogy as a whole is the first great cinematic masterpiece of the twenty-first century. It has certainly inspired me to start reading Tolkien's original novels.[30]

How can such seemingly frivolous, escapist fare inspire such allegiance? Actor Christopher Lee (Saruman) points to the timeless and timely aspects of Tolkien's story: "It's a mixture of myth, legend, and what feels almost like contemporary history in that there's a sense in which the story almost parallels the behavior and reactions, the mentalities and morals, ideals and beliefs of our world today."[31] Literary scholar Ralph Wood explains the perennial appeal of Tolkien's vision:

> The reason why readers repeatedly return to it—not to escape from but *into* Reality. We learn from the hobbits and their allies that the drama of everyday life is full of fantastic adventure and challenge, that it contains epic horrors and blessings, that our smallest deeds belong to a huge universe of meaning, that we are working out nothing less than eternal destinies, that we have hope of victory only through courage and trust, love and loyalty, friendship and faith.[32]

This reminds me of my transforming, boyhood experiences of cinema. Movies didn't call me away from reality but toward my best intentions. The finest films nurtured the nobility buried beneath my surface, lurking within my God-given heart. I joined a community at the movies, even while alone, in the dark. My vision was expanded, my nascent faith enlarged. This was general revelation in action.

Embracing Creation

While historical films are often associated with nostalgia, fantasy films like *The Lord of the Rings* hark back to prehistoric times. They are not postmodern but premodern, freed from the realm of time and history. Tolkien's primordial visions are both pantheistic and panentheistic, laden with magic, touched by the divine. As a medieval scholar, Tolkien was steeped in Norse legends and pagan rites. Yet rather than reject them, he appreciated the codes of honor that infused a pre-Christian world. He gathered from assorted fairy tales to fashion his own subcreation—an enchanted world that resembled our own. Tolkien demonstrates that we need not fear a neo-pagan culture. We have ample creative resources to recount the true myth of Christ's death and resurrection amid a resacralized world.

While it is easy to admire the courage exhibited by Frodo's fellowship, *The Lord of the Rings* trilogy extends considerable compassion toward the seemingly evil. Tolkien suggests that Lord Sauron had noble reasons for consolidating power in one ring. The Orcs who serve him did not begin as monsters. Even Gollum had a different bearing as Smeagal, before he was consumed by greed for his "precious" ring. While we cheer for Legolas, Gimli, and Aragorn to overcome these dark forces, we are reminded that even the most contorted figures had a brighter heritage. Tolkien affirms the pagan traditions but pushes past their sense of doom.

> In pagan cultures, whether ancient or recent, mercy is granted only to the weak and helpless, never to the strong and undeserving, lest they be denied justice. For Tolkien the Christian and Augustinian, the injustice of the powerful cannot be broken by force but only by mercy and grace. And because evil is a perversion and distortion of the good—never having any positive existence of its own—no creature in *The Lord of the Rings* lies beyond redemption. Not even Sauron was evil in the beginning.[33]

Tolkien recognizes the realities of Adam and Eve's fall in Genesis 3. *The Rings* trilogy illustrates the tragic results of the fall. But Tolkien's vision also reminds us of the *imago Dei*, humanity created and celebrated by God in Genesis 1 and 2.

Tolkien also extends the same sense of wonder and care toward creation. As *The Two Towers* begins, the fellowship has been split up, with Merry and Pippin captured by Uruk-hai. The hobbits escape to Fangorn and find allies in the Ents, the talking, treelike creatures led by the venerable Treebeard. The Ents have a long view of history, a geological or "green" sense of time.[34] The dark wizard Saruman declares war on Middle Earth, endangering the lush forests around Isengard. Treebeard recognizes death creeping across the land via the dreaded Orcs: "They come with fire, they come with axes . . . gnawing, biting, breaking, hacking, burning. Destroyers and usurpers, curse them." Peter Jackson draws

Conclusion

parallels to clear-cutting of our endangered environment. Tolkien himself suggested that although we may know the end of God's story, "The Christian has still to work, with mind as well as body, to suffer, hope, and die; but he may now perceive that all his bents and faculties have a purpose, which can be redeemed. So great is the bounty with which he has been treated that he may now, perhaps, fairly dare to guess that in Fantasy he may actually assist in the effoliation and multiple enrichment of creation."[35] Treebeard and the Ents join the fellowship of elves, dwarves, and humans to repel Saruman's Uruk-hai army. Nature itself joins with all kinds of creatures to preserve Middle Earth. The crown of creation is not humanity but the Sabbath, creation preserved and resting on the seventh day.

The Lord of the Rings is about cooperation across cultures. We follow an ensemble in action, given an overwhelming task. They must resist evil, flee from temptation, and renounce power. The diverse group is small in number, not especially gifted, definitely not likely to strike fear in their enemies' hearts. But their strength arises from intense loyalty and solidarity. At the end of *The Fellowship of the Ring*, when a depressed Frodo attempts to journey alone, Sam comes alongside because, "I made a promise." What revelation and emotion rises from Sam's simple pledge: "I cannot carry it [the ring] for you, Mr. Frodo, but I can carry you." This ragtag assortment of elves, wizards, and hobbits is a modest collection of surprising role models. Each has a particular (but limited) perspective. As a dwarf, Gimli knows the mountains and the mines. As an elf, Legolas can navigate the woods. They both depend on the other to survive and thrive. Ralph Wood notes the similarities to the first-century church:

> Not only do they trust each other implicitly; they also have a shared faith in an unfailing guide (the wizard Gandalf) as well as undying devotion to a transcendent good (the destruction of the Ring). Rather like the early disciples of Jesus, they are a communion of the *unlike*—including such historic enemies as a dwarf and an elf. Even though they have been splintered into three sub-groups, they still function as mini-communities maintaining a profound solidarity with each other.[36]

As Aragorn and Legolas, actors Viggo Mortensen and Orlando Bloom captured the romantic side of heroism. They are strong and beautiful. Jackson altered Tolkien's story to give Arwen (Liv Tyler) a more active role befitting contemporary understanding of women. But Frodo, Sam, and the hobbits represent more reluctant warriors. They don't seek glory or fame. They'd be content to stay home, gathered around a fire in the comfort of the Shire. Frodo repeatedly admits to wishing the ring had never come to him. But Gandalf reframes the question: "That is not for us to decide. We must decide what to do with the time given us." Circumstances call us to rise and respond.

The hobbits' humble bearing suggests the heroic capacity residing in unexpected people and places. Movies usually focus on extraordinary people—warriors, crime fighters, and superheroes. *The Lord of the Rings* celebrates the small, the ordinary, and the unlikely. The Lady of the Forest reminds Frodo, "Even the smallest person can change the course of the future." Ralph Wood admires how "Tolkien shows that true victories over evil are won not for the sake of the valiant but for the little people—the unheralded and the defenseless."[37] I initially considered the multiple endings attached to *The Return of the King* a sign of weakness. Peter Jackson's faithfulness to the book seemed to drain the conclusion of its power. Why did he have to take us back to the Shire after such a stirring wedding and coronation? Aren't movies supposed to end with beautiful people, robed in splendor, ruling from on high? Jackson's affection for Frodo seemed to blind his judgment, sending us on a literal rabbit trail back to the Shire.

But perhaps I misunderstood Tolkien's intent. The fellowship did not take on the task for profit or glory. The battles were fought to return to life as they knew it—a modest existence in a remote village. In Tolkien's novels, the Company of Nine do not take up arms with shouts of "Liberty, Equality and Fraternity."[38] Their battle cry is decidedly local: "The Shire!" When Frodo is down, Sam motivates him with memories of home: "Do you remember the taste of strawberries?" Memories can animate and call us to action. Frodo and company have seen more than they could ever convey. Like all war veterans, they have witnessed a shadowy side of life that will never leave them. But they didn't join the fellowship to pursue personal wealth or fame; they fought for a community. In *Return of the King*, Frodo declares, "We set out to save the Shire, Sam, and it has been saved, but not for me." Ralph Wood suggests that in Tolkien's world, "The most hopeful means of combating modern evils is to be found in small communities of the weak and emarginated who overcome modern self-aggrandizing individualism by refusing all coercive power."[39] This connects the dots between God's questions. How do we remember who we are? By joining with our brothers and sisters, forming communities in action. We discover where we are as we answer, "Who is my brother or sister?" These are the bonds of fellowship that triumph and endure, resisting temptation, overcoming evil.

Theologian Ray Anderson offers clues for locating Jesus within *The Lord of the Rings* or our contemporary culture. He suggests:

If there are two sides to humanity, Jesus will be found on the wrong side. He was not a religious person, though he lived amid a religious society that prized appearance and cultivated piety as a discipline of outward form. Where lines were drawn between the sacred and the profane that tended to dehumanize and marginalize common people, he acted with uncommon decency toward those whose dignity was shredded by the disgrace that comes from misfortune, mistreatment and moral failure.[40]

This is the province of filmmakers, getting in touch with the brokenness of their characters and our world. *The Lord of the Rings* movies confirm our dual nature, highlighting our weaknesses and embracing our noble calling. We cannot manage things alone, but in community we become more than conquerors. Our mission is to work with creation, preserving the beauty around us, preparing for the glory to come.

Remembering Our Story

How do we connect these cinematic stories to the shaping story unfolding within the Bible? Despite Jean-Francois Lyotard's oft-repeated claims regarding our incredulity toward metanarratives, the size and scale of postmodern movies suggests otherwise. In *The Two Towers*, Samwise Gangee reminds a discouraged Frodo of their place in a much larger narrative. Sam points out, "By all rights we shouldn't even be here. But we are. It's like in the great stories, Mr. Frodo. The ones that really mattered. . . . Folks in those stories had lots of chances of turning back, only they didn't. They kept going. Because they were holding on to something." In a world of competing claims, Sam suggests that not all stories are created equal. We must hitch our individual narratives to the much grander story still unfolding. In our introduction, we noted how Balthasar described God's story as "theo-drama." We are bit players in a cosmic passion play. But our choices, our decisions, our connections to the community players matter. Brian McLaren has more recently recovered the power of narrative theology and our need for communal recognition of "The Story We Find Ourselves In."[41] Like Frodo, we will undoubtedly face seasons of discouragement. We must have friends like Sam who will remind us of our place within the divine drama. In *The Drama of Doctrine*, Kevin Vanhoozer challenges us to see ourselves as essential actors on God's cosmic stage. We must *perform our faith*, everyday, in tangible and dramatic ways.

Like the Company of Nine determined to return the ring, Jesus's disciples were galvanized by shared events. They acted on faith, even if circumstances made them question and doubt. They had some evidence that Jesus was the Christ. Watching Jesus heal the blind or raise the dead should have been sufficiently convincing. The transfiguration of Jesus on the Mount of Olives came closest to putting the mark of the divine on the man from Galilee. But fear and doubts and alternative plans continued to undercut the disciples' convictions. The crucifixion spun the twelve off in various directions. From Thomas's doubt to Judas's suicide, those who witnessed this central act of history responded in a variety of ways. The question, "Were you there when they crucified my Lord?" became a confusing lived reality.

The unexpected death of a close friend sends the burgeoning community into crisis. Will they rally? Will they be able to solve the riddle of Jesus's passing? With the resurrection, suddenly all of Jesus's veiled teachings make sense. (Remember how Anna's miraculous resurrection changed our perspective of Benigno in *Hable con ella*?) All the morbid allusions to what might happen were wiped away by a reality that exceeded their wildest dreams and imagination. (Remember Sylvia's final walk through the garden in *Finding Neverland*?) In a blatant act of restoration, Peter's threefold denial of Jesus was reversed by three questions on the beach. In the Gospel of John, Jesus reinstates Peter by flashing back to his earlier denial. In Jesus's presence, time is collapsed into a single defining moment. (Remember the test put before *Donnie Darko*?) For Jesus, it came when he rose from the grave. For Peter, it arrives when Jesus names his worst fears and embraces him anyway. The liar, cheater, and killer within us may be exposed. (Remember the ending of *Memento*, when Leonard's flagrant self-deception was revealed?) But Jesus pushes past the worst moments in our personal history. He erases the regret we cannot forget. (Remember how the doctors in *Eternal Sunshine* failed to heal Joel and Clementine's emotional scars?) Yet Jesus doesn't erase Peter's pain just for Peter. He has a much larger vision. The restoration of an entire community arises from forgiveness. The real plan is people, gathered together, owning up to their worst inclinations (*Crash, Mystic River, No Man's Land*) and pressing on toward a higher mark (*Hotel Rwanda, The Lord of the Rings, Spirited Away*). We have a high calling to get over ourselves and on to each other. As the Holy Trinity engages in mutual interdependence (*perichoresis* in Greek), so we gain strength, power, and wholeness in community, in relationship with one another and with our tripartite God. That is ultimate reality, richer than (but reflective of) our finest movies and our grandest dreams. We may walk into darkness, but some day we shall see with the most piercing, comforting, and restorative light.

The biblical word for this peaceful vision is *shalom*. Walter Brueggemann describes its rich meaning to the Hebrew community: "*Shalom* at its most critical can function as a theology of hope, a large-scale promissory vision of what will one day surely be. As a vision of an assured future, the substance of *shalom* is crucial, for it can be a resource against both despair and an overly eager settlement for an unfinished system."[42] This is the type of community we've been seeking since chapter 1. This is the dream that keeps me coming back to movies for more sneak previews of coming glory. I want to join a fellowship characterized by liberty and justice for all. I want to reside in a city of joy, a peaceable kingdom.

Teaching Aids and Mnemonic Devices

Art is far and away the most educational thing we have, far more so than its rivals, philosophy and theology and science.

Iris Murdoch[43]

The recurring themes of nostalgia, memory, and amnesia flowing through our culture's most resonant films suggest a genuine crisis within the postmodern mind. We have forgotten who we are and where we came from. The challenges and opportunities for educators are considerable. How do we communicate to a distracted audience? Where do we begin the story within a fractured narrative? The complex, discontinuous plots of postmodern movies suggest that mind games are preferable to rote memory. Straightforward information has failed to captivate young minds. We will have to rediscover the story for ourselves, infusing it with all the mystery, adventure, and wonder found in *The Lord of the Rings*. Tolkien proved that, with enough research and imagination, it can be done. The worldwide embrace of his Christian vision demonstrates that God's story remains as compelling as ever. Can we muster theological imagination equal to Tolkien's storytelling?

Jesus offered two basic ways to stay focused. To God's question, "Where are you?" Jesus proposed a tangible frame of reference. He turned to one of the oldest, most readily repeatable Old Testament truths, the Hebrew *shema*: " 'Love the Lord your God with all your heart and with all your soul and with all your mind.' This is the first and greatest commandment" (Matt. 22:37–38). To God's second question, humanity's social dilemma, "Where is your brother?" Jesus responded with a practical piece of advice: "Love your neighbor as yourself" (Matt. 22:39). The simplicity of such a snappy retort must not be forgotten amid our distracted and discordant age. The problems are obvious, the prescription clear. Yet, somehow, the working out of such ancient wisdom still vexes me.

Where is the Spirit of God when you need her? In Genesis she hovers over the water, bringing order to chaos. As ancient, enduring wisdom, she surprises me through common, everyday (and yet still, unlikely) means. In Revelation, she invites all who are thirsty to "Come" to a wedding banquet.

I solved my memory problems at a local Episcopal church. What a surprising twist! I had always been attracted to the most timely and relevant expressions of faith. So why was I suddenly longing for ancient liturgy? I wanted something timeless, mysterious, beyond words. I still appreciate the urgency that drives the young and the restless toward theological hot spots. But after a quarter century of chasing the Spirit from place to place, I finally settled down long enough for God to catch me. The *Raging Bull* for Jesus took a knee. Paused. Reflected. The flicker in the candles whispered. The stained glass started to move. A whiff of incense transported me. No, it's not perfect. How could any community that made space for me be anything but flawed? But it offers plenty of room for tears or confession. Birthdays are noted. Death dates as well. These are real effects, both general and special.

Most of all, it is helping me to remember. In following the church calendar, I have discovered where Halloween came from (All Saints Day!). I now understand that Advent is more than a countdown to Christmas; it is the start of the church year, coming after Christus Victor, the last Sunday of the spiritual calendar. I am part of a remember religion, rooted in ritual. The Jewish tradition is founded on the exodus, which is celebrated at Passover every year. The Christian tradition is founded on the death and resurrection of Christ, which is celebrated at Easter every year. But just in case we can't wait that long, Jesus fused the two traditions into one transcendent act of remembrance: the Eucharist. Our problems of memory are resolved by regular worship. We are reminded each week, in the body and blood of Christ, what has happened and how we have been transformed. The bread and wine humbles us and elevates us. We are put in our place: a little lower than angels, worthy of the ultimate sacrifice.

The Eucharist is a communal action; it reminds us that we are not alone; we are part of a global communion that transcends space, place, and time. On All Saints' Day we reach across the centuries, finding ourselves within a great chain of being, identifying us as both insignificant and essential. I am just another in a long line of God's followers. As Jesus passed the cup to the disciples, our priests pass it to us. We are here simply to hand things off. Frodo may have carried the ring to Mount Doom, but the fellowship carried him during the journey. As Jesus served his disciples, so we serve others. In the Eucharist, we recover our sense of purpose, our place in community.

We may not fully understand why Jesus asked us to do this in remembrance of him, but it does tide us over until he comes. In the meantime, I keep thinking about that heavenly country that keeps getting mentioned. And I make the sign of the cross to mitigate my tendency to separate and isolate the Father, Son, or Holy Spirit. I am reminded, every time I pray, that I am not alone. The Holy Trinity invites me to join their community, to follow their conversation, to join their sacred song. Sometimes I praise God through the natural world. Other times I find Christ revealed in Scripture. The Holy Spirit still sneaks up on me, in the dark. But much to my surprise, that transcendent moment now occurs more often in the Eucharist than in the movies. What a surprising conclusion to this highly cinematic story.

Top 250 Movies as Voted by IMDb Users

(JANUARY 1, 2007)
www.imdb.com/chart/top

Rank	Rating	Title	Votes
1.	9.1	The Godfather (1972)	187,063
2.	9.1	The Shawshank Redemption (1994)	225,519
3.	8.9	The Godfather: Part II (1974)	105,771
4.	8.8	The Lord of the Rings: The Return of the King (2003)	170,046
5.	8.8	Buono, il brutto, il cattivo, Il (The Good, The Bad and The Ugly, 1966)	52,061
6.	8.8	Casablanca (1942)	90,555
7.	8.8	Schindler's List (1993)	134,372
8.	8.7	Pulp Fiction (1994)	192,073
9.	8.7	Shichinin no samurai (The Seven Samurai, 1954)	49,021
10.	8.7	Star Wars: Episode V—The Empire Strikes Back (1980)	143,802
11.	8.7	Star Wars (1977)	180,769

Rank	Rating	Title	Votes
12.	8.7	One Flew Over the Cuckoo's Nest (1975)	97,558
13.	8.7	Rear Window (1954)	57,482
14.	8.7	The Lord of the Rings: The Fellowship of the Ring (2001)	212,320
15.	8.6	12 Angry Men (1957)	43,495
16.	8.6	Raiders of the Lost Ark (1981)	123,986
17.	8.6	The Usual Suspects (1995)	141,065
18.	8.6	Cidade de Deus (City of God, 2002)	54,611
19.	8.6	Dr. Strangelove or: How I Learned to Stop Worrying and Love the Bomb (1964)	86,666
20.	8.6	The Lord of the Rings: The Two Towers (2002)	167,923
21.	8.6	Goodfellas (1990)	98,978
22.	8.6	Psycho (1960)	72,832
23.	8.6	Citizen Kane (1941)	80,512
24.	8.6	C'era una volta il West (Once Upon a Time in the West, 1968)	28,482
25.	8.6	North by Northwest (1959)	48,584
26.	8.6	Memento (2000)	129,443
27.	8.5	The Silence of the Lambs (1991)	122,937
28.	8.5	Lawrence of Arabia (1962)	42,376
29.	8.5	It's a Wonderful Life (1946)	55,395
30.	8.5	Sunset Blvd. (1950)	24,310
31.	8.5	Fabuleux destin d'Amélie Poulain, Le (Amelie, 2001)	88,875
32.	8.5	Fight Club (1999)	166,717
33.	8.5	American Beauty (1999)	148,421
34.	8.5	The Matrix (1999)	194,623
35.	8.4	Vertigo (1958)	46,536
36.	8.4	Apocalypse Now (1979)	89,385
37.	8.4	Taxi Driver (1976)	68,481
38.	8.4	Eternal Sunshine of the Spotless Mind (2004)	89,829
39.	8.4	Se7en (1995)	126,158
40.	8.4	Paths of Glory (1957)	20,883
41.	8.4	Léon (The Professional, 1994)	80,592
42.	8.4	To Kill a Mockingbird (1962)	42,561
43.	8.4	Chinatown (1974)	36,700
44.	8.4	American History X (1998)	91,325
45.	8.4	Der Untergang (The Downfall: Hitler and the End of the Third Reich, 2004)	28,681
46.	8.4	The Third Man (1949)	26,030
47.	8.4	The Pianist (2002)	51,354
48.	8.3	Monty Python and the Holy Grail (1975)	84,432

Rank	Rating	Title	Votes
49.	8.3	M (1931)	18,039
50.	8.3	The Treasure of the Sierra Madre (1948)	14,920
51.	8.3	Sen to Chihiro no kamikakushi (Spirited Away, 2001)	42,328
52.	8.3	The Bridge on the River Kwai (1957)	30,447
53.	8.3	Das Boot (The Boat, 1981)	39,137
54.	8.3	L.A. Confidential (1997)	91,436
55.	8.3	Alien (1979)	86,749
56.	8.3	A Clockwork Orange (1971)	91,715
57.	8.3	The Maltese Falcon (1941)	26,698
58.	8.3	Requiem for a Dream (2000)	76,936
59.	8.3	Hotel Rwanda (2004)	31,844
60.	8.3	Metropolis (1927)	17,770
61.	8.3	The Shining (1980)	74,332
62.	8.3	Double Indemnity (1944)	16,739
63.	8.3	Reservoir Dogs (1992)	98,400
64.	8.3	Saving Private Ryan (1998)	136,267
65.	8.3	Singin' in the Rain (1952)	28,263
66.	8.3	Rashômon (1950)	17,609
67.	8.3	Sin City (2005)	96,705
68.	8.3	Raging Bull (1980)	39,503
69.	8.3	Modern Times (1936)	15,327
70.	8.3	The Manchurian Candidate (1962)	19,412
71.	8.3	Aliens (1986)	85,682
72.	8.2	Rebecca (1940)	16,477
73.	8.2	The Great Escape (1963)	28,852
74.	8.2	Some Like It Hot (1959)	34,831
75.	8.2	Touch of Evil (1958)	16,222
76.	8.2	All About Eve (1950)	18,135
77.	8.2	2001: A Space Odyssey (1968)	85,873
78.	8.2	Million Dollar Baby (2004)	53,808
79.	8.2	Amadeus (1984)	50,033
80.	8.2	The Departed (2006)	47,526
81.	8.2	Det Sjunde inseglet (The Seventh Seal, 1957)	15,117
82.	8.2	La Vita è bella (Life Is Beautiful, 1997)	52,486
83.	8.2	Jaws (1975)	66,445
84.	8.2	The Sting (1973)	32,762
85.	8.2	Forrest Gump (1994)	130,096
86.	8.2	Strangers on a Train (1951)	15,533
87.	8.2	Terminator 2: Judgment Day (1991)	105,613

Rank	Rating	Title	Votes
88.	8.2	Batman Begins (2005)	98,874
89.	8.2	On the Waterfront (1954)	18,874
90.	8.2	Braveheart (1995)	124,476
91.	8.2	The Wizard of Oz (1939)	52,173
92.	8.2	Mr. Smith Goes to Washington (1939)	16,428
93.	8.2	The Elephant Man (1980)	24,156
94.	8.2	Kill Bill: Vol. 1 (2003)	101,800
95.	8.2	Blade Runner (1982)	97,235
96.	8.2	Full Metal Jacket (1987)	67,854
97.	8.2	The Incredibles (2004)	59,865
98.	8.2	The Apartment (1960)	16,030
99.	8.2	City Lights (1931)	11,451
100.	8.2	The Big Sleep (1946)	14,245
101.	8.2	High Noon (1952)	17,125
102.	8.2	Nuovo cinema Paradiso (Cinema Paradiso, 1988)	20,494
103.	8.2	Donnie Darko (2001)	90,221
104.	8.2	Notorious (1946)	15,147
105.	8.2	Fargo (1996)	86,258
106.	8.2	Ran (1985)	17,420
107.	8.1	Crash (2004)	72,107
108.	8.1	Star Wars: Episode VI—Return of the Jedi (1983)	114,038
109.	8.1	Finding Nemo (2003)	66,729
110.	8.1	The Great Dictator (1940)	15,711
111.	8.1	Once Upon a Time in America (1984)	29,576
112.	8.1	Cool Hand Luke (1967)	20,214
113.	8.1	Mononoke-hime (Princess Mononoke, 1997)	29,780
114.	8.1	The Sixth Sense (1999)	129,410
115.	8.1	Le Salaire de la peur (The Wages of Fear, 1953)	5,080
116.	8.1	V for Vendetta (2005)	73,858
117.	8.1	Unforgiven (1992)	43,361
118.	8.1	Indiana Jones and the Last Crusade (1989)	82,809
119.	8.1	Ben-Hur (1959)	28,780
120.	8.1	Kill Bill: Vol. 2 (2004)	75,112
121.	8.1	Back to the Future (1985)	95,157
122.	8.1	Oldboy (2003)	30,392
123.	8.1	Annie Hall (1977)	30,645
124.	8.1	The Killing (1956)	10,522
125.	8.1	Wo hu cang long (Crouching Tiger, Hidden Dragon, 2000)	66,651
126.	8.1	Yojimbo (1961)	13,585

Rank	Rating	Title	Votes
127.	8.1	The Green Mile (1999)	87,532
128.	8.1	Life of Brian (1979)	46,630
129.	8.1	The Princess Bride (1987)	71,404
130.	8.0	The Deer Hunter (1978)	40,531
131.	8.0	Platoon (1986)	50,238
132.	8.0	The Graduate (1967)	39,181
133.	8.0	It Happened One Night (1934)	11,364
134.	8.0	Per qualche dollaro in più (For a Few Dollars More, 1965)	15,119
135.	8.0	Gladiator (2000)	129,700
136.	8.0	Butch Cassidy and the Sundance Kid (1969)	28,101
137.	8.0	Le Notti di Cabiria (Nights of Cabiria, 1957)	4,021
138.	8.0	Gandhi (1982)	22,296
139.	8.0	The African Queen (1951)	18,481
140.	8.0	Kind Hearts and Coronets (1949)	5,531
141.	8.0	Amores perros (Love's a Bitch, 2000)	24,983
142.	8.0	Ladri di biciclette (The Bicycle Thief, 1948)	11,111
143.	8.0	Toy Story 2 (1999)	55,835
144.	8.0	The Adventures of Robin Hood (1938)	10,656
145.	8.0	Diaboliques, Les (Diabolique, 1955)	5,301
146.	8.0	La Battaglia di Algeri (The Battle of Algiers, 1966)	4,438
147.	8.0	Shadow of a Doubt (1943)	8,901
148.	8.0	8½ (1963)	12,216
149.	8.0	Lola rennt (Run, Lola, Run, 1998)	44,969
150.	8.0	Brief Encounter (1945)	4,758
151.	8.0	Stand by Me (1986)	43,087
152.	8.0	The Night of the Hunter (1955)	11,233
153.	8.0	The Wild Bunch (1969)	15,122
154.	8.0	Die Hard (1988)	80,103
155.	8.0	The Conversation (1974)	14,863
156.	8.0	Harvey (1950)	11,021
157.	8.0	Smultronstället (Wild Strawberries, 1957)	8,523
158.	8.0	Dog Day Afternoon (1975)	23,192
159.	8.0	The General (1927)	9,477
160.	8.0	Duck Soup (1933)	13,776
161.	8.0	Nosferatu, eine Symphonie des Grauens (Nosferatu the Vampire, 1922)	12,782
162.	8.0	Patton (1970)	20,090
163.	8.0	Glory (1989)	29,077
164.	7.9	The Day the Earth Stood Still (1951)	14,375

Rank	Rating	Title	Votes
165.	7.9	Das Cabinet des Dr. Caligari (The Cabinet of Dr. Caligari, 1920)	6,462
166.	7.9	Gone with the Wind (1939)	40,054
167.	7.9	Spartacus (1960)	23,872
168.	7.9	Ying xiong (Hero, 2002)	39,967
169.	7.9	Groundhog Day (1993)	63,029
170.	7.9	The Gold Rush (1925)	9,206
171.	7.9	Toy Story (1995)	62,332
172.	7.9	Finding Neverland (2004)	40,069
173.	7.9	Trainspotting (1996)	72,460
174.	7.9	The Grapes of Wrath (1940)	11,095
175.	7.9	Magnolia (1999)	64,198
176.	7.9	The Exorcist (1973)	48,497
177.	7.9	A Christmas Story (1983)	28,332
178.	7.9	The Philadelphia Story (1940)	14,517
179.	7.9	The Big Lebowski (1998)	74,708
180.	7.9	Mystic River (2003)	47,833
181.	7.9	Heat (1995)	65,298
182.	7.9	La Belle et la bête (Beauty and the Beast, 1946)	3,993
183.	7.9	Shrek (2001)	91,459
184.	7.9	Twelve Monkeys (1995)	84,484
185.	7.9	King Kong (1933)	17,881
186.	7.9	Big Fish (2003)	55,956
187.	7.9	Cinderella Man (2005)	25,647
188.	7.9	El Laberinto del fauno (Pan's Labyrinth, 2006)	5,266
189.	7.9	Ed Wood (1994)	33,634
190.	7.9	Before Sunset (2004)	19,744
191.	7.9	The Hustler (1961)	11,735
192.	7.9	Judgment at Nuremberg (1961)	5,466
193.	7.9	The Terminator (1984)	81,190
194.	7.9	The Lady Vanishes (1938)	6,987
195.	7.9	Snatch (2000)	69,054
196.	7.9	The Best Years of Our Lives (1946)	8,567
197.	7.9	Walk the Line (2005)	36,322
198.	7.9	Out of the Past (1947)	4,345
199.	7.9	Bride of Frankenstein (1935)	7,278
200.	7.9	Wallace & Gromit in The Curse of the Were-Rabbit (2005)	19,061
201.	7.9	In the Heat of the Night (1967)	10,213
202.	7.9	Hotaru no haka (Grave of the Fireflies, 1988)	12,829
203.	7.9	Stalag 17 (1953)	10,124

Rank	Rating	Title	Votes
204.	7.9	Sleuth (1972)	6,651
205.	7.9	Witness for the Prosecution (1957)	7,457
206.	7.9	Bonnie and Clyde (1967)	18,141
207.	7.9	Young Frankenstein (1974)	30,778
208.	7.9	The Thing (1982)	28,368
209.	7.9	Hable con ella (Talk to Her, 2002)	19,926
210.	7.9	Rosemary's Baby (1968)	19,325
211.	7.9	Lock, Stock and Two Smoking Barrels (1998)	51,512
212.	7.9	The Straight Story (1999)	21,053
213.	7.9	Manhattan (1979)	17,553
214.	7.9	Sling Blade (1996)	26,920
215.	7.9	Frankenstein (1931)	10,026
216.	7.9	The Prestige (2006)	19,581
217.	7.9	Du rififi chez les hommes (Rififi, 1955)	2,913
218.	7.9	Scarface (1983)	52,782
219.	7.9	Arsenic and Old Lace (1944)	15,532
220.	7.9	Anatomy of a Murder (1959)	6,030
221.	7.9	Monsters, Inc. (2001)	56,142
222.	7.9	Quatre cents coups, Les (The 400 Blows, 1959)	9,960
223.	7.9	Kumonosu jô (Throne of Blood, 1957)	5,628
224.	7.9	Tengoku to jigoku (High and Low, 1963)	3,195
225.	7.9	Pirates of the Caribbean: The Curse of the Black Pearl (2003)	105,726
226.	7.8	All Quiet on the Western Front (1930)	9,985
227.	7.8	The Man Who Shot Liberty Valance (1962)	10,400
228.	7.8	Roman Holiday (1953)	13,755
229.	7.8	Doctor Zhivago (1965)	14,846
230.	7.8	The Searchers (1956)	14,513
231.	7.8	The Lost Weekend (1945)	4,462
232.	7.8	Bringing Up Baby (1938)	12,905
233.	7.8	A Streetcar Named Desire (1951)	14,446
234.	7.8	Little Miss Sunshine (2006)	22,488
235.	7.8	Brazil (1985)	42,182
236.	7.8	Haine, La (Hate, 1995)	9,847
237.	7.8	Planet of the Apes (1968)	28,427
238.	7.8	United 93 (2006)	18,280
239.	7.8	Umberto D. (1952)	2,553
240.	7.8	His Girl Friday (1940)	9,835
241.	7.8	Ikiru (Living, 1952)	7,100
242.	7.8	Mulholland Dr. (2001)	52,755

Rank	Rating	Title	Votes
243.	7.8	Seppuku (Harakiri, 1962)	1,642
244.	7.8	In Cold Blood (1967)	4,168
245.	7.8	Festen (The Celebration, 1998)	16,851
246.	7.8	Dial M for Murder (1954)	11,546
247.	7.8	The Killing Fields (1984)	12,943
248.	7.8	A Man for All Seasons (1966)	6,389
249.	7.8	Der Himmel über Berlin (Wings of Desire, 1987)	10,253
250.	7.8	To Have and Have Not (1944)	6,009

The formula for calculating the Top Rated 250 Titles gives a true Bayesian estimate:

weighted rating (WR) = $(v \div (v + m)) \times R + (m \div (v + m)) \times C$ where:

R = average (mean) for the movie = (rating)

v = number of votes for the movie = (votes)

m = minimum votes required to be listed in Top 250 (currently 1,300)

C = the mean vote across the whole report (currently 6.7)

For the Top 250, only votes from regular voters are considered.

Appendix B

The IMDb's Top Films
of the 21st Century

(JANUARY 1, 2007)

Ranked by Position within the Top 250 Films of All Time

4.	The Lord of the Rings: The Return of the King (2003)
14.	The Lord of the Rings: The Fellowship of the Ring (2001)
18.	Cidade de Deus (City of God, 2002)
20.	The Lord of the Rings: The Two Towers (2002)
26.	Memento (2000)
31.	Le Fabuleux destin d'Amélie Poulain (Amelie, 2001)
38.	Eternal Sunshine of the Spotless Mind (2004)
45.	Der Untergang (The Downfall: Hitler and the End of the Third Reich, 2004)
47.	The Pianist (2002)
51.	Sen to Chihiro no kamikakushi (Spirited Away, 2001)
58.	Requiem for a Dream (2000)
59.	Hotel Rwanda (2004)

The IMDb's Top Films of the 21st Century

(April 15, 2008)

Ranked by Position within the Top 250 Films of All Time

12.	The Lord of the Rings: The Return of the King (2003)
16.	City of God (2002)
19.	The Lord of the Rings: The Fellowship of the Rings (2001)
27.	Memento (2000)
28.	The Lord of the Rings: The Two Towers (2002)
39.	Amelie (2001)
42.	The Departed (2006)
44.	There Will Be Blood (2007)
48.	The Lives of Others (2006)
51.	Eternal Sunshine of the Spotless Mind (2004)
54.	No Country for Old Men (2007)
55.	Pan's Labyrinth (2006)
56.	The Pianist (2002)
58.	Spirited Away (2001)
62.	Requiem for a Dream (2000)

68. Der Untergang (2004)

77. Hotel Rwanda (2004)

79. Sin City (2005)

89. The Prestige (2006)

103. Batman Begins (2005)

111. Oldboy (2003)

117. Donnie Darko (2001)

122. Kill Bill: Vol. 1 (2003)

124. Ratatouille (2007)

125. Into the Wild (2007)

126. Million Dollar Baby (2004)

127. Gladiator (2000)

129. The Bourne Ultimatum (2007)

144. Amores Perros (2000)

145. Finding Nemo (2003)

147. The Incredibles (2004)

149. V for Vendetta (2005)

153. Children of Men (2006)

159. Letters from Iwo Jima (2006)

163. Crash (2005)

165. Snatch (2000)

174. Juno (2007)

176. Kill Bill: Vol. 2 (2004)

179. Crouching Tiger, Hidden Dragon (2000)

182. Little Miss Sunshine (2006)

190. American Gangster (2007)

217. Big Fish (2003)

222. Grindhouse (2007)

223. Mystic River (2003)

230. Once (2006)

233. Mou gaan dou (2002)

234. Hot Fuzz (2007)

240. 3:10 to Yuma (2007)

245. Shaun of the Dead (2004)

247. Hero (2002)

248. Pirates of the Caribbean: The Curse of the Black Pearl (2003)

Notes

Preface: A *Hornet's Nest*

1. Death Cab for Cutie, "Soul Meets Body," *Plans*, compact disc, Atlantic Records, 2005.

2. *Leonard Maltin's Movie Guide* was first published in 1969, but it took off with annual editions that coincided with the videotape boom. My most heavily worn copy came from 1980. For the current edition, see Leonard Maltin, *Leonard Maltin's 2008 Movie Guide* (New York: Signet, 2007). See also, Ephraim Katz, *The Film Encyclopedia* (San Francisco: Harper, 1979).

3. Andrey Tarkovsky helped me appreciate the space that movies provide, rearranging time and organizing a world so we might better process our own. See Andrey Tarkovsky, *Sculpting in Time: The Great Russian Filmmaker Discusses His Art*, trans. Kitty Hunter-Blair (Austin: University of Texas Press, 1989).

4. Greg Garrett, *The Gospel according to Hollywood* (Louisville: Westminster John Knox, 2007), xiii.

5. For a more complete background on this fervent era, see Ryan Gilbey, *It Don't Worry Me: The Revolutionary American Films of the Seventies* (London: Faber & Faber, 2003).

6. Robert Sklar, *Movie-Made America: A Cultural History of American Movies* (New York: Vintage Books, 1994).

7. Peter Biskind chronicles the idealistic rise and somewhat cynical co-opting of Coppola, Lucas, and Spielberg in *Easy Riders, Raging Bulls: How the Sex-Drugs-and Rock 'n Roll Generation Saved Hollywood* (New York: Simon & Schuster, 1999).

8. When he first read George MacDonald's *Phantastes*, C. S. Lewis recalls, "I saw the common things drawn into bright shadow. . . . In the depth of my disgraces, in the then invincible ignorance of my intellect, all this was given me without asking, even without consent. That night my imagination was, in a certain sense, baptized; the rest of me, not unnaturally, took longer" (C. S. Lewis, *Surprised by Joy: The Shape of My Early Life* [New York: Harcourt, Brace & Company, 1955], 181).

9. Andre Bazin, *What Is Cinema?* (Berkeley: University of California Press, 1968).

10. Andrew Sarris, *The American Cinema: Directors and Directions, 1929–1968* (Berkeley: Da Capo, 1996).

11. Among the first serious film books I repeatedly checked out of my local library were: Louis Gianetti, *Understanding Movies* (Englewood Cliffs, NJ: Prentice-Hall, 1972); James Monaco, *How to Read a Film* (New York: Oxford University Press, 1977); and Molly Haskell, *From Reverence to Rape* (New York: Holt, Rinehart and Winston, 1974).

12. My first exposure to serious movie criticism was Pauline Kael's collection of reviews from 1972 to 1975, titled *Reeling* (New York: Little Brown, 1977).

13. *Los Angeles Times* film critic Kenneth Turan celebrates smaller, independent films in *Never Coming to a Theater Near You* (New York: Public Affairs, 2005).

14. Roger Ebert dabbled in low-budget, exploitation filmmaking, serving as screenwriter of Russ Meyer's camp classic, *Beyond the Valley of the Dolls* (1970).

15. This is the dark side of their story, where success squelched idealism. See the latter portion of Biskind, *Easy Rider, Raging Bulls*.

16. Robin Wood, "Papering the Cracks: Fantasy and Ideology in the Reagan Era," in *Hollywood from Vietnam to Reagan . . . and Beyond* (New York: Columbia University Press, 2003).

17. Ibid., 147.

18. Ibid., 148.

19. J. Hoberman, "The Film Critic of Tomorrow, Today," in *American Movie Critics: From the Silents Until Now*, ed. Phillip Lopate (New York: Library of America, 2006), 535.

20. Lawrence S. Friedman, quoted in Christopher Deasy, *Screen Christologies: Redemption and the Medium of Film* (Cardiff: University of Wales Press, 2001), 121.

21. Michael Blowen quoted in ibid., 122.

22. The worst of my anti-art excess can be found in my documentary, *Purple State of Mind* (2008), where my college roommate reminds me that I once told him, "God doesn't like artists because they ask too many questions."

23. For a magisterial take on the theatrical roots of Christian revelation, see Hans Urs von Balthasar, *Theo-Drama: Theological Dramatic Theory*, vol. 1, *Prolegomena*, trans. Graham Harrison (San Francisco: Ignatius Press, 1988).

24. J. R. R. Tolkien, "On Fairy-Stories," in *Essays Presented to Charles Williams*, ed. C. S. Lewis (Grand Rapids: Eerdmans, 1966).

25. Ibid., 81.

26. Jürgen Moltmann, *The Spirit of Life: A Universal Affirmation* (Minneapolis: Fortress, 1992), 34.

27. David Hay and Kate Hunt, "Is Britain's Soul Waking Up?" *The Tablet*, June 24, 2000, 846; and David Hay and Kate Hunt, "Understanding the Spirituality of People Who Don't Go to Church," Research Report, University of Nottingham, 2000.

28. George Barna, *Revolution!* (Wheaton: Tyndale, 2005), 48–49.

29. See esp. Jolyon Mitchell, "Theology and Film," in *The Modern Theologians: An Introduction to Christian Theology since 1918*, 3rd ed., ed. David F. Ford (London: Blackwell, 2005), 736–59.

30. For more on the calling of artist, read Makoto Fujimura's compelling talk from the International Arts Movement's (IAM) 2007 Redemptive Culture Conference, "Being a Child of the Creative Age," www.makotofujimura.blogspot.com/search?q=being+a+child.

Chapter 1 Methodology: Into the *Darko*

1. Death Cab for Cutie, "I'll Follow You into the Dark," *Plans*, compact disc, Atlantic Records, 2005.

2. One of the more insightful theologies rooted in our current context is Miroslav Volf, *Exclusion and Embrace: A Theological Exploration of Identity, Otherness, and Reconciliation* (Nashville: Abingdon, 1996).

3. The tragic statistics speak for themselves in the research commissioned by Gabe Lyons and summarized by David Kinnaman, *unChristian: What a New Generation Really Thinks about Christianity . . . and Why It Matters* (Grand Rapids: Baker Books, 2007).

4. Among the dueling studies assessing the heart of generation Y are Barbara Schneider and David Stevenson, *The Ambitious Generation: America's Teenagers, Motivated but Directionless* (New Haven, CT: Yale University Press, 1999); Christian Smith and Melinda Lundquist Denton, *Soul*

Searching: The Religious and Spiritual Lives of American Teenagers (New York: Oxford University Press, 2005); Chap Clark, *Hurt: Inside the World of Today's Teenagers* (Grand Rapids: Baker Academic, 2005).

5. Paul Schrader, "Canon Fodder," *Film Comment*, September/October 2006, www.filmlinc .com/fcm/so06/filmcanonintro.htm (accessed January 17, 2008).

6. Elaine Pagels, *Beyond Belief: The Secret Gospel of Thomas* (New York: Vintage Books, 2003); Dan Brown, *The Da Vinci Code* (New York: Doubleday, 2003).

7. Among the most accessible introductions is Bruce Metzger, *The Canon of the New Testament: Its Origin, Development, and Significance* (New York: Oxford University Press, 1997).

8. Among his enduring contributions are his criticism in Paul Schrader, *Transcendental Style in Film* (Berkeley: Da Capo Press, 1972); his screenwriting in *Taxi Driver* (1976) and *Raging Bull* (1980); and his directing of *Light Sleeper* (1992) and *Affliction* (1997).

9. Schrader cited Alexander Sokurov's *Mother and Son* (1997), the Coen brothers' *The Big Lebowski* (1998), Wong Kar Wei's *In the Mood for Love* (2000), and Pedro Almodóvar's *Talk to Her* (2002).

10. Damien Cave, "Reel World Domination," http://dir.salon.com/story/mwt/fea ture/2002/10/31/film_literacy/index.html (accessed October 31, 2002).

11. Rudolph Arnheim, "The Film Critic of Tomorrow," in Lopate, *American Movie Critics*.

12. Ibid.

13. www.bfi.org.uk/sightandsound/topten/.

14. www.afi.com/tvevents/100years/movies.aspx.

15. Jonathan Rosenbaum, "List-o-Mania, or How I Stopped Worrying and Learned to Love American Movies," *Chicago Reader*, June 26, 1998, www.chicagoreader.com/movies/100best.html (accessed January 17, 2008).

16. Jonathan Rosenbaum, *Essential Cinema: On the Necessity of Film Canons* (Baltimore: Johns Hopkins University Press, 2004).

17. Jimmie Hicks, "Frank Capra (Part 3)," *Films in Review* 44, no. 3–4 (March/April 1993): 114.

18. Andre Mouchard, "10 years later, *Shawshank* finds redemption on TV," *Orange County Register*, January 29, 2004.

19. *Empire Magazine*, January 2006.

20. The history of the IMDb can be found at www.imdb.com/help/show_leaf?history or at the equally evolving Wikipedia.

21. William Goldman, *Adventures in the Screen Trade* (New York: Warner Books, 1983).

22. Deasy, *Screen Christologies*, 16–17, notes the omission of religion in John Hill's introduction to *The Oxford Guide to Film Studies*, ed. John Hill and Pamela Church Gibson (New York: Oxford University Press, 1998).

23. Margaret R. Miles, *Seeing and Believing* (Boston: Beacon, 1996).

24. Friedrich Schleiermacher, *On Religion: Speeches to Its Cultured Despisers*, trans. John Oman (New York: Harper & Row, 1986), 29.

25. Hans Urs von Balthasar's imaginative and Christocentric theology informs much of my methodology. See esp. *The Glory of the Lord: A Theological Aesthetics*, vol. 1, *Seeing the Form* (San Francisco: Ignatius Press, 1982).

26. Jürgen Moltmann, *The Coming of God: Christian Eschatology*, trans. Margaret Kohl (Minneapolis: Fortress, 1996), xi.

27. David Dark, *Everyday Apocalypse* (Grand Rapids: Brazos, 2002), 10.

28. Moltmann, *Spirit of Life*, 17.

29. Dark, *Everyday Apocalypse*, 12.

30. Moltmann, *Spirit of Life*, 17.

31. For a quick insight into ongoing Dutch Calvinist debates regarding "common grace," I recommend, Richard J. Mouw, *He Shines in All That's Fair: Culture and Common Grace* (Grand Rapids: Eerdmans, 2001).

32. Sallie McFague, *Life Abundant: Rethinking Theology and Economy for a Planet in Peril* (Minneapolis: Fortress, 2001), 119.

33. David Bentley Hart, *The Beauty of the Infinite: The Aesthetics of Christian Truth* (Grand Rapids: Eerdmans, 2003), 255.

34. Paul Avis, "Divine Revelation in Modern Protestant Theology," in *Divine Revelation*, ed. Paul Avis (Grand Rapids: Eerdmans, 1997).

35. I am grateful for the insights of Crystal L. Downing in *How Postmodernism Serves (My) Faith: Questioning Truth in Language, Philosophy, and Art* (Downer's Grove, IL: InterVarsity, 2006), particularly her discussion of the deconstructionist philosophy of Jacques Derrida.

36. Jürgen Moltmann, "Natural Theology," in *Experiences in Theology: Ways and Forms of Christian Theology* (Minneapolis: Fortress, 2000), 73.

37. N. T. Wright, *Simply Christian: Why Christianity Makes Sense* (San Francisco: Harper, 2006).

38. H. D. McDonald, *Theories of Revelation: An Historical Study, 1700–1960* (Grand Rapids: Baker Books, 1979), 275.

39. Nancey Murphy, *Beyond Liberalism and Fundamentalism: How Modern and Postmodern Philosophy Set the Theological Agenda* (Harrisburg, PA: Trinity Press International, 1996).

40. Moltmann, *Experiences in Theology*, 11.

41. Ibid., 15.

42. Ibid., 16.

43. For further reading, see my article, "Buying Time: *21 Grams, In America, Eternal Sunshine*," *Mars Hill Review* 24 (2004): 159–64 (or online at www.get-culture.com).

44. Hans Urs von Balthasar, *The Glory of the Lord: A Theological Aesthetics,* vol. 1, *Seeing the Form,* trans. Erasmo Leiva-Merikakis, ed. Joseph Fessio and John Riches (San Francisco: Ignatius Press, 1982), 50.

45. Jacques Maritain, *Art and Scholasticism with Other Essays,* trans. J. F. Scanlan (1930; repr., Whitefish, MT: Kessinger Publishing, 2003).

46. Balthasar, *Glory of the Lord*, 38.

47. Craig Detweiler and Barry Taylor, *A Matrix of Meanings: Finding God in Pop Culture* (Grand Rapids: Baker Academic, 2003).

48. Balthasar, *Theo-Drama*, vol. 1, *Prolegomena*.

49. Ibid., 125.

50. Kevin J. Vanhoozer, *The Drama of Doctrine: A Canonical-Linguistic Approach to Christian Theology* (Louisville: Westminster John Knox, 2005).

51. Richard Viladesau, *Theological Aesthetics* (New York: Oxford University Press, 1999), 107.

52. I offer more detail on these distinctions in Craig Detweiler, "Life Outside the Faith Ghetto," *Relevant Magazine* 14, May–June 2005. Also found at www.relevantmagazine.com/pc_article .php?id=7550.

53. A great phrase attributed to Ken Gire, *Reflections on the Movies: Hearing God in the Unlikeliest of Places,* Reflective Living Series (Colorado Springs: Chariot Victor Publishing, 2000).

54. Tarkovsky, *Sculpting in Time.*

55. Among the articles bemoaning the declining influence of film critics are Patrick Goldstein, "Critics' Voices Become a Whisper," *Los Angeles Times,* August 15, 2006; David Carr, "Studios Turn Thumbs Down on Film Critics," *New York Times,* May 29, 2006, www.nytimes.com/2006/05/29/ technology/29Carr.html?_r=1&scp=5&sq=David+Carr%2C+Film+Critics&oref=slogin.

56. As a French Catholic critic, Andre Bazin serves as a foundational starting point for both *film studies* and *theology and film*. See his two-volume collection of essays, Andre Bazin, *What Is Cinema?* (1968; repr., Berkeley: University of California Press, 2004).

57. George Barna, "Christians and the *Da Vinci Code*," www.barna.org/flexpage.aspx?page=perspective&perspectiveID=4 (accessed January 24, 2006).

58. Larry J. Kreitzer, *The New Testament in Fiction and Film: On Reversing the Hermeneutical Flow* (New York: Sheffield Academic Press, 1993), 19. This is the first of four different volumes in which Kreitzer has applied a reverse hermeneutic to biblical studies. Subsequent studies have addressed the Old Testament, the Gospels, and the Pauline letters.

59. Larry J. Kreitzer, *The Old Testament in Fiction and Film: On Reversing the Hermeneutical Flow* (Sheffield: Sheffield Academic Press, 1994), 13.

60. Ibid.

61. I appreciate the helpful challenge offered by Melanie J. Wright in *Religion and Film: An Introduction* (London: I. B. Tauris, 2006). For my initial response, see "Seeing and Believing: Film Theory as a Window into a Visual Faith," in *Reframing Theology and Film: New Focus for an Emerging Discipline*, ed. Robert K. Johnston (Grand Rapids: Baker Academic, 2007), 29–50.

62. Robert Jewett, *Saint Paul at the Movies: The Apostle's Dialogue with American Culture* (Louisville: Westminster John Knox, 1993), 7.

63. Ibid., 9.

64. Ibid., 8.

65. Robert K. Johnston, *Reel Spirituality: Theology and Film in Dialogue* (Grand Rapids: Baker Academic, 2000).

66. H. Richard Niebuhr, *Christ and Culture* (London: Faber and Faber, 1952).

67. Robert K. Johnston, *Reel Spirituality: Theology and Film in Dialogue*, 2nd ed. (Grand Rapids: Baker Academic, 2006), 164.

68. Schleiermacher, *On Religion*, 18.

69. Graeme Turner, *British Cultural Studies: An Introduction*, 3rd ed. (New York: Routledge, 2003), 2–3.

70. I am indebted to the insights of Seung Hyun Chung, "The Missional Ecclesiology in Contemporary Hyperreal Culture" (PhD diss., Fuller Theological Seminary, 2007).

71. Stuart Hall, "Encoding/decoding," in *Culture, Media, Language: Working Papers in Cultural Studies, 1972–79* (London: Routledge, 1980), 128–38.

72. A good example of this phenomena is the hip-hop community's embrace of Brian DePalma's remake of *Scarface* (1983).

73. Clive Marsh, *Cinema and Sentiment: Film's Challenge to Theology* (Milton Keynes, England: Paternoster, 2004).

74. Lynn Schofield Clark, *From Angels to Aliens: Teenagers, the Media, and the Supernatural* (Oxford: Oxford University Press, 2003).

75. *Carl Th. Dreyer: My Metier*, directed by Torben Skjodt Jensen, Criterion Collection DVD, 1995.

76. For a lively discussion of the conflicts that arise from this shift, I recommend the introduction to Robert Anthony Orsi's acclaimed *The Madonna of 115th Street: Faith and Community in Italian Harlem, 1880–1950*, 2nd ed. (New Haven, CT: Yale University Press, 2002).

77. David D. Hall, ed., *Lived Religion in America: Toward a History of Practice* (Princeton, NJ: Princeton University Press, 1997).

78. Orsi, *Madonna of 115th Street*, xiii.

79. Downing, *How Postmodernism Serves (My) Faith*, 223.

80. Hall, *Lived Religion in America*, ix.

81. C. S. Lewis, *Screwtape Letters* (San Francisco: HarperSanFrancisco, 2001), 135.

82. There are discrepancies between the general user ratings and the Top 250. The top-ranked films from the 2000s lists almost all the same films but in a slightly different order. By only rounding a film's ratings off to the nearest tenth, all the 8.0s are clumped together in ways that makes differences between the lists negligible.

83. *Donnie Darko*, written and directed by Richard Kelly, Newmarket Films, 2001.

84. www.boxofficemojo.com.

85. Richard Kelly, *Donnie Darko: The Director's Cut*, Newmarket Films, 2004.

86. Clark, *Hurt*.

87. Roland Orzabel, "Mad World," from Tears for Fears, *The Hurting*, compact disc, Mercury Records, 1982.

88. Adam Burnett, "'*Donnie Darko*: The Director's Cut.' The Strange Afterlife of an Indie Cult Film," www.indiewire.com/movies/movies_040722darko.html.

89. A poll organized by Britain's *Hotdog* magazine placed *Donnie Darko* as the second greatest cult movie of all time, ranking higher than *The Wizard of Oz* and *The Rocky Horror Picture Show*. See Daniel Saney, "'Wicker Man,' 'Donnie' Best Cult Films," www.digitalspy.co.uk/movies/a27861/wicker-man-donnie-best-cult-films.html, January 3, 2006.

90. Richard Kelly, "Director's Commentary," *Donnie Darko*, DVD (Fox Home Entertainment, 2001).

91. Richard Kelly, "Director's Commentary on Deleted and Extended Scenes," *Donnie Darko*, Fox Home Video, 2002.

92. R. C. Hilborn traces Edward Lorenz's evolving metaphors that led to the Butterfly Effect in *Chaos and Nonlinear Dynamics: An Introduction for Scientists and Engineers* (New York: Oxford University Press, 1994).

93. See Preface, n. 28.

94. evilmatt-3, "Beautiful, Terrifying," www.imdb.com (accessed December 2, 2001).

95. Lwjoslin, "The Dreams in Which I'm Dying Are the Best I've Ever Had," www.imdb.com (accessed May 23, 2002).

Chapter 2 *Memento*: Duped in Film Noir

1. Lewis, *Surprised by Joy*, 177.

2. Cornelius Plantinga Jr., *Not the Way It's Supposed to Be: A Breviary of Sin* (Grand Rapids: Eerdmans, 1995).

3. Paul Schrader, "Notes on Film Noir," in *Schrader on Schrader* (London: Faber & Faber, 1992).

4. One of the best takes on film noir's historical context is Sheri Chinen Biesen, *Blackout: World War II and the Origins of Film Noir* (Baltimore: Johns Hopkins University Press, 2005).

5. Among the most fascinating and wide-ranging rereadings of film noir is Paula Rabinowitz, *Black and White and Noir* (New York: Columbia University Press, 2002).

6. For more on film noir as an urban phenomena, see Edward Dimendberg, *Film Noir and the Spaces of Modernity* (Cambridge, MA: Harvard University Press, 2004).

7. Reeve Robert Brenner, *The Faith and Doubt of Holocaust Survivors* (New York: Free Press, 1980); Leon Weliczker Wells, *Shattered Faith: A Holocaust Legacy* (Lexington: University Press of Kentucky, 1995).

8. Eric226, "Awful and Essential," www.imdb.com (accessed November 25, 2002).

9. Harry Knowles, review of "*Requiem for a Dream*," http://aronofksy.tripod.com/requiemaicnreview.html.

10. dj bassett, "Didn't Like It Much At All," www.imdb.com, April 24, 2005.

11. schnofel, "A Rather Disappointing Effort," www.imdb.com (accessed September 29, 2004).

12. dj bassett, "Didn't Like It Much at All."

13. Hakapes, "Violence without Sense," www.imdb.com, March 16, 2005.

14. John Powers, "Once upon a Time in the East," *L.A. Weekly*, October 9, 2003.

15. Quentin Tarantino, "The *Playboy* Interview," *Playboy*, November 2003, 59–62.

16. Todd Aftershock, "A Legend in Our Times," www.imdb.com, April 27, 2004.

17. C. K. Dexter Haven, "Vile, Endless, Horrid," www.imdb.com, August 27, 2006.

18. Patrick McGee, *From* Shane *to* Kill Bill: *Rethinking the Western* (Oxford: Blackwell, 2007), 242.

19. Zardoz74_2000, "Bold, Brilliant and Totally Badass," www.imdb.com (accessed March 18, 2005).

20. *The Departed*, written by William Monohan, directed by Martin Scorsese, DVD (Warner Home Video, 2006).

21. One of the many "facts" Leonard Shelby dispenses in the movie. I got the idea to incorporate Leonard's quotes into this chapter from an IMDb user: wkbeason, "Innovative Narrative Structure Makes for a Powerful Viewing Experience," www.imdb.com (accessed July 9, 2002).

22. Scott Timberg, "Indie Angst," *New Times*, Los Angeles, March 15–21, 2001, 15.

23. Ibid.

24. Anthony Kaufman, "Remembrance of Things Lost," *IFC Rant*, March/April 2001, 27.

25. Ibid., 28.

26. Miroslav Volf, *End of Memory: Remembering Rightly in a Violent World* (Grand Rapids: Eerdmans, 2006), 33.

27. The anti-Semitic *Protocols of the Elders of Zion* was first published in Russia in 1903. It is the source for many of the conspiracy theories suggesting a Jewish plot to takeover banking, the media, and so forth. An excellent documentary called *The Protocols of Zion* was made by Marc Levin in 2005.

28. Some clues were revealed via the official Web site, www.otnemem.com, created by Christopher Nolan's brother, Jonathan. Among the most comprehensive efforts to organize the facts of the film was the one made by Andy Klein in "Everything You Wanted to Know About *Memento*," http://archive.salon.com/ent/movies/teative/2001/06/28/memento_analysis (accessed June 28, 2001).

29. Umberto Eco, *The Role of the Reader: Explorations in the Semiotics of Texts* (Bloomington: Indiana University Press, 1984).

30. Murphy, *Beyond Liberalism and Fundamentalism*, 88.

31. Ibid., 12.

32. Karl Popper, *The Logic of Scientific Discovery* (1935; repr., London: Routledge Classics, 2002), 94.

33. Moltmann, *Experiences in Theology*, 18–19.

34. Murphy, *Beyond Liberalism and Fundamentalism*, 154.

35. Ella Taylor, "Time Warped," *LA Weekly*, March 16–22, 2001, 36.

36. Christopher Nolan, interviewed by Daniel Argent, "Remembering *Memento*," *Creative Screenwriting*, March/April 2001, 49.

37. Christopher Nolan, screenwriter, *Memento*, DVD (Sony Pictures, 2001).

38. Argent, "Remembering *Memento*," 47.

39. Aptly pointed out by Andrew O'Hehir in his review of "Insomnia," *Slate*, May 24, 2002, http://dir.salon.com/story/ent/movies/review/2002/05/24/insomnia.

40. "Q and A with Christopher Nolan," by Electric Artists, www.christophernolan.net/interviews_qa.php.

41. Pseudo-geordie boy, "Confusion, Uncertainty and Paranoia as an Art Form: Possibly," www.imdb.com, January 25, 2001.

42. Argent, "Remembering *Memento*," 48.

43. Ibid.

44. See Stanley Grenz and John R. Franke, *Beyond Foundationalism: Shaping Theology in a Postmodern Context* (Louisville: Westminster John Knox, 2001).

45. Murphy, *Beyond Liberalism and Fundamentalism*, 154.

46. Argent, "Remembering *Memento*," 49.

47. Kaufman, "Remembrance of Things Lost," 28.

48. Timberg, "Indie Angst," 16.

49. Ibid.

50. *Memento*, Limited Edition, DVD (Sony Home Video, 2002).

51. A guide to navigating the Limited Edition double DVD can be found at www.dvdtalk.com/features/002208.html.

52. Kristina, "Absolutely No Spoilers Here—READ THIS REVIEW INSTEAD!!!!" www.imdb.com (accessed April 19, 2001).

53. ltlrags, "An Unforgettable Trip into the Mind of a Man with No Memory," www.imdb.com (accessed March 18, 2002).

54. Moltmann, *Experiences in Theology*, 19.

Chapter 3 *Eternal Sunshine*: The Risky Rewards of Romance

1. Daveprice55, "Thank God for Carrey," www.imdb.com, January 25, 2005.

2. IllyriasAcolyte, "The Greatest Romantic Movie Ever," www.imdb.com, February 24, 2007.

3. Two of the more rapturous reviews came from Jack Matthews, "It Pulls Perfect Blank Job," *New York Daily News*, March 18, 2004; and David Edelstein, "Forget Me Not," *Slate*, March 18, 2004, www.slate.com/id/2097362. Both called the movie about memory loss "unforgettable."

4. Among many books on the subject of romantic comedies, the splashiest is Ed Sikov, *Screwball! Hollywood's Madcap Romantic Comedies* (New York: Crown, 1989).

5. C. S. Lewis, *The Four Loves* (Fort Washington, PA: Harvest Books, 1971), 9.

6. These core questions form the backbone of David L. Ulin's hagiographic essay, "Why Charlie Kaufman Is Us," *West Magazine, Los Angeles Times*, May 14, 2006, 116.

7. "Charlie Kaufman: A True Original," Associated Press story, March 23, 2004.

8. Charlie Kaufman, audio commentary on the Special Two-Disc Collector's Edition, *Eternal Sunshine of the Spotless Mind*, DVD (Universal Home Video, 2004), 65-minute mark.

9. Beck, "Everybody's Gonna Lose Sometime," *Eternal Sunshine* (Original Motion Picture Soundtrack, 2004).

10. A more detailed chronology for *Eternal Sunshine* can be found at http://en.wikipedia.org/wiki/Eternal_Sunshine.

11. Stephanie Zackarek, "Brilliant Mistake," http://dir.salon.com/story/ent/movies/review/2004/03/19/eternal_sunshine/index.html?source=search&aim=/ent/movies/review (accessed March 19, 2004).

12. Kimberley Jones, "Something More Than Just Cerebral: An Interview with Charlie Kaufman," *Austin Chronicle*, March 19, 2004, www.austinchronicle.com/gyrobase/Issue/story?oid=oid:202887.

13. "Charlie Kaufman: Writer, Executive Producer, *Eternal Sunshine*," April 8, 2004, http://cgi1.usatoday.com/mchat/20040408003/tscript.htm.

14. Volf, *Exclusion and Embrace*, 92.

15. Charlie Kaufman, *Eternal Sunshine of the Spotless Mind: The Shooting Script* (New York: Newmarket, 2004).

16. Brian Miller, "The Sit-Down: An Interview with director Michel Gondry and Screenwriter Charlie Kaufman," *Seattle Weekly*, March 17, 2004, www.seattleweekly.com/2004-03-17/film/the-sit-down.php.

17. Ibid.

18. Anecdotes in this section are taken from Michel Gondry's commentary, *Eternal Sunshine of the Spotless Mind*, Special Two-Disc Collector's Edition DVD (Universal Studios, 2005).

19. Emily Blunt, "Jim Carrey: A Bountiful Mind," www.bluntreview.com/reviews/carreyeternal.html.

20. The most obvious scriptural parallel is found in the book of Esther, which fails to mention God amid Esther's maneuvering on the Hebrews' behalf.

21. I appreciate the insights of David L. Smith in "*Eternal Sunshine of the Spotless Mind* and the Question of Transcendence," *Journal of Religion and Film* 9, no. 1 (April 2005), www.unomaha.edu/jrf/Vol9No1/SmithSunshine.htm.

22. Alexander Pope, *Selected Poetry*, ed. Pat Rogers (New York: Oxford University Press, 1998), 55.

23. Michelle L. Brown, "Castrating the Nun in Pope's 'Eloisa to Abelard,'" Winner of James Madison University's "Write On" contest, 2001.

24. Jones, "Something More Than Just Cerebral."

25. Rob Blackwelder, "Messing around in Kaufman's 'Mind,'" www.planetout.com/entertainment/interview.html?sernum=680.

26. www.imdb.com/chart/female.

27. Carmen-d, "If You're Lucky This Movie Will Change Your Life!" www.imdb.com (accessed December 26, 2004).

28. Jilske, "This Movie Can CHANGE Your Life ;-)," www.imdb.com, December 24, 2001.

29. Composer Mike, "Best Gift from France since the Statue of Liberty," www.imdb.com, January 20, 2005.

30. Stanley Cavell, *Pursuits of Happiness: The Hollywood Comedy of Remarriage* (1981; repr., Cambridge, MA: Harvard University Press, 2006).

31. Zygmunt Bauman, *Life in Fragments: Essays in Postmodern Morality* (Oxford: Blackwell, 1995), 156, quoted in Volf, *Exclusion and Embrace*, 21.

32. "Interview with Charlie Kaufman," http://o-a.mymovies.net/synopsis/default.asp?filmid=1773&exp=5&s=1&n=7.

33. Roland E. Murphy and Elizabeth Huwiler, *Proverbs, Ecclesiastes, Song of Songs*, New International Biblical Commentary (Peabody, MA: Hendrickson, 1999).

34. Phyllis Trible, "Love's Lyrics Redeemed," in *God and the Rhetoric of Sexuality* (Philadelphia: Fortress, 1978), 144–65, quoted in Murphy and Huwiler, *Proverbs, Ecclesiastes, Song of Songs*, 242.

35. Paul K. Jewett with Marguerite Shuster, *Who We Are: Our Dignity as Human; A Neo-Evangelical Theology* (Grand Rapids: Eerdmans, 1996), 208–9.

36. Rabbi Akiba, "Mishnah Yadayim 3:5" (second century AD).

37. Ariel and Chana Block, quoted in Murphy and Huwiler, *Proverbs, Ecclesiastes, Song of Songs*, 236.

38. Ibid.

39. Carl W. Ernst, "Interpreting the Song of Songs: The Paradox of Spiritual and Sensual Love," in *Song of Songs: Erotic Love Poetry*, ed. Judith Ernst (Grand Rapids: Eerdmans, 2003).

40. Moltmann, *Spirit of Life*, 259–63.

41. Murphy and Huwiler, *Proverbs, Ecclesiastes, Song of Songs*, 176.

42. Ibid.

43. Kaufman, audio commentary on the Special Two-Disc Collector's Edition, *Eternal Sunshine of the Spotless Mind*, DVD (Universal Home Video, 2004).

44. Ibid.

45. Ibid.

46. Christopher Orr, "Unforgettable," *The New Republic*, September 28, 2004, http://209.212.93.14/doc.mhtml?pt=FUXhBFeSnNxhGoCSB3QXoS%3D%3D.

47. Murphy and Huwiler, *Proverbs, Ecclesiastes, Song of Songs*, 175.

48. Viewer responses posted on the movie Web site, www.eternalsunshine.com, and then reprinted in booklet form for the Special Two-Disc Collector's Edition of *Eternal Sunshine of the Spotless Mind*, DVD (Universal Home Video, 2004).

49. Kaufman, audio commentary on the Special Two-Disc Collector's Edition, *Eternal Sunshine of the Spotless Mind*, DVD (Universal Home Video, 2004).

50. The Korgis, "Everybody's Got to Learn Sometime," *Dumb Waiters* (Rialto Records, 1980).

Chapter 4 *Crashing* into the Ensemble Drama: Communities in Crisis

1. Willie Nelson, "My Heroes Have Always Been Cowboys," *Blue Skies*, CBS Records, 1981.

2. The most probing insights on the violent aspects of the cowboy myth is Richard Slotkin's three-volume survey concluded by *Gunfighter Nation: The Myth of the Frontier in Twentieth Century America* (Norman: University of Oklahoma Press, 1998).

3. Willie Nelson and Waylon Jennings, "Mamas Don't Let Your Babies Grow Up to Be Cowboys," *The Outlaws* (RCA Records), 1978.

4. Richard Mouw opened his online blog, "Mouw's Musings," by connecting the dots between MySpace and God's space, "Launching a New Blog: MySpace," www.netbloghost.com/mouw/?m=200612 (accessed December 4, 2006).

5. Found in Robin Wright, "The New Tribalism," *Los Angeles Times*, June 8, 1992, H1.

6. Volf, *Exclusion and Embrace*, 20–21.

7. MatthewinSydney, "A Highly Enjoyable Ensemble Road Movie—Funny Stuff," www.imdb.com, June 22, 2006.

8. I still refer back to my classes in family systems and the excellent resource by Edwin H. Friedman, *Generation to Generation: Family Process in Church and Synagogue* (New York: Guilford Press, 1985).

9. Ark-Flash, "Don't Believe the Hype," www.imdb.com, May 3, 2007.

10. Linda Cowgill, "Writing the Ensemble Film: The Gang's All Here," *Creative Screenwriting*, April 8, 2005, www.plotsinc.com/sitenew/column_art_10.html.

11. Volf, *Exclusion and Embrace*, 48.

12. For a brilliant and rigorous meditation on God as a character, see Jack Miles's Pulitzer Prize–winning *God: A Biography* (New York: Alfred A. Knopf, 1995).

13. Dietrich Bonhoeffer, *Life Together*, trans. John W. Doberstein (San Francisco: Harper & Row, 1954), 37.

14. Among the many biblical passages that refer to the sins of the father are Ps. 79:8; Isa. 14:21; 65:7.

15. Paul Thomas Anderson, *Magnolia: The Shooting Script* (New York: Newmarket Press, 2000).

16. www.igs.berkeley.edu/library/election2006/Prop83.html.

17. Dennis Lehane, *Mystic River* (New York: William Morrow, 2001).

18. David Sterritt, "Mystic River Runs Deep," *Christian Science Monitor*, October 10, 2003, www.csmonitor.com/2003/1010/p16s01-almo.html.

19. kashuu1 from Japan, "Tragic Travesty of Tragedy—Is This Really What You Meant, Mr. Eastwood," www.imdb.com (accessed December 11, 2005).

20. Mark Greene, "Am I the Only One Who Thinks This Movie Sends a Terrible Message?" www.imdb.com (accessed February 22, 2006).

21. Mattias Petersson, "Second Time Around," www.imdb.com (accessed November 8, 2005).

22. Nizmeister, "I Guess You Need to Read the Book," www.imdb.com (accessed October 21, 2003).

23. Linkinem41, "Isn't It Ironic? Don't You Think?" www.imdb.com (accessed August 8, 2006).

24. Rodney Clapp, *A Peculiar People: The Church as Culture in a Post-Christian Society* (Downers Grove, IL: InterVarsity, 1996).

25. Stanley Hauerwas and William Willimon, *Resident Aliens: Life in the Christian Colony* (Nashville: Abingdon, 1989).

26. John Spano, Paul Pringle, and Jean Guccione, "Church to Settle with 45 Accusers," *Los Angeles Times*, December 2, 2006, A1.

27. Sam Howe Verhovek, "Church Abuse Claims Settled," *Los Angeles Times*, December 12, 2006, A24.

28. Volf, *Exclusion and Embrace*, 258.

29. Bonhoeffer, *Life Together*, 27.

30. Ibid.

31. A complete history of the festival is available at www.cityofangelsfilmfest.org.

32. Lawrence Kasdan (writer/director), *Grand Canyon* (Twentieth Century Fox, 1991).

33. Paul Haggis interview, "I Stole Liberally from Robert Altman!" www.totalfilm.com/features/paul_haggis (accessed February 8, 2006).

34. Rai, "Roller-Coaster of Emotions," www.imdb.com (accessed May 1, 2005).

35. jaime_serrat, "It Should've Been Titled, 'Trash,'" www.imdb.com (accessed October 16, 2005).

36. PeterDecker, "*Crash* Is a Made-for-Television Kind of Film," www.imdb.com (accessed March 20, 2006).

37. www.totalfilm.com/features/paul_haggis.

38. Volf, *Exclusion and Embrace*, 74–75.

39. For a comedic take on the madness of the war in the Balkans, check out the Academy Award–winning *No Man's Land* (MGM Home Video, 2001). Bosnia-Muslim director Danis Tanovic implicates all sides in the conflict, showing how an inability to listen or empathize results in a chaos comparable to ancient Babel (Gen. 11:1–9).

40. Terry George, ed., *Hotel Rwanda: Bringing the True Story of an African Hero to Film* (New York: Newmarket Press, 2005), 88.

41. Terry George, "Timeline: The Rwandan Crisis," in George, *Hotel Rwanda*, 101.

42. Keir Pearson, "The Beginning," in George, *Hotel Rwanda*, 20.

43. Terry George, "My Promise," in George, *Hotel Rwanda*, 23, 25.

44. Anne Thompson, "The Struggle of Memory against Forgetting," in George, *Hotel Rwanda*, 54.

45. ksapmorgan, "Very Disturbing and Eye Opening," www.imdb.com (accessed April 13, 2005).

46. Rakesh Thind, "One of the Most Inspiring Films I've Ever Seen," www.imdb.com (accessed December 16, 2004).

47. Anhedonia, "A Brilliant Movie That Deserved a Best Picture Oscar-Nomination," www.imdb.com, February 16, 2005.

48. Condor335, "A Genocide Movie without Genocide," www.imdb.com (accessed March 21, 2006).

49. Attila the Pooh, "Dumbed Down, Sentimental, Superficial Version of History," www.imdb.com, February 24, 2006.

50. Nicola Graydon, "The Rwandan Schindler," in George, *Hotel Rwanda*, 44.

51. George, "My Promise," in George, *Hotel Rwanda*, 23.

52. www.thepeaceplan.com.

53. Tina Daunt, "After 'Rwanda' Drawn to Darfur," *Los Angeles Times*, December 22, 2006, E1.

54. Gavin Smith, "Rules of Engagement," *Film Comment*, May/June 2006, www.filmlinc.com/fcm/mj06/united93.htm.

55. Greengrass's breakthrough film, *Bloody Sunday* (2002), also re-created a horrific real-life event with startling accuracy.

56. pwhitmar, "Prayers," www.imdb.com (accessed April 28, 2006).

57. saraemiller1, "Gut and Heart Wrenching," www.imdb.com (accessed April 28, 2006).

58. Spydamang, "United 93 Is Unbelievably Real, Not to Mention Inexplicably and Heart Wrenchingly Powerful. It's a Film Not Just for a Nation, but for the Entire World," www.imdb.com (accessed July 17, 2006).

59. The most seminal early study of our frontier mythology is Frederick Jackson Turner, *The Frontier in American History* (1920; repr., New York: Dover Publications, 1996).

60. Karen Dodwell, "From the Center: The Cowboy Myth, George W. Bush, and the War in Iraq," *Americana: The Journal of American Popular Culture* (March 2004).

61. Moltmann, *Spirit of Life*, 131.

62. Moltmann, *Experiences in Theology*, 309–10.

63. For much more on this loaded topic, see Miroslav Volf, *After Our Likeness: The Church as the Image of the Trinity* (Grand Rapids: Eerdmans, 1998).

64. Moltmann, *Experiences in Theology*, 324–26.

65. Ibid., 328–29.

66. Ibid., 331.

67. Volf, *Exclusion and Embrace*, 128.

Chapter 5 *Talk to Her* (and Him and Us): Everyday Ethics

1. Bob Dylan, "Need a Woman," *The Bootleg Series, Vol. 1–3*, compact disc, Columbia Records, 1991.

2. William Booth and Sonya Geis, "And This Year's Oscar Goes to Social Issues," *Washington Post*, March 5, 2006, A1.

3. An entertaining history of the entire regrettable cast of characters is contained in Hunter James, *Smile Pretty and Say Jesus: The Last Great Days of PTL* (Athens: University of Georgia Press, 1993).

4. Two of the more damning documentaries on the subject are Kirby Dick's Oscar-nominated, *Twist of Faith* (HBO Films, 2004), and Amy Berg's *Deliver Us from Evil* (Lions Gate Films, 2006). In both cases, the directors allow the accused to incriminate themselves with institutional indifference.

5. A gripping history of the sorry affair is unspooled by director Alex Gibney in *Enron: The Smartest Guys in the Room* (HDNet Films, 2005).

6. Stephen Glass was the subject of director Billy Ray's chilling film, *Shattered Glass* (Lions Gate Films, 2003).

7. Dan Barry, David Barstow, Jonathan D. Glater, Adam Liptak, and Jacques Steinberg, "Times Reporter Who Resigned Leaves Long Trail of Deception," *New York Times*, May 11, 2003, http://query.nytimes.com/gst/fullpage.html?res=9403E1DB123FF932A25756C0A9659C8B63&scp=1&sq=Times+Reporter+who+resigned+leaves+long+trail+of+deception.

8. Directed by Michael Mann, *The Insider* (Walt Disney Home Video, 1999) tracks how tobacco executive Jeffrey Wigand was courted then hung out to dry by *60 Minutes* due to internal corporate business and politics.

9. "Final Figure in '60 Minutes' Scandal Resigns," Associated Press, March 25, 2005.

10. This question was raised with humor and insight by Jennifer Ayres in her presentation, "'Good Evening, Godless Sodomites': *Comedy Central's* Contribution of Religious and Political Satire to the Public Sphere," at the American Academy of Religion, November 18, 2007.

11. For a more complete take on the Oscars, see my article, "The Bigger Picture—Oscars 2008: Power, Corruption, Lies," www.relevantmagazine.com/pc_article.php?id=7612, February 21, 2008.

12. Douglas Groothius, *Truth Decay: Defending Chrstianity against the Challenges of Postmodernism* (Downers Grove, IL: InterVarsity, 2001).

13. Nancy Pearcey, *Total Truth: Liberating Christianity from Its Cultural Captivity* (Wheaton, IL: Crossway Books, 2005).

14. Balthasar, *Glory of the Lord*, 19.

15. Ibid., 34.

16. Robert K. Johnston put *Million Dollar Baby* into dialogue with *The Sea Inside* in his book *Reel Spirituality*, 227–37.

17. Diane Lynne, "The Whole Terri Schiavo Story," WorldNetDaily, March 24, 2005, www.worldnetdaily.com/news/article.asp?article_ID=43463.

18. Abby Goodnough, "In Schiavo Feeding-Tube Case, Notoriety Finds Unlikely Judge," *New York Times*, March 17, 2005, www.nytimes.com/2005/03/17/national/17greer.html.

19. Abby Goodnough, "Schiavo Dies, Ending Bitter Case over Feeding Tube," *New York Times*, April 1, 2005, www.nytimes.com/2005/04/01/national/01schiavo.html.

20. A sense of the vitriol emanating from both sides of the aisle can be discerned from Michael Medved's response, "My 'Million Dollar' Answer," *Wall Street Journal*, February 17, 2005, www.opinionjournal.com/la/?id=110006305.

21. A Web site and a DVD attacked Eastwood as a "million dollar bigot." See www.milliondollarbigot.org (accessed May 12, 2007).

22. Alistair Deacon, "A True 'Hollywood Classic,'" www.imdb.com (accessed March 26, 2005).

23. Movieguy1021, "Million Dollar Baby: 9/10," www.imdb.com (accessed February 17, 2005).

24. Bernard Weinraub, "The *Playboy* Interview: Clint Eastwood," *Playboy*, March 1997, 59–64.

25. HollywoodAM, "Leave Your Personality on 'Eject' When This Slides into 'Play,'" www.imdb.com (accessed July 22, 2005).

26. mbrent711, "Terrible Movie in Many Ways," www.imdb.com (accessed July 19, 2005).

27. Ivanhoe Vargas, "Another Subtle Story by Clint Eastwood," www.imdb.com (accessed January 30, 2006).

28. Darren DeBari, "Million Dollar Baby Is a Knockout!" www.imdb.com (accessed February 28, 2005).

29. IronboundFW, "Million Dollar Baby," www.imdb.com (accessed February 10, 2005).

30. FilmSnobby, "He Doesn't Train Girls," www.imdb.com (accessed February 14, 2005).

31. Amy Taubin, "Online Interview with Clint Eastwood," *Film Comment*, January/February 2005, www.filmlinc.com/fcm/1-2-2005/ceint.htm.

32. David Hubbard, *Proverbs*, Communicator's Commentary (Waco, TX: Word, 1989), 24.

33. Ibid., 25.

34. Don S. Browning, *A Fundamental Practical Theology: Descriptive and Strategic Proposals* (Minneapolis: Fortress, 1991), 10.

35. Ray S. Anderson, *The Shape of Practical Theology* (Downers Grove, IL: InterVarsity, 2001).

36. Moltmann, *Spirit of Life*, 83–98.

37. Nancy C. Murphy, *Bodies and Souls, or Spirited Bodies?* (Cambridge: Cambridge University Press, 2006), 22.

38. William F. May, *The Physician's Covenant: Images of the Healer in Medical Ethics* (Louisville: Westminster John Knox, 2000).

39. William Butler Yeats, "The Lake Isle of Innisfree," originally published in *The Rose* (1893); also see Yeats, *The Collected Poems of W. B. Yeats*, ed. Richard J. Finneran, 2nd rev. ed. (New York: Scribner, 1996).

40. Carrie Rickey, "Two Men Get Lost in Love," *Philadelphia Inquirer*, December 25, 2002. This article is no longer posted.

41. Pedro Almodóvar, "A Self Interview," www.clubcultura.com/clubcine/clubcineas tas/almodovar/hableconella/autoentrevistaeng.htm.

42. Ibid.

43. Stephanie Zacharek, "Talk to Her," http://dir.salon.com/story/ent/movies/re view/2002/11/22/talk_to_her/index.html (accessed November 22, 2002).

44. Abigail17, "What Is There to Like?" www.imdb.com (accessed July 6, 2003).

45. theman5, "Can't Get Past Society's Views," www.imdb.com (accessed November 13, 2004).

46. Danisaley, "Moving, Morally Emotive, a Fantastic Concept, Truly Remarkable, Individual Film," www.imdb.com (accessed October 17, 2005).

47. Jono-73, "Love Is the Saddest Thing When It Goes Away," www.imdb.com (accessed September 25, 2005).

48. Zacharek, "Talk to Her."

49. Almodóvar, "A Self Interview."

50. Balthasar, *Glory of the Lord*, 125.

51. David Sterritt, "A Course in Miracles," *Christian Science Monitor*, November 22, 2002, www.csmonitor.com/2002/1122/p14s03-almo.html.

52. Ella Taylor, "Dead Alive," *LA Weekly*, December 11, 2002, www.laweekly.com/film+tv/film/dead-alive/3337.

Chapter 6 *Finding Neverland*: Nostalgia and Imagination in History

1. Jacques Ellul, *The Presence of the Kingdom*, trans. O. Wyon (New York: Seabury, 1967), 138.

2. Frederic Jameson, "Nostalgia for the Present," *South Atlantic Quarterly* 88, no. 2 (Spring 1989): 517–37.

3. Bob Dylan, "Like a Rolling Stone," *Highway 61 Revisited*, Columbia Records, 1965.

4. Joni Mitchell, "Woodstock," *Ladies of the Canyon*, Asylum Records, 1970.

5. David Lowenthal, *The Past Is a Foreign Country* (Cambridge: Cambridge University Press, 1988).

6. Among the exquisite costume dramas from director James Ivory and producer Ismail Merchant are *The Bostonians* (1984) and *The Remains of the Day* (1993). For a detailed recollection, see Robert Emmet Long, *James Ivory in Conversation: How Merchant Ivory Makes Its Movies* (Berkeley: University of California Press, 2005).

7. Among recent volumes, see Pam Cook, *Screening the Past: Memory and Nostalgia in Cinema* (London: Routledge, 2005); Susan Aronstein, *Hollywood Knights: Arthurian Cinema and the Politics of Nostalgia* (New York: Palgrave Macmillan, 2005).

8. Svetlana Boym, *The Future of Nostalgia* (New York: Basic Books, 2002).

9. Linda Hutcheon, "Irony, Nostalgia and the Postmodernism," University of Toronto, www.library.utoronto.ca/utel/criticism/hutchinp.html.

10. Boym, *Future of Nostalgia*, 4.

11. Hutcheon, "Irony, Nostalgia and Postmodernism."

12. Dolores Hayden, *The Power of Place: Urban Landscapes as Public History* (Cambridge, MA: MIT Press, 1997).

13. Marcel Proust, *Remembrance of Things Past*, trans. Joe Johnson (New York: NBM, 2007).

14. Hutcheon, "Irony, Nostalgia and Postmodernism."

15. Vivian Sobchack, "'Surge and Splendor': A Phenomenology of the Hollywood Historical Epic," in *Film Genre Reader II*, ed. Barry Keith Grant (Austin: University of Texas Press, 1995), 281–303.

16. Addie-7, "An Old-Fashioned Hero, Brilliantly Portrayed," www.imdb.com, June 29, 2001.

17. www.wwiimemorial.com/archives/factsheets/inscriptions.htm.

18. Eldakim, "The True Definition of Being a Man," www.imdb.com, June 7, 2006.

19. Josh Young, "The Slate," *VLife—Daily Variety*, October 2005, 54.

20. Manohla Dargis, "Roll the Fairy Tale, Fade to the Fists," *New York Times*, June 3, 2005, http://query.nytimes.com/gst/fullpage.html?res=9402E1DE1738F930A35755C0A9639C8B63&fta=y (accessed January 17, 2008).

21. Rene Rodriguez, "Crowe's Desperation Scores a TKO," *Miami Herald*, June 3, 2005, 11G.

22. Roger Ebert, "Cinderella Man," http://rogerebert.suntimes.com/apps/pbcs.dll/article?AID=/20050602/REVIEWS/50523002/1023 (accessed June 2, 2005).

23. Chris Docker, "Simple Crowd Pleaser," www.imdb.com, August 31, 2005.

24. Flagrant-Baronessa, "Dangerously Close to Being 'Just Another Movie about Boxing,'" www.imdb.com, August 30, 2006.

25. ignatiusloyala, "Good but . . . ," www.imdb.com, January 10, 2006.

26. George Orwell, *1984* (New York: Harcourt, Brace, 1949), 177.

27. Maurice Halbwachs, *On Collective Memory*, trans. Lewis A. Coser (1950; repr., Chicago: University of Chicago Press, 1992).

28. Paul Ricoeur, "Memory, History, Forgiveness: A Dialogue between Paul Ricoeur and Sorin Antohi," *Janus Head* 8, no. 1 (2005): 15.

29. Jonathan Rosenbaum, "Life Is Beautiful," *Chicago Reader*, November 1998, http://onfilm.chicagoreader.com/movies/capsules/16982_LIFE_IS_BEAUTIFUL.html (accessed January 17, 2008).

30. Richard Schickel, "Fascist Fable," *Time*, November 9, 1998, www.time.com/time/magazine/article/0,9171,989504,00.html (accessed January 17, 2008).

31. *Life Is Beautiful*'s reign proved short-lived as its $57 million gross was eclipsed by *Crouching Tiger, Hidden Dragon*. See Brandon Gray, "Weekend Box Office," www.boxofficemojo.com/news/?id=1853&p=shtm (posted January 13, 2001).

32. Paul Ricoeur, *Memory, History, Forgetting*, trans. Kathleen Blamey and David Pellauer (Chicago: University of Chicago Press, 2004).

33. sford-20, "Excellent Movie," www.imdb.com, January 6, 2007.

34. Elie Wiesel, *From the Kingdom of Memory: Reminiscences* (New York: Summit Books, 1990), 239, cited in Volf, *Exclusion and Embrace*, 234.

35. Zygmunt Bauman, *Modernity and the Holocaust* (Ithaca, NY: Cornell University Press, 1989), 74, quoted in Volf, *Exclusion and Embrace*, 77.

36. Volf, *Exclusion and Embrace*, 77.

37. Jonathan Marlow, "Florian Henckel von Donnersmarck: Among *The Lives of Others*," www.greencine.com/central/node/48 (accessed August 21, 2007).

38. Jesse3, "The Most Underrated Film of 2006," www.imdb.com, January 17, 2007.

39. Brigid O'Sullivan, "Outstandingly Great Movie," www.imdb.com, March 8, 2007.

40. For a shocking look at how Christians in America are perceived by the next generation, read Kinnaman and Lyons, *unChristian*.

41. Another German film, directed by Marc Rothemund, *Sophie Scholl: The Final Days* (2005), chronicles the trial of the brave Scholl and her fellow students/truth tellers in The White Rose resistance movement.

42. Cited in Balthasar, *Glory of the Lord*, 101.

43. Richard Gladstein, "Feature Commentary with Filmmakers," *Finding Neverland* (Miramax, 2004).

44. Marc Forster, "Feature Commentary with Filmmakers," *Finding Neverland* (Miramax, 2004).

45. Imagination serves as the hope within daunting circumstances in Marc Forster's previous film, *Monster's Ball* (2001). For a more complete meditation on that movie, see "An Ambiguous Joy: Marc Forster and *Monster's Ball*," chap. 6 in Robert K. Johnston, *Useless Beauty: Ecclesiastes through the Lens of Contemporary Film* (Grand Rapids: Baker Academic, 2004).

46. Anthony Lane, "Lost Boys: Why J. M. Barrie Created Peter Pan," *New Yorker*, November 22, 2004. Also found at www.newyorker.com/archive/2004/11/22/041122 (posted February 13, 2001).

47. Volf, *End of Memory*, 28.

48. Gladstein, "Feature Commentary with Filmmakers."

49. For more on the link between children, art, and the kingdom, check out painter Makoto Fujimura's address to the 2007 International Arts Movement's (IAM) conference, "Being a Child of the Creative Age," at www.makotofujimura.blogspot.com (posted March 3, 2007).

50. Harry Haun, "Peter Pan Complex," *Film Journal International*, www.filmjour nal.com/filmjournal/index.jsp (also found at www.allbusiness.com/services/motion pictures/4426411-1.html).

51. Marc Forster, quoted by Dennis Harvey in "Directors," *Daily Variety*, January 15, 2002, A18.

52. Sapphira Gratz, "Beautiful & Sweet Film," www.imdb.com (accessed February 6, 2005).

53. Marcin Kukuczka, "The Film for All That Can Still Find 'Child' in Themselves," www.imdb.com (accessed March 13, 2005).

54. Naoum, "The Reparation of Magic!" www.imdb.com (accessed March 18, 2005).

55. Shanfloyd, "The Beauty in It All," www.imdb.com (accessed April 19, 2005).

56. Ciprian Cucu, "What Is the Meaning of Life?" www.imdb.com (accessed March 4, 2005).

57. Walter Brueggemann, *Hopeful Imagination: Prophetic Voices in Exile* (Philadelphia: Fortress, 1986), 4.

58. Ibid., 6.

Chapter 7 *Spirited Away* by Fantasy: Tending the Garden

1. Quoted but uncited in Antonio Monda, *Do You Believe? Conversations on God and Religion*, trans. Ann Goldstein (New York: Vintage Books, 2007).

2. Steven Horn, "Interview with Hayao Miyazaki," http://movies.ign.com/articles/ 371/371579p1.html (accessed September 20, 2002).

3. Daniel Cappello interviews Margaret Talbot, "Q & A: The Animated Life," *New Yorker*, January 17, 2004, www.newyorker.com/archive/2005/01/17/050117on_onlineonly01.

4. Tolkien, "On Fairy-Stories."

5. Antti Aarne and Stith Thompson, *The Types of the Folktale: A Classification and Bibliography*, 2nd rev. ed. (Bloomington: Indiana University Press, 1995); Vladimir Propp, *Morphology of the Folktale*, ed. Louis A. Wagner, trans. Laurence Scott (Austin: University of Texas Press, 1968).

6. William Steig, *Shrek!* (New York: Farrar, Straus, and Giroux, 1990).

7. Madeleine L'Engle, *Walking on Water: Reflections on Faith and Art* (Wheaton: Harold Shaw, 1980).

8. The preachable possibilities of Disney movies is explored by Philip Longfellow Anderson in *The Gospel in Disney: Christian Values in the Early Animated Classics* (Minneapolis: Augsburg Fortress, 2004).

9. Charles W. Brashares, in *The Christian Century*, 1938, cited in Mark I. Pinsky, *The Gospel according to Disney: Faith, Trust, and Pixie Dust* (Louisville: Westminster John Knox, 2004), 27.

10. Cited in Pinsky, *Gospel according to Disney*, 8.

11. Among the most detailed biographies is Neal Gabler's massive *Walt Disney: The Triumph of the American Imagination* (New York: Alfred A. Knopf, 2006).

12. Cited in Pinsky, *Gospel according to Disney*, 2.

13. *The Wizard of Oz* reportedly cost Metro Goldwyn Mayer $2.78 million but grossed only $2.05 million in its initial release. See www.boxofficemojo.com/movies/?id=wizardofoz.htm.

14. Frederick Buechner, *Telling the Truth: The Gospel as Tragedy, Comedy, and Fairy Tale* (San Francisco: HarperCollins, 1977), 79.

15. Ibid.

16. Guillermo del Toro, www.panslabyrinth.com.

17. Ibid.

18. Michael Guillen, "Pan's Labyrinth—Interview with Guillermo del Toro," www.twitchfilm.net/site/view/pans-labyrinthinterview-with-guillermo-del-toro/ (accessed December 16, 2006).

19. Ibid.

20. Ibid.

21. Tolkien, "On Fairy-Stories."

22. Jon Boorstin, *Making Movies Work: Thinking Like a Filmmaker* (Los Angeles: Silman James, 1995).

23. Jürgen Moltmann, *The Future of Creation* (Philadelphia: Fortress, 1979), 10.

24. For a more complete take on the first Matrix movie, check out my thoughts in Craig Detweiler, *A Matrix of Meanings: Finding God in Pop Culture* (Grand Rapids: Baker Academic, 2003).

25. Moltmann, *Future of Creation*, 10.

26. Alan Moore and David Lloyd, *V for Vendetta* (New York: DC Comics, 2005).

27. Richard Dawkins, *The God Delusion* (Boston: Houghton-Mifflin, 2006); Sam Harris, *The End of Faith: Religion, Terror, and the Future of Reason* (New York: W. W. Norton, 2004).

28. Moltmann, *Future of Creation*, 10.

29. Todd Gilchrist, "Interview: David Lloyd," http://dvd.ign.com/articles/722/722102p1.html (accessed July 31, 2006).

30. One of the primary texts on character animation comes from two of Disney's "Nine Old Men," the men who drew almost all of the foundation films: Frank Thomas and Ollie Johnston, *The Illusion of Life: Disney Animation* (New York: Disney Editions, 1995).

31. Ibid., 13.

32. Robin McKie, "A Dog's Life," *Observer*, September 18, 2005, http://film.guardian.co.uk/interview/interviewpages/0,,1572937,00.html.

33. M. Faust, "Cracking: An Interview with Wallace and Gromit Creator Nick Park," ArtVoice.com, vol. 4, no. 40, http://artvoice.com/issues/v4n40/cracking (accessed October 6, 2005).

34. Ched Meyers, "Theological Animation," Bartimaeus Cooperative Ministries, http://bcm-net.org/wordpress/theological-animation/.

35. Brent Schlender, "Pixar's Magic Man," *Fortune*, May 15, 2006, http://money.cnn.com/magazines/fortune/fortune_archive/2006/05/29/8377998/index.htm.

36. Peter Rainer, "Cold Heart," *New York Magazine*, June 16, 2003, http://nymag.com/nymetro/movies/reviews/n_8779.

37. Cathy Booth, "The Wizard of Pixar," *Time*, December 14, 1998, www.time.com/time/magazine/article/0,9171,989819,00.html.

38. Joe Ranft, "Interview with Joe," www.pixar.com/artistscorner/joe/interview.html (accessed January 2002). Joe's animated life was tragically cut short in a car crash. His creative legacy lives on in Pixar's films.

39. Igenlode Wordsmith, "The Film That Launched a Thousand Rats," www.imdb.com, October 6, 2007.

40. Jason Adams, "JoBlo.com Interviews *Cars* Director John Lasseter," http:///www.joblo.com/index.php?id=13476 (accessed November 7, 2006).

41. Doug Bunnell and Sharon Gallagher, "Interview with Pete Docter," *Radix* 26, no. 1 (2001), www.radixmagazine.com/page1PeterDocter.html.

42. John Lasseter revealed the relationship between Pixar's subjects and technology to Adams, "JoBlo.com Interviews *Cars* Director."

43. Roberta Smith, "It's a Pixar World. We're Just Living in It," *New York Times*, December 16, 2005, www.nytimes.com/2005/12/16/arts/design/16pixa.html?_r=1&oref=slogin.

44. www.calarts.edu/aboutcalarts/history.

45. Schlender, "Pixar's Magic Man."

46. www.pixar.com/companyinfo/history/index.html.

47. Adams, "JoBlo.com Interviews *Cars* Director."

48. Neal Gabler, "When You Wish upon a Merger," www.dvrepublic.com (accessed February 5, 2006).

49. For a scathing critique of cultural exporters like Disney and how they undermine Christian faith, see Michael Budde, *The (Magic) Kingdom of God: Christianity and Global Culture Industries* (Boulder, CO: Westview, 1997).

50. Gabler, "When You Wish upon a Merger."

51. Schlender, "Pixar's Magic Man."

52. Smith and Denton, *Soul Searching*.

53. Ibid., 171.

54. www.metacritic.com/film/awards/.

55. Horn, "Interview with Hayao Miyazaki."

56. "Interview: Miyazaki on Sen to Chihiro no Kamikakushi," trans. Ryoko Toyama, *Animage*, www.nausicaa.net/miyazaki/interviews/sen.html (accessed May 2001).

57. Ibid.

58. Ibid.

59. Xan Brooks, "A God among Animators," *Guardian*, September 14, 2005, http://film.guardian.co.uk/interview/interviewpages/0,,1569689,00.html.

60. "Interview: Miyazaki on Sen to Chihiro no Kamikakushi."

61. James W. Boyd and Tetsuya Nishimura, "Shinto Perspectives in Miyazaki's Anime Film *Spirited Away*," *Journal of Religion and Film* 8, no. 2 (October 2004), www.unomaha.edu/jrf/Vol8No2/boydShinto.htm.

62. Ibid.

63. "Interview: Miyazaki on Mononoke-hime," trans. Ryoko Toyama, ed. Deborah Goldsmith, www.nausicaa.net/miyazaki/interviews/m_on_mh.html (accessed July 1997).

64. Ibid.

65. Ibid.

66. Danherb, "Wonderful Coming-of-Age Story, Beautifully Pictured," www.imdb.com (accessed June 2, 2005).

67. Tomimt, "Wonderful Animation," www.imdb.com (accessed February 2, 2005).

68. Glen B. Wang, "A Movie Where Many Childhood Dreams Are Reborn," www.imdb.com (accessed May 3, 2005).

69. Matti-Man, "The Audience Is Even More Interesting Than the Film," www.imdb.com (accessed January 24, 2005).

70. "Moriarity's Rumblings from the Lab #14: Interview with Miyazaki," *Cool News*, www.aintitcool.com/node/4413 (accessed September 21, 1999).

71. Cappello, "Q & A: The Animated Life."

72. Brooks, "God among Animators."

73. Thomas Molnar, *The Pagan Temptation* (Grand Rapids: Eerdmans, 1987), 91.

74. Ibid., 148.

75. Ibid., 163.

76. Ibid., 107.

77. McFague, *Life Abundant*, 102.

78. Mircea Eliade, *The Sacred and the Profane: The Nature of Religion* (New York: Harcourt, Brace, 1959), 205.

79. McFague, *Life Abundant*, 102.

80. Ibid., 150.

81. Alistair McGrath, *The Re-Enchantment of Nature: Science, Religion, and the Human Sense of Wonder* (London: Hodder & Stoughton, 2002), 13–14.

82. Lynn White, "The Historical Roots of Our Ecological Crisis," *Science* 155 (1967): 1203–7.

83. E. O. Wilson, *The Creation: An Appeal to Save Life on Earth* (New York: W. W. Norton, 2006).

84. McFague, *Life Abundant*, 72.

85. Ibid.

86. McGrath, *Re-Enchantment of Nature*, 16.

87. Jürgen Moltmann, *God in Creation: A New Theology of Creation and the Spirit of God* (Minneapolis: Fortress, 1993), 13.

88. Ibid., 98.

Chapter 8 Conclusion: Mnemonic Devices

1. Death Cab for Cutie, "Someday You Will Be Loved," *Plans*, compact disc, Atlantic Records, 2005.

2. Bill McKibben, "Old McDonald Had a Farmer's Market—Total Self-Sufficiency Is a Noble, Misguided Ideal," www.incharacter.org/article.php?article=87 (accessed Winter 2007).

3. Christopher R. Little, *The Revelation of God among the Unevangelized: An Evangelical Appraisal and Missiological Contribution to the Debate* (Pasadena: William Carey Library, 2000), 94.

4. Moltmann, *Spirit of Life*, 40.

5. The apostle Paul quotes this Psalm in Rom. 10:18 as part of an extended discussion of the Israelites' rejection of the Good News. Just because everyone can see it (or hear it) doesn't mean they will embrace God.

6. Frank Burch Brown, *Good Taste, Bad Taste, and Christian Taste: Aesthetics in Religious Life* (New York: Oxford University Press, 2000).

7. Bruce A. Demarest, *General Revelation: Historical Views and Contemporary Issues* (Grand Rapids: Zondervan, 1982), 250.

8. Robert Johnston, "Of Tidy Doctrine and Truncated Experience," *Christianity Today*, February 18, 1977, 11.

9. Schleiermacher, *On Religion*, quoted in Demarest, *General Revelation*, 95.

10. Robert K. Johnston, "Rethinking Common Grace: Toward a Theology of Co-relation," in *Grace upon Grace: Essays in Honor of Thomas A. Langford*, ed. Robert K. Johnston, L. Gregory Jones, and Jonathan R. Wilson (Nashville: Abingdon, 1999), 160.

11. McDonald, *Theories of Revelation*, 7–8.

12. Avis, *Divine Revelation*, 12.

13. Demarest, *General Revelation*, 123.

14. Karl Barth and Emil Brunner, *Natural Theology: Comprising "Nature and Grace" by Professor Dr. Emil Brunner and the Reply "No!" by Dr. Karl Barth*, trans. Peter Fraenkel (Eugene, OR: Wipf & Stock, 2002).

15. Peter L. Berger, *A Rumor of Angels: Modern Society and the Rediscovery of the Supernatural* (New York: Penguin, 1970), 67.

16. Karl Barth, *The Humanity of God* (Louisville: Westminster John Knox, 1960).

17. Avis, *Divine Revelation*, 5.

18. McDonald, *Theories of Revelation*, 275.

19. Moltmann, *God in Creation*, 59.

20. Moltmann, *Spirit of Life*, 7.

21. Balthasar, *Glory of the Lord*, 80.

22. Tolkien, "On Fairy-Stories," 72.

23. Brian Sibley, *The Lord of the Rings: Official Movie Guide* (Boston: Houghton-Mifflin, 2001), 25.

24. Ibid., 83.

25. Ibid., 110.

26. Ibid., 115.

27. Minionlost, "Wow!" www.imdb.com (accessed December 11, 2001).

28. Bonnie 91, "The Fellowship of the Ring: Not Just a Movie, but the Door to Another Dimension," www.imdb.com (accessed April 14, 2006).

29. Jed Salazar, "Beautiful Perfection," www.imdb.com (December 19, 2002).

30. James Hitchcock, "The First Great Cinematic Masterpiece of the Twenty-First Century," www.imdb.com (accessed February 4, 2004).

31. Sibley, *Lord of the Rings*, 8.

32. Ralph C. Wood, "Tolkien the Movie and Tolkien the Book," www3.baylor.edu/~Ralph_Wood/tolkien/ReviewFellowshipMovie.pdf.

33. Ralph C. Wood, "Visual Adventure and Aural Quest: Peter Jackson's Rendering of *The Two Towers*," www3.baylor.edu/~Ralph_Wood/tolkien/ReviewTwoTowersMovie.pdf.

34. Andrew Light, "Tolkien's Green Time: Environmental Themes in *The Lord of the Rings*," in *The Lord of the Rings and Philosophy: One Book to Rule Them All*, ed. Gregory Bassham and Eric Bronson (Chicago: Open Court, 2003), 155–60.

35. Tolkien, "On Fairy-Stories," 84.

36. Wood, "Visual Adventure and Aural Quest."

37. Ralph C. Wood, "The Lure of the Obvious in Peter Jackson's *The Return of the King*," www3.baylor.edu/~Ralph_Wood/tolkien/ReviewReturnKingMovie.pdf.

38. Ralph C. Wood, "J. R. R. Tolkien: Postmodern Visionary of Hope," in *The Gift of Story: Narrating Hope in a Postmodern World*, ed. Emily Griesinger and Mark Eaton (Waco: Baylor University Press, 2006), 343.

39. Ibid., 334.

40. Ray Anderson, *The Soul of Ministry: Forming Leaders for God's People* (Louisville: Westminster John Knox, 1997), 179.

41. Brian D. McLaren, *The Story We Find Ourselves In: Further Adventures of a New King of Christian* (San Francisco: Jossey-Bass, 2003).

42. Walter Brueggemann, *Shalom* (St. Louis: Chalice, 2001), 5.

43. Iris Murdoch, *The Fire and the Sun: Why Plato Banished the Artists* (Oxford: Clarendon, 1977), 86.

Movies Cited

Cars (d. Lasseter and Ranft, 2006), 312n42, 312n47

Chicken Run (d. Lord and Park, 2000), 236

Chinatown (d. Polanski, 1974), 140

Chronicles of Narnia: The Lion, the Witch, and the Wardrobe, The (d. Adamson, 2005), 29

Cinderella Man (d. Howard, 2005), 51, 189, 192, 195, 196, 197, 198, 211, 215, 216

Cinema Paradiso (d. Tornatore, 1988), 11

Citizen Kane (d. Welles, 1941), 25, 26

City of God [Cidade de Deus] (d. Meirelles and Lund, 2002), 50, 66, 67

Corpse Bride (d. Burton and Johnson, 2005), 241

Crash (d. Haggis, 2004), 9, 51, 126, 140, 141, 142, 143, 155, 157, 158, 163, 231, 250, 276, 304n36

Creature Comforts (d. Park, 1989), 236

Crouching Tiger, Hidden Dragon [Wo hu cang long] (d. Lee, 2000), 52, 228, 254, 309n31

Darfur Now (d. Braun, 2007), 149

Dead Man Walking (d. Robbins, 1995), 35

Deathtrap (d. Lumet, 1982), 69

Deliver Us from Evil (d. Berg, 2006), 133, 305n4

Departed, The (d. Scorsese, 2006), 49, 50, 71, 72, 91, 299n20

Devil Came on Horseback, The (d. Stern and Sundberg, 2007), 149

Diner (d. Levinson, 1982), 132

Dinner at Eight (d. Cukor, 1933), 128

Do the Right Thing (d. Lee, 1989), 48, 139, 140

Donnie Darko (d. Kelly, 2001), 23, 52, 53, 54, 55, 56, 57, 58, 276, 298n83, 298n85, 298n88, 298n89, 298n90, 298n91

Double Indemnity (d. Wilder, 1944), 64

Downfall, The [Der Untergang] (d. Hirschbiegel, 2004), 48, 51, 189, 192, 202, 203, 204, 205, 206, 207, 208, 215, 216

Elizabeth (d. Kapur, 1998), 191

Emma (d. McGrath, 1996), 191

Enron: The Smartest Guys in the Room (d. Gibney, 2005), 305n5

Eternal Sunshine of the Spotless Mind (d. Gondry, 2004), 9, 30, 50, 94, 95, 96, 97, 98, 99, 100, 101, 102, 103, 104, 105, 106, 107, 108, 109, 112, 114, 115, 116, 117, 118, 119, 120, 231, 246, 250, 276, 301n8, 301n9, 301n10, 301n13, 301n15, 301n18, 302n21, 302n43, 303n48, 303n49

Everything Put Together (d. Forster, 2000), 211

Evil Dead (d. Raimi, 1981), 55

Far from Heaven (d. Haynes, 2002), 24

Fight Club (d. Fincher, 1999), 30, 100

Finding Nemo (d. Stanton and Unkrich, 2003), 52, 237, 238, 240

Finding Neverland (d. Forster, 2004), 51, 190, 192, 208, 209, 210, 211, 212, 213, 215, 216, 276, 309n43, 309n44

Flags of Our Fathers (d. Eastwood, 2006), 201, 202

Following (d. Nolan, 1998), 83, 91

For a Few Dollars More [Per qualche dollaro in più] (d. Leone, 1965), 124

Forrest Gump (d. Zemeckis, 1994), 192

Game, The (d. Fincher, 1997), 100

Gandhi (d. Attenborough, 1982), 190

Girlfight (d. Kusama, 2000), 163

Gladiator (d. Scott, 2000), 51, 189, 192, 195, 196, 215

Glory (d. Zwick, 1989), 192

Godfather, The (d. Coppola, 1972), 10, 12, 25, 27, 32

Godfather: Part II, The (d. Coppola, 1974), 10

Golden Compass, The (d. Weitz, 2007), 259

Good Night and Good Luck (d. Clooney, 2005), 157, 158

Gosford Park (d. Altman, 2001), 128

Grand Canyon (d. Kasdan, 1991), 140

Grand Hotel (d. Goulding, 1932), 128

Green Mile, The (d. Darabont, 1999), 30

Hero [Ying xiong] (d. Zhang, 2002), 52, 228

Hornet's Nest (d. Karlson and Cirino, 1970), 7, 8, 14

Hot Fuzz (d. Wright, 2007), 49

Hotel Rwanda (d. George, 2004), 51, 126, 144, 145, 146, 147, 148, 152, 153, 155, 267, 276

Howard's End (d. Ivory, 1992), 190

Howl's Moving Castle [Hauru no ugoku shiro] (d. Miyazaki, 2004), 218

Human Nature (d. Gondry, 2001), 94, 96

In America (d. Sheridan, 2002), 38

In the Mood for Love [Fa yeung nin wa] (d. Wong, 2000), 295n9

Inconvenient Truth, An (d. Guggenheim, 2006), 253

Incredibles, The (d. Bird, 2004), 52, 237, 238, 240, 241

Insider, The (d. Mann, 1999), 159, 306n8

Insomnia (d. Nolan, 2002), 83, 84

Internal Affairs [Mou gaan dou] (d. Lau and Mak, 2002), 71, 72

Into the Wild (d. Penn, 2007), 26

Intolerance: Love's Struggle throughout the Ages (d. Griffith, 1916), 128

Invisible Children (d. Poole and Russell, 2006), 149

It Happened One Night (d. Capra, 1934), 109

It's a Wonderful Life (d. Capra, 1946), 25, 56

Jaws (d. Spielberg, 1975), 10

Juno (d. Reitman, 2007), 95, 112, 160

Kill Bill, vol. 1 (d. Tarantino, 2003), 68

Kill Bill, vol. 2 (d. Tarantino, 2004), 68

Killing Fields, The (d. Joffé, 1984), 192

Kingdom of Heaven (d. Scott, 2005), 196

L.A. Confidential (d. Hanson, 1997), 65

Lady Eve, The (d. Sturges, 1941), 110

Lady in the Water (d. Shyamalan, 2006), 26

Last Tango in Paris (d. Bertolucci, 1972), 11

Last Temptation of Christ, The (d. Scorsese, 1988), 55

Lawrence of Arabia (d. Lean, 1962), 190

Letters from Iwo Jima (d. Eastwood, 2006), 48–49, 189, 196, 201, 202

Life Is Beautiful [La Vita è bella] (d. Benigni, 1997), 200, 201, 210, 309n31

Light Sleeper (d. Schrader, 1992), 295n8

Little Children (d. Field, 2006), 133

Little Miss Sunshine (d. Dayton and Faris, 2006), 51, 126, 128, 129, 155

Lives of Others, The [Das Leben der Anderen] (d. Donnersmarck, 2006), 49, 189, 206, 207, 208, 215, 309n37

Lock, Stock and Two Smoking Barrels (d. Ritchie, 1998), 67

Lord of the Rings, The (d. Jackson, 2001–3), 257, 268, 270, 271, 272, 273, 274, 275, 276, 277

The Fellowship of the Ring (d. Jackson, 2001), 270, 273

The Two Towers (d. Jackson, 2002), 270, 272, 275

The Return of the King (d. Jackson, 2003), 219, 269, 271, 274, 314n37

Lost Highway (d. Lynch, 1997), 70

Lost in Translation (d. Coppola, 2003), 49

Love's a Bitch [Amores perros] (d. Iñárritu, 2000), 48, 50, 66

Magnolia (d. Anderson, 1999), 30, 133, 140, 303n15

Maltese Falcon, The (d. Huston, 1941), 64

Master and Commander (d. Weir, 2003), 195

Matrix, The (d. Wachowski and Wachowski, 1999), 230, 231, 233, 234

Matrix Reloaded, The (d. Wachowski and Wachowski, 2003), 231

Matrix Revolutions, The (d. Wachowski and Wachowski, 2003), 231, 232, 234, 239

Meet the Parents (d. Roach, 2000), 128

Memento (d. Nolan, 2000), 9, 30, 48, 50, 57, 62, 63, 70, 73, 74, 75, 76, 77, 78, 79, 80, 81, 82, 83, 84, 85, 86, 87, 89, 90, 91, 100, 101, 231, 246, 250, 257, 263, 276, 300n28, 300n36, 300n37, 300n38, 300n50

Michael Clayton (d. Gilroy, 2007), 160

Million Dollar Baby (d. Eastwood, 2004), 30, 48, 51, 159, 161, 162, 163, 164, 165, 166, 167, 168, 170, 171, 172, 173, 174, 175, 176, 177, 179, 180, 182, 183, 198, 306n16

Monster's Ball (d. Forster, 2001), 211, 309n45

Monsters, Inc. (d. Docter and Silverman, 2001), 52, 237, 239, 240, 243

Mother and Son (Mat i syn, d. Sokurov, 1997), 295n9

Motorcycle Diaries, The [Diarios de motocicleta] (d. Salles, 2004), 191

Mulholland Dr. (d. Lynch, 2001), 50, 70, 71, 91, 100

Munich (d. Spielberg, 2005), 157, 158

Mystic River (d. Eastwood, 2003), 48, 51, 126, 133, 134, 135, 136, 137, 154, 276, 303n17

Nashville (d. Altman, 1975), 11

Nativity Story, The (d. Hardwicke, 2006), 131

No Country for Old Men (d. Coen and Coen, 2007), 72, 94, 160

No Man's Land (d. Tanovic, 2001), 49, 145, 153, 155, 276, 304n39

Oldboy (d. Park, 2003), 50, 67, 68

On the Waterfront (d. Kazan, 1954), 163

Pan's Labyrinth [El Liberinto del fauno] (d. Toro, 2006), 48, 207, 223, 224, 225, 226, 254, 311n18

Passage to India, A (d. Lean, 1984), 194

Passion of Joan of Arc, The (d. Dreyer, 1928), 45

Passion of the Christ, The (d. Gibson, 2004), 29, 31

Patton (d. Schaffner, 1970), 190

Philadelphia Story, The (d. Cukor, 1940), 109

Pianist, The (d. Polanski, 2002), 51, 189, 192, 202, 203, 204, 215, 216

Pirates of the Caribbean: The Curse of the Black Pearl (d. Verbinski, 2003), 52, 228, 229, 256

Planet of the Apes (d. Schaffner, 1968), 188

Prestige, The (d. Nolan, 2006), 48, 50, 84, 85

Pride and Prejudice (d. Wright, 2005), 191

Princess Mononoke [Mononoke-hime] (d. Miyazaki, 1997), 218

Protocols of Zion, The (d. Levin, 2005), 300n27

Pulp Fiction (d. Tarantino, 1994), 9, 10, 65, 66, 69, 125

Purple State of Mind (d. Detweiler, 2008), 294n22

Queen, The (d. Frears, 2006), 190, 191

Raging Bull (d. Scorsese, 1980), 13, 15, 70, 71, 90, 163, 259, 278, 295n8

Raiders of the Lost Ark (d. Spielberg, 1981), 10, 12

Ratatouille (d. Bird and Pinkava, 2007), 237, 239

Remains of the Day, The (d. Ivory, 1993), 308n6

Requiem for a Dream (d. Aronofsky, 2000), 50, 65, 66, 299n9

Return of the Secaucus Seven (d. Sayles, 1980), 132

Rocky (d. Avildsen, 1976), 163, 168

Rocky Horror Picture Show, The (d. Sharman, 1975), 298n89

Room with a View, A (d. Ivory, 1985), 190

Rules of the Game, The [La Règle du jeu] (d. Renoir, 1939), 128

Saving Private Ryan (d. Spielberg, 1998), 191

Scarface (d. De Palma, 1983), 298n72

Schindler's List (d. Spielberg, 1993), 145, 151, 199, 203

Sea Inside, The [Mar adentro] (d. Amenábar, 2004), 306n16

Seabiscuit (d. Ross, 2003), 198

Sense and Sensibility (d. Lee, 1995), 191

Shake Hands with the Devil: The Journey of Roméo Dallaire (d. Raymont, 2004), 148

Shane (d. Stevens, 1953), 299n18

Shattered Glass (d. Ray, 2003), 306n6

Shawshank Redemption, The (d. Darabont, 1994), 25, 26, 27, 30, 32, 34, 204, 295n18

Shrek (d. Adamson and Jenson, 2001), 52, 220, 221, 241, 254

Signs (d. Shyamalan, 2002), 38

Sin City (d. Miller and Rodriguez, 2005), 50, 69, 70, 91

Subject Index

escapism, 16
eschatology, locus of, 51–52. *See also* fantasy; nostalgia
ethics, 51, 159–62, 165–66, 170–74, 181. *See also* ecclesiology, locus of
eucatastrophe, 16
Eucharist, the, 278–79
euthanasia, 51, 165–66, 172–74. *See also* ethics
evil, 38, 222–23
experience, religious, 263–65

facts, 78–80
fairy tales. *See* fantasy
faith, 36, 86–88, 119. *See also* interpretation
fantasy, 52, 220–23, 225–28, 243
feelings, human, 263–65
film noir, 50, 63–65, 72

general revelation, 15–16, 30–41, 48, 250–54, 258–68. *See also* special revelation
genocide, 143–44, 148–50
grace, 15, 34–35. *See also* general revelation

Hall, Stuart, 44–45
hermeneutics, 42–43, 78–80, 86–88. *See also* faith
heroism, 273–74
historical films, 51
history, analysis of, 199–202. *See also* memory, human

identity, human. *See* individual, autonomous
imagination, 13, 214–16. *See also* aesthetics, theology of
IMDb, 26–28, 45, 46–49, 298n82
individual, autonomous, 49–50, 123–24, 265–66
Internet, the, 125. *See also* community
Internet Movie Database (IMDb). *See* IMDb
interpretation, 42–43, 78–80, 86–88. *See also* faith
interventionism, United States, 151–53

Jewett, Paul, 43
Johnston, Robert K., 43

Kreitzer, Larry, 42

Lasseter, John, 240–42. *See also* Pixar
Law, the. *See* special revelation
life, human, 173
locus, cinema as, 42–43
Los Angeles, 138–40

love, human. *See* anthropology, locus of; relationships, postmodern

magic, 226–27. *See also* fantasy
McDonald, H. D., 37–38
memory, human, 50, 76–78, 277–79. *See also* anthropology, locus of
methodology, subjective. *See* metier
metier, 45–46
mirror. *See* reference, frame of
Miyazaki, Hayao, 243–49
molestation, child, 132–33
Moltmann, Jürgen, 38, 266–67
moralistic therapeutic deism, 243
Murphy, Nancey, 173
MySpace, 125. *See also* community

narrative theology, 42–43
narrator, unreliable, 74–75, 88
Nathan, David and, 90
natural theology, 35, 259
nature, care for, 251–53, 272–73
nature, human, 173
neo-noir, 63–65
neo-paganism, 249–54
Nietzsche, Friedrich, 106
noir, 50, 63–65, 72
nostalgia, 51, 192–94, 199–202, 214–16

objectivity. *See* individual, autonomous; truth
observer, detached. *See* individual, autonomous
Orthodox churches, revelation and, 35
other, the, 126, 143–44, 148–50, 151–53. *See also* community; ethics

paganism, new, 249–54
panentheism, 251–53, 264. *See also* general revelation
pantheism. *See* neo-paganism
perichoresis, 153–54
Pixar, 237–43. *See also* Disney, Walt
Pope, Alexander, 106–8
practical theology, 170–74. *See also* ethics
practice, religious. *See* religion, lived
prevenient grace, 15. *See also* general revelation
production design, 227–30. *See also* fantasy
Protestants, revelation and, 34–35
Proverbs, 170
purity, politics of. *See* genocide

reason, faith and. *See* faith
reference, frame of, 50, 80–82. *See also* anthropology, locus of

relationships, postmodern, 50, 109–10, 111–12, 114–15, 119–20. *See also* anthropology, locus of

religion, lived, 46, 47

remarriage, comedy of, 109–10. *See also* relationships, postmodern

response, audience, 44–45

revelation, general. *See* general revelation

revelation, special. *See* special revelation

reverse hermeneutic, 42–43

revisionism, historical, 76–78. *See also* memory, human

Roman Catholicism. *See* Catholic Church, the

romantic comedies, 50

ruach, 260

Schiavo, Terri, 165–66

Schleiermacher, Friedrich, 264

science fiction, 230–31

secrets, communal, 132–33, 136–38

shalom, 276–77

sin, 62–63, 72

Song of Songs, 113–16

special revelation, 33–34, 262–63, 265–66. *See also* general revelation

Spirit, the, 35, 37–38, 260, 262

subjectivity, methodological. *See* metier

terror, war on, 52. *See also* fantasy

theodicy, 38

theo-drama, 40–41. *See also* aesthetics, theology of

theophany. *See* aesthetics, theology of

tribalism, new, 126. *See also* community; ethics; genocide

Trinity, the, 153–55, 254

truth, 37–38, 41, 78–80

unity, dramatic, 130

unreliable narrator, 74–75, 88

via media, 47. *See also* religion, lived

Wesley, John, 264–65

wind, God's, 260

wire fu, 228–29

Wright, N. T., 37